By the River

To Aubri:

To continue your
journey into
Chinese language
& culture!

[signature]

9/21/2019

CHINESE LITERATURE TODAY BOOK SERIES

By the River
Seven Contemporary Chinese Novellas

Edited by

Charles A. Laughlin

Liu Hongtao

and Jonathan Stalling

UNIVERSITY OF OKLAHOMA PRESS : NORMAN

This book is published with the generous assistance of China's National Office for Teaching Chinese as a Foreign Language, Beijing Normal University's College of Chinese Language and Literature, the University of Oklahoma's College of Arts and Sciences, and *World Literature Today* magazine.

Library of Congress Cataloging-in-Publication Data

Names: Laughlin, Charles A., 1964– editor. | Liu, Hongtao, 1962– editor. | Stalling, Jonathan, editor.
Title: By the river : seven contemporary Chinese novellas / edited by Charles A. Laughlin, Liu Hongtao, and Jonathan Stalling.
Other titles: Seven contemporary Chinese novellas | Chinese novellas
Description: First edition. | Norman : University of Oklahoma Press, 2016. | Series: Chinese literature today book series ; 6
Identifiers: LCCN 2016012896 | ISBN 978-0-8061-5404-6 (paperback)
Subjects: LCSH: Chinese fiction—20th century—Translations into English. | Chinese fiction—21st century—Translations into English. | China—Social life and customs—Fiction.
Classification: LCC PL2658.E8 B9 2016 | DDC 895.13/0108—dc23
LC record available at https://lccn.loc.gov/2016012896

By the River: Seven Contemporary Chinese Novellas is Volume 6 in the Chinese Literature Today Book Series.

The paper in this book meets the guidelines for permanence and durability of the Committee on Production Guidelines for Book Longevity of the Council on Library Resources, Inc. ∞

1 2 3 4 5 6 7 8 9 10

Contents

Introduction

Charles A. Laughlin

WITH LIU HONGTAO

The seven novellas presented here, curated by coeditor Liu Hongtao, give English readers a rare glimpse into the heart of contemporary Chinese fictional writing. The authors range from established novelists such as Wang Anyi and Han Shaogong to authors who have only recently started attracting the attention of foreign publishers and translators, such as Chi Zijian and Xu Zechen, and to Fang Fang, Li Tie, and Jiang Yun, who are well known in China but virtually unknown in the West. Taken as a group, these novellas create a tapestry of historical experience and contemporary life in China that is as attentive to their characters' inner lives as to the events and landscapes of their times.

The Chinese novella, or *zhongpian xiaoshuo*, is the mainstay of modern Chinese fictional art. Ranging from twenty or thirty thousand up to around a hundred thousand characters, novellas have been important in the evolution of modern Chinese literature and have been institutionalized in contemporary Chinese literary culture. The first award of a national prize for five novellas written between 1977 and 1980 got the ball rolling in the beginning of the New Era, and since then novellas have been included in every issue of the prestigious literary magazines *Renmin wenxue* (People's literature), *Shouhuo* (Harvest), *Shi yue* (October), *Hua cheng* (Flower city), and *Da jia* (Master). One of the contributors to this volume, Xu Zechen, is an editor at *People's Literature*, and has stated that most of the space in most literary magazines is occupied by novellas, and furthermore that the readership for novellas far exceeds that for short stories. Xu attributes this niche occupied by the novella to the balance it strikes between the Chinese reading public's insatiable appetite for stories and the fast pace of their life, which does not leave enough time to read many full-length novels.[1] There may be some truth to this, although the pace of life in China today is many times faster than it was when the novella achieved this exalted status back in the early 1980s. However, Xu also mentions another important factor: the usefulness of the novella form as source material for television and film scripts due to its particular length and scope.[2]

From the point of view of European literature, the idea that there needs to be a form of fiction that is longer than a short story but shorter than a novel is probably not a universally held perspective. "It was not until late in the 18th and early in the 19th c.," according to J. A. Cuddon, "that the *novella* was fashioned into a particular form according to certain precepts and rules." In addition to its length, "the general characteristics of the genre were its epic quality and its restriction to a single event, situation, or conflict. It concentrated on the single event and showed it as a kind of chance. The event ought to have an unexpected turning point (*Wendepunkt*) so that the conclusion surprises even while it is a logical outcome."[3] The novella presents in some detail a significant episode or more in the life of one central character. In contrast, the short story tends to focus on the intersection of a very small number of characters over a short period of time, while the full-length novel often spans the entire life of at least one of its principal characters, and may even extend beyond one generation.

From a narrative standpoint, therefore, the novella performs a unique role. Its mission is not the encyclopedic rendition of a fully formed world, but rather to tell a whole story, often of a relationship between the central character and one or more other characters. Scenes from childhood or other stages in the lives of these characters may appear in the form of flashbacks or digressions, but narrative attention is primarily devoted to a progression of events among the central characters over weeks, months, or years that achieves closure less often in death or historical cataclysm than in a simple parting of ways or the resolution of a central conflict. Indeed, novellas are less committed to closure than novels, and often end without a clear resolution. The ability to return, to reflect on a past that has already been depicted, and then to continue to move forward is part of the special roominess of the novella; it allows characters to develop, to respond to changes in their lives not once but often several times. This makes it an attractive form for writers who want to keep actively writing and publishing for their readers without being burdened with the task of completing full-length novels.

Cuddon identified German writers as "the most active practitioners" in the production of novellas, and added that "the *Novelle* has . . . flourished in Germany more than anywhere else."[4] That may have been the case in the past, but since then, Germany certainly has been superseded by

China: the novella is the native habitat of modern Chinese fictional production and publication. If we go back to the beginning, however, it was a German novella—Johann Wolfgang von Goethe's *Die Leiden der jungen Werthers* (The sorrows of young Werther, 1774)—that set the history of the Chinese novella in motion.

Traditional Chinese fiction before the twentieth century came in the form of short stories and extremely long novels; this can be traced to the origins of vernacular fiction in the form of oral storytelling. The storytelling session placed a tight limit on the length of a narrative unit: one session could only amount to a short story. These stories could be strung together into extremely long, episodic sagas, such as *The Three Kingdoms*, *Outlaws of the Marsh*, *Journey to the West*, and *Dream of the Red Chamber*. But these longer narratives were not expected to project an overarching plot structure as was the case in European fiction. And because Chinese readers never tire of an endless narrative, these stories could extend themselves as long as their authors could sustain them.

The idea of structured dramatic action as opposed to the cyclical linkage of an indefinite number of episodes came into China at the beginning of the twentieth century thanks to works like Goethe's "Werther." Translated into Chinese by Guo Moruo in 1922, this story of an aristocratic artist who falls madly in love with a woman who is already betrothed to another provided an archetypal text for the romantic generation of modern Chinese writers in the 1920s, most famously represented by Yu Dafu's novella "Sinking" (1921). In addition, Goethe's work introduced the theme of love outside of wedlock, which is a common subject in the Chinese novella. Most of the novellas in this anthology concern relationships among three or more people, including subtle attractions between people who are married to others, or are soon to be. Others involve challenges with romantic attachments. Rarely do they result in actual infidelity, but they do collectively acknowledge that what attracts people to one another and what leads to marriage are often different, and people's sense of frustration with their everyday lives often leads to new associations and desires that either come to an early end or are never fulfilled.

The relative prevalence of women writers among Chinese authors of novellas is striking, and is borne out by the gender balance of the contents of this anthology, in which the percentage of female authors far exceeds that of the other volumes in this series. Women also figure prominently as pioneers of the novella in the first half of the twentieth century, from Xiao Hong (1911–1942) to Eileen Chang (Zhang Ailing, 1925–1995). This is not to say that there are not male contributors to the genre; some of the most compelling modern Chinese male authors are prolific novella writers. They range from Yu Dafu (1896–1945) to Xu Dishan (1893–1941), Mao Dun (1896–1981), and Shen Congwen (1902–1988), and include a great number in contemporary China, including Wang Meng (1934–), Ah Cheng (1949–), Han Shaogong (1953–), Zhang Chengzhi (1948–), and Liu Heng (1954–). Even so, novellas by male authors often focus particularly on women, especially in the early twentieth century. Could it be that the relational focus, more open-ended structure, and moral ambiguity of the genre bespeak gendered thought processes and modes of communication?

Speaking as an author, Xu Zechen relates his struggles with the novella form: because he did not know quite what was expected of it in contrast to the short story and the novel, his experimentation with the form led him to view it in terms of vivid metaphors—trench warfare, for example, as opposed to guerrilla fighting or protracted war, or to holding his breath: "It is very difficult to hold the breath for either too long or too short a moment." Possibly his most compelling description, however, is more abstract: He points out that all his stories about Beijing are novellas, and in every case "I was searching, excavating, questioning, and proving ideas through trial and error. In all of these stories, I did not know the results beforehand, nor did I know how to get to the places where the characters might eventually go, or where the complicated and equivocal relationships between them (and me) and this city might go."[5] Thus for Xu the writing of novellas is an inherently improvisational endeavor, writing blind, as it were, without a road map. Yet precisely because of this, it evinces a vigorously concrete world and conveys human truths that are difficult to formulate.

Few Chinese novellas have been published in English translation, perhaps because they create awkwardness for publishers.[6] Publishers much prefer the novel due to its coherence at book length. If the three or four novellas in a single-author collection are not organically related to each other, the collection can seem incoherent in comparison not only to a novel, but also to a collection of stories, in which the greater number and diversity of voices can lend more of a sense of comprehensiveness. By putting a variety of recent practitioners together in a single volume, Liu Hongtao hopes that this collection strikes a balance among different regional cultures, life in the city and the countryside, and different eras of modern history.

Yet there is an additional common thread: rivers appear in most of the stories, lending the grouping an unexpected coherence. Xu Zechen's coming-of-age story "Voice Change" is punctuated by references to the local river, where flooding in the upper reaches has led to all manner of flotsam that one of the characters seems to spend his days scooping out with a hook. And though the primary setting of Li Tie's "Safety Bulletin" is the heavy-industry landscape of an electrical power station, a key scene between the protagonist and his love interest occurs outside the plant as they stroll along a nearby river. In Jiang Yun's "Beloved Tree," a woman's epic journey to Chongqing to find her estranged mother dramatically concludes as she slowly emerges, ragged and unkempt, from the river's edge onto the bank, eliciting the astonishment of her mother's other children, who have never seen her before. In Fang Fang's "Love and Its Lack Are Emblazoned on the Heart," the "true love" between a woman and her now-deceased fiancé is dramatized by "long walks along the river, holding hands and returning late." Later, as she slowly moves toward loving another man, the man she sees in her dreams emerging from the mist on a riverbank finally transforms from the man she lost into her new-found love. The rivers depicted here are generally not named, and they are rarely the site of momentous events, but even in these scenes in which nothing or very little "happens," meaning accumulates in often silent, reflective moments.

There are even more examples, as you will see in the pages that follow, and this recurrence of the river image is no coincidence: rivers are the lifeline of human community. They offer an entry and exit point between the hometown and the world outside, allowing for both chance encounters and final farewells. But they are also the scene of communal domestic activities like bathing and washing clothes, with all the attendant joking and gossip. Even if in the twenty-first century rivers in more urban landscapes no longer play such a practical community role, this universal social legacy confers an archetypal quality on them that draws characters toward them for contemplation and emotional transactions.

In an age when television, film, and new media often place a greater emphasis on the young economic elites of the twenty-first century, these novellas evince a refreshing emphasis on the lower end of the middle class, even in urban settings. While Han Shaogong's protagonist Old Yin in "Mountain Songs from the Heavens," portrayed as a dirt-poor peasant, has access to fame and opportunity because of his extraordinary musical talents, the characters in most of the other stories are generally not college graduates but rather factory workers, schoolteachers, street vendors, or rural villagers. The lives they lead are not on the surface dramatic or remarkable. This thick stratum of society tends to be marginalized and stereotyped in popular culture, while in this collection we are exposed to its dreams, yearnings, and conflicted subjectivities.

Liu Hongtao has observed that much of the Chinese fiction that has been influential in translation shares an almost obsessive fascination with the distant past and sometimes outrageous and gratuitous violence, while the world of these novellas, although not without violence, is less melo-dramatic, more down-to-earth, and more up-to-date. Back in the 1940s, the Shanghai author Eileen Chang (Zhang Ailing) described the writers of her day as striving so hard for the dynamic and heroic in their fiction that they forgot the rich complexity of "the placid and static aspects of life," which she says "have eternal significance: even if this sort of stability is often precarious and subject at regular intervals to destruction, it remains eternal. It exists in every epoch. It is the numinous essence of humanity."[7] Chang, a modern master of the novella, seems almost to be interpreting the fictional image of a river, and in a collection of essays that happens to be titled *Written on Water*. Even though the novellas in this collection are not bombastic, or grand, or (usually) dramatic, through their engross-ing subtlety—which is in part achieved though the added length of the novella form—they plumb the depths of the psychic and mythic beneath the surface of the everyday. It is precisely those details that resonate on a deeper level—whether because of historical and cultural undertones or psychic, philosophical, and symbolic overtones—that leave the reader not with simple answers to moral and political questions, but with the vivid feeling of being challenged by a compelling artistic vision that will, at least temporarily, leave them looking at the world through different eyes.

Notes

1. Xu Zechen, "Novellas, Contemporary Chinese Literature, and My Writing," tr. Xu Shiyan, *Chinese Literature Today*, vol. 5, no. 2 (2016): 26–27.

2. Ibid.

3. J. A. Cuddon, "Novella," in *A Dictionary of Literary Terms* (London: Deutsch, 1977).

4. Ibid.

5. Xu Zechen, "Novellas, Contemporary Chinese Literature, and My Writing," 29.

6. The only other example I am aware of before this volume is Joseph S. M. Lau, C. T. Hsia, and Leo Ou-fan Lee's classic *Modern Chinese Stories and Novellas, 1919–1949* (New York: Columbia University Press, 1981), which presents a mix of short stories and novellas that I think gives readers a much better sense of the fabric of modern Chinese fiction than reading several novels or collections of short stories.

7. Eileen Chang, "Writing of One's Own," in *Written on Water*, edited by Eileen Chang and Andrew Jones (New York: Columbia University Press, 2005), 6.

By the River

The Beloved Tree

Jiang Yun

TRANSLATED BY CHARLES A. LAUGHLIN

It was 1890, or 1891; a man packed his things for a journey. He left the road by the ocean, and followed a path through a thicket dense with grasses and trees, on his way around the island. Later he borrowed a horse, and he continued to travel along the island's length. All along the way people hailed him, saying "*Haëre maï to maha!*" which means "Please join us for a meal." He smiled but continued on his way. Later someone did stop him: it was a woman as hot and brilliant as the sunlight.

"Where are you going?" she asked him.

"I'm going to Itia," he answered.

"What for?"

"I'm looking for a woman."

"There are many beautiful women in Itia; is that what you want?"

"Indeed."

"If you like, I can give you one; she is my daughter."

"Is she young?"

"Yes, she is."

"Is she healthy?"

"Yes."

"Good; please bring her to me."

And just like that, the European Gauguin found his treasure, a bride with skin like golden honey, in Itia. He used a horse to take his bride, his happiness and his inspiration, back to his island home.

Two years later, this man departed; he boarded a ship from Tahiti back to France. His woman sat on the stone edge of the pier, her two sturdy feet immersed in the warm sea water. The flower that she always wore behind her ear had withered and fallen onto her knees. A group of women, Tahitian women, gazed at the retreating steamer, at the man going far away, and they sang an ancient Maori song:

Ye gentle breezes of the south and east
That join in tender play above my head,
Hasten to the neighboring isle.
There you will find in the shadow of his favorite tree,
Him who has abandoned me.
Tell him that you have seen me weep.

—Paul Gauguin, *Noa Noa*[1]

1. Meiqiao and Sir

Meiqiao was sixteen when she married the man they all called "Sir." He was much older than she, by maybe twenty years, so of course she wasn't his first wife. His first wife had died of consumption, leaving him with a boy and a girl. When he married Meiqiao, his boy had already gone to Beijing for school, while the girl was almost thirteen, living with her grandparents in the countryside.

Meiqiao had her conditions for marrying Sir. At the time she was already attending a normal college, Women's Normal, so she agreed to marry him only on the condition that she be allowed to complete her studies. "I will marry you if you'll let me study," she said, "even if you have to wait until I'm seventeen." This last part she said ominously, as if she were defying him. But honestly, who was she to lay down conditions? That's the kind of girl Meiqiao was, always throwing caution to the wind. Of course, you couldn't tell that just by looking at her; her doe-eyed face was childlike, tame, with moist red lips pursed like a baby's. She was the image of innocence. There she sat, doing embroidery by the window, and she looked up when she heard the door. The expression of surprise when she raised her head was like something out of a painting, and it lodged itself in Sir's heart for fifty years.

—

It was a small town; at least to Meiqiao it was small. Meiqiao yearned for a larger place, a bigger city. To be more specific, this "bigger" city bore the name of Paris.

Meiqiao wanted to be an artist.

Seventy or eighty years ago, Meiqiao's town was undoubtedly drab and gray. Northern cities often have this kind of dark gray color. If you stand at a higher elevation, for example up on that thousand-year-old seven-story pagoda east of town, the place might seem as quiet as a fish submerged in water, the way the gray roof tiles wrap the body of the town like fish scales. Meiqiao found it depressing, so she used her paintbrush to revise the town's appearance, repainting the roof tiles a brilliant red. An expanse of roofs painted red covered the earth, rising like steam, roaring, as if a fire had started. Sir stated his opinion—"Terrifying!"

At the time, Meiqiao was already pregnant, and it was getting too hard for her to get around for her to continue attending classes. Sir used the evening hours to help her keep up with her assignments. In the daytime she sat alone in the empty compound with its double courtyards, bored to tears. The sun's rays seemed to inch along interminably. She reached out to grab them, then opened up her hand: her palm was full of sunlight. She grabbed again, squeezing hard, but when she opened her hand, it was only a handful again. She had so much time on her hands; when would it ever end? Meiqiao sighed as she listened to the cicadas in the trees, their chirring cries making her feel empty inside.

Sir was a disciplined man—stern, stodgy, not much for talking and laughing—all appropriate to his station in life. Sir was the dean of the normal college in the city, and its mathematics teacher. His achievements in this field were well known near and far. In terms of his family rank, he actually was not the eldest, but everyone referred to him as if he were, calling him "Da xiansheng"—"Sir," mostly as a token of respect.

Sir, who as a teacher had seen all kinds, discovered to his great surprise that his new bride, his humble little lady, was exceptionally intelligent. When he started to give her math lessons at home, she instantly solved every problem. Trying to conceal his excitement, he began to experiment, pushing her harder or leaping ahead, even setting traps for her, but nothing was too difficult for her. She was like a horse—a proud young filly—and mathematics was a vast prairie in which she could gallop freely to her heart's delight. Sir started to become frustrated, wanting to trip her hooves, looking everywhere for obscure and unusual problems, but who could stop her? Like Liu Bei's jinxed horse, at the moment of truth she would leap across the Tan River.[2] The glass shade of the kerosene lamp was polished snow-white, and the flame danced on her face, giving the profile of her lowered head an unreal, faraway quality. Sir thought of the poetic description of Lin Daiyu in *Dream of the Red Chamber*—"Her mind more agile than Bi Gan"—and suddenly he was gripped with foreboding.[3]

Now Meiqiao would no longer be Meiqiao, but "Mrs. Sir." Everyone's "Mrs. Sir." Getting used to this name would take more than a day or two. At first when people called her "Mrs. Sir," she blushed up to her ears, sensing that she was being teased. Only at school did her classmates still call her by her name. Sir was a man of his word, and sure enough, after the wedding he sent her back to the Women's Normal College. Only there was she still Fan Meiqiao, even "Miss Fan." Her group of friends took to calling each other "Miss": Miss Zhang, Miss Li, Miss Fan. The Women's Normal College was in a Western-style building, one of those colonial affairs with a stone foundation, soaring Roman pillars, a pointed Gothic roof, and halls that were eternally gloomy with a booming echo. Earlier, Meiqiao had not realized that she loved this place; now she knew for sure.

Less than a month after giving birth to her first child, Meiqiao ran back to take her final exams. In the hot July weather, her full breasts swelled painfully, and the milk oozed out in streams. In no time, the front of her blouse was soaked. The examination proctor kindly stopped in front of her, wondering whether he should give her a handkerchief. She wished she could disappear into a crack in the earth. Swallowing tears of humiliation, she swore never to have a baby again.

But that was not something she could control. Those little creatures, those babies, kept coming one after another in spite of her. After Number Two and Number Three came, before she knew it she had Number Four inside. Her body was just too good, like a fresh, fertile field: casually toss some seeds and you get a bumper crop. She tortured herself, running lap after lap on the college exercise field, practicing long jumps in the sand pit, her legs bruised blue and purple, but those warm, weird lumps of flesh seemed to have become part of her body and would not go away. She took croton berries and castor oil to purge them, and even hid charms on her body to induce an abortion. None of this, however, could stop those lumps of flesh from growing bigger and maturing by the day. Her mother-in-law, Sir's mother, came in from the countryside after she gave birth to Number Two and said, "Mother of Lingxiang, quit going to that school and making a fool of yourself. Even if you're at the top of the class, what good will it do with these kids here?" Her own mother also tried to reason with her, saying, "Don't be so stubborn; just accept your fate. Who can overcome fate with her will?" And Sir? He didn't say anything out loud, but those arguments were written into his gaze. Meiqiao avoided that gaze, and persisted, and that persistence took endurance. For what should have been a three-year course, because she alternated periods of study with time off, it wasn't until the sixth year that this extraordinary and painful journey came to its conclusion: Meiqiao finally received her Women's Normal College diploma with its bright red stamp.

She ran to her mother's house, diploma in hand, laughing as she entered the gate, hot tears streaming from her eyes.

Sir heaved a great sigh, and thought, *It's about time we had some peace and quiet around here.*

Number Four was getting bigger every day in her belly, and she did quiet down, maybe even too much. She had never been much of a talker, but now she had practically become mute. It was as if she had used up all of her energy, and her eyes became dull and distracted. The northern summer was winding down, but Indian summer had arrived. She moved a bamboo bench out under the tree to cool off, her belly rising up like a hill. It was a locust tree, no one knew how old, with dense branches and leaves, sprinkling rich shade over half of the courtyard. Locust trees were the most common in this city, practically a symbol of the city. Meiqiao hated the tree's old and decrepit look, so on one of her paintings she changed it, taking her revenge by mischievously painting the leaves blue. A vast blue grove of locust trees, it had a surging, roiling power, so that at first glance it looked like a rough, stormy sea, bursting with passion and . . . evil.

Shortly before the baby was due, late one night Sir was startled awake by Meiqiao's screams. She was having a nightmare. In terror she grabbed his hand, saying, "I'm going to die!" and burst into tears. In all their years together, not once had she ever wept like this, crying right in front of him so weak and helpless, unrestrained and overwhelmed with sorrow—she had always kept a respectful distance from him as if he were her father. Sir was paralyzed by her weeping, panicking in his heart, yet from his lips came the words "What nonsense, how could that happen? Dr. Hu is the best obstetrician . . ." But no sooner had he said it than he realized this was not the kind of assurance she was looking for.

The birth did turn out to be difficult; the fetus was out of position. Dr. Hu, who had studied in Japan, tried everything he knew, but in the end he had to take out scalpel, scissors, and obstetric forceps. Meiqiao had endured two excruciating days and one night of labor; it was a life-or-death struggle. After that came postpartum depression, anorexia, fever, silence, inexplicable weeping and sobbing. The child was taken away by a wet nurse; Meiqiao hadn't produced a drop of milk, so at least she was saved the past troubles of stopping the milk after weaning. The infant was just a little thing, less than five pounds, like a skinned cat; his head had been stretched by the forceps so that it resembled a long purple eggplant. One look at the baby made her shudder with disgust, disgust mixed with pity.

Sir invited his mother-in-law in to stay with her during the first month. Meiqiao's mother sat cross-legged on the kang, chatting delicately about one thing or another. She could have said one hundred, one thousand, sentences, and Meiqiao would still have ignored her. She wasn't speaking or eating, either. She couldn't even keep a bowl of Qinzhou yellow millet porridge down. It was almost like morning sickness. She became thinner, more haggard and withered, every day. Her mother was at her wits' end, and began to cry. "Meiqiao, it's like you don't want a perfectly good life, and now you're making yourself die!"

Her comment cut to the quick. It was shocking, the kind of thing only one's own mother could say. After she said it, she went home moaning. Out of sight, out of mind. But that didn't work for Sir. He couldn't put her "out of sight"; he couldn't run away from the situation. One day when he came home from work, he called their eldest daughter, Lingxiang, over to him and gave her something. Lingxiang carried the object into her mother's room and called out, "Ma." She climbed onto the kang and handed it to her.

Meiqiao took hold of it and froze for a moment. Gradually her hands began to tremble, and she pulled Lingxiang to her bosom in a tight embrace. She felt Lingxiang's body, so warm, tender, and fragrant; she drew in the warmth and scent of this little creature. She was saved.

It was an appointment letter, for a teaching position at a public elementary school.

———

After the New Year celebrations, Meiqiao became an elementary schoolteacher. First she taught fourth grade arithmetic, and later she began to teach art. It goes without saying that this job was Sir's doing. Most people have to work hard to find employment, but for Sir it was as simple as saying the word. Only for Sir, whether to say that word was a very difficult decision. Sir was perfectly clear about what was wrong with this girl: she dreaded being doomed to the ordinary life of a housewife in a courtyard house; her lush young body resisted that life. But what could be done about it? Saving one life is better than building a seven-story pagoda, after all.

The weather had not yet become warm, but Meiqiao had already traded her cotton-stuffed clothes for spring clothes, a bright indanthrene blue gown with a green cashmere sweater on top. That green was fresh and confident, clear and bold like spring grass. Despite having carried four children, Meiqiao's body had actually not changed much. Standing there, she still cut a striking figure, with the pristine look of someone who could go through the muck without getting dirty. This fresh person went out every morning and came home in the evening, and even with all the chalk or watercolor paint on her hands, the ink or chalk dust on her clothes, she still looked fresh and bright. The world outside, the vast land, nourished her. In fact, she was not all that enthusiastic about teaching; it was the outside world that she loved.

The public school was about a fifteen-minute walk from home. Her teaching load was not heavy. What's more, there was a happy surprise, in that a classmate from the Women's Normal College, the one they had called "Miss Zhang," also happened to be on the faculty at this school. Miss Zhang had graduated some years before Meiqiao (don't forget that Meiqiao was held up by one pregnancy after another) and returned to her hometown, a county town about thirty miles away from this city known for its grapes and rice vinegar. Over time they had lost touch with each other, but they had never imagined that they would run across each other in this place, much less as colleagues! Meiqiao was overjoyed.

"Oh, my, my!" she cried. "I had no idea where you'd gone. I thought I'd never see you again, and here you are right outside my back door!"

"That's right! I've been lying in wait for you!" Miss Zhang replied.

Their eyes flashed, sparkling as they had when they were students, but of course they were not students anymore. They both suddenly felt time whoosh past them, like a strong wind past their ears, and for a moment it left them at a loss.

"I got married," Miss Zhang said.

In the old days, Miss Zhang had been a pretty but masculine young lady, with broad shoulders, a long neck, thick eyebrows, and a body that seemed that it would be as straight as a poplar forever. They teased her with the nickname "Boy Beauty." This proud "Boy Beauty" once boasted that she would be a virgin for life. It appeared that she still had the same broad shoulders, long neck, and straight figure, but that oath from the past had gone up in smoke.

That day, the two reunited old friends had lunch at a place outside the school gate run by some people from Shandong. Meiqiao treated. They even had a little Zhuyeqing, that fine liquor infused with real bamboo leaves, both clear and green. When you take it into your mouth, it has a wondrous flavor. With cups in hand, the two of them shared their experiences since they had parted ways. Meiqiao's story was quickly disposed of: it consisted only of having children, one after the other, now up to the fourth. Miss Zhang, however, had a much more complex and dramatic tale: resisting an arranged marriage, eloping, running away with the man she loved—it was a story of the era.

"Oh my goodness," Meiqiao couldn't stop saying. Because of the wine, because of her excitement, her cheeks bloomed like peaches, hot and feverish. "Miss Zhang, you're really something else!"

But Miss Zhang taught for only one more term at the elementary school before resigning. Her husband had received an unexpected invitation to teach at a school in Wuhan, and during summer vacation, in the hottest part of the summer, she left this city to hurry to that furnace on the Yangtze River. Just before she left, she came to bid farewell to Meiqiao. She gave Meiqiao her address and said, "Write to me!"

Meiqiao nodded, her emotions surging.

"If you have a chance, please come south for a visit."

Meiqiao reflexively nodded, but tears began to spill from her eyes. She would probably never have such a chance, not ever. She turned around, and when she looked back, her friend was already out of sight; the courtyard was empty, dappled with shade. The sound of birds chirping seemed to come out of nowhere, growing in volume, covering up everything. *Chirr-lyao—chirr-lyao—chirr-lyao*—it was the sound of prophesy.

---

2. Along Comes Xi Fangping

One day Sir came home and said to Meiqiao, "Have someone tidy up a guest room. A teacher from Beijing has come, and he couldn't find a place to stay. I offered to put him up for a few days."

Meiqiao's house, No. 16 First Street, was a double-courtyard compound with a small wing off to the side. The various rooms, large and small, totaled more than twenty. Although there were lots of children and others living there in the bustling household, there were always empty rooms that were not being used. Meiqiao had a servant clean up a western room in the back courtyard. Instead of a traditional heated kang bed, it had a brass bed with a spring mattress.

The guest was Xi Fangping.

When she heard the name, Meiqiao could scarcely suppress a laugh. Wasn't that a character out of *Strange Stories from a Chinese Studio*?[4] He looked the part, too, with long, thin eyebrows and fair skin. Upon hearing that "a teacher from Beijing" was coming, she had initially assumed that he would be a severe old man, not a young, cultured scholar with almost feminine beauty.

In fact, Xi Fangping was a former student of Sir's, maybe even his favorite. His family was poor; he had been brought up by his widowed mother. He managed to get into Beijing Normal College and had just graduated when Sir invited him back to teach. It goes without saying that Sir was very fond of this young man.

That night, Sir held a banquet at home to welcome Xi Fangping, to which he invited several of his other students. He took out a special liquor he had stashed away—a jar of his hometown specialty, an excellent fruit wine made from persimmons—and regaled everyone with the wonders of this "blossom wine." Host and guests enjoyed themselves throughout the meal. Halfway through it, Meiqiao entered the room to pour tea, in part to remind Sir not to drink too much. Xi Fangping, whose face was already red, ceremoniously stood up and held out his wine cup in a toast. "Mrs. Sir," he cried, his face growing even redder. Everyone could see that he'd probably had enough. "We've put you to so much trouble, a toast to you!"

Throwing his head back, he downed it in one gulp, and tears seemed to well in his eyes. How could these be the eyes of a man? Meiqiao smirked and said, "It's no trouble. The room was empty anyway, right?"

Of course, rooms are meant to be occupied. If not by people, then by ghosts. Meiqiao smiled again as this thought crossed her mind: *Why do I keep thinking about ghosts today? Probably it's because of this "Xi Fangping's" name.* Carrying a lamp, she returned to the back courtyard. The banquet up front had not yet dispersed, but the people in back were already asleep. The wet nurses with their charges were all in dreamland; to the north, east, and south, all was pitch-black, except for the western chamber, where there was a lamp with a small flame, gently swaying and waiting for the night guest to come in. Meiqiao quietly pushed the door open and walked in as if to check to make sure that nothing was amiss. Her own shadow, huge and black, cast on the wall, actually gave her a start.

That night Meiqiao had a dream, a crazy dream, like she was floating in the air. In the dream she was her old self, as she was before she married, sixteen years old, with short hair just down to her ears, wearing a white blouse and a dark blue skirt, standing under a grape trellis. Someone walked over and said, "So this is where you are, this is where you've been hiding, waiting for me to find you!" That person, the one talking, was the Meiqiao of today.

———

At the breakfast table the next morning, Xi Fangping blushed as soon as he set eyes on Meiqiao.

This made people uneasy. The wife of a teacher is not someone who would normally make one blush or one's heart beat faster. A teacher's wife is supposed to be caring, proper, quiet, and warm, like a serene tree in autumn. But the "teacher's wife" in front of him, this brilliantly radiant and fetching woman, this woman whom he didn't dare look in the eye, was simply in a league of her own!

I must quickly find another place to live, he thought.

Later, after they got to know each other, she let him see her paintings. That was an opening: upon seeing those burning and suggestive roof tiles, those wavelike surging and sinister locust tree leaves, those contorted and darkly sorrowful faces, he was astonished and amazed. He softly caressed them with his hand, and lovingly, compassionately, said, "You unyielding prisoner . . ."

---

3. Lingxiang

Of all the children, Lingxiang was the most dependent on her mother.

Four children, and one wet nurse for each: it was Lingxiang's wet nurse who had the toughest job. During Meiqiao's month-long lying-in after her birth, the infant drank only her mother's milk. When Meiqiao had to go back to school and handed her over to a wet nurse, forget it: she would not take the wet nurse's breast for anything. She closed her eyes, opened her mouth wide, and wailed like it was the end of the world, crying until her wrinkly little face turned from red to blue. It seemed that she would rather chew on her own poor little fist and starve than to "accept grain from Zhou."⁵ Even worse, when she started crying, half a city away in the school, as if on cue, Meiqiao's breasts tingled, and before she knew it, two hot streams were flowing uncontrollably. In no time at all, her blouse was soaked.

Meiqiao's eyes were soaked, too.

Several times she couldn't take it, and she sneaked out of the school gate, hiring a rickshaw to take her home so she could come to her child's rescue. As soon as Lingxiang was brought toward her bosom, the infant would burrow her head into her mother's breasts with a vengeance, desperately grabbing for her nipples, with her two tiny hands oh so tightly embracing the life-saving nourishment, like a dangerous little wild animal.

Meiqiao had no other choice. She was forced to surrender to this little daughter of hers. From then on, early every morning before she left for work, she would give her her fill; at noon she would rush back in a rickshaw and feed her another meal. At night she still had her sleep with her wet nurse, but if she heard her cry in the middle of the night, she would get up and give her a late-night snack. Meiqiao's breasts were so full and generous! Over the course of the year, Lingxiang grew beautifully, white and fat, her two little arms puckering like tender lotus roots; she could have done advertisements for any dairy company. But Meiqiao lost weight at an alarming rate, until one day her milk mysteriously dried up.

She had learned her lesson. As soon as the subsequent children were born, Meiqiao immediately handed them over to a wet nurse. Not a one of them ever got to drink a drop of their own mother's milk, and so they were just that little bit more distant from her.

They each had their own wet nurse to care for them, spoil them, and protect them. Lingxiang's nurse, however, left the household early on. Lingxiang had not nursed on the woman's milk, but she had been held to her bosom morning and night over those many childhood years, so even if she had been a rock, she would have felt some warmth. When the nurse left, it was the first heartbreak she had experienced in life. She didn't know why her nurse had left so suddenly. Only later—much later—did she learn the reason: it was because her own child had developed a terminal illness. Lingxiang had just turned four, and they had her sleep with her younger brother Linghan and his wet nurse. The wet nurse held Linghan at one end of the great big kang, while Lingxiang slept at the other end. She had to get up to relieve herself in the middle of the night, so she called the wet nurse. When the wet nurse ignored her, she quietly wept to herself.

When Linghan's wet nurse opened her eyes the next morning, she discovered that Lingxiang's end of the kang was empty: the little princess was gone! Frightened out of her wits, she jumped off the bed, running into the courtyard to look for Lingxiang, but she was nowhere to be found. She was afraid to call her name out loud, and was at her wits' end when she looked up and noticed that the door to the south chamber was ajar, leaving a wide crack open: that was the room where Lingxiang had slept with her own wet nurse. She rushed in to find the little princess curled up in a ball on the great big kang, her face streaked with tears, sleeping, her arms wrapped around her wet nurse's pillow, and the wet nurse's cotton quilt tangled around her body . . .

Meiqiao heard about what had happened during the day, so in the evening she carried bedding over and took the little troublemaker in her arms. Lingxiang, a little bashfully, burrowed her little head into her bosom, and didn't move. Suddenly she called out, "Ma!" and said, "Is it really you?"

Meiqiao suddenly felt her nose get that prickly feeling inside; she tightly hugged her child and said, "It's me, it's me! Who else would it be?" Lingxiang began to sob, and hot tears fell on Meiqiao's chest like drops of candle wax. Meiqiao held the heartbroken little girl all night, and asked herself, *Who does this girl remind me of?*

Later, Lingxiang asked Meiqiao a question: "Mama, could there ever be a day when you wouldn't want me anymore, like the wet nurse?" Meiqiao answered, "Silly girl, treasure, how could I ever not want you?"

Meiqiao did not realize that all children are prophets.

Meiqiao could not figure out why this child seemed to be in a constant state of terror. Every time Meiqiao went out and returned a little late, as soon as she came back the girl would lunge at her and embrace her tightly, unwilling to let go, as if she had lost her and had just gotten her back. At times, early in the morning, before she opened her eyes, this child would suddenly run into her room in a panic and caress her face with her hands, saying, "Mama, you're here!" as if she were checking to make sure.

Meiqiao looked at the child, at her huge black eyes, and wondered, *What is it that this girl is afraid of?* When she had this thought, a hint of the disappointment and unease at the unpredictability of life would sweep through her heart.

Now, finally, Meiqiao would know the answer.

How did it all begin? The eight-year-old Lingxiang had no idea, but she knew that something terrible had happened, and there was great danger ahead. That atmosphere of danger, like the pungent fragrance of locust tree blossoms, permeated the air that May, finding its way into every pore. In the daytime, you wouldn't have known that something had happened in this family. Everything was as usual. Dad left early in the morning, dressed up nicely, called a rickshaw, and went to work. Ma went out early, too, also dressed nicely, but she went to work on foot, not in a rickshaw. The weather had been getting hotter every day, and both Ma and Dad began wearing new unlined gowns made of light cotton. Dad's was moon-white, while Ma's was imprinted with tiny flower petals like stars on a pink background. When they walked past, a puff of new cloth smell would waft by.

But the sun must always set, and the night will always come. The danger revealed itself under the cover of darkness. Dinner was a prelude, an overture to the menace. Ma had not come home for dinner several nights in a row. There was a shadow over Dad's face, and he did not speak. His teeth seemed to be working especially hard at chewing. Everyone knew that a storm was coming. The whole family waited with bated breath, trembling with fear. Even the littlest brother, Lingtian, who had just turned two, the apple of his dad's eye, was unusually quiet. The whole meal passed silently and was over quickly, and then everyone went to their own rooms, still not daring to breathe easily. The wet nurses got into bed early with their charges and went to sleep. The female servants and male workers huddled in the dormitory in the side courtyard, talking in hushed tones. Everyone was waiting, waiting for a big storm—there would be no shelter or escape, even in the dreams of deep sleep. Everyone's ears had become hypersensitive, so that even the sound of a leaf dropping to the ground could be heard, not to mention the creaking of a door. When the door creaked, it was like the fuse for a bundle of explosives. The footsteps of the lady of the house, *click-clack click-clack*, seemed about to shatter the heavens, life and death hanging between the footfalls. At this moment, everyone was sure that whatever was going to happen was going to happen now.

It might have been called an argument, but actually, all anyone could hear was Sir bellowing and roaring. When Sir got angry, it was terrifying; even the ground would shudder. But gradually came the sound of an answer. It was not loud, but it was full of rage and passion, a kind of fearless and desperate passion, which in a way was even more frightening. That kind of fearless, desperate excitement could destroy. This was the great menace, the peril that had been hanging over their heads. Sir bellowed, roared, even smashed things, but that was only a prelude, like the clouds around the moon, merely providing a dark backdrop for the menace to come.

When the argument reached its frenzied climax that night, Sir became violent. He suddenly gave the woman a slap so heavy it could have made the earth move, like the lethal slap you would use to kill a fly. It was aimed not only at Meiqiao, but at Sir himself. The blow knocked Meiqiao to the ground, and she began to bleed from her nose and mouth. The sight of blood made him freeze from head to toe. Meiqiao slowly struggled back up. She wiped her face with her hand and found it smeared with blood, then pressed that bloody hand against the whitewashed wall. A bright red handprint suddenly jumped out of the wall like a little red devil. Meiqiao looked at it, and then, without a word, she smiled and sauntered out of the room.

The next morning, everyone saw the consequence of the violence. Meiqiao's face was terribly swollen and bruised. But she maintained her composure, and with her hair done flawlessly, her summer dress as neat as could be, and her head raised high, she simply walked out the door. On her way out she gave some instructions to the wet nurses, as if it were an ordinary morning just like any other. Lingxiang chased after her, grabbing her and hugging her, and once she was able to hesitantly break free of those clasping little arms, she walked away without a backward look, saying, "Treasure, go to school."

That day was an ordeal. Every minute was torture for Lingxiang. She was distracted in class, clumsy when she walked, and had no interest in eating. Minute by minute, she yearned for the sun to climb down, she waited for the darkness, longing for the quiet of night—she even hoped that there would be arguing. She told herself that today was really no different from yesterday, the day before, and the day before that, like all the days in the past, no difference whatsoever. This was not a special day at all; it was not an unlucky day. She pulled herself up straight and resolutely comforted herself, but she could not help but give in to wave after wave of trembling, as if she had developed a fever. The passing of the day felt like a hundred years. Finally the sun went down, and the whole family was together again in the dining room—except for Mommy. But that didn't matter; after all, had she not been gone yesterday, the day before, and for many days? Sir's face was gloomy, and once again the whole family was on edge. His chewing, however, did not seem so fierce; it had lost that murderous quality, and besides, he ate almost nothing. Lingxiang's heart was suddenly tangled into knots; she didn't know what was going on.

Later people saw Lingxiang standing alone in the courtyard. When Big Sun the cook saw her, he came out and asked in a hushed voice, "What are you doing here?" Lingxiang said, "I'm waiting for my ma." Missus Yang, a servant, came out to relieve herself, and she too whispered, "What are you doing here in the pitch dark?" The answer again was, "Waiting for my ma." Everyone knew this girl's temperament, that she couldn't be talked out of anything, so they just let her be. Gradually the courtyard descended into silence, while she stood alone under the locust tree for most of the night.

The locust tree was in full bloom, and the fragrance of the blossoms was thick enough to cut through. In years past when the tree had burst into bloom, Big Sun would knock down the flowers in big clumps with a stick, then wash them and mix them with flour to make locust flower sweets for the children to eat. He loved to say, "The time is ripe, the scene is fine—have a taste." But this year Big Sun didn't have the heart to have them "have a taste." Probably for this reason, the locust tree flowers were much thicker than in previous years, the fragrance much more intense than before, more powerful, and needless to say it was a strong, baleful odor.

The dew had fallen. Like tears from the tree falling drop by drop, it was an inexpressible sorrow. Some insects began calling. Lingxiang's legs were sore and swollen, and she could hardly stand up anymore. Passion-flowers and flowering plums were about to bloom by the wall, and morning glories were already climbing up the frame. They were all from seeds sown by her mother, or plants that she had brought in. In the back courtyard she had also planted roses, Chinese roses, and herbaceous and tree peonies. Mom loved those full, rounded flowers with their brilliant and intense colors. She would always say, "This courtyard is too plain!" so she used those flowers to dress it up.

Flowers, please hurry up and bloom! Lingxiang called out from the depths of her heart. Once the flowers bloomed, Ma loved the courtyard. This year, maybe it was only because the flowers seemed to be blooming too late, too slowly, like a betrayal, that Ma had begun to hate home? Lingxiang suddenly shuddered, and wept desperately.

"Creeeeak—" went the door. It was the sound of mercy. Lingxiang could hardly believe her ears. This merciful sound was followed by the click-clack of footsteps, and then the dark shadow of the one she loved came to a stop in front of her, asking her in astonishment, "What are you doing here?" As if her mother had just come back from the dead, she lunged into her bosom, wailing, "I thought you were never coming back!"

As Meiqiao embraced her tightly, the girl sobbed and her body trembled. With her bruised face, the mother caressed and fondled her daughter's dew-soaked hair. She called out her name, "Lingxiang, Lingxiang, treasure!" Then, holding her in her arms, she took her into her back courtyard room. She pulled out a towel to dry her hair, made her bed, and took off her clothes, as if she were a tiny little child, less than four years old, who had just left her wet nurse . . . she put her to bed, and when she was fast asleep, she stared at the child's face for a long, long time—beautiful, so hard to part with, her own flesh and blood—and said, "Treasure, my treasure, go to sleep."

And then she was gone.

The house was dark, except for a single light in the study, like the eye of a judge, or the eye of a god. Meiqiao walked toward that light. She entered the room and saw Sir, who silently stood up. The two of them silently gazed at each other for a long time. Then Meiqiao knelt on the floor, knelt down and kowtowed to Sir.

The night was strangely quiet, no arguing. From top to bottom, the whole family's hearts were being pulled at, and they listened intently, anticipating a storm that never came. It was as if this were the stillest, quietest night for a very long time, a silent night. They all breathed a sigh of relief. This night, everyone in the household slept deeply, sweetly, without a single dream among them.

Only in the morning, when the sun came up, did they realize that their world had changed.

That morning, the flowering plums suddenly exploded into bloom, the whole tree a brilliant, dazzling pink, like the sunset clouds. Their solemnly quiet courtyard was illuminated by this pink sunset, but Lingxiang's wait for her mother's return would not end this time, not ever.

4. Blossom Wine, Persimmon Trees, and More

There is a place called Emei Ridge. This isn't the Mount Emei in Sichuan; this one is in Hedong. It's the biggest plain in Hedong. Hedong is well known for its persimmons, like the lines in *Romance of the Western Chamber*: "What dyed the frosted forest red at dawn? In the leaving man's tears / the trees drown." That frosted grove was not maple, but persimmon. The persimmons in autumn, once the frost hits, become as red as blood; it's a marvel of Hedong.

On Emei Ridge, the persimmons blanket both the hills and the highlands. The persimmons of Emei have a special property: they can be used to make wine. Not ordinary wine, but "blossom wine." What is blossom wine? If you pour it into a cup, filling it slowly up to the brim, a cluster of foam will gradually "blossom" in the middle of the cup, the tiny bubbles sticking together, lining up like trotting horses, rolling outward toward the inner rim of the cup until they reach the edge and vanish. This is called "galloping blossoms," which in this case means the wine is 30 percent alcohol. If those clusters of blossoms pile up along the sides and form a solid ring, it's called a "full bouquet," which means the wine is somewhat stronger, almost 40 percent. If the blossoms pile on top of each other in layers and the whole cup is covered with a flower ball, there's a name for that, too; it's called "story upon story." Wine like that is fully 55 percent alcohol! This is called "classifying wine by blossoms," and it is a legend of Hedong. Brewing wine from persimmons is an art, and it is passed down through the generations in utmost secrecy. It is transmitted along a single line, but only to daughters-in-law, not to daughters. It is almost like a secret martial arts technique: the raw material for the wine must be hollow persimmons that are gathered after the first frost at Emei Ridge. The wine made with these hollow persimmons has threadlike strands in it; this is the finest blossom wine of all.

Blossom wine has a long history. It is luscious and mellow, with a lingering and pleasant finish; most remarkably, once it goes down, it clears out your blood vessels, like newly dredged rivers, quickening the flow. It can be an effective vehicle for medicine: "It carries a hundred drugs into the twelve arteries." If you have bruises from being hit or falling, it has a wondrous effect as a salve; it works as soon as you dab it on. In short, it's a treasure among treasures.

In later times there was a scholar named Yang Shenxiu who took this blossom wine to the capital. This Yang Shenxiu hailed from Emei Ridge; every time he went home for a visit, he would bring back some of the ancient brew and invite guests over for a banquet to celebrate his return. Perhaps even Kang Youwei and Liang Qichao tried this nectar! Raising their cups under lamplight, cups containing "galloping blossoms," "full bouquets," and the rolling foam of "story upon story," they would have opened their hearts and drunk freely, splendid in both thought and discourse, discussing their great plans for reform—how exhilarating it must have been!

And then there's the Guangxu emperor. Come to think of it, he should also have partaken of this fine wine: Guangxu and his true love, "classifying wine by blossoms," sharing the marvels of this nectar.[6] The fair lady would burn incense and offer libation under the moonlight for benediction, singing, "May his majesty enjoy a long life and a happy marriage with grace far-reaching as the rain and dew." Those cups surely were filled with this blossom wine! The froth filling the cup is like a heart full of joy; what could be more appropriate to offer to the heavens? What lovely dreams this innocent couple must have harbored in their hearts. Yet these dreams would vanish even more quickly than the bubbles in the cups; once the heads of the Six Gentlemen fell, blossom wine was not seen again in Beijing.[7]

Stars moved, constellations turned, and many years later the Japanese devils came. That year the devils got into Emei Ridge and the Great Highland. Those little guys truly had an eye for quality. They quickly became enamored of that ancient Emei brew; the wonder of "classifying wine by blossoms" left them gawking. They kept crying, "How wondrous, how wondrous! Yoshhhhi!" Of course, it wasn't enough for them to cry out in praise; they had to have the secret! The next year when the persimmons bore fruit, the harvest was at hand, and the time for brewing was near, they issued an "invitation" to the best winemaker in the highland. They encamped in the village that had the best wine cellar, so they were just waiting for harvest time and the picking of the fruit. The invaders couldn't contain their excitement, and they began to warble and hum the harvest songs of their hometowns.

Suddenly one day, a great wind came in the middle of the night. Never before had an autumn wind so terrible, so ferocious, been seen in the history of the highland. The only thing that could be heard all night was the tens of thousands of persimmon trees on the mountains and in the meadows, roaring, howling, weeping. By morning, when everyone crawled out of bed, they found that in all of Emei Ridge, not a single tree still had fruit. In this greatest of meadows in Hedong, in one night all the persimmon trees over hill and dale had dropped all their fruit, the children they had nurtured for ten months, as if by agreement. In one night, the fallen red persimmons turned Emei Ridge into a sea of blood. And that was not the end of it. Immediately thereafter, a vast blue fog swallowed the whole of Emei Ridge in one gulp. In an instant the bright sky became dark, and the darkness was blacker than hell, so that if a person held out his arm, he could not even see his own fingers. The dogs of the dozen or so villages throughout the highland barked continuously, thinking the Heavenly Dog had swallowed the moon and the sun. The roosters lost their bearings, crowing in the middle of the night. This great fog lingered for three days and three nights, and on the fourth day the sky cleared and the sun came out. The sun shone down on a plain of tragedy: as far as the eye could see, every single fallen persimmon had rotted to bursting—they had all committed suicide under the cover of fog. The whole of Emei Ridge, hundreds of square miles, was littered with the sleeping souls of those fallen heroes.

Just like that, the Japs' plans for winemaking vanished into thin air.

This is our Hedong, our beloved homeland. Do you know the history that lies behind it? One day about five thousand years ago, a man came here; he came deep into the plain and looked around. He saw the vast yellow earth extending off in all directions, and two great rivers, the Yellow and the Fen, converge in the bosom of this vast expanse. The landscape here had a bizarre configuration, like a gigantic womb. On this plain, the earth, the deep soil, exposed its secret, sacred, and fertile womb to the heavens without any modesty whatsoever. This man was stunned, moved by this openness, moved by this motherly openness of the earth. He could not contain himself; he knew it was the grace, beauty, and goodness of the earth, and that it was an inspiration and a sign. He cleared the ground to make an altar, gathering some earth for incense, and respectfully, gratefully knelt down, prostrating himself again and again before this Mother Earth. From then on, people called this Fenyin sui—the womb of the earth. It is the place where Xuanyuan, the Yellow Emperor, cleared an altar.[8]

After many years, some two thousand years later, another man came. He came by boat, upstream on the Yellow River, and entered the Fen to make a sacrifice to Mother Earth. That day on the Fen, thousands of boats raced each other, surrounded by the sounds of flutes and singing and the rippling autumn breezes. The boatmen sang their river songs in unison, and a flock of wild geese passed over their heads. This man alighted from his boat onto the riverbank and ascended the "Sui"—the place where

Xuanyuan, the Yellow Emperor, had cleared an altar so long ago, and which was now the site of a majestic temple complex. He ascended the Temple of the Earth, and looking far off into the distance, he reflected on the passage of those two thousand years. He was overwhelmed with emotions, and involuntarily broke into a chant:

> *The autumn winds arise and white clouds soar,*
> *The grasses wither and wild geese return to the south . . .*

This man, whose name was Liu Che (Emperor Wu of the Han Dynasty), at that moment was no longer a Son of Heaven overlooking all of creation; he was simply a poet who felt the tragedy of history and the sadness of existence. He continued,

> *Storied barges fill the Fen River,*
> *They cross the middle currents and traverse white waves*
> *Flutes and drums sound, and they sing boatmen's songs*
> *But when the joys reach their peak, laments mount*
> *Young and strong only a while, we've no choice but to age!*

Thus was a classic poem for the ages, "Song of Autumn Winds," born on this broad plain, before the womb of the great, fertile earth. And with it was also erected a magnificent Autumn Wind Tower.

Another two thousand years or so had passed when Sir came. He ascended the Autumn Wind Tower. It was 1939, the year the provincial capital fell to the enemy. Sir delivered his family from the fallen city, then returned to his hometown, Emei Ridge, to find refuge. Little did he know that Emei Ridge, too, would soon fall beneath the enemy's iron hooves. Sir's reputation had somehow become known to the Japanese, and they actually wanted him to serve them as a county magistrate! They brought one emissary after another to him, so many that they trampled his threshold to pieces. One day such an agent came to visit, and Sir didn't even wait for him to speak. He told him that he was just in time to join him in ascending the Autumn Wind Tower on this clear day after the first frost. Sir's village was located not far from the Autumn Wind Tower. Not suspecting what Sir might be up to, the visitor said only, "What a fine idea!" and followed Sir and two or three friends off to the Autumn Wind Tower. Actually, neither the tower nor the Temple of the Earth was the original. The rivers had flooded and changed course many times, and the two structures had to be rebuilt in different places, ultimately being located in a village called Temple Entrance. But what difference did that make? At least the Autumn Wind Tower was still standing on our territory. Sir lit three incense sticks that day. He first worshipped at the

Temple of the Earth, then ascended the eighty-one steps of the Autumn Wind Tower, one level at a time. He looked down, and suddenly the Yellow River, the Fen, and the vast expanse of the loess plain were all spread out beneath him. The autumn wind was strong; the persimmon trees had already dropped all their fruit, and the only things left were the frosted leaves, red as a sea of blood, also lying beneath his gaze. Sir let out a great sigh, and began to speak to the emissary: "Do you know what this place is? I think you must know: it is the Sui of all the land of China, the place where Xuanyuan the Yellow Emperor made sacrifices to Mother Earth. Here, even the persimmon trees have a conscience and would not dare to forget their ancestors. Do you think I am inferior even to the trees?"

The emissary was stunned into silence.

Sir continued, "How tall is this Autumn Wind Tower? Do you know? I'll tell you, it is thirty-three meters high, eleven zhang. If a person were to jump from here, not even the gods could save him! Today I might as well leap from here, and take a lesson from the passion and righteousness of those Emei Ridge persimmons of ours!"

Having said this, Sir wound himself up to leap off, but he was held back firmly by the friends who had come with him. The emissary was so frightened he ran away.

The next day the emissary brought more Japanese with him, and they pushed their way into Sir's village, surrounding his house. But they went away empty-handed. Sir and his family had abandoned the place, leaving only a guard dog behind, which barked fiercely at the intruders. The Japanese searched thoroughly inside and out: they upended the water vats, shattered the washbasins, smashed the wine jars, destroyed the wok and stove, then finally took out a gun and shot the big black dog that would not stop barking.

Sir and his family had run away into the Zhongtiao Mountains, where his wife and mother's family were—meaning, of course, his new wife.

---

5. Daping, and the Days in the Mountains

At first, no one dared bring up "remarrying" to Sir's face. He had visibly aged. It was as if he had grown ten years older in an instant, his jet-black hair now flecked with silver strands. At night he could frequently be heard coughing, a hollow-sounding hack that carried a long way in the quiet, causing pain to those who heard it. Of course, in the daytime he was still that "Sir" who commanded respect; deep wounds and humiliation had not changed the usual dignified and proper deportment of a "Master."

The youngest of the four children was only two years old. He didn't understand, and every once in a while he would blurt out, "Where's Mommy?" Other than the baby, no one else ever brought up that woman in Sir's presence again. It was half a year later when that child got the measles; somehow his wet nurse got infected, too—a peasant woman, she had never had measles. Sir had no choice but to bring in his own elderly aunt from back home to help out. By this time his mother had been gone for more than three years, and his aunt realized that when she passed on, there would be no one left to help out Sir, no one on earth. Her heart ached for him. Those thoughts were like a knife being twisted in her heart. Taking matters into her own hands, she brought in a woman for him from the hometown, a woman by the name of Daping.

Daping was the opposite of the woman before her in every way. That woman was a scholar, a schoolteacher, while Daping had never gone to school. She didn't even know a basketful of bowl-sized characters. The previous woman had a face as small as your hand and a willowy waist, while Daping had a face like a platter, a big behind, and a thick waist, heavy and solid, as steady as a millstone. Sir didn't know whether to laugh or to cry, but Daping didn't say a word. She came right in and picked up the gravely ill child, wrapping the motherless baby in her ample, warm, soft bosom, and her eyes showed nothing but a glow of sympathy. With this, whatever it was Sir had wanted to say went back down.

From that moment on, for the rest of his life, those words of rejection would never emerge from his lips.

At first Sir practically ignored this woman, acting like she didn't exist. Every morning she brought him a brass basin for washing his face, and every evening she brought him a basin for washing his feet. No matter how late he lingered in his study at night, when he retired to his bedroom, that footbath would be waiting for him—and it was always steaming hot. On the kang platform, the bedding was already rolled out, and the brass bed warmer was already inside the quilt, bulging like the belly of a pregnant woman. On the bedside table was a pot of hot tea, covered with a cotton warmer, like it was wearing a padded jacket. The quilt was made of that kind of homespun material with crude red squares, and it was bright, so just looking at it made a person feel warm. It was the style of his hometown.

Daping's influence gradually pervaded the entire household. At first it was Lingtian, the three-year-old: suddenly he was wearing tiger-head shoes and a tiger-head cap, scampering about the courtyard showing off his flowery red and green tiger feet with the character for "king" written on them. This living, breathing tiger cavorted around the courtyard for the whole winter. Before long, the whole family was wearing homemade thick cotton shoes, called "kick down the mountain"—they had thick padded cotton soles, and the uppers were coated with tung oil. The shoes all had brightly colored green and red insoles inside, and the uppers were decorated with a variety of embroidered designs: "Peonies of Wealth," "Magpies on Cherry Blossoms," "Pluck the Cassia in the Moon Palace" (indicating success on the imperial exam), and interlocking swastika patterns. The dinner table was now graced at each meal with a platter of colored steamed buns, dyed green and red, adorned with dates—this was a specialty of Sir's hometown. And a dish of oil-fried peppers, deliciously fragrant and vividly red, was essential at every meal, to sandwich inside the hot buns, another authentic treat of Sir's hometown. Before anyone knew it, Daping's homey influence had added a hearty filling to the household and family.

In the month leading up to the New Year, there was one snowfall after another, and the icicles hanging from the eaves had grown to over a foot long. It was cold enough to freeze a person's ears off, but inside the house it was warm and cozy. The coal in the stove popped as it burned, and a brass kettle sat on the stovetop. The dates soaked in liquor had been opened, and the preserved persimmons, too. The liquored dates had been handpicked by her one at a time, each one perfectly formed. The persimmons she piled up in a crock, inserting an apple in the center. Both the dates and persimmons had been sealed tightly with white hemp paper, and now that they were opened, the whole house was filled with the aroma of liquor and dates, and a peculiar kind of warm and soft fruity fragrance came right up to your face, enshrouding you as if it were meant to fill every pore. The dates and persimmons were arranged on a big platter and placed on the long table under the window. As soon as you drew aside the door curtain and walked in, the fragrant air would hit you in the face. Sir was taken aback at first, but then he felt a little sad: long ago at this time of year, there would have been either wintersweet or narcissus on that table. When he looked at these simple bright-red and honest fruit, the rims of his eyes reddened.

That night when she brought the basin for his footbath and turned to leave, Sir reached out and grabbed her arm.

"You don't look down on me?" he began.

She started to cry—the stone finally spoke, the iron tree blossomed. Tears blurred her vision, and she asked, "Look down on you for what?"

"I'm so old," Sir said huskily.

She shook her head, and the tears began to fall. She turned and bent her head, using her hand to wipe them away. Sir was touched by the gesture.

What a fool he had been! Feeling compassion for her, he knew he must be good to this woman for the rest of his life.

That was the twenty-third of the twelfth month, when the kitchen god went back to heaven. Outdoors the air was filled with the sound of bursting firecrackers, pip-pip pop-pop, brash and lively. It was a day of celebration.

—

The whole family moved into Daping's family home. It was in a little mountain village nestled in the foothills of the Zhongtiao Mountains. The Zhongtiao range is full of treasures, including all kinds of minerals, from bronze to bauxite and others. Medicinal herbs grew all over the mountains—astragalus, chuanqiong, calamus. Each spring, right after the Waking of Insects, people would go into the mountain to gather calamus. The luckier and more experienced herbers might also find the rare cordyceps (caterpillar fungus). Walnuts were another of the place's treasures, and so were persimmon trees. In winter, after the first snow, in the mountain gullies or on the slopes on the sunny side, the large persimmon leaves would still be on the trees, glistening proudly in the reflection off the snow, like the reddest agate, unparalleled in their beauty. People were enlivened and moved at the sight.

To Sir, those days in the mountains were like a retreat from the world, but Daping took to them like a fish to water. From working the bar to mill the grain, to working the shuttle for weaving, shouldering the pole to carry buckets of water, gathering medicinal herbs in the mountain, clearing fields for crops—there was nothing she couldn't do. The male and female servants had all scattered by this time; only Big Sun and his wife remained in the kitchen, loyally following them. A few cave rooms and a large courtyard in the foothills were now this family's home. The courtyard was empty, so the next spring Daping took out the pick and hoe and turned the soil, sowed seeds, brought in some chicks and a milk goat, and made it into a functional peasant household. By summer the squash was flowering, and eggplants and beans were climbing the trellises and blooming, here yellow, there purple, flowers large and small, making a blaze of color, dancing with bees and butterflies. Sir took up his brush to write the words "Contented in Bamboo Hedges and Thatched Hut"; he didn't have calligraphy paper, so he wrote it on the white rag paper they used to paper windowpanes. It looked like an expression of high ideals, but in fact he was filled with discontent over things he could do nothing about.

Lingxiang was sixteen years old at the time, and had not yet graduated from high school. Her older little brother, Linghan, was almost fifteen, and the two of them were at home because the war had interrupted their studies. When summer was almost over, someone made his way to this mountain village all the way from Xi'an, asking to take Linghan to his school. This person was also one of Sir's students, and he had taken risks to come. The plan was just to take Linghan to school, but at the last minute Lingxiang suddenly blocked the way.

"Take me with you," she said.

Lingxiang had never been one to speak brusquely, but she meant what she said and her words carried weight. Apart from Sir, everyone in the family was a little afraid of her—the servants, the younger siblings, even Daping. Truth be told, even Sir had certain misgivings about this eldest daughter of his, as well as an inexpressible tenderness for her. She was eccentric, cold, taciturn; she kept to herself and seemed not to be close to anyone in the family. Sir knew the reason for this, and precisely because he knew, he was all the more helpless. As things progressed, it got so he felt nervous when he was alone with her, stiff and unnatural.

In the turmoil of war, a young girl out on her own was a cause for worry, not to mention the family's straitened financial circumstances— how could they provide for two students away at school? Sir was filled with worry; after much hesitation, he said simply, "Maybe some other time." When Lingxiang heard this, she was silent for a long time, then suddenly dropped to her knees. When Sir saw this, his heart was flooded with pain, as if it were being pierced by thousands of arrows. On this child's face, in her eyes, he could clearly see someone else, who seemed to be inhabiting her body. This kneeling girl was like the showdown in a cliffhanger, a life-or-death ultimatum, uncompromising, resolute, and filled with righteousness.

The next day, the man took not only Linghan with him down the mountain, but Lingxiang as well. They had traveled some distance before Lingxiang could bear to turn around; she knew that her father would be standing beneath the persimmon trees at the village entrance, a head of gray hair . . . she was afraid he would see the tears in her eyes.

---

6. I Have Something to Tell You

But Lingxiang was destined to leave. She had been waiting for this day since she was eight years old. It was an immutable destiny, and it was a summons.

She got to Xi'an and easily tested into the third year of high school;

the school naturally provided her room and board. And thus she became a "displaced student." For her, school was not a difficult matter, and others could not guess the happiness she hid within. Of course, life was hard from day to day; how could rootless wandering be easy? But there were thousands of displaced students; she wasn't the only one. She could handle hardship, but this was something she hadn't known. The little amount of money she was able to bring from home, she spent with the utmost care; every penny hurt. Later she stumbled across an opportunity to write for newspapers, and then she even got a column in one—"Diary of a Wandering Student," writing about the sights and sounds of occupied areas. This way she had a little bit of income. It wasn't much, but she saved it up so that it was enough to be useful.

The fact that this student was able to take on two of Sir's children as students showed that they were more than mere acquaintances. She did not like to beat around the bush, so one day when the man came to the school to visit, she suddenly put him on the spot, like a knife to the heart: "Do you know anything about my ma?"

It had been many years since this syllable "ma" had escaped her lips. It had been stuck in her throat and in her heart, where she couldn't either spit it out or swallow it. She had never called Daping "Ma," even though she knew she deserved the name. One year when she had typhoid and her fever would not go away, Daping never left her side for seven days and nights; it was Daping who personally washed all her soiled clothes. During the illness, when Daping leaned over her with that platter-like face, she felt the warmth radiating from her body, and when she came close to her, that warmth washed through her body in waves, bringing tears to her eyes and making her nose tingle. Still, she could not utter that word, that fateful word; if it came out of her mouth, she would surely collapse.

Never in his wildest dreams had Sir's student imagined that this child would pin him to the wall with such a question. His face fell with the shock, and he could only stutter and shake his head. But this sixteen-year-old girl had an expression on her face that frightened him, the expression of a warrior ready for battle, along with a look of despair like a black hole. He thought to himself that it would be cruel to her to sugarcoat the truth, so he answered, "I have not been in touch with her for a long time, several years."

"So, when you last heard from her, where was she?"

"Hankou."

Hankou, she thought to herself, swallowing hard. *It's not all that far, hardly at the edge of the earth.* Her expression made Sir's student very uneasy, and then he said, "But I'm sure she's not in Hankou anymore. Xi Fang-ping, er, in the last letter he wrote, they . . ." he stopped for a moment. "They were about to leave the country."

Leave the country! Lingxiang closed her eyes, and her body went cold, as if all her blood vessels were blocked by ice and had frozen into a trans-lucent tree. Her clenched fists had also become ice chunks, her legs col-umns of ice. Her father's student thought she might be about to cry, but she didn't. Gradually she came back to life, with the flush of blood and breath, and said, "Thank you."

Sir's student privately let out a long sigh, thinking that the matter was over and done with. But a few days later she came to his house, and ran him through with another question: "Do you have Miss Zhang's address?"

Once again he was shocked, at a loss about how she could have known this crucial name "Miss Zhang." Without waiting for him to speak, she relentlessly continued: "Miss Zhang is in Hankou, right? When they went to Hankou, it was to seek refuge at Miss Zhang's in Hankou, right?"

Step by step he was forced into a corner, with no escape. She eyed him like a predator that had just spotted its prey. He shook his head. "Let me see . . ."

Three days later, her father's student gave her what she needed: Miss Zhang's address. He thought it over for three days and three nights before he came to this painful decision, this concession. He thought that if he did not give her a clear direction, who knew what kind of blind blunder-ing about this kid was capable of? This girl was the kind of person who would follow a road into a dark alley, the kind of person who would rush at a wall without turning her head, the kind of person who would know-ingly jump over a bed of hot coals. He saw this with the greatest clarity, and he also saw the great danger embedded within. Besides, this child was impossible to refuse; in her heedless fury she was like a blind man riding a blind horse, and the longing and pain that had been building up by the day since she was a little girl made him helpless before her. He said, "You have to remember, you're the one who made me betray Sir's trust."

———

A month later, the girl was on the road. The day after she received a reply from Miss Zhang, she set out right away. She left a note for her father's student, which said, "No matter how long I live, I will never forget your kindness." It was only a month until exams and winter vacation, but the child could not wait another day: she had already waited eight years, three thousand days, and she had used up all of her patience. Who knew in this month to come, in these thirty bright days and dark nights, what sort of unexpected thing might happen? This child had lacked any sense of security since she was small. She did not trust *time*.

Her destination was clear: Sichuan, Chongqing, Greenwood Pass. But as for the rest, she was at a loss. She carried what little money for the journey she had, a little dry food, and embarked on a long-distance bus. All she knew was that the bus was going south, to Shiquan. As long as it was headed south, she could not go wrong—wasn't Sichuan south of Shaanxi? The bus was unbelievably crowded, stopping and starting frequently along the way, and the road, which had already been terrible to start with, was full of craters that had been blown into it by Japanese bombs. She was sitting in the rear, so she was thrown into the air innumerable times, her head bumping into the roof, her bones rattling so hard she felt like she would fall apart. But the bus did not arrive in Shiquan that night as scheduled; it made it only as far as a place called Ningshan. Everyone got off the bus for refreshments; while the others made their way to a lamb and dumpling stew place, she went to a tea stall. She asked for a bowl of boiled water, and used it to soak a biscuit she had brought with her to eat.

For the first time in her life, she was alone on a night bus. All around her it was pitch-black; only the beams of the bus's headlights were moving, as if they were slashing a wound through the darkness. Others on the bus were snoring, but she couldn't sleep; she wasn't the least bit sleepy. Her eyes were wide open, looking at the strange pitch-black world outside the window. Waves of terror flooded her heart. She was afraid that she wouldn't know which direction to take; would she really be able to get where she wanted to go? Chongqing, Greenwood Pass, in this limitless blackness, the name captured her imagination; it seemed unreal, as if it were a part of heaven, the bus station of heaven. She heard what sounded like some kind of delicate stones being clicked together; suddenly she realized it was the sound of her own teeth chattering.

The bus arrived at Shiquan. The little town was still asleep, and the air was crisp and piercingly cold; it smelled of crops, dung, and the river—the fragrance of the human world. With the arrival of this clumsy bus and its occupants, there was a flurry of activity, and the little main street came to life. It was then that Lingxiang's courage returned to her; as she watched the gradual rising of the sun, she thought, *All roads lead to Rome, so why not also to Greenwood Pass?*

Further ahead and to the west should be Hanzhong, but people were saying that the road had been bombed out, and vehicles couldn't get through. Lingxiang came across some displaced students from the northeast while she was waiting for a bus. They were going to Chongqing, too. So Lingxiang joined their group. They started out on horse carts and then donkey carts, and then they continued on foot, one section at a time, mile after mile, one step after another, approaching the rivers and mountains of Sichuan. Finally they got to Hanzhong, where they were fortunate enough to get on a truck that was going to Guangyuan, which would put them in Sichuan. At Guangyuan they got onto a boat.

The boat plied the waters of the Jialing River, taking them farther downstream. It was a long wooden boat; there were eight crewmen working the oars, an older man at the rudder, and a woman who did the cooking. Apart from the wandering students, there were just two merchants and a schoolteacher. The boat was hauling freight, so the passengers were tucked in among the bundles. As they journeyed on, they were nourished by the wind and slept under the skies; you could say they had their share of hardships, and there would be days when they did not get a single meal. Even more frequent were the times that they spent the night in ruined temples, in someone's ox pen, or in a mountain cave. To them this boat was like Noah's Ark: it made them feel like they were being rescued. The bamboo matting over the cabin hung low, but it felt safe, like the domed ceiling of a cave dwelling. The two long bed boards were level and steady, like the most comfortable kang in the world. The woman's whole-grain rice cooked with chili peppers and dried bamboo shoots was the most delicious food in the world. The cries of the boatmen in unison on deck—*yo-ho, yo-ho!*—were the sound of a peaceful world. Lingxiang stretched out her body in the cabin and fell asleep amid the boatmen's peaceful cries, full of life's joy and sorrow.

When she awoke, the cabin was very quiet and dark, and all sound seemed to be extremely far away. For a moment she forgot where she was. The rhythmic rocking of the boat was like a huge cradle, a long-lost cradle. Those hands that had rocked her! She felt confused for a while, like she was dreaming. Just then she heard voices outside the boat, distinct voices. It was the displaced students; they were on the deck. Everybody was on deck. A boy started singing with a wavering voice, "My home is on the Songhua River . . ." The word "river" made her remember where she was. For the first time in her life, she had come to a great river . . . The cries of *yo-ho, yo-ho!* were the cries of the Sichuan waterways, the voices of the ancient state of Shu! As she quietly listened, tears began to fall from her eyes, and she wept.

Close to evening, the boat moored at Sword Pavilion, and the captain looked at the sunset on the horizon, saying, "We've got good weather, we've got a tailwind, and we're going downstream!"

To be sure, they were going with the flow, with the wind at their backs. In three days they had made it to Hechuan. Just then a squadron of enemy airplanes flew toward them over the river, on their way to bomb Chongqing. The planes dropped a few bombs into the river; the water surface burst into blossoms, and one bomb struck the back of their boat. The boat was tossed by towering waves, and all the passengers and crew, the captain and the cook, the merchants, the schoolteacher, even the students who had passed through so many trials and had nearly reached their destination, all of them ended their lives at the bottom of the river.

Only one person survived, and that was Lingxiang.

———

After Hechuan came Beipei, and after Beipei was Chongqing, and between Beipei and Chongqing there is a little town called Greenwood Pass. Greenwood Pass has a bamboo grove on the slope alongside the river. Beyond the bamboo grove there are some grass huts, and one of those huts was occupied by an ordinary refugee couple, the man a teacher, and the woman also a teacher.

That day, near dusk, the woman was by the hearth preparing dinner. From the hut next to her, the sound of coughing emerged in percussive waves—it was the cough of a man with consumption. A group of children were spinning wooden tops in a small clearing past the bamboo grove. The winter sun had long since sunk into the river, and the water had transformed into a rushing river of blood. A person came walking over from the river, limping, in tattered clothes, and climbed up the stone stairs to the slope one at a time. Gradually the black top of her head appeared, then her face, her upper body, and her legs and feet. She made her way into the clearing past the bamboo grove. The playing children were wide-eyed, looking at this unexpected visitor. The visitor asked the children something, and a little girl, maybe five or six years old, turned and ran to the hut, yelling, "Ma! Ma! There's a beggar asking for you!"

Hearing this, the woman teacher emerged from the hut, her hair tousled, some bits of green vegetable stuck to her hands, the smell of smoke clinging to her. At first she didn't recognize the visitor, and said, "Who is it?" Suddenly her mouth fell open, and she stood stock still as if nailed to the spot. Her face and hands immediately turned white, as if all the blood in her body had been instantly sucked dry. She stood there like a pale, transparent exclamation mark. She locked her gaze on the visitor who, step by step, was limping toward her. When she was only inches away, she said, "You told me you would never abandon me. I've thought about what you said every day for the last eight years. I came here to tell you something: you aren't worth my longing for you like this!"

And with that, she turned and left.

"Lingxiang! Treasure—" the woman teacher—Meiqiao—cried out loudly, as she collapsed to the ground.

7. The End of the Legendary Romance

Since the beginning of winter, Xi Fangping had coughed constantly. Meiqiao wanted to buy a brazier for him, but she didn't have the money to buy coal—coal was more expensive than gold! So she warmed up sheets of straw tissue paper and applied layers of it to his back. She roasted mandarin oranges on the fire, drizzled honey on them, and had him eat them on an empty stomach every day. She boiled pears in the drinking water and made porridge out of radishes. In short, she used every folk remedy she had heard of, one after another, but that cough seemed to be getting worse all the time.

At night he coughed even harder, and she would cradle him against her like a baby.

"Does that feel better?" she would always ask.

"Much better," he would always answer.

In the warmth of her bosom, he was all the more frail. Often they would embrace like that until dawn. Sometimes he would say, "It would be wonderful if we could sleep on a heated kang!" She would hold him tighter and say, "Yes, the south is fine in so many ways, except for that." She knew that these were not the things he wanted to say in his heart; he also knew that she knew.

They were avoiding a word, a reality: consumption, tuberculosis. But in their hearts they were clear that they had run up against it, run up against the god of disease. They were able to hide the terror they felt when they were in front of each other. On sleepless nights, as they lay in the damp, chilly southern hut, it was always trivial domestic matters that they talked about, or little things about the north, like millet porridge, like baked persimmons in winter, like a steaming bowl of tounao—that was the finest winter delicacy of their hometown.[9] The percussive and dramatic coughing assaulted her like waves of electricity, making her tremble with fear. All she could do was hold him tighter, thinking over and over again, *God, this is my man, my one and only, you can't take him away from me . . .*

One night he brought up something about his mother, who had already passed away. He said that in their Hedong hometown they had a custom: newlywed brides had to give their husbands a keepsake, a piece of embroidery, something like a wallet, but not like any ordinary wallet. It wasn't for keeping money or holding tobacco, it was for—teeth! "Do you know how we use it? When you get old, your teeth start falling out, until eventually they're all gone. This purse is for those lost teeth. As your teeth come out, they go into this purse, and at the end you must take it with you to the next world, and you can't be short a single tooth. Women have to make two of these wallets, or tooth purses: one for their husbands and one for themselves. It means 'till death do us part'; it is a solemn pledge to stay together forever.

"My ma carried one of those embroidered tooth bags, with mandarin ducks embroidered on a red satin background. The other one my dad took away with him, but his wallet was empty inside—he left us alone in the world before he was old enough to lose teeth. He disappointed that tooth purse . . ."

He embraced Meiqiao, his woman, as he told this story. Her body, ripe like berries, warm, powerful, and robust, pulsing with blood, made him intensely needful of her and unable to bear the thought of their being apart. What a wonderful body! He pressed his face close to hers, and suddenly he began to weep.

A week later, something new appeared next to his pillow, a piece of embroidery, very small, with a red cloth background, a sawtooth border, and two colorful mandarin ducks embroidered on it: it was crude and garish, but it was sewn so touchingly that every stitch pierced him to the heart. Another one, also embroidered with a stunning pair of mandarin ducks, was still clutched in her hand. Meiqiao leaned down and, with her dark eyes fixed on his face, said one word at a time—"Xi Fangping, you listen to me: you must not disappoint that tooth purse!"

As she finished speaking, her tears began to fall.

And that is their story: legendary in the beginning, but not at the end. When two beautiful youths with lofty hearts and the determination to be together in life and death become mired in such abject hardship, it shows that not all romantic elopements end with a dramatic landing on the banks of the Seine in Paris, in the old neighborhoods of London, or under the cherry blossoms of Ueno Park. Usually they end up as just another impoverished couple in the world.

—

In reality, the moment Lingxiang set eyes on Meiqiao, she had already forgiven her. Seeing her emerge from the grass hut in a cloud of smoke, her hair mussed up, her clothes covered in patches, bits of green vegetable leaves stuck to her hands, she forgave her. Or, even earlier, when the boat she was taking was sunk by a Japanese bomb, and everyone on it was buried under the waves, those wandering students who came with her who were like brothers to her, in that moment in which their young, vigorous lives suddenly vaporized into smoke, she forgave her. Yet she still uttered those words; those words that had been stuck in her throat, suspended from her heart, had to be spoken. Only when she had said them could she return to being a good-natured and warm-hearted child, a girl with compassion.

---

8. Famine

Many more years went by.

This was the year of drought, catastrophic drought. Not only people in the countryside, but even city people were starving.[10] All of the cities, except maybe Beijing and Shanghai, had descended into famine conditions. In Lingxiang's city, many people were bloated, their bodies so swollen that their skin glistened, their faces and heads unusually large, like rubber people. Lots of young women were not getting their periods. These victims of bloating could sometimes buy "nutritional items" like bran biscuits with an authorization from the hospital.

Everyone was focused on trying to find food, coming up with all kinds of ideas. The wild vegetables on the outskirts of town had long since been eaten up, so tofu dregs and the bean cakes used for feeding livestock were now the popular foods that people were fighting over. They invented a beverage called chlorella; it was a kind of algae that grew on ponds, green and glittery. Supposedly it was very nutritious. Preschool and elementary school children would line up to get a tea jar full of chlorella to drink. The idea of supplying bran biscuits to people with bloating was another innovation of the times.

That year Lingxiang was thirty-seven years old, and the mother of two children. One was twelve, the other ten, both in their growth spurts, the time when you never get full no matter how much you eat. The food rationed to them was of course hardly enough. The rations of meat and eggs they received on holidays like the Chinese New Year were not even enough to fill the gaps between their teeth. So they had to buy large amounts of the expensive grain and foods. Fortunately this was within Lingxiang's means. Her husband was a high-ranking laborer in a large industrial concern, and she herself was a teacher at a college. Their monthly salaries plus the little savings they had were all used up on food, and there wasn't any money left over.

The day that wages were doled out every month was the busiest day of all for Lingxiang. Early in the morning, she would pack some food and ride the bus twenty miles to visit her father. Her father, Sir, had served as the principal of a higher vocational school ever since the Communist victory. The school was not in the provincial capital, but was located in a small town, where the transportation was not all that convenient. Sir was not only the principal; he also had to teach, and was writing books as well. He relished the isolation from the world and the quiet atmosphere of the little town.

The school was situated on the banks of the Fen River, with a large campus that conveyed an impression of grandeur. Its buildings were all designed by Soviet architects: clumsy, solid, big, and lavish. This kind of complex always had an auditorium with a soaring spire with a red star on top like the Kremlin. Sir's house was a separate structure, a Western-style bungalow, red brick with stone steps leading up to it, with a long porch in front. The courtyard was large, with pomegranate, Chinese toon, and date trees, while Daping cultivated the open spaces and planted all kinds of vegetables, even growing corn and other grains.

In the 1960s, a little bit of farming could save your life.

Sir's four children had scattered, gone from his side—only Lingxiang was close by. At least once a month, a Sunday would be Sir's holiday. He and Daping would start making preparations several days in advance. Daping would take her basket and wait in long lines to buy precious sugar and dessert cakes, not to mention the relatively good brands of cigarettes and other sought-after goods. A figure like Sir would occasionally be able to enjoy some special allotments, but not much, and he would save them all up so he could "use the good steel to make sharp knives." Early in the morning on those Sundays, Daping would already have mixed the fragrant dumpling filling—pork and cabbage, or lamb and radish—in a big basin. Daping's dumplings were really something to see, with thick skin and lots of filling, their bellies bulging, all fat and white, neatly arranged on several trays. Just the three of them, even at their hungriest, could not possibly eat up several trays of dumplings. The leftovers would be boiled, chilled, and piled neatly into a lunchbox. Sir would say, "Go on and take them home."

Lingxiang always left as soon as she finished lunch; Sir and Daping never tried to keep her. Daping arranged those dessert cakes and sugar, one at a time, in Lingxiang's bag. Lingxiang would always bring a little bit and take home way too much. If she refused, Sir would get angry and say, "It's not for you; take it home for Mingming and Liangliang to eat!"

It wasn't just dessert cakes, sugar, and cooked dumplings; often there would be freshly dried vegetables—eggplant strips, dried radish, beans, and so forth—packages and packages of them. And cartons of cigarettes, Qianmen or Phoenix brand. It was always Sir who personally took out the cigarettes, wordlessly packing them into her bag.

Obviously, with Qianmen or Phoenix, he couldn't say it was for Mingming or Liangliang. Lingxiang's husband didn't smoke, either. Those cigarettes didn't seem to make any sense. Lingxiang understood, but she never let on. She'd pick up all the packages, large and small, and go out the door. After walking a ways, she'd turn and look back. Daping would be on Sir's arm, the two of them still watching her from the gate.

By then, though, Lingxiang needed to be getting to her next stop: the provincial capital twenty miles away.

—

In the early 1950s, Xi Fangping and Meiqiao went back home, to the city of sadness, with their one little girl.

Their return to the north was naturally for health reasons; Xi Fangping couldn't go through another cold and clammy southern winter. Thus, when he received an appointment letter from a middle school in the capital of his home province, he thought, *This is my capitulation to old age.*

He taught mathematics at that middle school, and Meiqiao went to be a "queen of children" in a primary school.[11] They rented two rooms on the east side of a courtyard house not far from the middle school. They built a little kitchen by themselves. This had been their home for ten years; from this courtyard, their daughter got into a university in Beijing. After graduation she was assigned to Gansu Province to help develop the border areas.

Then came the famine, catching everyone unprepared. Just two years before, the government had made such a big deal out of the communal dining halls where you could eat for free, as if communism had already arrived. But the famine came so fast. Meiqiao was actually quite a thrifty woman; she knew how to pinch her pennies. But no matter how prudent she was, she would have had no way to make them a full three meals a day, and no matter how she pinched those pennies, she couldn't stretch that pathetic few pounds of flour and rice and the three and a half ounces of cottonseed oil each person was rationed every month. For three years, because of his tuberculosis, Xi Fangping had been resting at home, collecting his labor insurance, and Meiqiao's salary as a primary schoolteacher was in any case pretty humble; it was hard enough to afford expensive grains, so imagine how much harder it was to buy nutritional supplements! Meiqiao saved all the flour and rice for Xi Fangping to eat, while she ate steamed buns made from dried vegetables and bran; she saved up the oil to stir-fry dishes for Xi Fangping, while she ate pickled and salted vegetables. At the New Year that paltry pound of meat was practically all fat; she melted it into pork oil and used the leftover cracklings as filling, along with radish and cabbage, to make steamed dumplings for Xi Fangping.

"What about you? Aren't you going to eat?" Xi Fangping asked uncomprehendingly as he picked up his bowl.

She was smoking a cheap cigarette, the cheapest kind of plain-wrapper cigarettes. This was a habit she had picked up as a young woman, and was the last remaining trace of her previous life. She took a long drag and answered, "You go ahead and eat; I have to correct homework," or she might have said, "Just now when I took the dumplings out of the steamer, I ate a couple while they were hot." Xi Fangping didn't believe her, and pressed her, fixing his gaze on her. Her expression didn't change. "Look at you! Your only flaw is you're so old-womanish; nowadays my appetite is bigger than ever, and I can't wait until dinner . . . I can eat a lot more than before; I've even gained some weight."

Her face in fact was plumper, with a blinding glow. Xi Fangping knew: that was bloating.

He lost his temper: "Meiqiao, do you think I'm a fool? That I'm blind?"

Meiqiao's face suddenly become very serious, and she glared at him. Slowly she began, "I'm healthy, I can live on anything. You're in bad shape; you need nourishment to survive—without it you won't live more than a few days! You listen to me: I'm not about to let you leave me halfway; I wouldn't be able to bear to live—you have to save yourself, and save me! Close your eyes, harden your heart, and eat!"

She said "eat" ferociously, as if the word weighed a ton, and her eyes reddened around the rims.

One day Lingxiang went to the capital for a conference. After dinner there were no activities planned, so she went to Meiqiao's house. In all these years, Lingxiang was the only one of the four siblings who had been in touch with Meiqiao. As far as Linghan, Lingshuang, and Lingtian were concerned, there had never been such a person in the world. Only Lingxiang wrote her a letter every month, sending some money because she knew they were struggling. Sometimes when she had to go to the capital for work or for a meeting, she would stop by to say hello, but of course she never spent the night there, because Xi Fangping was there, and so it would have been putting them out. Xi Fangping always made her feel awkward and uncomfortable; she didn't know how to act toward him. In her whole life, she had only heard her father mention Xi Fangping's name once, and that was many years ago, one New Year's Eve, while the whole family was eating the holiday meal together. That night Sir had too much to drink; suddenly he pointed at everyone with his chopsticks and inexplicably blurted out, "You mark my words: Xi, Fang, Ping, this man, is the enemy of our whole family!"

At the time, Linghan, Lingshuang, and Lingtian all turned to look at their oldest sister as if she were a common enemy. Their eyes said, "Listen to him! Listen! You dare to call that criminal your parent!" They all knew that Lingxiang had been in touch with Meiqiao for years, that she couldn't let her go. It made them angry, like she had betrayed the family, betrayed her father. For them, "Meiqiao" and "Xi Fangping" were the same person. But what could they do to Lingxiang? Even the Japs' bomb couldn't do anything to her. Lingxiang was not angry, only taken aback. It had been so many years! She thought her father had already put that behind him, but in fact it was not . . . behind him.

She was shocked.

When Lingxiang came out of the conference that day, she went to see Meiqiao at the courtyard house, which was getting messier and more crowded every day. Seeing that a lantern was burning in the kitchen, she decided to go in. She pushed open the door and saw Meiqiao sitting on a stool next to the stove eating a bran bun. Upon hearing the noise, Meiqiao raised her head—Lingxiang was frightened out of her wits: her face was swollen up like a rubber mask! Lingxiang stared blankly for a moment, then walked over and snatched that black lump of stuff out of her hand and took a bite. Her tears began to flow.

The next Sunday, Lingxiang came again, carrying an assortment of packages. She didn't say anything. The big sack held grain, the high-quality kind, along with dried noodles, millet, and cornmeal. In the small packages were sugar, fruit candies, and eggs. She took them out one by one, straight-faced, as if she were angry with someone. These things, these life-saving supplies, covered half of the kang bed. Meiqiao's hands caressed one thing and then another, and she wept.

That is how her monthly visits started. In the past, she had gone every month to see Sir; now she had extended her itinerary over twenty miles, and Sir's place had become a transit station. Before, she would empty out her backpack at her father's, but now she would empty out half and leave half inside for Meiqiao. Before, when she visited her father, she would leisurely while away the time, but now as soon as she put down her lunch bowl and chopsticks, she would have to take off in a hurry. At first she didn't know how to explain it to Sir; she would come up with some clumsy excuse for having to leave early, saying something like Mingming was not feeling well, or Liangliang was ill, or there was something going on at home. She wouldn't look Sir in the eye when she said these things. Suddenly one day she discovered she didn't need excuses anymore; that day, he quietly put a carton of Phoenix cigarettes into her bag. As if struck by a lightning bolt, she knew. Sir, her father, his heart was like "a clear mirror hanging on high"—kind and wise, like the revered magistrates of yore.

They just couldn't mention it. She wouldn't say anything, and neither would he; they wouldn't let the secret out. It was like they had a tacit understanding. What was different was that she was taking a lot more away from Sir's house than she used to. It made her uneasy; without any explanation, her father would direct Daping to pack this and send that. Lingxiang wanted to stop him, but he wouldn't relent. If she squeezed his hand, he would sigh and say, "It's not like I'm giving them to you!" She knew; of course she knew for whom her more than seventy-year-old father, in a time of famine, a time of hunger, was scrimping and saving those little bits of food. That made her uneasy, and very sad.

She made sure that Meiqiao ate every meat-filled dumpling she brought for her, one after the other; fierce as Yama, the King of Hell, she compelled her to eat everything in the lunchbox, without anything left over. This was the one thing, the one solitary thing, she could do for her white-haired old father.

9. The Beloved Tree

The three years of famine passed, but the greater calamity had not yet come. A period of peace and prosperity began. Those monthly visits continued, and became a habit. Now when the day came, Meiqiao was able to make dumplings and other dishes for Lingxiang.

Meiqiao's dumplings were different—delicate, refined . . . just like her. Lingxiang praised them as she ate, and Meiqiao sat opposite her, smoking.

"Your dumplings are tasty, too; they just look kind of ugly."

"Those are Daping's," Lingxiang blurted out.

Meiqiao froze, the cigarette smoldering between her fingers. After some time she laughed quietly and said, "Is your father still the same?"

"What do you mean?"

"Old-fashioned, tyrannical, unreasonable, narrow, dirty, growing his grimy fingernails out so long, making noise when he eats."

Lingxiang abruptly put down her chopsticks and glared fiercely at Meiqiao, her father's former wife: "In all these decades, I have never once heard the word 'no' come from my father's lips, and in all these decades, Dad has never said a single word of complaint about you . . ."

"He doesn't say it out loud, but inside he is cursing me!" Meiqiao interrupted her. "Inside he curses me eighty times a day! He said to me himself, 'Meiqiao, you betrayed me and left me; I will curse you eighty times a day' . . ." She choked and her eyes reddened, and the long ash fell from her cigarette with a plop onto the table. She averted her face. "Your dad, is he okay?" Her voice conveyed a mix of pain and tenderness.

"He's fine," Lingxiang answered.

He was not fine, but Lingxiang was not aware of it. He hadn't told any of his children. In his breast pocket he carried a positive diagnosis of prostate cancer. The doctor had told him to check into the hospital for surgery, but he wouldn't. He would never believe in the knives and scissors of Western medicine, or in the mythology of modern medicine. He really *was* old-fashioned. He was receiving treatment from an old friend who was a doctor of Chinese medicine; the friend gave him one prescription after another for herbal medicine and pills, and he obediently and respectfully consumed them all. His friend said, "Sir, you know that the only thing herbal medicine can cure is the curable diseases."

He smiled; how could he not catch the meaning? He replied, "Brother, I know you're not a god, and you don't have a prescription that will bring the dead to life."

He hid in his study, organizing his things, his book manuscripts, his lectures; the sweat and blood of his entire life had accumulated here, drop by drop. The times of his life were also all here. He caressed them, lovingly lifting each page, bidding farewell to them all. He straightened out the books on his bookshelf, with their traditional and modern bindings, each volume an old friend and confidante, sticking with him through thick and thin for decades; they were truly loyal. Full of gratitude, he pulled out one after another, lifting its cover and flipping through the pages, until suddenly a slip of paper fluttered out of one like a great big butterfly flip-flopping through the air down to the floor, where it landed near his foot.

It was a letter on fine rice paper that had a watermark on it—"One and Only Studio." That was what he used to call his study.

He picked it up and saw some characters written with a brush: "Mei, you hateful woman, are you well . . ."

This unsent letter, one that would never be sent, had somehow gotten into that book years ago. His hand began to tremble, and he couldn't stay standing. All those decades of the past came blowing at him like a great storm, and with them came longing. His eyes filled with tears.

The next time Lingxiang came to visit him and Daping, he told her that the next week he would be going to the capital for a conference, and asked, "Can you go with me?"

It was a meaningless meeting he could easily miss, the kind he would usually not even consider attending, but this time he was full of enthusiasm. This excited attitude made Lingxiang suspicious. She waited until the two of them were seated together on the train to the capital, and asked him, "Dad, what's going on? Tell me the truth."

Sir thought for a while, looking out the window. "I want to see your mother . . . do you think it would be all right?"

—

In the middle of the 1960s—1965, to be exact—this northern city had no cafes, no teahouses. The two of them, Sir and Meiqiao, met at . . . the railway station.

In the waiting room.

Transportation was not well developed in this city; it wasn't on one of the main railroad arteries, so not many trains passed through every day. By two or three in the afternoon, most of the trains had come and gone, so it was fairly quiet in the waiting room.

Meiqiao arrived.

Lingxiang pushed Sir in her direction, pointing Meiqiao out to him. What he saw was . . . an old lady. As the old lady walked straight toward him, she went backward in time, back to sixteen-year-old Meiqiao, with her lips as moist and red as flowers, and those big eyes glistening like crystal-clear water, startled, like the eyes of a deer. Sir had treasured this image in his heart for over forty years, and it had not faded. For a moment he was confused about what connection this old lady with frosted temples had to his Meiqiao.

Lingxiang called her "Ma" and stood up; he stood up, too. Now they were face to face at a train station. That face that would never be young again, that withered face, suddenly filled him with grief. More than forty years had blown past like a great wind, blowing so hard he could hardly steady himself, and he couldn't keep his eyes open. They gazed at each other dumbfounded for a long time, while travelers came and went around them. Lingxiang said, "Have a seat," and they sat down, one on the left and the other on the right, with Lingxiang in the middle. Nobody knew what to say, and in the end it was Lingxiang who broke the silence: "You must be hot."

Meiqiao shook her head and said, "Not really."

"I'll get some sodas." Lingxiang stood up and left.

Big electric fans slowly turned above their heads, making a humming sound. For a while the train station in the afternoon was shrouded in a strange silence. The sounds retreated into the distance, people, trains, loudspeakers, receding ever farther like the ebbing tide. The only things left uncovered were the two of them, like rocks eroded by time. Sir fumbled around for a while and took a pack of Phoenix cigarettes out of his pocket. He pulled one out and offered it to Meiqiao: "Have a smoke?"

Meiqiao took it in her hand and said, "All right."

He pulled one out for himself, too, then fished out a lighter, but he couldn't get it to light. Meiqiao took it from his hand and got a flame on the first try. The graceful little flame swayed, so pretty yet sad, it was moving to watch. Meiqiao lifted it to Sir's face, and he leaned forward to light his cigarette, taking two deep drags, but then coughed till the tears came out. Meiqiao lit her own, and the two of them sat there, smoking.

"How have you been?" Sir began.

"Not bad," Meiqiao answered, "and you?"

"Fine."

Meiqiao puffed out a cloud of smoke; it had a spicy and familiar rich flavor, a flavor she liked.

"Those cigarettes, was it you who had Lingxiang bring them to me?" Meiqiao suddenly asked.

Sir froze.

"And all those other things?"

"Not entirely," Sir said hastily.

Meiqiao's heart was also a clear mirror. She was perfectly clear as to where that life-saving food, those grains like precious gems, those cakes, that sugar, had all come from. She did not refuse; she accepted his loving gesture.

"One does not give thanks for great kindness . . ." Meiqiao averted her eyes, then quietly, but with extraordinary clarity, repeated, "One does not give thanks for great kindness." Her voice caught.

"Meiqiao, don't say that."

"Sir, I won't say anything."

At this point, neither of them knew what to say next. They merely gazed at each other. The words they had wanted to say had turned into curling plumes of cigarette smoke. It was as if they had met at a train station after thirty-four years only to have a smoke together. Once his cigarette was finished, Sir put it out and said, "Yesterday I went to First Street and had a look around. No. 16—" He paused for a moment. No. 16 First Street was once their home. "No. 16 is still there; it's a primary school now, but that tree, that great locust tree, such a fine tree, is gone. Someone cut it down."

Long, long ago, she would always color the leaves of that tree a seething and surging blue in her paintings; how unruly her heart was in those days. She laughed.

"I know," she replied. "It's been cut down for many years. Funny you should mention it. I happened to be passing by that day; in all those years I had never gone back there, but of all days it was that one, and I saw the workers cutting it up, two of them, pushing and pulling on their great saw. They would rasp back and forth, and tears would stream out of the cut; they would rasp some more, and another string of tears would come. I saw it with my own eyes; the tree was crying . . ."

She stopped and turned her face away.

That face of hers had time etched into it, the years had left their traces, and it had an honesty about it. Meiqiao, the one and only Meiqiao, had aged irretrievably. The afternoon sun shone in through the expansive windows, so that her whole figure was bathed in sunlight, everything that had disappeared, never to return, bathed in light. The light was almost spiritual. From a distance a train was approaching, sounding its whistle. It was the train that Sir was about to board, the train that everyone was about to board. His eyes were full of tears.

He wanted to say, "Meiqiao, in the next life, if we were to cross paths, would I still remember you?" But he did not say it.

Notes

------

1. The paragraphs before the song paraphrase Gauguin's story; Gauguin's book concludes with this song, given here in O. T. Theis's English translation. Paul Gauguin and O. F. Theis, *Noa Noa* (New York: N. L. Brown, 1920), 148.

2. Liu Bei is one of the heroes of *The Three Kingdoms*, one of the masterpieces of traditional Chinese fiction. The novel narrates the rivalry among various states and their ambitious leaders after the disintegration of the Han Dynasty. The horse was considered unlucky because of superstitions about his markings, but he proved his worth by saving Liu's life as he was pursued to a river's edge by assassins.

3. Another masterpiece of traditional fiction, *Dream of the Red Chamber* is Cao Xueqin's largely autobiographical account of the opulent world of his youth. It tells the story of the strange young boy Jia Baoyu and the various girls in his extended family with whom he is in love. Lin Daiyu, a brilliant and beautiful but sickly cousin, is his true soul mate, but their story ends tragically. The admiring comparison to Bi Gan, a brilliant prime minister of the ancient Shang Dynasty who was brutally

slaughtered along with most of his family by his nephew, the last Shang king Zhou, foreshadowed this tragic ending.

4. Pu Songling's *Liaozhai zhiyi* was an extremely popular collection of romantic ghost stories from the Qing Dynasty. Xi Fangping's namesake is the title character of one of these stories, who, like most of the protagonists of these stories, is a handsome, sensitive young scholar on the way to the capital to participate in the civil service examinations.

5. The reference here is to the legend of Boyi and Shuqi, two brothers of extraordinary virtue who survived the end of the ancient Shang Dynasty: though they ran to the rising Zhou state to seek refuge, and hated the Shang rulers, they attempted to prevent the Zhou conquest over the Shang for reasons of filial piety and loyalty to the ruler. Though this action was treasonous, their lives were spared by someone who recognized their moral fiber; but they could not bear to live off the produce of the Zhou Dynasty, and fled to Shouyang Mountain, where they eventually starved to death.

6. The reference here is to Consort Zhen (1876-1900), Guangxu's favorite, who encouraged reform and Westernization. She drowned in a well in the Forbidden City under mysterious circumstances, likely also a victim of the backlash against the 100 Days Reform (see note 7).

7. The Six Gentlemen (Tan Sitong, Lin Xu, Yang Rui, Liu Guangdi, Kang Guangren, and Yang Shenxiu) were young and visionary government ministers in the service of the late Qing Dynasty emperor Guangxu, who was also young and under their influence advocated modernizing reforms similar to the Meiji Restoration in Japan, which had launched Japan into a period of increasing industrial modernity and military might. But the model of a Westernized constitutional monarchy was distasteful to conservative forces in the Manchu court, and led by the Empress Dowager Cixi, the reforms were aborted after only one hundred days (thus the reform movement has often been referred to as the Hundred Day Reform), the Guangxu emperor was deposed, and the Six Gentlemen were executed. One of them, Yang Shenxiu (1849–1898), was indeed from the Hedong area of Shanxi.

8. The Yellow Emperor is the legendary progenitor of the Chinese people.

9. Tounao is a kind of breakfast broth thickened with wheat flour and containing chunks of mutton and tendons as well as lotus pod and Chinese yam.

10. The Great Famine of 1959–1961 was largely caused by the misguided economic policies of the Great Leap Forward, which began in 1958.

11. "King of Children," as in the title of a novella by Ah Cheng made into a film in 1987 by Chen Kaige, is an old-fashioned term of scorn referring to humble primary schoolteachers.

Voice Change

Xu Zechen

TRANSLATED BY CHARLES A. LAUGHLIN

1

Old Man He was in the process of lecturing me when two guys came in from outside and took him away. Old He was fed up with me; his finger trembled as it pointed at my nose. "You can't even solve a simple problem like this," he said. "Did your lunch go down into your dog's belly?"

I said, "Yeah, Furball ate everything." The whole class burst into laughter; they knew our family had a yellow dog called Furball. She had a litter of puppies that were less than a month old. Having recently had puppies, Furball had to eat good food, so I fed her my lunch without Mom and Dad knowing. Rice's laughter was the loudest, like thunder rolling over the classroom desks. I loved the sound of Rice's voice, full and rich like a grownup's, solid on the inside and shiny on the outside, glowing like molten iron. When Rice laughed, everyone laughed along with him. Old Man He got even madder, taking his black fedora off with a trembling hand and slamming it on the lectern, revealing his bald head, which we rarely saw.

"Stop laughing!"

Suddenly two guys came in from outside—Midnight Liu's two sons; they were both big, heavy guys. Without saying a word, they each grabbed one of Old He's arms, pushing here and shoving there, moving him away like a wheelbarrow.

Old Man He cried, "What are you doing? Why are you arresting me?" Liu's two sons still didn't speak. Old He yelled, "Wait a minute! My hat!" But they remained totally silent, striding forward with their backs straight and their chests puffed out. By then they had already made their way to the paulownias at the school gate.

Everyone crowded to the window to watch. In one or two pulls, Rice tore away the newspaper that had just been pasted on, and then they stuck their heads right out the window. I stood at my desk, craning my neck to see outside the classroom door. The three figures of Old He and Midnight Liu's two sons came together in the shape of an airplane, with Old He as the nose. His head, baked by the afternoon sun, flashed a reflection of the sunlight, then disappeared outside the gate. Old Man He was not actually bald, it was just that he had very little hair, so unless you looked closely you could easily miss it. I guess that's why he always wore the hat, not taking it off at any time of the year. I had no way of knowing whether he took it off before he went to sleep, but anyway, he rarely took it off. He must have been really angry with me that day to have taken off his hat. I was angry with myself, too, for my inability to answer such a simple question.

But I didn't like Old Man He waving his finger at my nose and yelling at me in front of Rice and everybody. I took the hat off the lectern and spat into it, then spat again, but when I spat a third time, someone said, "Where's Old He's hat?" I hurried to hide it under my desk, using my shirt cuff to wipe off the spit.

Someone else asked about the hat, but then there was silence. Everyone went over to the window again; there was a crowd of people running by the school gate, but no one knew what they were up to. I took the opportunity to flatten out the hat and stuff it into my book bag, and then I walked over to the window as if nothing had happened, to look outside like everyone else. A few stragglers were still running past.

"Does this mean school is out?" Thirty Thousand asked Rice.

"Of course," said Rice. "Old Man He was arrested, so school is out!"

Thirty Thousand picked up Rice's book bag for him, and a bunch of kids ran out of the classroom with Rice. They wanted to see what was going on out there. I suspected it had something to do with Old He getting arrested; but as to why he had been grabbed, I had no idea. I picked up my book bag and went out the gate with them; they went west and I went east: I had to hide the hat.

"Blockhead," Rice called to me, "aren't you coming?"

"I have to go home and check on Furball."

"Heh-heh, okay." Rice began to laugh. "Fatten Furball up real good—I'm going to visit her in a couple of days."

Rice's "heh-heh" was not the laugh of a nice person, but it sure had a good sound to it. Only a grownup could have that kind of voice, heavy and solid, with a hint of raspiness. I had asked my mom, "Why is my voice so thin and shrill, like a little kid's?" and she had said, "If you're not a little kid, then what are you?" "But then how come Rice has a voice like a grownup?" "He's older than you," my mom said. "When you get older, your voice naturally changes. Anyway, what's so great about booming like a stovepipe?"

I thought it was great. Rice could make everyone listen to him; it was all because his voice was different from everyone else's. He'd say, "You're just a bunch of little kids, squealing with milk on your breath!"

Not all of us were younger than Rice. Thirty Thousand, Whole Table, and Crooked Neck Danian were his same age, but their voices didn't sound good. As I went past paulownias and locust trees, holding tight to my book bag and running toward home, my heart was full of fear: I had actually sneaked Old Man He's hat away with me. I didn't dare raise my head and say hello to the few people who were running past me to the west, although I was full of curiosity about where they were going. What on earth were they going to see?

That year I was thirteen, and I was holding two different "puppies" in my heart—one was terror and the other was curiosity. Just like Furball's puppies, they had shiny fur, and once they woke up, they couldn't stay still.

2

I wasn't sure where it would be safest to hide it. I shut myself in my room and looked everywhere, but I didn't feel right no matter where I put it. My sister was in the courtyard hurrying me to go out and see what was going on; she too was anxious to find out what could possibly have happened on West Avenue. All I could do was grit my teeth and stuff it under my bed, and in order to prevent anyone from crawling under there and looking around, I put a pair of my stinky socks by the bed. The smell was enough to bring tears to a blind man. Before I went out, I wanted to have a look at Furball's four little puppies, but my sister couldn't wait any longer and pulled me away with her. I could only whistle in the direction of the straw bed by the wall. Furball heard me and said, "Arf." The four puppies chimed in, whining.

On the street there were people running along with us. When we were almost to West Avenue, we ran into Mom, who was talking to Chive, telling her she should come to our house for dinner that night, but Chive was waving her arms no. My sister said, "Mom, there's something happening on West Avenue. Aren't you going to have a look?"

"Go home!" Mom said. "There's nothing to see over there!"

"So what's going on over there? I'm dying to know!"

"Lord Laozi came down from the sky, that's what!" Mom was irritated. "Come back with me! Chive, listen to your auntie. I'll make you something nice to eat."

Chive still didn't want to go, and she pouted as she said, "Look, look, I wanna go see."

I cautiously asked, "Is it Old Man He?"

My mom glared at me. "Get back home for dinner!"

Sis had already dragged me on past them, but Mom continued to yell from behind us.

I had guessed right: a crowd had gathered outside the entrance to the Production Brigade headquarters. They were standing on tiptoes trying to look through the tightly shut doors, unable to see anything but still stubbornly craning their necks. I could see a few people talking quietly into each other's ears, their expressions unclear. I moved closer to listen and managed to get the gist of it—Principal He was locked up inside. Sis asked Dongfang's mom, who was standing beside her, what was happening, but she said, "Who knows? I heard it's got something to do with Yaya, but I dunno." Sis wanted to ask more, but then everyone quieted down, and Wu Tianye, the branch Party secretary, came out of the headquarters entrance, waving his hand and saying, "Everybody go on home. If you've got business to do here, come back tomorrow."

The crowd dispersed. Sis cocked her head and looked at me. "Does it have something to do with Yaya?"

How would I know?

"Yaya" was Chive. She's around twenty years old. She's an idiot; her brain doesn't work right. She smiles at everyone she sees and asks whether they've eaten. She was called Yaya seven years ago, and didn't get called Chive until Old Man He took her into his house. When she was called Yaya, she was an orphan; her dad died when she was nine, and then one day her mom disappeared. Some people said she ran off with someone; anyway, she never came back. All Yaya could do was wander about the village. She would play with someone's cat or goose, and the owner would usually invite her in at mealtime. Wu Tianye was already the Party secretary back then; he told everyone to take turns feeding Yaya: as long as she was alive, they would keep taking care of her. Apart from her three meals, though, nobody bothered with anything else for Yaya. She was always dirty and disheveled, her face so grimy it looked like she was wearing a mask, and she ran around outside even on rainy days. Later, when Old Man He came to be our schoolmaster, he took pity on Yaya, who was eating everyone's food but had no one looking out for her, so he said to Wu Tianye, "Why don't I just take her in?" Old He was not from these parts; they said he was from some big place in the north. He showed up here alone and became the schoolmaster. My dad said, "You can tell he's the teacher type, wearing that hat all the time, indoors and out."

The day Yaya was brought to Old Man He's front door, he just happened to be picking through a bunch of chives that someone had given him. He stood up with a handful of chives and said, "We should change your name; let's call you Chive."

And so she became Chive. Those who were used to calling her Yaya kept calling her Yaya; everyone else called her Chive. Two days later, Yaya had transformed into a clean and fresh Chive. Old Man He helped her wash and comb her hair, and made two sets of new clothes for her. People who had been around said, "You know, Yaya's pretty good-looking, like the girls in the city." I had never seen what city people looked like, but if Chive looked like them, I guess they had four things going for them: clean, white, pretty, and they had new clothes to wear. After she washed her face, Chive was even fairer than my sister, and that's the honest truth.

After a while, Chive started treating Old Man He like her father, and routinely called him Dad. Old Man He was happy about it, as if he were delighted to have an idiot daughter. He taught her to read and write and to do arithmetic problems. I doubt if she could learn that stuff in her whole life; even I, with an undamaged brain, had trouble with problems that were a little complicated, so I couldn't believe a simpleton like her would ever get them. It was hard to even imagine it. But there was progress in some other areas, like speaking and looking at people. Before, once Chive had opened her mouth, she wouldn't shut it, and drool would dangle from the corners of it. But now it's different; now she can pull her saliva back before it dribbles out. Her gaze has also become more focused. Before when you stood facing her, you always felt like she was looking at two other people, and in two different directions to boot. Her gaze wandered, like chickens, ducks, and geese, with each eye taking care of its own side. When Chive just stands there without talking, she looks even better than a normal person. Of course, you can't give her anything good to eat, because as soon as she sees it, her mouth and eyes all go their separate ways again.

Everyone knew Old Man He was good to Chive, but Dongfang's mom meant that Old Man He's arrest had something to do with Chive.

Someone was calling me, and I could tell right away that it was Rice. Thirty Thousand, Whole Table, and a couple of other kids from class were right behind him. "How big are the puppies?" Rice asked. "Can you give me one?"

"They're still little," I said. Actually it wasn't up to me; who the puppies would go to when they got to be a month old was my parents' decision. Even before Furball had given birth, a bunch of people were lining up for puppies. I didn't want Rice to know I had no say in the matter; they would look down on me.

My sister said, "Rice, why did your dad put Schoolmaster He in the lockup?"

"Why don't you ask him?" Rice said. "It has nothing to do with me. I didn't lock him up." He waved a hand at the bunch behind him, and they all went off together. I envied him his wave, and that rich and solid "Let's go!"—so commanding, so unlike us with our flimsy arms and spindly legs and our shrill voices. Just as they were about to leave, Rice reminded me, "Don't forget to set one aside for me, the more the better."

"There aren't any."

"What do you mean?"

"Mom and Dad already gave them away."

"Fuck!" Rice said. "I spoke up before they were born, and now they're gone?" He threw a rock and hit a locust tree ten meters away. "It's just a stinking little dog. Fuck! If you won't give one to me, then to hell with it!"

When we got home, Chive was sitting in the kitchen helping Mom start the fire. Busying herself with the fire like that, she looked prettier than other girls. Sis asked Mom again, "Why did they arrest Old He?" Mom gave her a look and signaled her to keep her mouth shut with Chive there. Chive had dinner at our house, but when she got halfway through the meal, she stopped and said: "Chive won't eat; Dad didn't eat."

"We've got his set aside," Mom said. "You eat yours."

———

3

I was frightened awake in the middle of the night by a nightmare about the hat. I dreamt that it grew thirty-two skinny legs like a spider, and it skittered up my back and suddenly grabbed my neck. I screamed and woke up, wiping the sweat off my forehead, then relaxed when I realized that it was only a dream. I climbed out of bed and, with the help of the moonlight, pulled the hat out from under my bed. It had gone back to its normal shape. I carefully inspected its rim and didn't find any legs. I threw it back under the bed; I had to think of a way to get it out of there.

The next morning, Sis woke me up. "Quick!" she said. "They're gonna struggle Schoolmaster He!" It took me a while to come to my senses, then I jumped to the floor from my bed. "Struggle how?"

"Parade him through the streets!"

The sound of drums and gongs began from West Avenue. The gongs were those big bronze gongs, the drums were ox-hide drums. If you didn't know better, you would think an opera troupe was in town. When I went to the well to wash my face, I saw Chive playing with Furball and her four puppies. She was holding two of the puppies against her bosom, one in the crook of each arm, kissing each of them on the mouth, with lullaby sounds coming out of her throat. It was hideous.

"Keep your hands off my puppies!" I shouted.

Chive was so frightened that she let one arm drop, sending that puppy tumbling to the ground, and as the other arm became unbalanced, the other pup went down, too. The puppies yelped nonstop from the fall. I ran over with my face and hands still dripping with water, and hurriedly picked them up and coddled them. "Oooh, poor babies! You had a big fall!" Chive bowed her head and looked up at me. Knowing she had messed up, she stood off to one side, pouting and pulling at her clothes.

"What are you looking at? You almost killed them!" I howled.

Chive started crying with a great big "Waaah!" Swinging her arms, she cried, "I want my dad! I gotta look for Dad!"

My mom ran out of the kitchen, drying her hands with her apron. "Don't cry, Yaya, don't cry! Who's been picking on you?"

Chive pointed at me: "Him! He's yelling at me!"

"Don't cry, Yaya, I'll give him a beating!" She pretended to hit me. "See, I'm hitting him. I'll chop him up and feed him to the dogs!"

Chive laughed and stamped her feet. "Chop him up! Chop him up and feed the puppies! Hee-hee!" But then she grew quiet and looked like she was going to cry again. "I want my dad! I gotta look for Dad!"

Mom said, "You can look after you've eaten. That's a good girl, Yaya." Then she said to me and Sis, "What are you standing there for? Are you waiting for me to bring breakfast out here for you?"

We didn't do a proper job of eating. Sis and I were anxious. The drums and gongs on West Avenue were booming up to the skies, even making our table vibrate. I didn't dare say anything. Mom and Dad were both shielding Chive, afraid she'd find out that Old He had been captured and struggled. What's the big deal? They'd beat him up, then wheel him around the streets a few days. I just wanted to know what it was that He had done.

I ran into some schoolmates on the street. They were all on their way to West Avenue. Old Man He had been arrested, so of course there was no school. It seemed like all the passersby in Flower Street had come, and they were thronged in front of the door of Brigade headquarters. There were two drummers at the gate, and one person ringing a gong: *boom boom boom bonnnng, boom boom boom boom bonnnng!* I had just pushed my way in when one of the doors opened, and Midnight Liu's younger son came out, waving his hands at the crowd—"Stand clear! Back off! Back off! Get out of the way!" Everybody stuck out their asses and backed off. The other door opened, and Old Man He was pushed out by Liu's older son. He was in a really weird getup.

Like the soul-reaper Bai Wuchang in the comics, He was wearing a tall, pointy white cap, and around his neck a huge card was hanging, on which was written

A Beast in Human Clothing
Old Yet Indecent.

Old He came out through the gate with his head bent down, and the drums and gongs, which had just fallen silent, began booming again, then again came to a stop. Wu Tianye also came out. Because everyone had quieted down, his voice seemed unusually loud. Wu Tianye said: "Fellow villagers, these past two days I've been wracked by a headache and a heartache! When I saw those letters of accusation, I felt like my eyes were going to explode, and I couldn't close my mouth. I could never have imagined, even in my dreams, and I bet no one in Flower Street would ever dream, that our Schoolmaster He, the teacher who teaches our Flower Street children to read and write, is a beast in human disguise! That he had such filthy intentions when he adopted our Flower Street orphan Yaya! Fellow villagers, how young Yaya is, our Chive, only twenty years old! Such a fine age, and yet she was destroyed by him, this swine! This brings shame on our Flower Street! Tell me, what should we do? What should we do?"

Midnight Liu's two sons shouted in unison, "Beat him to death! Beat him to death!" followed by a surge of sound from the drums and gongs.

Wu Tianye waved his hand, and the sound stopped. He said, "Beating him to death is wrong, but Flower Street's cry for justice must be answered; Yaya and the people of Flower Street deserve some kind of satisfaction. The Brigade has discussed it: we'll parade him through the streets to make an example of him. We cannot accuse good men falsely, but evil men will not get away! All right, let it begin!"

The drums and gongs sounded again. In front were Midnight Liu's two sons, who were dragging Old Man He, one man on each arm. As they passed in front of me, Old He raised his eyes, and I quickly hid myself behind another onlooker. He walked another few steps, and then the drums stopped again. Everyone was wondering what was going on. Then a bunch of kids' voices broke the silence as if reciting lessons:

Our schoolmaster should die for such crimes; he is inhuman. Our schoolmaster is worse than a beast; he is a dirty old man. Seven years ago he had his evil idea and took in the stupid girl so he could ride her like a horse. We saw him hit Chive; we saw him scold Chive; we saw him commit every evil. Parade him on the street; criticize him in a struggle session: down with all shameless vermin!

I quickly came out from where I'd been hiding behind someone and saw that there were seven or eight little kids from lower grades in three rows, walking behind Old Man He with their eyes fixed on his back. I went over for a look, and found that a big white card had been hung on He's back, covered with brush-written characters. No wonder the kids were reciting those slogans so perfectly—they were reading them off the card! Still, I had to hand it to them; there were several characters I wasn't sure I knew. I stared at some of the blurry characters and began to feel that the harder I looked at them, the more familiar they seemed, until I finally realized they were in Old Man He's own handwriting. Nobody in Flower Street could write so beautifully in the Yan script—Old Man He had taught us that this kind of fat and solid calligraphy was called Yan script. It was really hard to believe that Old Man He had written the very words that were cursing him, and cursing him so directly and fiercely.

I knew a little bit about that stuff that grownup men and women do together. Rice and the other guys were always talking about those parts of men's and women's bodies. Rice himself had told me that he saw a naked couple having sex in the reed patch off Eighth Street; they were steadily pumping away, the guy's naked butt going up and down like a pile driver. I won't say who it was, but I know. When Rice got to the part about the naked butt, he started drooling out of the corners of his mouth, like someone who ate too much fatty meat on New Year's and still had oil smeared all over his mouth. But to be honest, I had never seen Old Man He and Chive doing anything. I always pass behind He's house when I walk the ducks; all I have to do is turn my head, and I can see as clear as day even where they put their teacups in there.

But these sons of bitches all chimed in and said they saw them. I'm sure I don't know how they managed that.

The crowd would move forward for a while and then stop. As soon as they sounded the drums and gongs, those little bastards started reciting the lines off of Old Man He's back. The crowd was unruly. West Avenue was narrow enough as it was, and with all those people jostling around, it was chaotic, and I soon got separated from my sister. Another reason for the confusion was that everybody was arguing with everybody else about what was going on. As far as I could make out, there were three main opinions. One was that Old Man He ought to get what was coming to him, a man of his age wearing that fedora all day long like some kind of VIP, when all along he'd been so rotten and evil inside, taking a girl in off the streets with such filthy schemes in mind. It's a good thing she was an idiot; if she were a proper girl, how could she go on living with that shame? How could she get married and have kids? The second point of view was totally different from the first. So what if she's an idiot? A stupid girl is still a girl. Yaya is a woman, too; if it weren't for her mental defects, that face of hers, that skin as white as jellied bean starch, how many Flower Street girls could compare with her? And the third point of view was naturally another story altogether; they thought that nothing had happened at all, that Old Man He had been in Flower Street for seven years and had always been good to people, especially Yaya; though she was a simpleton, she was dear to him. How could he do such a thing? I wouldn't believe it even if you beat me to death.

"Then why was he arrested, and why is he being paraded around Flower Street?"

"Who knows what scoundrel framed him? There're more and more in Flower Street who eat human food but don't shit human shit!"

Since there were these different views, the crowd split off into smaller groups. Some of them were following the parade participants around to observe and shout along with them, "Down with Old Man He, beat him to death!" There were even people spitting on him and throwing rocks. Another group was looking on coolly with their arms folded, talking to each other in twos and threes, their eyes fixed on the marchers in front. The third group was clustered at the back of the throng; in fact, they had come out on West Avenue but weren't following the parade, just stopped in places along the side of the road, their long faces showing anger, mumbling to themselves about how Old Man He had been wrongly accused. I turned my head to look for my sister and heard them cursing people, including Midnight Liu's two sons. Now only two or three of the seven or eight little kids were reciting. The ones who had left had been pulled out of the reciting squad by their ears by these folks. They scolded their sons or young relatives: "You little rascal! Itching for a beating, are you? I'll teach you to make a spectacle of yourself!"

The parade group continued along the street, with more drums and gongs and more reciting. Later I heard some grownups say it was the first time they had ever seen someone alternately being paraded around and indicted like that; they wondered if it was what foreigners did. I ran back to the front group just out of curiosity. I saw gobs of spittle, rocks, and clods of mud with moss on them being thrown at Old He from all directions. They were scooping those clumps of mud up from the base of the wall. I didn't throw anything at Old Man He, because I didn't know if he had done anything wrong. And I didn't dare; he was my teacher, he taught me all my lessons, and I had his hat hidden under my bed. As soon as I remembered the hat, I got nervous. I had really screwed up this time; did I think taking his hat would get me a meal or something?

Later I thought I should have brought the hat out with me and given it back to him to put on. That tall dunce cap had already been knocked off him. Midnight Liu's sons tried to put it back on him a bunch of times, but it always got knocked off. The boys got impatient and pretended they didn't see, stepping on it so they wouldn't have to pick it up again. So the rocks, mud, and spit were falling directly on that nearly bald head of his. Blood started to flow, and gobs of spit started to hang down and sway, but Old Man He didn't make a sound, as if he'd suddenly lost the ability to speak.

For heaven's sake, say something! Why don't you talk?

———

4

Just when the procession had turned from East Avenue onto Flower Street, Chive came running toward them, her arms swinging wildly. The wind had blown her hair back, and her breasts were bouncing around. Through the people banging drums and gongs, she saw Old Man He with his head down, looking at his feet.

"Papa!" Chive cried. "What are you doing? I was looking for you yesterday!"

Old He's head shot up, and he opened his mouth to say something, his dry lips split and bleeding in two places. Midnight Liu's two sons immediately pulled his arms straight, but Chive had already lunged in front of them. She gave each of Midnight Liu's sons a slap on the arm. "Why did you take my papa?" As she tried to grab Old He, she suddenly saw the card hanging from his neck. She tilted her head and looked at it for a while, then pointed at it and said, "Pa, let's go home and I'll make dinner for you. What's this writing?"

The gongs and drums stopped, and everyone stood staring at Chive. Midnight Liu's sons were stunned at first, too, but then they loosened their grip on Old He to push Chive, and Chive cried out, her hands crazily grabbing and scratching at them. The two sons had nowhere to hide.

Old Man He said hoarsely, "Chive, you go on home, go home."

Chive said, "Pa, he hit me, I wanna fight him!" She took a swipe across Midnight Liu's son's face, leaving two bloody scratches. The boy felt the pain, and when he rubbed it with his hand and saw blood, he let out a wild cry and went berserk, ripping Chive's blouse almost completely off, exposing half her chest and one plump white breast. Old Man He lunged forward to cover her, but the two Liu boys tightly gripped his arms, and Old He could only cry out. The veins bulged out on his neck and forehead, and his scalp started bleeding again. The surrounding onlookers rose up onto their tiptoes.

Someone said into my ear, "Blockhead, how does it look?"

"How does what look?" I said, then turned my head to see who was asking. It was Rice.

"*That*, of course," he said, smiling at me devilishly, making a cupping gesture with his right hand.

My face immediately got hot. "I didn't look! I was looking at Old Man He's bald head."

"Didn't look at what?" Thirty Thousand's head poked out from another direction. "Who said they're small, small what? I think your heart's throbbing for it!"

"It's not throbbing." I wasn't even sure what to say.

"I'll bet you're throbbing somewhere!" Whole Table's face also poked out from somewhere.

Thirty Thousand pushed Whole Table back and said, "I'm gonna ask you again, can you give us one of those puppies or not?"

"Ask my mom and dad; they already promised them all to other people."

Rice looked at Chive's chest and wiped his mouth. I saw my mother coming. She pulled Chive off to the side to straighten her clothes, and Chive struggled a bit before she relented. She still wanted to give Midnight Liu's son more scratches. Rice was staring hard at Chive the whole time and said, "If you're not gonna give me one, the hell with it! Let's go!" Thirty Thousand and Whole Table took off, with a few of the others trailing behind them.

They went off in such a self-satisfied huff, it made me feel bad. All the kids in class hang out with Rice; wherever he goes, there's always a big crowd following behind him, looking really happy. It was like they were happy no matter what they were doing, but not me. I'm often off stewing by myself, like I've got something on my mind all day. What it is I'm thinking about, I couldn't really say. One time I spent two days trying to figure it out, and decided the problem might have something to do with my voice. My voice was high and shrill, and Rice probably thought I didn't deserve to hang out with him. There was nothing I could do about that. I couldn't do anything about the fact that he wanted a puppy, either; my mom had said she'd promised them all to people already, and my job was just to raise them for a month. So I take care of them. And anyway, I love those little things.

The procession came back to order after the confusion. My mom had finally gotten Chive away. "Chive is a good girl," Old He said to my ma. "Believe me, I did absolutely nothing immoral with her! You have to believe me. It doesn't matter if they hound me to death, but if they ruin Chive, how will she get along in life?" He made my mom take Chive home. Chive didn't want to go, but Old He said, "Be a good girl, Chive, go home and make dinner for your dad. Dad will go around town one more time and then come home to eat."

They started beating the drums and gongs again. Mom took Chive's hand and led her home. By now the number of people throwing garbage at He was dwindling.

The parade didn't end until the middle of the afternoon, and I was starving. Finally the clamor of the drums and gongs also died down, with only an occasional listless clatter, because the kids reciting off the card had all gone home after the second-to-last lap. Without the reciting, the people with the drums and gongs had no choice but to bang away some more. When I got home, there was no one there. I found a piece of flat bread and started munching on it while I went to the base of the wall to look for the puppies—but I only saw Furball and two of the pups. I went around the whole wall, looking in every corner, but there was no sign of the others. As I was standing in the courtyard in a daze, my sister came back. I asked her, "Where are the puppies?"

"I was about to ask you," she said. "I've been looking all over for them! Did you give them away to someone?"

"I didn't!"

"For goodness' sake," she said, "all you think about is eating! We have to search for them!"

I took the half-eaten bread with me and went out through the gate to look for the puppies. When you need to look for something, you realize that Flower Street is not a small place after all. What was small were the two puppies: all they'd have to do is burrow into some corner and you'd never find them. I whistled as I searched, hoping the little puppies could hear me. East Avenue, West Avenue, Flower Street, I looked everywhere and didn't find anything. Parched with thirst, I went to the canal. There were boats moving along it, and there was loading and unloading going on at the stone docks. Some people were squatting on the stone steps, chatting away with cigarettes between their fingers. I asked them, "Have you seen our puppies?"

"Are your puppies named Zhang or named Li?"

All they wanted to do was make fun of me, so I said, "They're named You!"

I saw a puppy at the Second Dock. He was squatting in the bushes, with his head sticking out and his jaw on the ground. I whistled to him and clapped my hands, but the little guy didn't move. I got mad and grabbed him by the ear to drag him out, but the only thing that came out was his head! Under his neck was some freshly congealing blood; his body was nowhere to be seen, but his little eyes were wide open. I screamed in terror and fell backwards on my ass. I sat there for a long time, and the wet mud soaked coolness into my pants. The cake I had just eaten was doing somersaults in my belly and wanted to come back out, but I held it. I gave the skin between my left forefinger and thumb a hard pinch, and the tears began to flow.

After a while I broke off a few branches and dug a hole behind the bushes. It was sunset by the time I buried the little puppy, and dusk had draped itself over the canal. The water was grayish-brown. A boat went by, splitting the canal in two.

I was afraid to keep looking, afraid I would find the other puppy's head.

How could he have died here like this? I couldn't figure it out. The wound looked like it was from a knife, but it also looked torn and bitten. Who killed my puppy?

When I got back to Flower Street, I ran into Whole Table, and he said, "I found a puppy."

"Where?"

"At Rice's house."

I turned and ran straight for Rice's house. Whole Table said, "What's the hurry? It's not going anywhere!" Then he ran with me to Rice's house. The gate to the compound was standing open, and Rice, Thirty Thousand, and Crooked Neck Danian were in the courtyard playing with a puppy. It was our puppy, all right. They kept rolling him over and making him get up.

"Puppy!" I called out to him.

The puppy rolled over and stood up. He ran toward me, staggering from dizziness. I picked him up and held him, and he squealed with joy.

"It's yours?" Rice stood up; his voice always sounded like it came up from his belly. "Whole Table picked him up on the street."

"Yeah."

"You want to take him home?"

"Yes!"

"It's not easy to pick up a dog," said Rice.

"It's not as if there's puppies all over the place," Crooked Neck Danian said.

I looked at them. I couldn't figure out what they were getting at.

"It should be worth something to you to get him back," Thirty Thousand said.

"What do you have in mind?"

Rice scratched his head and couldn't think of anything interesting, but after a while he said, "What if Chive . . . ah, never mind, that would be hard to do." Then he laughed, "Fuck, you don't have anything fun!"

"The hat! Old Man He's hat!" Whole Table said. "He's got it, for sure!"

I hesitated. I wanted to take the hat to Old He so he wouldn't have to get hit on his bare scalp with rocks and mud and stuff. What's more, he had caught a cold in the afternoon, so his nose was running and he was sneezing constantly.

"If you don't want to trade, forget it! Put the dog down."

"I'll trade."

Once I brought the puppy home, I took out the hat, flattened it to stick it into my jacket, and ran back to Rice's house. Rice took the hat and pushed and pulled it around until it was back to its original shape, and then the bunch of them started tossing it around the compound like a flying saucer. They had just started playing when I heard Wu Tianye cough—he had more phlegm than he could cough up in a whole day. Rice quickly hid the hat in the hay in the ox pen. He was afraid of his dad, just like I was afraid of my mom.

———

5

———

Chive was restless. After eating dinner at our house, she wanted to run as soon as she put down her bowl. When the time for the next meal came, Mom sent me to get her. My sister wouldn't go; she said she had enough people to do chores for without taking care of an idiot. Mom scolded her. "So what if she's an idiot? These guys don't have any conscience." Sister felt wronged and said, "Don't say 'these guys' or 'those guys.' Which 'guys' are you talking about?"

"I mean *you* guys," Mom said. "I really can't imagine what goes through your mind every day. I just don't get it. Who would believe that a good man like Old Man He is capable of such inhuman behavior? Wu Tianye said someone reported him, but who? Why won't he tell us? I say he's being framed!"

Sister said, "Ma, I thought Wu Tianye was your cousin or something, a relative!"

"Good grief, what a cousin! He couldn't be any farther removed. I'd rather claim a pig as my cousin!"

For years Mom had had it in for Wu Tianye. She'd curse him as soon as his name came up. She'd call him mean, always scheming to give people a hard time. Back when he was the village chief, he was already rotten. Everyone in the village was foraging for peanuts, and he wouldn't let them eat a single one! At first he made the brigade commanders run around in the fields and monitor everybody; when quitting time came, they would pull everyone's mouths open and inspect them for chewed-up peanut bits. Later that wasn't good enough, so he had them all rinse their mouths in the field at quitting time. They would spread a layer of sand on the ground and make everyone spit onto the sand; anyone who had sneaked some peanuts into their mouth would spit out white water. It didn't matter how much spit you tried to swallow. My mom said everyone was tightening their belts and going down into the fields to work, but not him; he would leisurely walk around with his hands behind him, turning his head this way and that like a field mouse, occasionally reaching into his pocket for a couple of peanuts that he would toss into his mouth.

What my mom meant in scolding my sister was this: a person should be able to eat what she wants; other people shouldn't say bad things about her.

Of course, Sister wasn't that kind of a person, she just didn't want to run around, so I had to go.

Old Man He's house was a small freestanding compound behind the school. I knocked for the longest time, but there was no response, so I started yelling, "Chive! Chive!" But the only answer I got was some lazy honks from the two geese in the courtyard—from the sound of them, they were probably famished. Who knew where that idiot had gone off to. I looked all around the compound gate, and Rotten Egg's mom saw me. She told me that Chive had headed west. I went in the direction she pointed, following an alley all the way to the end. Society's wife, who was holding her baby, told me that she had turned south, and so I looked south. After I passed Five Bushel Channel, I saw Chive jogging. I called, "Chive! Chive!" But the south wind was rushing in her ears, and she didn't hear. I was going to shout again when I saw something being tossed up from behind a row of haystacks by the drying ground ahead—something black, something round, like a big upside-down mushroom. I immediately stopped.

Then I saw Rice, Thirty Thousand, Whole Table, and Crooked Neck Danian running between the haystacks, their crazy shouts carried over by the wind. Chive was running forward, she was running toward the hat. As she ran she shouted, "The hat! That's my papa's hat! Where did you get my papa's hat?'"

When she got close, Rice and the guys stopped, and no matter how she screamed, they wouldn't give it to her. They just exchanged creepy looks and laughed. I didn't dare go over there; I was afraid they would say that they got the hat from me. They let the hat fly again, and they passed it between them, toying with Chive. Chive couldn't get at the hat, so she sat down on the ground in frustration and started bawling at the top of her lungs, picking up clods of dirt and throwing them in all directions. Rice and the others probably were afraid someone would discover them, so they teased her for a while and then took the hat and ran away.

I caught up to her after they had gotten pretty far away. Chive wanted the hat. I said, "Hat-schmat! Let's eat first and then talk."

"I want the hat first, then eat! My dad will catch cold! He'll sniffle! His eyes will water! He'll sneeze!"

I said, "Eat first, and then the hat."

"Get the hat, and then I'll eat!"

"Eat first, then I'll go and get the hat for you."

"Really?" Chive stopped crying. She looked up at me and held out her little finger, which was smeared with mud: "Promise and hope to die?"

Why not? I held out my own little finger and hooked it with hers: "Hope to die." Chive was suddenly all smiles. She got up off the ground and didn't even bother to wipe the mud off her pants. "Okay," she said, "let's eat, eat!"

Chive wanted me to go get the hat as soon as she'd cleaned up her bowl. The stupid idiot! My mom said, "Okay, I'll make him go find it and bring it back to you." But where was I supposed to go? I said, "I don't know where it is." Mom shot me a look, and I said, "Okay, okay, I'll go look for it right now." If I didn't agree, she wouldn't go with Mom to the vegetable garden. I went out the gate and wandered aimlessly until I got bored and headed over to see Old Man He get paraded through town.

There wasn't really anything to look at—same as before, drums and gongs. They had found five new kids to recite the lines. The content was about the same, just a little change in the wording. Apart from that, the card on his chest had been replaced, and there was new writing:

He looks like a scholar

But he is a beast in human garb

It was still Old Man He's own calligraphy. It wasn't written as carefully as the last one; he probably was losing his patience. With his head bowed, Old He was being paraded as his tears and snot flowed down. His cold was getting worse, and he coughed occasionally. The same two people were still banging on the drum and gong, but their energy was flagging, I guess because the crowd was thinning out. This kind of public spectacle was a little monotonous; after a few rounds, there weren't too many people who wanted to follow anymore. Old Man He would even raise his head from time to time and look around, maybe because there were so few people throwing rocks and spitting at him that he was feeling lonesome. The only ones with spirit were Midnight Liu's two sons; they still seemed as fired up as they had been at the very beginning, which was really something.

I went along with the procession through a lap around West Avenue, East Avenue, and Flower Street, then went off to the stone dock. The water in the canal had risen, and the flow had gotten more turbulent and muddy, tumbling down from the upper reaches. I heard that there had been heavy rains up there, and flooding, and some old houses had even been washed away. There was a crowd at the dock watching Chen He fish stuff out of the canal. He had attached two bamboo poles together and put an iron hook on the front, and he was using that to pull out whatever came floating down from the flooding upstream. By the time I got there, the dock was cluttered with dead pigs, cats, tree roots, pot lids, wooden cabinets, and benches. Everyone was saying that with his hooking skills, sooner or later Chen He would pull out a millstone.

But he had not pulled out a millstone by sunset. I went back home at dusk and found that another puppy was missing. I looked for it for a long time but didn't find it. So I went to look at the animals Chen He had picked up at the stone dock. There was a dead puppy, but it wasn't ours. By then the sky was already black.

——

6

——

The next morning, I went out to look for the puppies again. First I looked on the three streets, asking everyone I saw. Then I went to take a look around the canal bank and the nearby bushes and reeds. Nothing. I went back to the dock, and Chen He was still fishing things out of the canal, and he did pull out a bunch of dead dogs, but none of them looked like ours. It was strange. Later I ran into Han's uncle. He said he had just seen a puppy on Eighth Street and I should go have a look. I asked him what color it was, and he said he hadn't seen it clearly, it was just a fleeting glimpse, like he just saw a head flash by. I went south to look.

Eighth Street was on the south side of Flower Street. There were open fields there that you had to cross a graveyard to get to, so people didn't go there very often. I had no idea at the time that the puppies might have run so far away; I just went that way without thinking. I went along by fits and starts, entering the graveyard. There were pine trees growing between the graves, so it was dark and chilly in there, and my heart raced. If it hadn't been broad daylight, I would rather have died than go to that place. Once I'd gotten most of the way through the graveyard, I started to hear voices, which scared me so much I wanted to turn back around. But then I thought the voices sounded familiar, like iron: it had to be Rice. I couldn't make out what he was saying. I bent over and looked between the graves, and finally I saw a person moving between the graves and the pine trees.

The sunlight was coming down through the trees, and I walked in that direction toward the patches of ground the sun was shining on. The talking was getting louder, and it wasn't just one person.

Someone said, "Take them off."

Someone else said, "Take it off!"

A third person said, "Pull them down lower."

Then it was Rice's voice: "Do you want it or not?"

I walked ahead along the grave mounds, and suddenly heard Chive say, "Give it to me! Give it to me!"

Someone laughed coldly, and then someone else; it was probably Thirty Thousand and Crooked Neck Danian. I looked across a grave mound and saw Rice and Whole Table talking into each other's ears, both with their arms crossed over their chests. Thirty Thousand and Crooked Neck Danian were each seated on top of a grave, and Thirty Thousand was using his right forefinger to spin Old Man He's fedora.

"Hurry up!" Thirty Thousand said with a strange smile. "See? The hat's right here!"

I didn't dare go any closer, so I hid behind a grave and stuck my head out to watch. They shouted and then shouted again. Behind a grave mound I could see the back of Chive's head, then her neck, and before I knew it I could see her naked back, and then when she started running toward Thirty Thousand, my God, Chive's whole body was naked white skin;

her butt was so big, it looked like two balls. Suddenly something leapt up into my throat, and I let out a loud belch; it scared me so much I quickly squatted down to hide. Rice called out tentatively, "Who's there?"

The other four cautiously looked around them. "Who? Where is he?"

For some time there was no sound. Chive had stopped in mid-stride.

Crooked Neck Danian said, "There's no one there; you must have been hearing things!"

Rice said, "It sounded like someone belched just now. Maybe I imagined it."

Thirty Thousand laughed disdainfully and said, "Who would come to this godforsaken place? Rice, are you going first?"

"You go first," said Rice. "I'll wait."

Thirty Thousand said, "I think you should go first. Or maybe Whole Table?"

Whole Table said, "Danian should be first. Isn't he always talking about how big his thing is? Why don't you give it a try?"

Crooked Neck Danian also gave a sarcastic laugh. "I was just kidding," he said. "Thirty Thousand should go. Didn't you say you can do this in your sleep? You've done it so many times."

Chive called out again, "Give me the hat! My dad's hat!"

I stretched out my neck and belched again. There was no way I could hold it in, considering what I had just seen! Chive turned around and ran toward me, and I saw her fat white breasts bouncing up and down, and then that black tuft between her legs. Seeing Chive like that made me panic, and my heart was racing so fast I felt like it was about to float away. I honestly couldn't hold back that burp, and to let it rip I had to stretch my neck longer and longer.

"Quick!" Rice said. "There *is* someone!"

Thirty Thousand and the others turned around and were about to run away, but Rice stopped them and said, "See who it is first!"

Once I heard that, I knew I was dead, and I started running away as fast as I could. Crooked Neck Danian was yelling behind me, "It's Blockhead!"

Rice said, "After him! Don't let him get away!"

The whole bunch of them was behind me. They yelled as they chased me, telling me to stop. How could I stop? I was wishing I could grow four wings out of my armpits. I didn't realize I could run so fast, and they couldn't catch up to me. There were some people up ahead, and they didn't dare keep up the chase. They turned and took another road toward Flower Street. I stopped and collapsed onto my ass. I could feel my legs getting shaky.

I sat for the length of time it would take to smoke two cigarettes, then remembered that Chive was still in the graveyard, and I got up to look for her. She had put on her clothes and was coming toward me. She had buttoned her shirt up wrong. As soon as she saw me, she said, "The hat! My dad's hat!"

"Rice and those guys have the hat."

"I want the hat! Give me the hat!"

I was afraid she'd get stupid on me and not do what she was told; she didn't even seem to know that she had just taken all her clothes off, and she was pulling at my clothes telling me to give her the hat. I said, "Okay, then let go." She finally let go and said, "I want it today."

"Okay," I said. "But you'd better not to take off your clothes anymore."

"Uh-huh. I won't. I want the hat."

I led Chive toward Flower Street. Alongside the road there was a drainage ditch. There wasn't a lot of water in it, but there sure was a lot of grass. As we walked along I lost sight of her, and when I turned to look, I saw her squatting by the ditch with her head cocked to one side. I called to her, but she was saying, "Puppy, puppy." My heart almost stopped; I had almost forgotten about the pups. I ran over, and she was pointing at something in the grass and reeds. "Puppy! Puppy!"

As soon as I saw it, I had to cover my mouth. Sure enough, it was the pup we were looking for, but his head was the only thing there . . . this time his eyes were shut. I pulled Chive up and headed for home. I didn't want to see any more, and I didn't want to bury this one in a hole like I did the last one. The whole way home, Chive was mumbling, "Puppy . . . puppy . . ."

―――

7

―――

When we got home, I told Mom and Dad about the dead puppy. When I reported it, I was squatting by the dog pen, instinctively worrying about the other two. The whole family squatted around me, everyone clamoring to guess, but we couldn't figure out why there was nothing but a head. What kind of animal enjoys that kind of hobby? We couldn't imagine. We hadn't offended anyone. But the puppies' bodies were gone just the same. Just thinking of those two little heads made my body all tingly and set my teeth to grinding loudly, and I had goosebumps all over. It made my hair stand on end.

"Someone must have it in for us," my sister said.

"Who the hell would have it in for us?" I said.

"What do you mean 'have it in for us'?" Mom said. "If people are out to get us, they wouldn't go after two puppies."

"No matter what, it doesn't hurt to take preventive measures," said Pa. "They're nowhere to be seen, but we're right out here in broad daylight. We have to put a stop to it once and for all."

"Give them away," Mom said, "right now."

Giving them away before they were even a month old . . . my heart made a loud ba-bump. I knew they had to be given away sooner or later, but now that the time had come, it still felt miserable, and I couldn't snap out of it. My mom patted me on the back of the head. "What are you standing there for? Go take them to Stars' and Pumpkin's families." I was holding the puppies and not moving, and Mom continued, "Are you waiting for someone to kill them, too?"

I jumped up, picked one up, and ran out. "I'm going to take you to Stars' house," I said to the puppy, my heart aching so much the tears were falling. Furball was barking in the basket, and the puppies were yelping, too.

When I went by Rice's house, I hid the puppy in my jacket and quickly flashed past their gate. Rice and the rest of them were all home; Thirty Thousand, Whole Table, and Crooked Neck Danian were cackling about something. When I came back from Stars' house, they were still laughing. Then I took the other puppy to Pumpkin's house, and when I went past there again, the laughing had ended. Their gate had one door open and the other one closed. I stopped, and the idea that suddenly came to me gave me a start.

Scared stiff, I walked into their compound through the gate. There was no one in the courtyard. I ran straight for the ox pen and the pile of hay. If you didn't look hard, you would have missed the hole in the middle of the haystack. I silently leaned over and got it as soon as I thrust my arm in. I stuck it in my jacket and ran away. It was only after I came out of the courtyard gate that I discovered there wasn't anyone around me. Then I could feel how violently my heart was beating.

I got it. I had actually stolen something from someone else's home.

My mom was boiling water in the kitchen, and she casually asked, "Did you get them delivered all right?"

"Yep," I said, and immediately went into my room.

I stuffed the hat under my bed, then sat on the bed in a daze, thinking about whether or not I should give it to Chive. She's a stupid girl; one slip of the tongue and I'd be exposed. I didn't feel comfortable about it. Finally I decided to ask my ma.

"Where did you get it?" Mom asked.

"I picked it up from in front of the gate at Rice's house," I said with my head down. "Principal He has cuts on his head, and he has a cold."

"Don't give it to Yaya, or she'll make trouble. Take it straight to Principal He."

"Is he locked up at Brigade headquarters?"

"I don't think so," Mom said, and then asked my pa, "Where is Principal He being held?"

"Wherever it is, it isn't Brigade headquarters." My dad was repairing his fishing net. "The clinic is in Brigade headquarters, and there's people going in and out of there all the time. Nobody has said they've seen him locked up in there."

Where Principal He was being kept was a problem—a problem I had overlooked the past two days. Where exactly he was, my mom and dad didn't have a clue. Sister brought Chive in from outside, and Chive immediately wanted the hat from me. I looked at my ma, and she told me to bring it out. Mom straightened out the fedora until she got it back in shape, and said to Chive, "Yaya, we found the hat. Let Blockhead take it to him, okay?"

"No!" Chive said. "I bring it, it's my pa's hat! I want to see my pa!"

"You can't take it," my mom said. "The branch Party secretary said that if you take it to him, he'll lock up your dad for the rest of his life, and you'll never see him again."

"Really?"

"Really."

"Okay . . . I won't take it to him." Chive rolled her eyes and said to me, "You bring it to him right now!"

"Yeah, I'll go right now." I found a bag to put the hat in, swung it across my shoulder, and went out the door. I went to the stone dock to see what Chen He was fishing out of the canal and then came right back. The water in the canal was still rising; for sure it was raining upriver. When I came in the door, I hid the hat in my jacket, then shook the empty bag for Chive to see. "See, I took the hat to your pa."

Chive was all smiles. "That's great!" she said. "My dad's eyes and nose won't be running anymore."

Even if his eyes and nose were running, there was no one to see it—there was no procession that day. My dad went to the stone dock in the morning and heard Midnight Liu say they were going to hold off on the parades for a couple of days. Everyone was tired; after some rest they would start up again. His two sons were both at home sleeping. Some people at the dock asked Midnight Liu where Old He was being kept, and Midnight Liu waved his hand and said he didn't know; those two bastard boys of his just came home and didn't say a word. They might as well have been Wu Tianye's own sons.

—

8

—

With all the puppies now gone, Furball circled around the nesting basket. She went outside the courtyard gate, then suddenly turned around and scurried into the house. She ran up to the basket and stood there staring, whining sadly. We gave her food, but she wouldn't eat much; she just sniffed at it a little, and that was it. When I called her, she came and pressed her neck against my leg, nudging me, her eyes brimming with tears. I tried to comfort her: "Don't feel bad, Furball, you can have another litter of puppies." I don't know if she understood, but she went out the door wagging her tail. And she didn't come back . . . we didn't hear a sound even when it got dark.

Sister said, "She went to look for her puppies, right?"

Even if she was looking, she wouldn't find anything now; she knows to come home when it gets dark. Feeling uneasy, I wolfed down a few mouthfuls of rice, then went out to look for Furball. I was afraid she might end up like those two little puppies, only a head left.

Furball wasn't a puppy, though; she would come running at the sound of my voice. I hit the streets with one thing on my mind, making all kinds of sounds—whistling, calling, and talking to myself. People walking past me turned their heads to look at me, wondering if I had some kind of mental problem. I walked several streets and roads, especially around Stars' and Pumpkin's houses, but she was nowhere to be found. It was weird. We had raised Furball for six years, so she should have been able to find our house with her eyes closed.

The moon that night looked like the curved blade of a thin knife, hanging blood-red in the middle of the sky. The water in the canal was black, but there were a few lamps shining dimly on boats. I couldn't see my own shadow on the ground. Some weird bugs were calling from the bushes. My mouth was getting numb from whistling so much; my throat was getting dry from talking to myself; but I still couldn't find Furball. The bloody thin knife moon moved. By the time I got to the abandoned mushroom house, it was already pretty late.

The mushroom house was on the bank of the canal. It was huge, with five big connected rooms. In the past they used it to grow mushrooms. Later, for some reason, they stopped growing mushrooms there, and left it to deteriorate. The tiers of mushroom beds were gradually dismantled and removed, leaving only the empty rooms. The door was always locked, and not even sunlight could get in. But I went in there a lot in the summer; I'd get in through a ventilation duct in the back of the building. A bunch of us would often climb in there after swimming in the canal. One kid refused to go in; it was dark and clammy, and the moldy stench made it hard to breathe. Good-for-nothing kids liked to climb in and piss and shit inside, so it really stank in there. When there was a little light, you could see flies, dung beetles, and emaciated mice skittering across the floor.

That night the mushroom house was like a big black monster. It made my hair stand on end just to look at it. I walked carefully along the wall, making sure to be light with my hands and feet, but suddenly one of my feet slid in what felt like it must have been some shit, and I cried out. Apart from my cry, everything was quiet, and the noises of insects became a part of the silence. I was shaking my foot, getting ready to wipe it on the grass by the river, when I heard a whimper. I halted, and heard a whimper again.

"Furball?" I quietly called out.

A whimper.

"Furball!" I cried louder.

Furball's whining also grew louder, and when I was sure it was coming from inside the mushroom house, I got up the courage to stick my head in the ventilation duct.

"Furball, what are you doing in there? Come out of there!"

Furball whined sadly in response.

Suddenly a human voice spoke from inside. "Is that Blockhead?" It shocked me so much I shrank back, and the voice added, "It's me, Principal He."

"Pr—Principal He, why are you in there, too?"

"I've been in here for days, but Furball has only been here since this afternoon."

"Why would she be in there?"

"Rice and those guys strung a rope through her nose and fastened her in here."

"Rice??"

That motherfucker, why would he coop Furball up in here? I stuck my head in the duct, but I couldn't see anything; I could only smell the pungent odor of mold and urine, and a little whiff of blood. Old He coughed, and Furball whined along with him. I held my breath as I climbed into the mushroom house, or the stench would have just about killed me. It was slippery underfoot—who knows what I'd stepped in this time. It was so dark, I couldn't see my hand in front of my face; only Furball's eyes were reflecting light.

"I can't see, Principal He."

"You'll get used to it after a bit."

A little while passed, but I still couldn't see well. Furball was in front, whining as she barked; Old He was back a ways. I could hear phlegm in his throat that he couldn't spit out. The two of them were just black shapes. I held out my hand toward Furball's shadowy figure and touched a rope. Furball yelped in pain.

"Don't touch the rope," Old He said. "It's threaded through her nose."

What Old He meant was that Furball had a rope run between her nostrils like an ox. I knew that oxen that had been strung like that would be in terrible pain if you bumped the nose rope. I couldn't see clearly where it went through her nostrils, and I didn't have a pair of scissors to cut the rope with, so I climbed back out of the vent and ran straight home. Mom and Dad were both asleep, so I stealthily got a flashlight and scissors and ran back to the mushroom house. When I was halfway there, I remembered Old He's hat, so I went back to get it.

Lit up by the flashlight, the mushroom house was too dirty inside to look at. Old He and Furball, one with scars on his head, the other with blood on her nose, looked like ghouls in the flashlight's rays. Furball tragically moaned in the direction of the light. Old He covered his eyes; he couldn't stand the bright light, and it was a while before he started to move his hand away from his eyes. I gave the hat to him, but he didn't want it. He asked me to take it back and keep it for him. I didn't want it anymore: "It's best that I give it to you; it'll help treat your cold," I said, and I put it on his head, which hurt him so much that he grimaced. Old He held the flashlight for me while I went about cutting the nose rope. That fucking bastard Rice had tied a square knot hard against Furball's nostril, and it took forever for me to cut it free. Furball was quiet during the whole process, and when it was over, she eagerly licked my hand, tears rolling out of her eyes.

"Furball . . . Furball . . . ," I said. "Okay, let's go home."

Then I wanted to cut Old He loose as well, but he wouldn't let me. "I can't drag you into this," he said. "They'll just struggle me a few more days and let me go home."

"My mom told me Wu Tianye is rotten from the boils on his head to the pus coming out of his feet. You'd be better off running."

"Nothing doing; I can't let him win. If I run, it would play right into his hands, and our neighbors would all think I'd really done evil."

"You really won't run?"

"No."

"Okay. My mom and dad both say you're a good man." I was rubbing Furball's neck. "Chive is at our house, and she always wants to see you."

"You can't let her know I'm in this place; I'll be out of here in a few days." He took off the hat and wanted to give it back to me. "You take it. I'll get it back from you when they let me out."

But I didn't take it—I had enough trouble to deal with. I said, "You'd better keep it on," and I picked up Furball and started to leave. He told me to hold up, but I had already pushed Furball through the vent, and I was climbing out of it myself. The moon was high, and the grass made shooshing sounds under my feet. Everything I passed was covered with dew.

—

9

—

Early the next morning, Mom and Dad were chattering away in the courtyard; Furball was barking along with them. They were always like this: they'd get up really early, and then they wouldn't have anything in particular to do, so they would spend half the morning in a heated discussion about where to put a chicken feed bowl. I turned over, thinking I would go back to sleep, but then I felt like I had to pee, so I got up to go to the bathroom. Dad was squatting by the well platform sharpening a knife; Mom was washing clothes. They were not resting their mouths as they worked, but when they saw me, they stopped their discussion.

"Blockhead, why are you up so early?" my dad asked.

"To go to the can."

"Stay in bed," my mom said. "There's nothing going on anyway."

Of course I was going to stay in bed. The sun wasn't even up yet, and the sky above Flower Street was shrouded in a damp grayness. That's Flower Street; early mornings always seemed like cloudy days. When I came back from peeing, Dad was still sharpening his knife, and Mom was still washing clothes, and both of them were still mumbling about something. I went back to bed, and as soon as I turned my head, I fell back asleep. Then I had a dream, a dream that Furball had four more puppies, a black one, a white one, a yellow one, and a spotted one. Each puppy had a full coat of shiny long fur, so when they ran they looked like a big ball of fuzzy yarn. Furball was playing with the four puppies, yapping happily. Or at least she seemed happy when she first started barking, but as time went on, it didn't seem right, like she was in pain, like a desperate howl. That sound was more than I could bear, and the sadness woke me up.

When I opened my eyes, I still heard Furball crying. I sat straight up and listened carefully, and it really was Furball crying out in pain.

I craned my neck to look out the window, and I saw Furball crouching behind her basket, whining in pain. Dad waved to her, and Furball hesitated, but then she stood up and staggered over to him. Dad caressed her head and slowly pinned her under his left arm; then he suddenly thrust his right hand under her neck. Furball's body began to convulse fiercely, her yelps more wretched and terrifying, and her tail tucked between her legs. Dad let her go and she ran away, back to crouch behind her basket. Dad quickly hid his right hand behind him, but I saw the razor-sharp boning knife dripping with blood.

What was my dad doing? I started yelling, still on my bed, "Dad! Dad! Furball! Furball!" I put on my shorts and ran out of the house, yelling, "Furball! Furball!"

Dad said, "This has nothing to do with you. Go back inside!"

"You're killing Furball!" I screamed at him. "You're killing Furball!" Furball was breathing shallowly on the ground by her basket, her eyes half-closed, spiritlessly looking at me. She wanted to wag her tail at me, but she lifted it halfway a few times and it flopped down in mid-wag. I screamed again, "Furball! Furball!" She heard me and struggled to open her eyes, trying to use her forelegs to push herself up, but she didn't have the strength. She slowly shook her head at me, blood spurting out of her neck at each shake. I reached out with both arms and hollered, "Furball! Furball!" My tears began flooding down. Furball's coat suddenly stiffened, her soft fur straightening, and with a heroic swing of her head, she got her forelegs under her, and her hind legs followed . . . she stood up. As she walked toward me, swaying back and forth, blood continued to drip from her wound, but she managed to stand up straight all the way up to me. I squatted down, giving her my palm to lick, and then I lowered my head to look at the stab wound on her neck, but all I could see was a clump of blood dyeing her fur red and black. "Furball!" I said, and I wanted to hold her, but my dad pushed me down to the ground. Pa's knife once again plunged into her neck, and blood spurted onto my feet and legs. I wiped up a handful of blood, and started to really cry.

Furball was even more unsteady now, and the fur all over her body started to curl a little; it hung down and then stuck close to her skin, like a flower that was withering right before my eyes. Her hind legs gave out as her strength ebbed, and she sat down. Then her forelegs bent, one joint at a time, until she was kneeling, then lying down, getting lower and lower until her whole body was flat on the ground. Her jaw was resting on my left foot. She was trembling uncontrollably, and blood had started to ooze out of her mouth. She looked at me, the light in her eyes growing dimmer, like all kinds of things were flowing out of her, while less and less remained. Her eyes started to close as her breathing slowed, the warm breath on my foot lighter and softer, and tears oozed from under her eyelids. Her eyes were tightly closed, but two great big sticky tears rolled out of the corners. I felt her jaw shudder and then relax, and her whole body went soft. Furball's head lay tilted on my foot, motionless.

I said, "Furball. Furball." Furball couldn't hear me. Her ears had flopped down over her nose and eyes.

Dad put his knife down and came to help me up, and I punched him between his legs. He immediately covered his groin and bent over. "Are you crazy?" he said. "You want to die?"

"Why did you kill Furball??" Now I was furiously pounding my own thigh.

Dad moaned for a while in pain, then pulled me up with one hand. "Stand up straight!" he said. "You want me to not kill her and wait for someone else to kill her? Huh? Think about it, how many of our dogs did he kill? When someone has it in for you, how many more days do you think Furball would live?"

I didn't care. Furball was dead. I sat back down on the ground, rubbing her muzzle and silently crying. Her nose was still wet, and the scab from the nose rope was still there. Furball . . . Furball. I sat on the ground straightening out her fur, so she would look like she was just lying there, sleeping.

———

10

———

When Dad strung Furball up on the locust tree to gut her, I spent the whole day wandering around outside, without so much as a bite to eat. I couldn't eat; when I thought about Furball being dead, I didn't want to eat anything. That day I walked at least seven miles along the canal, hating Dad and hating Rice inside. I didn't know whether Rice and the others had also killed those two puppies, and I couldn't figure out why they would kill a perfectly good dog. The canal water was muddy as hell; it was definitely still raining upriver. I felt like all the water in the world was flowing into this canal. Midway through the afternoon, I passed through West Avenue and watched Old Man He's parade. He wasn't wearing his hat, just walking through the wind bareheaded. He wasn't bowing his head this time; his face was up, and he looked almost like a leader surveying the town. Now that he had lifted up his head, no one dared to spit on him or throw rocks, because his eyes were scanning the crowd around him, and he could see them clearly.

On the street I ran into Crooked Neck Danian. "I've been looking for you," he said. "Rice wants you to come to his house to hang out."

"I don't want to," I said.

"You won't give Rice face? But he sent me to get you. He said that if you go, we'll all be cool."

I hesitated for a while before saying, "Something happened at home." I couldn't go. They had killed Furball, and I had stolen the hat from Rice's house. There was no way I could go.

Crooked Neck Danian went off in a huff.

When I got back home, it was already sunset, and the quartzite pavement on the road reflected a blood-red glow. My mom was cooking something in the kitchen, and Sister and Chive were excitedly moving around the stove. Chive was rubbing her hands, saying, "Oh, it smells so good!" I smelled, it too, but the aroma made my stomach turn, and I wanted to vomit. My stomach felt like I had swallowed a bunch of dirty rocks. Chive said to me again, "Smells good, smells good!"

I yelled into her ear, "Good? The hell it smells good!"

Chive's mouth twisted, and she was about to cry. She said to Mom, "He's yelling at me! He's going to hit me!"

My mom said, "Don't cry, I'll hit him! You watch me hit him." Then she pulled me aside and asked me, "The, ah, meat . . . do you think you can eat it?"

I shook my head. "I'm not hungry." I went straight to my room. "I'm tired; I'm going to sleep for a while."

By the time Mom woke me up, it was pitch-dark. They were finished with dinner. The dishes they had set aside for me were sitting on the table—vegetables. I sat by the table and picked up a leaf with my chopsticks. I shook it a few times, but then put it back down. I couldn't eat; I had no desire to eat. I ate a bit of rice gruel with corn and got up. The moon had gotten bigger, like a blood-red half-pancake. The courtyard was quieter than ever—the world was missing some dog barking. My Mom carried out a big bowl covered with a cloth and handed it to me, saying, "Give this to Principal He. He may not have had a square meal for days."

I didn't have to guess at what was in the bowl. I took it and silently went on my way. Flower Street's night had been soundless for some time; everyone had their doors shut, though occasionally you could see slanted rays of lamplight shining on the stone path in front of people's gates, creating a bizarre blue glow. In front of the stone dock by the canal, a variety of things fished out by Chen He were spread out to dry. From a distance, the mushroom house was just a huge shadow. When I got to the back, I was about to talk into the vent when I heard the sound of someone opening the lock, and then the creak of the door opening, and a shadow went into the mushroom house. He suddenly turned on a flashlight, and Old He was bathed in light, his body curled up.

The beam of the flashlight swept around the mushroom house, and the two of them said nothing for a long time. Then the person took something out and held it in front of the flashlight: it was the fedora, and my heart skipped a beat. I thought, how was it that Old He didn't have his hat on during the parade? When the guy spoke, it gave me a start, that voice like raw iron. I could have sworn it was Rice, but as I continued to listen, I realized it wasn't—it was an older voice, and a voice that had little threads of some kind of unsettled stuff in it. It was Wu Tianye; he had endless phlegm. Wu Tianye waved the hat and said, "Old He, how did it feel during today's parade?"

Old Man He just snorted, paying him no attention.

"I know you hate me so much it makes the roots of your teeth itch," said Wu Tianye. He walked up to Old Man He and squatted in front of him, with the flashlight tucked into his armpit so it was still pointed at Old He's face. Gradually I began to make out the blurry outline and features of Wu Tianye's face. He was holding the hat with one hand, and tapping on it with the middle finger of his other hand. "This thing isn't bad at all; put it on, and you really look like somebody. No wonder everyone in Flower Street looks up to you like you're some kind of celebrity."

"Wu Tianye, what are you going to do to me?" Old Man He said.

"Nothing." Wu Tianye stood up, and with the flashlight tucked under his arm, he began to slowly walk around Old Man He, patting his own ass with the hat. "What can I do? All I can do is parade you around and struggle you."

"Just because you don't like the looks of the hat I wear, you persecute me?" Old Man He said, his voice trailing off in a fit of coughing.

"Principal He, you've got me all wrong. At first I thought it was just the hat that got to me. In a place like this, if you wear this kind of hat, you're several inches taller. But today I brought the hat back with me and found out it's no big deal when you put it on. The key is not in the hat. The key is you, you're a . . . what do the books say? An intellectual! Right, that's it; everybody admires you because you're an intellectual."

"You know very well I've honestly been raising Chive like she was my own daughter. It's one thing to ruin me, but you won't even let an idiot girl live in peace!"

"If she wasn't an idiot, this wouldn't have been an easy matter. Anyway, she can't say anything sensible."

"Wu Tianye, all these years and you still can't tolerate an outsider. I've been putting up with it all along, and you just come at me all the harder! Okay, then, let's see if you can persecute me to death!"

"You want to expose me?" Wu Tianye started laughing and turned off the flashlight. The mushroom house was plunged into pitch darkness. "Don't even think about it. How can you prove that you're innocent? You'd better save yourself the trouble." Wu Tianye fished a cigarette out of his pocket. He lit it and blew out a puff of smoke, then continued, "It's not that I can't stand outsiders; it's you who bugs me. Everybody in Flower Street says you're a good man. Are you really that good? I didn't believe it, so I wanted everyone to have a good look."

The flashlight came back on, and Wu Tianye put the fedora on Old Man He's head. "Come on, put it on, wear it tomorrow when we're parading you around; let the townspeople see that the great intellectual is capable of things even beasts wouldn't do." He took out another cigarette, lit it, and stuck it in Old Man He's mouth. "This place is full of bugs, it's damp; have a cigarette and fumigate it a little. It'll be good for your health. See, I haven't treated you all that badly."

Wu Tianye stood across from Old Man He, and the two of them were silent. They stayed that way until the cigarette was finished, at which point Wu finally locked the door and left the mushroom house. I listened to his footsteps get further and further away before I climbed into the house with the bowl I was carrying.

Old Man He asked, "Who is it?"

"It's me, Blockhead. I brought you some food."

I turned on my flashlight and shone it on the bowl, then turned my head while Old Man He took off the cover. I smelled the aroma, and it really was a mouth-watering aroma. My stomach made some gurgling sounds, but I still had no appetite.

"What kind of meat?"

"Dog."

"Furball?"

"Yeah."

Old Man He's chewing came to a stop, and he vaguely said, "Furball."

11

The parades of Old He were already losing their appeal; the people of Flower Street had lost interest, and they barely cast a glance his way anymore. But today was different: after casting a glance, they would take a second look, then a third. Clustered into small groups, they formed a big circle. Old Man He was wearing his fedora for the parade, and it gave everyone a strange feeling. Old Man He's hat was normally a symbol of honesty and dignity in Flower Street; it was knowledge, it was culture, it was something that made you stand in respectful silence when you saw it. Now it was combined with the cards in front and in back, cards that had the same old content, and the two things together felt a little off. What was awkward about it was hard to explain, but it made you think. That's why when people took a look at him, they stopped and stared at him. The people who were banging drums and gongs were encouraged and really threw themselves into it. Midnight Liu's two sons straightened their backs, cast off the laxity of the last couple of times, and walked like soldiers with a clickety-clack. The three kids reciting the slogans were new, too, their voices as crisp as radishes, with an emphatic rhythm.

Say what you will, this parade of Old He through the streets was entirely successful, at least in terms of the scene. I went along the whole way, too, all the while regretting that I hadn't kept Old Man He's hat safe, but at the same time not wanting to leave. Being dragged through the streets in a fedora was really something to look at.

Shortly before noon, the procession stopped in front of the gates to the Brigade headquarters, and Chive suddenly appeared out of nowhere. She immediately started kicking Midnight Liu's two sons, giving them one kick each. The two boys were not prepared, so they immediately let go to defend themselves against Chive. Chive was screaming and crying, cursing their mother and father, meaning Midnight Liu and his wife, saying she hoped their assholes would disappear. Midnight Liu's boys got riled up, grabbing at her hair and clothes and trying to push her away. Chive bit and scratched as much as she could, and she didn't stop even when Old Man He told her to. She sank her teeth into Midnight Liu's older son's arm, making him grimace in pain, and by the time she loosened her bite, his arm was already covered with blood. She screamed, "That'll teach you to arrest my pa!"

A kick from Midnight Liu's younger son sent her flying into the crowd, but fortunately there were people there to catch her before she fell down. The drums and gongs had stopped; the two drummers had crept off to the side with their mallets in hand, and two of the three reciting kids were bawling with fright. Some people started to make a ruckus, and Midnight Liu's boys chased after Chive in exasperation. Just as they assumed their attack positions, Wu Tianye came out of the Brigade headquarters and gave a loud shout, so the Liu boys didn't dare move.

The parade came to an end in this chaos. Chive wanted to drag Old Man He back home, but she was pulled back by others, and there was another round of kicking and cursing.

Furball and the puppies were gone, and the parade was over. I couldn't find anything to do. I couldn't fall asleep for the midday nap, either. I wandered on Flower Street like a person without a soul. Flower Street was boring, too. It was like everyone else had things to do, and I was the only idle one. After meandering around for most of the afternoon, I ended up going back to the stone dock to watch Chen He pull stuff out of the canal. He seemed to have developed a fondness for this scavenging, snagging anything he could see floating down the canal. When he fished out something good, he would quietly sell it to someone. Everyone joked that even if he couldn't get rich this way, it shouldn't be hard for him to fish out a good wife for himself.

As I was watching Chen He pull out a bamboo chair, Whole Table came running to find me. He pulled me aside to a spot where there weren't any people and said mysteriously that he had been looking everywhere for me, and finally he had found me.

"What's up?"

"Rice has an invitation for you."

"I have to do something in a bit."

"You'd better go anyway," Whole Table said with a devilish smile. "We all know who the little thief is."

"What do you mean, 'thief'?"

"I mean you took the hat from Rice's house."

"He's looking for me?" I was losing my nerve.

"You'll see when you get there."

Whole Table led the way, and I followed, going south all the way. In the distance I could see the graveyard coming into view, and I got scared, dragging my feet.

"Come on!" Whole Table said.

"What does he want with me?"

"Don't worry, it's definitely a good thing." Whole Table smiled wickedly again. "Rice wants to make friends with you."

"Making friends we can do in Flower Street; why do we have to go so far out of town?"

"Flower Street is inconvenient. Come on."

When we got into the graveyard, Whole Table stuck his thumb and forefinger in his mouth and let out a loud whistle. Another whistle came from the southeast. Whole Table said, "Over there," and I followed him over that way.

Rice and Thirty Thousand were each seated on a grave mound; it was Thirty Thousand who had Old Man He's hat now. Rice smiled at me. "So you made it," he said in that awesome iron voice of his. I nodded. Thirty Thousand was facing me and spinning the hat, saying, "Recognize this? It's back with us now." I didn't say anything, and my face started to get hot.

"Give me the hat!" Suddenly I heard Chive's voice. I spun my head around to see one of her arms being held by Crooked Neck Danian. The two top buttons of her blouse were undone, and her pants were gone. She was wearing only underpants, and her long white legs were exposed.

"Just do what you're told, and you'll get the hat for sure," said Thirty Thousand.

"What are you going to do?"

"It's not just what *we're* going to do, but all of us, including you," Crooked Neck Danian said. "We have some good fortune to share, and since you've come, you'll get yours as well."

"It's got nothing to do with me!" I spun around and started running.

"Don't let him get away!" said Thirty Thousand.

"Let him run," said Rice. "Tomorrow there'll be word of a new thief in Flower Street."

I had only run a few paces and stopped in my tracks. Whole Table walked over, pulled me by the arm, and said, "I think you'd better just wait here like a good boy." I compliantly walked with Whole Table over to where Rice was. Turning to face me, Chive called out, "You grab that hat back for me!"

Rice said, "If you don't quit your jabbering, I'll burn the hat!"

Chive rolled her eyes and didn't say any more.

Rice signaled something with his eyes to Crooked Neck Danian, and Danian awkwardly looked at me and said, "Let's have Blockhead go first." Rice said, "I was talking about her clothes." Danian rubbed his hands together for a long time, then said to Chive, "You'd better not yell, or else that hat will be gone." Chive nodded.

Danian rubbed his hands again, then started undoing the rest of the buttons on Chive's blouse. His fingers trembled constantly as he worked, and his face was red all the way down to his neck. Finally the blouse was unbuttoned. Chive had another small garment on underneath. Once he had taken off the outer blouse, it was as if he had set down a heavy burden. "I took it off! It's Thirty Thousand's turn!"

"We'd better leave that one on," Thirty Thousand said to Rice. "If we take everything off, when we lay her down, the grass will scratch her. If it hurts her so much she cries out, then what'll we do? What do you think?"

"Mmm, okay," Rice said. "Whole Table, you're up."

"What, me? For what?"

"Like we said, her underpants."

Whole Table's neck swelled. "M-m-me? Really take them off?"

Crooked Neck Danian said, "Fuck, what did you think? Nobody gets off the hook!"

Whole Table spat and said, "I'll fucking take them off, then. I'm not scared of anybody!" He walked up to Chive and laid out the clothes they had already taken off her between two of the grave mounds. "Lie down here," he said to Chive. With perfect timing, Thirty Thousand waved the hat at her. Chive obediently lay down. Whole Table knelt down and let a resounding fart, and even Chive started laughing. "You farted!" she said. "You let a fart!" Whole Table's whole head blushed red like a lobster, and he forced a smile. "I ate too much . . . too much." When his hand brushed against her groin, it jumped up as if it had been scalded, but he gritted his teeth, grabbed onto the panties, and pulled them down. Even the sound of breathing had disappeared from the graveyard, and everyone's necks were getting longer and longer. Chive giggled a bit because it tickled. Then we all saw the ink-black clump between her plump white thighs. Rice and the others leapt up on the grave mound and shouted, "Wow!"

Chive instinctively covered herself between her legs, and Thirty Thousand shouted, "Take your hands away!" She took her hands away but said, "It's cold."

"It won't be cold in a minute." Gesturing toward me with his chin, Rice said, "Now it's your turn."

"Me?"

"You."

"Brother," Crooked Neck Danian said, "you're gonna give the first battle to this punk? Isn't that being a little too good to him?"

"So, how about you?"

"Okay, let Blockhead do it."

Thirty Thousand barked at me, "Take your pants off!" I immediately clamped my hands down on my belt, because I knew what they wanted me to do: they were going to make me do it—do that thing—with Chive. "No way, not me!" Thirty Thousand said, "Then you will just have to be a good little thief. Have it your way!" Whole Table and Crooked Neck

Danian made their way over to me, each grabbing one of my hands. "You'd better stop pretending you don't want it," Crooked Neck Danian said. "You're wasting time." He pulled my pants off, and then my underwear, too. I was yelling and trying to jump, but I couldn't struggle free of them. I covered up my naked lower body, with nowhere to go. They threw my clothes to Thirty Thousand.

"Hurry up!" Thirty Thousand said, his face as red as a cooked crab, his eyes about to spit fire.

"I'm not going to do it!"

Rice lunged toward me and boxed my ear. "It's not up to you!" With one push he shoved me up in front of Chive. Rice's eyes were red, too, and with one hand he was rubbing a bulge below his waist. They separated Chive's legs and made me kneel between them, pulling my hands away. Rice yelled, "Look at it!" Following his pointing finger, I saw that place between Chive's legs. Suddenly I really had to pee, and there was a lightning flash in the front of my head—a blinding flash, so fast that it was gone as soon as it appeared. I broke loose from them, and then I put my hands back down on my privates and I peed. Right after that, I collapsed crookedly to one side and started puking. That black place on Chive made me feel really sick; my insides were churning around in my belly upside down and backwards.

I was puking in waves, worse than when I saw the puppy's head. My lower body was curled up on the ground, and I felt like I was going to throw myself up until there was nothing left, puking until I would literally vanish from the world. Chive saw me puking and wanted to get up and look after me, but Whole Table pushed her back down on the ground. Thirty Thousand kicked me in the butt and said, "You are so fucking useless!"

"What should we do?" Crooked Neck Danian was rubbing his fists in his palms.

Clenching his teeth, Rice said, "Fuck it! Who cares? Let's just do it ourselves!"

"How're we gonna do it?" Thirty Thousand asked. Crooked Neck Danian also came over, and in no time their excitement fed on each other.

"'Rock, paper, scissors'—whoever wins goes first, and nobody gets to back out!"

12

Crooked Neck Danian was the first winner.

Danian wriggled nervously, and Rice gave him a kick, saying again, "Nobody gets to back out!" Crooked Neck Danian pulled down his pants, and just as he lowered himself down on top of Chive, I lunged over there and pulled him off with all the strength I could muster. "Run away, Chive!" I said. "These guys are no good!" But Chive said, "No, I want Daddy's hat!" I put a deep scratch in Danian's ass, and he hollered; Thirty Thousand and Whole Table each grabbed one of my arms and dragged me off to one side.

"Keep him still!" Rice ordered, and then to Crooked Neck Danian he barked, "Get on with it!"

Danian gave a rough grunt; Chive screamed that it hurt, and told Danian to get off her. "I'm not getting off," he said. "It was hard enough to get it in. It'll be over in a second, in just a second." Chive started screaming again, but after a few times she stopped and started giggling instead, saying, "This is fun!" Then it was Crooked Neck Danian who let out a yell: "Aaaagh!" He rolled off her onto the grass as if he had just died.

Rock, paper, scissors: it was Whole Table's turn. Crooked Neck Danian pulled up his pants and held down my legs in Whole Table's place. Whole Table's grunting was even louder, like an ox. He took a longer time, but finished the deed with a great cry. My mouth was against the cogon grass on the ground, so I had to raise my head just to curse. Rice gave me a kick in the temple, and my whole head rang in confusion.

By the time I came to, Chive was screaming in pain. Crooked Neck Danian was yelling, too—he was back on top of Chive. I twisted my head and saw Rice sitting on a grave mound, happy as a clam, his pants around his knees, using a stalk of grass to pick his teeth. Thirty Thousand and Whole Table were still holding my arms and legs down. Crooked Neck Danian let out a long howl, then rolled off Chive and lay by her side like a pig. Chive was crying, without an ounce of strength left, mumbling through her tears, "You guys are all bad! Give me the hat! I'm gonna have my dad kill you guys! Kill you!"

"I'll give you the hat," Rice said. He got up and fastened his belt, then tossed the hat onto Chive's body. "Let him go," he said to Thirty Thousand and Whole Table. "Put this idiot girl's clothes back on her and let her go first."

They loosened their grip on me, but my arms and legs had gone numb, and it was a while before I could move them. Even my belly was numb.

They took the chance to cop a feel here and there as they dressed Chive. Then they gave her the hat and sent her back to Flower Street. Thirty Thousand told her she'd better not tell anybody, or not only would they take back the hat, but Old Man He might not escape with his life. Chive nodded, petrified with fear, and staggered away, saying to me, "I'm going back, to give Dad back his hat."

"What about this one?" Thirty Thousand asked.

"Leave him here," said Rice, stepping on my back. "If you say so much as a word about this, you'll really be in for it!" With that, he waved at the other three and left the graveyard.

The sun had set some time earlier, and the dark color of night rose up from the graveyard hidden in the pines. Once they'd gotten far away, I clambered up, found my clothes, and slowly put them back on, crying as I got dressed. Suddenly I heard a bone-chilling shriek from a bird, which scared me so much I ran zigzagging out of the graveyard. When I got on the road, I slowed down. My head was completely empty. I felt tired, totally exhausted. I walked for a while but then couldn't keep going, so I sat by the road, my eyes fixed on the gully by the roadside. I couldn't see anything, but gradually something came into view in the dim light of dusk. I shook my head to wake myself up, and I saw the shriveled-up head of a puppy. I got hit by another wave of nausea, and I started puking like it was the end of the world again.

My stomach was already empty, so I was puking up threads and clumps of blood, and my voice was chiming in louder and hoarser with each retch. Finally I was exhausted from puking, and I fell asleep collapsed in a heap by the road. I felt cold when I woke up, and I was covered with dew. The moon was up in the middle of the sky, and the treeline beyond the meadow was all blue-black, desolately blue and desperately black. I struggled up and started to walk toward Flower Street.

When I was almost there, I turned a corner, picked up a stone from the top of someone's crumbling wall, and headed toward the mushroom house. The door was locked, and everything was completely silent. I started smashing at the lock with the stone, which gave off sparks as it hit the iron lock. Old Man He called from inside, "Who's there? What are you doing?" I remained silent until I had smashed the lock open.

It was pitch-black inside, and it took a while for my eyes to adjust. I went straight over to Old Man He, and could just make out the rope he was tied up with. First I broke a stretch of rope that was fastened to a boulder; then I used my fingers and teeth to loosen the ropes on his hands and feet.

Old Man He said, "Blockhead, is that you? What are you doing?"

I stayed silent.

"You can't untie me!"

I still kept silent. Undoing all the ropes left me covered with sweat. "Go!" I screamed at him. "Get out of here now!" Then I went out the door.

When I got home, Mom and Dad were both still up, nervously pacing around the courtyard. They asked me where I'd gone off to like a wandering zombie for so long. I paid no attention to them and went straight to my room, where I took off my shoes and got into bed. I fell asleep with my clothes on.

The next morning, I was still asleep when my Mom anxiously yelled from outside my door, "Blockhead! Blockhead! Principal He is missing!" It took a huge effort for me to wake myself up. I slid off the bed, my whole body sore and aching. It was a bright, sunny day. My mom was still going on: "Principal He is gone! Chen He, who was fishing stuff out of the river at the stone dock, said he fished Old Man He's hat out of the water, but he didn't see the old man. Everybody's wondering whether Old Man He jumped into the river and drowned himself!"

"What?"

My mom looked at me with surprise and said, "What did you say?"

"I asked if Old Man He really drowned himself in the river."

My mom's face looked even more astonished, "Your voice!"

"What about my voice?"

"Your voice has changed!" Mom said. Dad was just coming back with his fishing spear on his shoulder. "Listen," Mom said to him, "don't you think Blockhead's voice has changed?"

"My voice has changed?" I repeated.

My dad cocked his head at me and said, "Yep, it sounds like it. It's a really deep voice!"

I grunted and . . . yes, it really *was* different, like the hard gleam of newly smelted iron.

Mountain Songs from the Heavens

Han Shaogong

TRANSLATED BY LUCAS KLEIN

1

Old Yin had a hump on his back, and sitting too long had bunched up the wrinkled cloth of his formalwear, like a curtain drawn long on one side and short on the other, making it look very odd indeed.

Old Yin, four bamboo chairs on his back, yawned at the bus stop, saw by the sky it was getting late, and asked all over for directions before he finally made it to the cultural center, moaning about the weather and the town the whole way.

Old Yin isn't an easy fellow to describe—for instance, his small head is hard to say anything about other than that it's kernel-like; not much can be said about his thick eyebrows, either, other than that they're like knives; his big ears, though, are like fans or sheets of paper, so that's better. Mr. Liu must have been unaccustomed to seeing such a granular head at the cultural center, so he waved his hands, *Get out, get out, no one here wants to buy any chairs. What do you think this is, a market?*

Old Yin dug out a slip of paper and gave it to Mr. Liu, which put a stop to his shooing.

"You're Maosan Yin?"

"Uh-huh . . ."

"Maosan Yin from Bianshan Cavern?"

"Uh-huh . . ."

"Wait, don't you have another Maosan Yin over there?"

Originally published in *People's Literature*, 2004; reprinted in the collection *Reportage Government*.

"We do?"

"That's what I'm asking you."

"In the village they call my big brother Herdsman Kuan, and my other big brother Herdsman Yi, and me I get to be Herdsman Yin. I don't like the name, but what can I do?"

He had an innocent face on his small head.

Mr. Liu looked over the meeting notice, black ink on white paper, properly official, and with nothing else to say brought him into the office. The office doorway was on the narrow side, so anyone coming in with four bamboo chairs would have to twist everything around, and the leg of one chair going sideways caught Mr. Liu right in the mouth. "What are you bringing all these chairs in here for?" A scream came from behind the chairs.

The granular head was still in the midst of all the twisting: "Sorry. These are sturdy, lightweight chairs, the kind the people on the street like, so my aunt said I should bring them over. My aunt said . . ."

Mr. Liu didn't give a whit about his aunt, and as he walked away massaging his mouth he panted to the director: "Who recommended this Mao what's-his-name? Is he here to pick cotton? Kill pigs? Play his country music? That half-ape looks like he was caught halfway through the evolutionary process."

The director of the cultural center was a local, and he had heard quite a bit about Old Yin, so he said not to look down on him, that he was not just some nobody, that he had even gotten a university education in Beijing, that he could play the erhu at five, and the suona as well—a couple of relatives of mine couldn't stop talking about him.

Mr. Liu chortled in disbelief, "Does he think Beijing is in Qiyang or Mayang?"—the names of two counties nearby—"or know whether the university gates face east? Just look at him and his head like a capon's; it smells like yams in here because of all his burps or farts. If he can hit seven notes singing, I'll come to work tomorrow standing on my head."

As he was speaking there was a scream outside, the kind that should only be heard when the world is ending. They ran out of the room to see one of their cashiers pointing a shaking finger toward the washroom, her face ashen: "In the ladies' room th-there's a . . . a . . ."

A man? A hick from the country? Mr. Liu ran into the women's room, where he found Small Head holding a corner of his shirt under his chin, meticulously tying the cord that held up his pants.

"Hey, hey—what are you doing in the women's washroom, you creep?"

"Oh, sorry, my eyes are no good . . . I just knew I'd make that mistake."

"Your eyes are no good—are you mute, too? Is it too much for you to ask, or grunt or something?"

Small Head walked through the door, sniffing the wall. "Something's not right, serious problems."

The words inked on the restroom door were no longer clear, having weathered in the sunshine and rain. Mr. Liu didn't want to get caught up in it: "Miss Lou has had heart problems. If she'd passed out, you'd be in big trouble, you know?"

Small Head smiled apologetically and walked past Mr. Liu to bend down to the woman on the floor behind him: "Sister, you didn't see anything. I can prove it. Don't worry . . ."

"Get back!" she screamed.

"All right, all right, I'll get back."

"What's wrong with you!"

Small Head backed up timidly. "I was just saying you didn't see anything, you have nothing to get upset about . . ."

"Did I want to see anything? Did I need to see anything? Of course I didn't see anything. I don't need you to tell me not to be afraid of my shadow, and I certainly don't need you to prove anything to me." The more she spoke, the less clear she was being, so upset had she been at Small Head's attempt to console her.

Small Head opened his eyes wide at Mr. Liu and the director: "I give her my guarantee, and she's still this mad? Did this lady take a spill today?"

What he meant was, Did she hurt her head when she fell?

———

2

———

Mr. Liu was one of the few college graduates around, as well as one of the more prominent artists in the town, and he often conducted the orchestras under the stage. Most people here didn't have much understanding about orchestras, and at the beginning they couldn't figure out why he was "waving his arms left and right." But they figured that he must have an important role to keep on waving like that for two hours and not get tired. Mr. Liu's theoretical acumen was good, too, and as he waved his fan back and forth, he could often be heard giving a clear and cogent analysis of any song he came across, such as what some scholar or other had said about one theme and two images and three developments and four particularities and five whatever else there might be, cooking up a theoretical broth out of any herbs available. He was especially emphatic about music being born in emotions: "The opera will determine when there will be a recitative and when an aria—pay attention. Do you sing 'The Internationale' with your head held high as you march toward the execution ground? Can you sing when your nose is running and your feet dragging?" This, a constant example of his, instantly enlightened the musicians.

Mr. Liu was a tireless teacher, modest and amiable, smiling all day like a bodhisattva, and he was constantly inviting friends over for tea or a smoke, or for a bowl of noodles, and he'd gladly cover for anyone running short on grain coupons. Since transferring from the orchestra to the cultural center, he'd hosted several amateur musicians from the country, who ate at his place and unwrapped their bedrolls there and began snoring, as if it were their free boarding house. Of course, his gregariousness served his own interests, too, such as his eagerness to be complimented, and within five minutes of coming through the door, anyone would be sure of all his accomplishments: he'd recently become a Party member, he'd been promoted to assistant director in the composition department, and he just might yet make deputy manager of propaganda. And of course he would be modest in the face of any flattery, as it had indeed been its own reward.

For two days he had again been honored with the task of leading the first creative group following the reconstitution of the cultural center, and he was determined to produce results in the face of the responsibility and expectations. He had reconfigured his notebooks from his student days into reams of lecture notes, to patiently explain mode, harmony, motivation, minor chords, the proper accompaniment for the theme of the revolutionary classic *Shajiabang*, and more. As he went on and on, at the peak of his lesson, an odd whine undermined the minor chords, sheer unharmonious and inappropriate noise—looking up, he found that it was emanating from a small head in the back row of the classroom.

"Hey!" He had forgotten the name of whomever he was addressing.

The students in the first row jumped, turning their heads to follow his gaze to the back of the room.

"Hey, hey—I'm talking to you!"

At the point his enraged gaze reached its object, the small head shook, awakened.

"Are you snoring back there? P-p-preposterous, snoring! The cultural center feeds you, so you think we have to give you a place to sleep, too—a place to snore?"

"I'm sorry, Mr. Liu, my eyelids are so heavy—so heavy."

"You want me to set up a bed for you, give you a pillow and blanket and tuck you in right here?"

"No, no, I don't need a bed, you're joking. This is such a rare opportunity, I'm here to study, so I shouldn't sleep." Everyone laughed as Old Yin slapped himself in the face, pinched his nose, gritted his teeth, and picked up his paper and pen.

"Comrades, comrades—do you know how much I put into preparing these classes for you?" Mr. Liu pounded the desk in aggravation, trying to regain the students' attention by puffing up his chest and returning to his chords with a show of pathos. But before he could finish explaining chords, before he could even begin his most important theoretical analysis, the shameless noise arose once again to disturb him, of course from the back row. If it hadn't been for Small Head being shoved by the person seated next to him, interrupting the offending snores and drool, Mr. Liu would have been in no mood to continue teaching that day.

"You just keep talking, don't mind me." Small Head had perceived the discomfort, lifting his chin to acknowledge Mr. Liu from afar.

"And what would you have me say?"

"Say something about chords."

Mr. Liu was in no mood to go on. He had planned to spend more time excogitating on his two works, so that everyone would have a sense of success in composition, but having lost his train of thought he had to cut things short, and he concluded so hastily that he left his fan on the desk when he went out of the room.

The purpose of the study group was not only training, of course, but the more pressing issue of composition: within four days, each student had to hand in one song, with the best piece to be entered into regional and provincial competitions. As overseer, Mr. Liu paced with his hands behind his back, examining their progress, analyzing this student's work for structure, improving another's lyrics. The students, at least, seemed to be putting effort into it, usually two to a desk, sharing an oil lamp between them when the electricity was cut, their heads buried in their writing, humming unfinished melodies in their throats. Some of their immature noises, such as the new variations attempted on their huqin or suona by the stream outside the cultural center, sounded asthmatic or even epileptic to Mr. Liu, or like acoustic constipation or an intestinal obstruction. Yet in his nervousness Mr. Liu found that he was missing a student, and passing Old Yin's door he noticed a colorful quilt draped over a human figure on the bed. The lingering scent of yam and pickled cabbage had not been aired from the clothes scattered beside the bed.

Unbelievable! Mr. Liu kicked a leg of the bed.

A capon-sized head peeked out from under the quilt, squinting: "Time to eat yet?"

"Fifty cents a day for missed work, all from the national budget, just for you to come here and sleep?"

"Oh, it's you, Mr. Liu. Didn't you say it wouldn't be due for four days?"

"And how many days would that make today?"

"There's still time."

"You may think you can take your time, but I don't. Look at yourself."

"Relax. I'm different, like a brooding hen—I nurture my music in my sleep."

"Or maybe you're like a spawning carp? Spawning every day out the window, for a song to shock the world with? Is that what you mean?"

"Oh, listen to you talk—you open your mouth and it's like you've eaten gunpowder. Don't rush me—if there's one thing I hate in this world, it's being rushed." Old Yin swallowed his saliva and pulled the quilt back over his head.

Mr. Liu almost passed out from anger, and he had half a mind to pluck this supposed hen out of its coop with a swift kick to the posterior to fly off wherever it was supposed to go. But then he figured, he is a peasant after all, and a member of the revolutionary classes for better or for worse, so let's not be impetuous; just grin and bear it instead.

In his anger he went looking for the center director, to make a forceful demand that as leader he reinstate discipline, to send that small head who'd come looking for a free meal packing, to let him know that whatever free meals there might be certainly wouldn't be for the likes of him. The director thought it over and decided it was best not to disturb anyone from Bianshan Cavern. Mr. Liu didn't understand. The director asked if he hadn't heard about Bianshan Cavern. The people out there are fierce. When other people go begging, say for alms for the god of wealth or the god of land, they sing and raise a racket, so whoever lives there ends up giving them money just so they'll go away, but only the people in Bianshan Cavern will simply stand silently in the doorway. Now, why would that be?

The director saw that Mr. Liu still didn't understand the peasants' predicament, so he told him about how the bandits of Bianshan Cavern had been suppressed one year, long after the bandits had been taken down everywhere else. Whether it was the Nationalists doing the suppressing or the Communists, the Bianshan Cavern bandits just wouldn't stay down. They'd rather be burned at the stake with their fat melting into frying oil stinking to high heaven before they'd let out half a cry. If they were punished by cutting, it would take all day to cut them, until the knife would get bent up from all the slashing, blood splashing as high as your head, a fresh coat of crimson on the walls, and never a peep from the one dying.

In those years during the Republic, it wasn't uncommon for people to carry wicker baskets of human hands or livers to hang up at the gates of the town as a warning about what would happen to bandits—to the point where pedestrians would rather take the long way around than cross the bridge. No question, the flesh on display was all from Bianshan Cavern.

The director's description of the human hands and livers made Mr. Liu's face go white with fear, and he quickly took his leave, on the pretense that he had to pick his wife up from work, promising himself that he wouldn't mention Small Head to the center director ever again.

For days, Mr. Liu went out of his way to avoid Old Yin. What he hadn't anticipated, though, was that when the four days were up, not only did Old Yin not hand in a blank sheet, but his time in bed did indeed seem to have brooded him a golden egg. Of the eight students, it was his "Mountain Ballad of the Plow" that was the best. Mr. Liu hummed the composition as he looked it over beneath a lamp, unable to believe his eyes. Out of professional duty, he had no choice but to admit that he could never have created anything as exquisitely beautiful as this—nor could any of his old classmates, whose glories he was endlessly praising, from the professional composer for the province orchestra, to the assistant editor of *Music* magazine, to the one who had taken on the duties of reinstating the subcommittees of the Musicians' Association. If you covered up the name of the composer, he could very easily have mistaken it for a grand maestro's masterpiece slipped in among the classroom assignments.

Who is he who plows the fields?
To plow well, one must plow deep.
Tell me not about the three-inch plow,
This is how we must plow now—
Not just four or five inches, even six inches is too shallow,
Hit seven inches or your field will fall fallow,
Only will a deep plow give a golden harvest . . .

Yet how could such plain, even rough lyrics be so soul-stirring when set to music? That was the oddity, the mystery, the miracle!

It must have been plagiarized, Mr. Liu thought spitefully. But the melody clearly resonated with the style and substance of the mountain ballads of the region, so it could not have been copied from the work of any master composer from anywhere else.

He resolved that he would clarify matters with Old Yin in person. At the time, there were a few students huddled around a table in the mess hall, eating and laughing, deep in conversation. Only Old Yin remained wordless, dignified and stately, his gaze fixated on his bowl, his chopsticks steadily and systematically picking up turnip slices from the serving dish, pausing in midair, and depositing them in his bowl, at which point they paused again before being conveyed to his waiting mouth. He didn't hear Mr. Liu's greeting. When Mr. Liu tapped him on the shoulder, he was met with impatience: "The Lord of the Underworld is always surrounded by hungry demons! Can't I eat without being rushed?"

Beside him another student said loudly, "It's Mr. Liu for you." Seeing that he hadn't responded, he shouted again: "Hey, it's Mr. Liu for you!" Yet his unswerving gaze did not waver, and his face remained expressionless.

The students stifled their laughter and explained to Mr. Liu that he was always like this, that he'd go catatonic the moment he started eating, and wouldn't even hear thunder.

No problem, no problem. Mr. Liu would just talk to him later.

———

3

———

It was no small matter for a master such as Mr. Liu to notice the profundity of Old Yin, that his songs had both an earthly quality as well as a Western structure; yet, while it may be hard to account for, it shouldn't be glossed over. A scrap of paper that Old Yin took to the bathroom, Mr. Liu noticed later, was the sheet music for a waltz that was based in Central Academy of Music instruction, yet it whooshed like a Russian whirlwind, bounding with its exotic accordion air beyond steppe and birch forest and floral skirts and borscht, an imitation that surpassed its original. The name of the composer should have been Maosanyinsky or Maosanyinoff, instead.

After reading many of his compositions, including the one on the scrap he'd wiped his ass with, Mr. Liu finally changed his own tune, inviting Old Yin over for tea and to smoke some quality tobacco. His appellation even changed: from *Hey, you* to "Comrade Mao."

Even "Mr. Mao."

Mr. Mao was of course reserved, his arms by his side, sitting straight, accepting the cigarette with his palm turned up, so cautious as he smoked that he ended up whistling, though he couldn't say where the air was coming in. No matter the source of the noise, though, he smiled shallowly, nodded slowly, and barely responded. Whatever he did say ended up a garbled mumble that was all but impossible to discern. Though he knew a thing or two himself, when meeting an intellectual he'd try to drop a word or two of cramped Beijingese into his country accent, but would end up neither sufficiently *−insky* nor *−inoff* enough, so anyone listening would struggle to safeguard both north and south, not to mention simultaneously administer urban and rural regions.

"Shit, the Socialist Education Movement was super fucking interesting!" He smiled broadly, then recollected, "One time Captain Gao went to the village, and he said, *Don't make a fuss, just bring enough for everyone to have an equail portion.* Well, Granny thought he meant she should bring *quail* for everyone, which scared her half to death, ha ha ha . . ." Mr. Liu didn't understand, but he smiled along politely. Only much later, having given it a great deal of thought and having asked for explication from others familiar with the issue, did he realize what Old Yin had been trying to say: when Old Yin was at university, his role in the Socialist Education Movement took him into the villages, where he met a work team captain whose accent was so thick that it led to a number of misunderstandings. He had brought this up following Mr. Liu's mention of the Central Academy of Music.

"Yah, Flower-Bridge Town is a heckuva grand place!" Old Yin flashed another smile, interrupting his host. "They say 'the masses' like '*them asses*'! Interesting, ain't it? When they have committee meetings in Flower-Bridge, they say: The revolutionary aspirations of them asses will wave like ten thousand miles of red flags flapping in the eastern breeze. We shall follow them asses, mobilize them asses, be vigilant against forces trying to provoke struggles of them asses against them asses, and be resolute in following them ass lines of Chairman Mao!" Mr. Liu didn't quite understand this, either, but again he smiled along politely. Only much later, having given it a great deal of thought and having asked for explication from others familiar with the issue, did he realize what Old Yin had been trying to say: when Old Yin heard the folksongs as sung by the people in his village of Flower-Bridge, he noticed how humorous the Flower-Bridge accent was. He had brought this up following Mr. Liu's comment about musical source materials.

When Old Yin laughed, he would stop abruptly and fall silent, or else mutter something, whistling on his cigarette, as if pondering the next funny thing to say. Mr. Liu stared anxiously at the long ash hanging from his cigarette and nervously offered him an ashtray; then he stared anxiously at his undulating larynx and nervously offered him a spittoon.

A false start here, a quick dash there, thoughts pinched off at the ends, unformulated opinions and non sequiturs, so much smoke and haze . . . such are the haphazard manners of any discussion of art. Having prepared fine tea and quality tobacco, not to mention a hearty meal, Mr. Liu was bound to be somewhat disappointed. He knew too little about Old Yin. Only much later did he realize that Old Yin was neither inattentive nor purposefully playing dumb to protect himself in a time when words so often brought on serious consequences. On the contrary, he said quite a bit that day, so it was no small feat that he hadn't headed off to bed to start snoring already.

He had drunk nothing all day. This is an important detail. Ordinarily it takes drinking to get drunk, but this time he got lightheaded, then sloppy, then wild, then incoherent and irresponsible in his speech, all without touching a drop. Dizziness from the heat of the sun—that's what Old Yin's thought process was like when he wasn't drinking. A sliced-up tongue—that's what Old Yin's words sounded like when he was sober. His taste for liquor had begun with the Zhuang people in their mountain settlements. At the time he had progressed from the high school of the Central Academy of Music into its undergraduate program, specially admitted as a peasant recruit to undertake Socialist Education and life experience in Guangxi. He loved the Guangxi opera *Sister Liu* as much as he loved the rice wine from the Guangxi province, and dreamt of one day composing an opera like *Sister Liu*. Drunk with an overabundance of dreams, after completing his Socialist Education he went AWOL, tracing the echoes of the Zhuang tunes into Yunnan, then entering Burma and India in a trance, before he was extradited back home two years later shackled in handcuffs and covered in lice. At the time all he knew was music, and he had no inkling of what borders might be. If he hadn't been a peasant, he'd probably still be rotting in prison.

Of course that put an end to his studies and any hope of a degree.

This past of his was by now something of a blur, and if it was unclear to others, it was just as unclear to him unless he'd had something to drink, so we can only get an outline. Nevertheless, even without drinking he looked like a lush, half-asleep, half-insane, saying *west* to anyone else's *east* and *down* to anyone else's *up*. To him Director Zhang was Tailor Li, he'd call Butcher Wang Principal He, and sometimes he'd stamp his feet at his own wife in the garden, cursing the crazy woman who was trying to steal his vegetables in broad daylight. His wife would get so upset she'd refuse to cook him dinner.

Of course, not making dinner wasn't a big deal, and even when they barely had enough rice to fill a pot with, he could still fill up on sleep, drinking just a bowl of cold water and leaving his wife and sons the yams and turnips, as he curled up in bed like a snake in brumation, whiling away another day. Back when he was a student in Beijing, he said, if ration coupons ran short, or he'd lost them, he could go a full day on just one meal, or even eat nothing for days straight, with no effect on his attendance record. He said he managed this by not exercising or running or taking any walks or doing laundry or going out or talking or laughing, not even looking or listening, just turning everything into sleep, curling into a ball to minimize his motions if he happened to wake up, and storing every molecule of heat to spend in going to class—to the point that eventually a slice of pork might even make him heave and wretch. He said that when he was abroad, gallivanting all over the place as part of a caravan, he'd often be unable to find anything to eat, so sleep was the surest and simplest way to ensure survival. So could he sleep? What a joke! It was those Burmese guys who really knew how to sleep, going as long as half a month at a time without eating or drinking, just slipping in and out of consciousness with their eyes shut, sustained by no more than a wisp of breath, inhaling all the nutrition they needed out of the air, they said, and getting their energy from the sun and moon—later he learned that this was called *yoga*.

As he put it, there was nothing special about this game called yoga, any more than there was anything special about sleeping, like pretending to be dead or at least mostly dead, curling up and not moving as a way to stave off hunger.

Back in his hometown, where he was able to eat a full meal, he still had a hard time breaking his habit of lying down wherever and whenever, regardless of whether it was day or night, so he always had a hard time earning anyone's trust. Sent down, he had been a citizen instructor for two years, but was then discharged by the school; he had loaded charcoal at the supply and marketing cooperative for a year, but was then discharged by the co-op. The production team captain could find nothing to do with him, so in the end he was made to look after cattle, if for no other reason than to keep the nutcase busy. He was happy looking after livestock; the scenery was excellent up there, he said, and the air was nice, too, with birds singing in harmony under clear skies, so it was a fine place to look after oneself. He'd play his bamboo flute all day long, morning till night, the six cows heeding its every call: they'd assemble to a gathering tune, advance to his march, and turn tail and head home when he played a nocturne from the West. He admired most a certain dun bull with a knack for music, which he claimed would wag its tail and wiggle its ears in time, and would low in a peculiar way every time it fell into a spell, as if it were humming along comfortably, like some kind of Mozart of the herd.

It was during that time that his squint got narrower, since at night he'd read by the light of three sticks of incense bound together because he didn't have the money to buy oil for his lamp. His alcohol dependency grew, too, so that he'd rather have nothing to eat than nothing to drink, and if his pockets were empty he'd head to the distillery and inhale deeply, so at least his nose could get a fix. One time a teacher at the school nearby implored him to write a song, offering him a jug of the first batch of Flower-Bridge's own brew by way of thanks. It must have weighed about ten pounds, which was far better than he could have expected, and he plopped down beside the jug and dipped his enamel cup into it repeatedly as he hummed to himself and wrote. So many dips in, and he realized his cups were getting lighter—he looked in and found that he could see the bottom of the jug and couldn't hear any sloshing when he shook it. He was so startled he jumped up and said, "What's this? The jug ain't leaking, and ain't no one else here, where'd all the liquor go?"

It was a full jug—how did it get so empty so fast?

As he exhaled, a dragonfly flying in front of his face was sent into a downward spiral, a drunken stumble of a tumble. As he took a piss, he tossed his cigarette butt into the puddle, where it flared up into a small explosion—not igniting fully like pure ethanol would, but still quite dangerous.

This was when he came to the realization that his body was flowing with flammable liquid, that he had become a jug himself.

His squinting eyes shot open, brimming with brightness; a red tide swept all sleepiness or senselessness from his body and straightened his hunched back, and even his voice gained more gravitas. In such a moment, not only was he free from drowsiness, and able to write excellent music, he also was able to reach a clear judgment on a number of complex questions, such as the realization that it had been he himself, and not his brother or his wife, who had finished the jug, and that this day was the first day rather than the third, let alone the fifteenth, day of the new year. In such a moment, he was able to stretch his arms and legs and go for a bout of radio calisthenics (which he'd learned in Beijing), and could walk over to the school and pick up a newspaper and read aloud from it in standard pronunciation (he was particularly interested in fighting in India and Burma, news of which had grown unfortunately rare). If he came across another music aficionado, he could accurately recall every last detail of operas such as *Sister Liu*, and he had copious information at his fingertips about compositions by maestros both Chinese and foreign, from Mozart to Liszt, from "Blind Abing" Hua Yanjun to Comrades Wang Luobin and Lei Zhenbang and He Zhanhao. Forget the hint of sharpness in his voice, or his slight lisp—he could open his mouth and hit any note, a precise and faultless middle C or a B-flat you could drill through iron with, completely independent of extraneous objects like tuning forks. Anyone in the field had to be impressed. He could pick up any instrument, erhu or pipa or flute or reed pipe or suona, and at least pass muster with it if not bring the sky crashing down. Even rocks in his hands, or the water running by his feet, or a leaf between his lips, or the chopsticks and rice bowl on his table—sounds could be wrested from each of these, or, more precisely, in his hands, music could be wrested from each of these.

Years later, a reporter on assignment to interview him about the lost greats of folk music traveled to Bianshan Cavern, and as he entered the mountain village he staggered as if he had vertigo, so struck was he by the clash of sceneries. A cat was being chased by a mouse, and he couldn't tell nightmare from reality. On the suspended cliff above him, with no pathway before or behind it, stood a goat, and he couldn't figure out how it had gotten there. Sometimes in a pumpkin patch there will grow a pumpkin of extraordinary size, as big as a table, while all the other pumpkins are either small as normal or wither on the vine, attracting attention from no one. Sometimes a flock of swallows will appear as if from out of nowhere, perching on an unfinished wall and turning it in an instant from white to black, but we'll never catch a glimpse if we try, no matter how many times we seek out such startling scenes. Walking up, the reporter was jittery, as if falling-down drunk, his own mind made irrational along with everything he saw in the mountains, inexplicable, come-as-it-may, audacious, and reckless. But he said he finally understood Old Yin, finally understood where his music came from.

The reporter never managed to interview Old Yin. I heard he got caught in a miasma, and both his legs swelled up and started to itch; I also heard he got so confused he lost all sense of direction, and could only catch the next truck transporting lumber out of the mountains.

But neither of these statements has ever been verified.

———

4

———

Mr. Liu worried a little less when he learned that Old Yin couldn't play the clarinet and could do little more than poke at a piano. Mr. Liu tried out all the students' assignments on the piano, after which he banged out a tempestuous fugue of his own, improvising a few extra flourishes to douse some of Old Yin's pride. Old Yin listened quietly, then lifted his eyelids, squeezed out a chuckle, stopped, chuckled again, and then said nothing.

"What did you think?"

"Fine. Yeah, fine."

"What did you like the most?"

"You have a very good memory. You're in good health."

This didn't sound like much of a compliment.

As he was about to leave, he turned around, remembering something: "The second *fa* was a bit short."

Fa was F. But only much later did Mr. Liu work out that "short" meant *flat*, or *low*, that they needed to bring someone in to tune the piano. If a note was "thin," it was weak, and then the mallet might be loose and they'd have to find a way to screw it in better. If a movement "hadn't eaten," it seemed unmotivated; if a movement "wasn't putting on weight" or was "not naughty" and was "nodding off," the progression needed variation. Then there were chords of various properties, which in his peculiar verbiage became "blood brothers," "cousins," "distant relatives," and "The Oath of the Peach Garden." He always sounded like he was talking about people rather than music. Or rather, notes for him weren't a matter of sound waves, but of individuals who needed to eat and drink and laugh and cry, individuals who had idiosyncrasies and could make mistakes. In which case every composer was the head of a large family, apron on, spoon-feeding chirping charges whose healthy development into notes he oversaw.

The shortness of the second F ruined Mr. Liu's mood, turning indignation into discord, and set him to toiling day and night, scouring his bookcase for anything he could find on ethnic folk music of the Hmong, Dong, Yao, and Thai—he needed to find better references than Old Yin, to compose a masterpiece worthy of a deputy director, so as not to stumble at the feet of some hick from the hills. In the end, he had a pile of crumpled drafts, but nothing he wouldn't be too embarrassed to hand in. When Old Yin's work ended up getting the nomination for the regional competition, he could do nothing but watch wide-eyed. Though in the end it was disqualified for the prize, because it did not "highlight class struggle" and "insufficiently embodied the spirit of the times," the name Mao Sanyin began to circulate, along with his background and habits and their odd circumstances.

Colleagues from all around began to ask Mr. Liu about Old Yin, about how a composition as sober as "Mountain Ballad of the Plow" could have been composed out of such reckless inebriation. One theory made it out of the county and then back in again: the night before his composition was due, a huge thunderstorm caused a power outage, on which night Old Yin emerged from beneath his blanket, bought three jugs of millet wine with what he had left over from selling the bamboo chairs, and set them before a lamp as an offering to the bodhisattvas.

He straightened his clothes as the corners of his mouth curled upward and then widened, like an announcer taking the stage. Actually, he was not smiling—only those who knew him well would appreciate this expression, a non-smiling smile that meant the liquor had begun to take hold, an expression that said the caretaker was ready to care for his charges, an expression with the intensity to face down the darkness beyond the lamp with gushing music, each moment of its composition sheer genius.

The district director of the Cultural Bureau had caught the music bug as an accordionist in the military, and he organized a conference on music composition all by himself, inviting composers from every province. This was where he had first encountered Old Yin, of whom he said, "We must not forget about that old drunk." Astonishingly, Old Yin didn't understand that leaders like to be praised, nor did he appreciate the significance of the opportunity, and he ended up bringing one of his sons to the event, so the kid could come to the big city and see the trains. And at the moment they touched its wheels, the train let out a whistle, shocking them both. "Look at you, afraid of a scratch," said the father. That's the story as the boy reported it. Obviously a seat-of-your-pants kind of kid, he ran in and out of the conference room, screaming up a storm, tearing up newspapers, knocking over teacups. He must have seen other kids outside the building clutching ragdolls and, always the good student, picked up a wooden board and dutifully started giving it water, walking it down the hall, and having it go pee—and when it wouldn't go fast enough, he took his own little pecker out of his pants and let out his own little yellow stream, right in front of the district director. In times like these of great tumult under heaven, Old Yin not only didn't chastise or berate his boy, he in fact did nothing a father should, and stood off to the side yawning rather than offering even a piece of candy to get things under control. He did eventually pull his son's pants back up, but a steaming puddle of urine remained on the floor, which certainly would not do.

It was when he yanked off his own oversleeve to wipe up the piss that the conference room really erupted with laughter.

He kicked away the board, dragged his son to the men's washroom in a fluster, and did not come back for some time. Mr. Liu saw the district director's face lengthen as he checked his watch, and with a pang of responsibility he rushed out to find Old Yin. Oddly, the men's room was empty, as was the women's room, as well as both washrooms on the second and third floors . . . The hall was structurally identical to both buildings of the reception center, their corridors meeting at the east corner, with other corridors connecting to the government services building, so its layout was somewhat confusing. Only when Mr. Liu made it as far as the kitchen adjacent to the canteen did he find Mao father and son looking anxiously around, as if they were lost. *You clod. No, you're the damned clod. You've got water in your brain. No, you've got water in your brain. I told you to come this way, but no, you wouldn't listen. Well, I told you to head upstairs, and you wouldn't listen. No wonder you're always lost, you never listen, it's like you were raised by pigs! You're the one who was raised by pigs—you never listen, either, and you're always lost, too . . .* Their bickering continued as they walked back with Mr. Liu, neither conceding anything, until any pretense of a father-son relationship had been lost, and their curses were both angry and sincere.

"Next time you come out, I should bring you two a cattle tether so you can't run away." Mr. Liu angrily wiped the sweat from his brow.

"A tether would be a good idea, a fine solution," Old Yin agreed vigorously.

"Just make sure the other end of the tether goes in my hand." The son added his endorsement.

The lunch bell rang, leaving too little time for speeches. "I look forward to hearing comments from each and every one of you, so that I can assiduously rectify whatever errors may remain, and resolutely critique revisionist art and cultural production, to grasp every last element of the work required." Old Yin stuttered through his closing statement, making it more grandiose than necessary.

Old Yin lowered his voice and asked Mr. Liu: "What if I added 'And tether our noses with proper thought, to lead us forever through the furrow that is the spirit of the times'?"

"Leave things like that out of it."

"Such a fine statement, can't I say it?"

"Director Tong is getting up to go eat, keep quiet."

"Fine, then." Old Yin turned toward the audience. "I almost said something else, but then Mr. Liu said I should keep quiet, so I won't say it. Thank you."

"No, say it, say it." The director seemed interested.

"Mr. Liu said I shouldn't."

"It's your mouth, not his."

Old Yin lowered his voice and asked Mr. Liu again, "So should I say it?"

"Do whatever you want to do." Mr. Liu was getting impatient.

"All right, I'll say it." Old Yin turned back toward everyone else and said, "So what was I going to say? You know, I had it right here, but now it's gone again." He scratched his head, as if he could no longer find what he had in mind to say.

Everyone scoffed.

Somebody reminded him: "You were just at 'revisionism.'"

"Oh, right, revisionism. So . . . so . . ." Old Yin coughed, carefully searching for the words, and continued, "Revisionism is sinister, it is anemic, and not only is it a plot against our beloved Chairman Mao, it's harming us even as we hold our meeting here, flapping our jaws nonstop, keeping us from getting a good nap in."

Some covered their mouths; others covered their stomachs, doubling over as the director pounded his fist against the table, futilely trying to restore order. Old Yin found this exceedingly strange, and he looked to his left and right and asked, "What's so funny? Did I say something wrong? Isn't revisionism the reason we can't take a nap?"

The laughter was interrupted by the sound of crying: his son had smashed his foot with a brick. The personification of unruliness, this kid was such a diligent student that when he saw some kids outside playing with building blocks, he decided to build a train station right there in the meeting room—who knows where the bricks came from—only to sustain a workplace injury once his wobbly station fell over. And so, as Old Yin hurried to rescue the injured, his discourse on revisionism remained forever unfinished.

5

Now, trading a boy's bricks for wooden building blocks, comes Miss Qin into our story.

The lead actress in the shows put on by the Cultural Propaganda Division (which was later renamed the Mountain Songs Theater Troupe), Miss Qin sang Old Yin's songs, and had said about them, "Only Mr. Mao's songs have that true flavor." But when she ran into Mr. Liu and waved at him repeatedly, he looked irritated and aloof, and she stuck out her tongue in embarrassment and finally understood what they say about loose lips. Immediately she turned her story around, saying that Mr. Mao's songs might have flavor, but Mr. Liu's had *depth*, and depth, well, depth was something that didn't just happen by wishing for it, but was something you'd have to have drunk inkwells to write convincingly. At every opportunity she gave Mr. Liu smoked plums, or moaned to him about sore shoulders and asked for back rubs, which finally got a smile out of him, maybe even a groan or two of satisfaction. If he'd had a tail, it would've been wagging.

Adhesive capsulitis can stave off danger. A master at this technique, she was in turns naïve, crafty, crafty in her naïveté, and craftily coming off as naïve, each utterance more ambiguous than the last, endlessly scheming, until she was sinisterly renamed "Capsulitis" or "Bursitis" or "Cheilitis" by her girlfriends. Professionally, she was the first singer in the troupe, having entered at a very young age, but she didn't have much formal education and couldn't even read sheet music, breaking into a sweat at the sight of a score, her throat stiffening, the notes catching in the back of her mouth, the tendons pulling in her neck, her shirt becoming drenched in sweat as if it had just been washed, and she still couldn't finish the line. But if it hadn't been for this deficiency, the breadth of her range and the richness of her tone would have put her in the provincial academy for sure, and the way Mr. Liu told it, one of his contacts would have recommended her all the way up to university for advanced training.

There were girls whose singing was no better than Miss Qin's who could nevertheless remain calm before a musical score onstage, and whenever they'd catch her looking too smug, they'd pick up some score and start soloing so she'd shut up, shuffling off to sit dispiritedly alone offstage, folding paper boats or crocheting a scarf. Sheet music had become the bane of her existence. Her singing was unparalleled, and her waistline and the look in her eyes were enough to command attention from every corner of the auditorium, but she still couldn't take that simplest and most basic step. So for far too long, someone had to teach her her songs line by line. It became a running joke, her greatest fault and her biggest worry.

Old Yin didn't see the performances very often, and he didn't know her very well, so he'd often end up calling her "Miss Kin" or "Missy Can" or even "Sister Chain" or some other fabricated name, whether out of intentional maliciousness or sheer confusion. He said once, "What's great about Missy Can is that she isn't very cultured." This was a stupid thing to say, bordering on crazy talk, and was neither taken very seriously nor inquired after by those who heard it.

Since no one asked, he didn't say anything else.

He also said once, "Qin is Herdsman Kuan's big goose, still throwing a fit even after he's taken all the birds' nests."

This was senseless, too, but even though those who heard it wanted to pursue the matter further, no one did.

And since no one asked, he didn't say anything else.

Miss Qin asked, though. Clutching the pages of Old Yin's newest work, her brow sweating, she said, "All these rising and falling semitones, even the singing instructors think they're too hard," and an illiterate girl like her, well, her eyes darkened just looking at it all; how was she supposed to sing this? Was this some kind of joke? Or was he trying to inflict harm? Even the illustrious Mr. Liu had failed to teach her—she'd falter in the higher registers like she was standing on a watermelon, and there aren't many of those that you're not going to lose your balance on. Mr. Liu even lost his temper, shouting, "Folk music is supposed to be about *lang ge li ge lang*, a pentatonic scale—*mi, so, la, do, re*—what's with all these semitones? If you want to play with that foreign stuff, this isn't how you do it." Mr. Liu even had something of a premonition: "Old Yin is so arrogant, he can't tell his glass is only half-empty. Is the music of the bourgeoisie making a resurgence?"

Old Yin probably remembered Miss Qin from that time with the building blocks, as he started gathering his belongings to make room for the visitor. "Don't worry, missy, don't worry, this song is actually right up your alley."

"You're drunk on cat piss!" Seeing the bottles on the table, and unable to bear the stench of alcohol, the female lead backed away toward the door where there was more ventilation, fanning her hand beneath her nose.

"You liked to fight as a girl."

"What does that have to do with anything?"

"You're still a young fool."

"What? You're the one who's a fool!"

"It's true, I am. I'm a fool and I like foolish people, and I like to sing foolish songs. Let me tell you, there's no need to be afraid of semitones. What are semitones? Semitones are your kids—and why would you be afraid of your own kids?"

"You're not being serious."

"I know you're not married, I'm just saying, for example. I'm saying, listen, the oxen in the hills, the goats, the chickens and ducks, the cars, the millstones, the saws, the bench planes, even the hawkers on the street, aren't they all semitones? Don't you fart in semitones?"

"Ugh, don't be vulgar!"

"Fine, no farting, we'll just talk about the hawkers. Have a listen to them on the street—all the kids are copying them, so how could a player such as yourself be having so much trouble?"

"Who's a player?"

"All right, all right, an actor—an actress, a people's actress. Aren't actors always using their eyes? Go up in the hills, all you've got is green, but after you've been looking long enough, maybe you find you start seeing a hundred different hues of green. All you've got is yellow, but look closer, and you get dozens of yellows. And color is music. Oh, there are a bunch of semitones in here, semitones of semitones. But, hey, how can a pentatonic scale cover everything? How are you going to sing everything in just five or even seven notes?" Old Yin was talking himself into a frenzy. "Paint a painting with only seven colors? Shit no! So should music have just seven notes? Shit no! All over the world you've just got people shitting all day long, and the more they shit, the more people talk about how brilliant they are!" Who knew where all his anger was coming from.

Miss Qin wasn't sure she understood. "Mr. Liu attended university, too, and he can read music, and play the accordion and the piano, but he said he can't sing this."

"Mr. Liu is a very smart man, with many credentials, and he's got a good complexion and isn't scrawny, is always walking around with fountain pens in his shirt pocket, and he's not deaf, obviously, since his ears are like a pig's."

Miss Qin couldn't help but laugh, and she laughed even harder when she envisioned Mr. Liu's big ears.

"Missy, have you ever heard a pheasant?"

"Of course I have."

"So sing like one."

Old Yin had Miss Qin crow like a pheasant, having her sing longer each time, until at one point he leapt up and took over the role of pheasant himself, taking a step, then lurching, then another step, until his voice developed a rhythm, an undulating melody, right out of his own score. Miss Qin was amazed. Ordinarily when she learned a song, she'd have to run through it seven or eight times before she got it, and here she was singing along, and in two or three turns it was like it had blown in on the breeze—if she could get this, she felt, she could get anything. Following Mr. Mao's instruction, she did everything she could to forget the notation—after all, didn't she just need to feel oxen and goats and chickens and ducks? Didn't she just have to have the force of hawkers selling fabric, or oil, or sugar, or ointments, or metalwork? Semitones rising and falling, what was so tough about that, at least to start with. Once the sound of a pheasant was in her head, taking her back to her childhood, to that village in the hills where she was brought up, she became overwhelmed by the wildness, the craziness—as well as the foolishness—of those years as they rushed back to her.

She was singing foolishly, foolishly and cheerfully. It felt less like singing than like flopping, flying, floating, overflowing, freely holding notes without knowing or caring where they'd come from or where they were going, stretching and coiling around whatever unutterable instances or worries she had in her heart—until tears of joy appeared in her eyes.

She was so surprised, she sat right down on the bed, eyes wide.

"All right, you get it but you don't get it, back to your roots." Whatever Old Yin meant by that.

"Mr. Mao, I . . . this song of yours is really great, really it is!"

"Of course, you have to like it!"

"I . . . it brought tears to my eyes! I've never sung so happily; look at me—I'm shaking. Mr. Mao, how could you even come up with something like this? What was your trick? Did you slip me some kind of elixir? I should punch you—or at least pinch you!"

She did, in fact, smack Old Yin really hard on the back. She must have felt like she'd gone too far, as she immediately stood up, grabbed the thermos, and ran to the boiler room to fetch more water. Looking back, she saw Old Yin still sitting there, bemusedly going over his score, oblivious to the fact that she had even left.

—

6

—

His song had had such an effect on Miss Qin that Old Yin poured himself into his writing even more, until he ended up having the kind of extravagant life he'd thought was reserved for landlords and capitalists: he ate seafood every day.

Brought in to write songs for the cultural center, he roomed with a young painter. The rank odor of the painter's feet was unbearable—every time he kicked off his canvas shoes was like an act of genocide. The young painter couldn't stand the way Old Yin ground his teeth at night, the way he talked in his sleep, or his intermittent startling cries. Nor could he stand his habit of inadvertently putting on others' clothes, using others' chopsticks and rice bowls, and constantly forgetting his key every time he left the room—that is, if he hadn't locked it inside to begin with. Even more unbearable was his unfailing willingness to ask to borrow money or grain coupons, which the shameless swindler would never repay. People even warned him, telling him that whatever money they lent him when he wasn't drinking would be beside the point, but what the hell kind of logic was that?

On a day like today, people were bound to think the sun had come up in the west. Old Yin suddenly looked to be the epitome of good health, and his clothes and bedding were all clean, though who'd done the washing no one knew. A new pail, washbasin, towel, and thermos sat at the head of his bed, though again, no one knew who'd bought them. He was even using such civilized accoutrements as a toothbrush and toothpaste, whitening all the yellow teeth in his mouth so it no longer had a sour stench. Yet his newly sparkling teeth would still chomp on tofu jerky and fermented fish, which naturally drew the young painter's astonished and envious gaze. Wrinkling his nose, he found the room had a feminine air, a scent only found on young women. There was no doubt about it: the room could never have been kept so incredibly clean without a woman's long, cold fingers. The problem was, an old guy like Mao Sanyin (though in fact he was not yet forty) didn't care—matter of fact, he didn't even seem to care who the woman might be, and when the young painter brought it up, he would only mutter about some Missy Can or Sister Chain, or something else he couldn't be free from.

He even took the two bottles of xiaoqu to be a gift from the painter, bowing to him: "You shouldn't have, really, you shouldn't have—what did I do to deserve this?"

"Am I suffering from meningitis? You expect me to give you gifts for some reason?"

"You mean you didn't buy them? Strange—do you think Director He bequeathed me some of his mead?"

"You really are clueless. What a waste, anybody giving you a bottle of anything. Just like you never pay me back the money I lend you."

"Money? You lent me money?"

"See? Just the other day you were beating your chest, promising you'd pay me back . . ."

"My brother, you should not make jokes like this. I'm a what-you-see-is-what-you-get kind of guy—short on cash but long on ambition. If I was a chicken in a past life, I didn't die owing you grain, and if I'm an ox in the next life, I'll depart without owing you grass. Don't joke like this, or you'll give me a heart attack!"

The young painter didn't know whether to laugh or cry.

Thank providence, the crazy old man had gone home only a few days prior. His new opera was unfinished, but the leaders had decided that he was beyond repair politically, and any libretto you gave him—a libretto whose lyrics had met with the approval of the steering committee—would come back with blatant lies about its having been eaten by a rat or blown away by the wind. Mr. Liu had demanded that he write a self-criticism once, to promise never to lose or make undue alterations to any libretto in the future; he stared blankly at Mr. Liu, without saying a word, then blurted out, "You want me to write a criticism? For being too lenient?"

The head of the propaganda committee could only say, "Revolution and production in the villages are important, or actually more than important, therefore Old Yin must go somewhere more than important."

Old Yin couldn't figure it out, and said his pigs back home were all in good health, and the seedlings hadn't had an infestation, so he could stay here and carry on composing, even if it meant giving up his stipend. But the head was adamant in his generosity, and sent Mr. Liu to take him to the station and buy him a ticket.

Crazy Old Yin of course never learned what happened next, that his songs had to be thawed out after being put in the freezer, or that Miss Qin made a name for herself singing his songs on the radio and television, winning a provincial prize and having her photograph taken with the governor. The political situation had already changed by this point, so oversight of creative works was no longer as tense as it had been. And when Miss Qin sang those songs they sounded effortless, no matter how hard people had thought they'd be when written out in notation, though they knew that they'd never heard anything like them before. Music like this was anomalous and new, drawing attention, particularly among the top students in the institutes and academies, throughout the cities in the province. Put it this way—it was the kind of song that could be led by a score but not described by a score, that existed simultaneously both within and without the score. Listening to music like this, someone might end up imagining all sorts of sounds—bird calls, the whir of the wind, instantaneous encounters with whistles sharp and dull—as if they were melodic, as if not a sound in the world didn't fit into some greater harmony, as if all the world's reeds and strings were but waiting for you to open your ears.

Naturally, these songs immediately became the target of exploration for some new faction or other, as if it were emblematic of this or that new -*ism*, which brought on new debates, and thereafter certain columns in certain periodicals. Meanwhile, the crazy old man was raising cattle up in Bianshan Cavern, totally unaware of any of this, aside from perhaps a phrase or two of Miss Qin on his radio receiver, somewhere in there amidst the crackle of static.

Once televisions appeared in the town, that receiver went from an occasional whine to an intermittent cough and then ultimately fell silent, even its crackle gone.

He went up the hill to check the cable and found a great length of wire flapping in the breeze—and no one had bothered to take care of it. Captain Wen was now selling rice noodles in the city.

As for -isms, he only learned what had changed when the high school teacher explained it to him after they ran into each other at the market. Later two other composers, who'd traveled quite a distance to see him, explained a bit more. He was squatting by the side of the road after digging up bamboo shoots, hoping to swap them for some coins, but before any buyers showed up, along came two graduate students asking about -isms.

"Whatism? You're joking, right, you need some -ism to write music? No, I don't need an -ism, and you don't need an -ism, either—all you need is a good drink. Yam wine will do if you don't have barley wine . . ." He practiced his Beijing accent with the students until his tongue was numb and they were looking at each other in utter confusion. He forgot to switch back when he got home, too, bewildering his poor wife with his rhotacizing—and he looked at her in utter confusion. "Are you sick?" She felt his forehead.

He had been talking about Mendelssohn and Bach, and about a madman on the street who didn't wait for his guests to understand him before he handed them two new songs right from his pocket—out of courtesy, since he didn't have any liquor on him, so the songs would have to do. Only later did he realize he'd given them the originals, since like an idiot he'd forgotten to make copies.

But since he was extremely happy, and since he'd begun to -ism, what did anything else matter? He liked music, he liked people who liked music, and he liked everything that made people as happy as music did, so sometimes he'd stand in his doorway inviting people in for a drink, waving to them on a whim, from which most people ran away in fright. When there was no one to talk to, he'd head up into the hills, find a rock or a tree, and pretend they were little kids needing to be calmed down, or monsters needing to be run out of town. One day a young woodsman heard the noises in the forest and ran over to take a look, figuring some people were up there fighting, only to find Old Yin all by himself, having it out with a thorn bush. "Last time you bit me, you bit me just a few days ago, you wanna die? If you're gonna bite, then bite right. You bite the same place each time, out of spite and ill intent, so I have to kill you or I deserve the people's wrath!" After pronouncing his verdict, Old Yin took out a knife and hacked the thorn bush to bits. Only then did he walk away, breathing hard.

Walking through the hills with no one to speak to, he grew much more talkative, as if his mouth were directly attached to his brain and nothing was there to control his thoughts: *So, do I want a drink? Nah, I can hold off a bit longer. And my knife? Strange, it was right here in the basket just a minute ago. Oh no, gotta piss again. Have to hold it till I get to the bushes over there.* And on and on, proclamations and declarations for the whole wide world to hear. Of course he prattled on about his time in the city, too, jabbering about the beautiful toothbrushes and toothpaste there and his days of bottles full of fine liquor, not to mention those fine friends of his who afforded him such a benighted lifestyle: Miss Qin, and Mr. Liu, and Director He, and that young painter he'd shared a room with. Oh, those were fine people, fine people indeed, and, oh, how nostalgic you get just thinking about them, how much you miss them. Had it really been three autumns since they'd parted, and had they really not kept in touch? How had they not sent him any requests for more songs? A song was a fine thing, as fine as liquor and which must also be drunk up, and which ran like blood in the veins of all the Miss Qins and Kins and Cans and Chains out there, no less than a baby needs to be brought to term and delivered.

When a letter did arrive from Missy Qin, imploring him to compose something for the newly reorganized Mountain Songs Theatre Troupe, his heart almost burst with joy. He curled up grandiosely on his bed and slept for three days straight, like a leopard in full crouch, carefully conserving his energy before pouncing for the kill. Everyone who knew him understood that he took music to be a form of manual labor, a form of physical exertion unfit for intellectuals with their lily-white hands, each lift of a pen like shouldering a plow, chiseling stone, or bearing a yoke, or a life-threatening leap that, once made, would make days pass into nights and nights pass into days, until, ribs visible from emaciation, he would collapse on the ground, his mouth agape and gasping for breath.

His new composition, a mountain-song opera in eight acts, he called *Heaven and Earth Are Great*, and to move this great mountain he had sold off his pigs, his home, and the lumber for which he was responsible, emptying his pockets of practically everything he could trade in for liquor— for his ammunition, waiting for ten enemy armies, or a hundred enemy armies, or a thousand, which would be bound and gagged and blindfolded and summarily executed. For him, *Heaven and Earth Are Great* was not music but the roaring blaze of a burning ethanol bomb ignited inside his body.

What he couldn't understand, though, was why it sank like a stone in the ocean once he sent it out.

Counting on his fingers, he realized that half a year had passed with no news. Were Mr. Liu and Mr. Wang and Mr. Li and the rest of those overfed guys not holding study groups anymore? Not concerning themselves with the peasants' extracurricular transformations of their objective and subjective conditions anymore? Not occupying the cultural front of the peasantry anymore? (He was oblivious to the fact that such terminology was not current anymore.) Was the cause of the proletarian revolution of arts and letters no longer to be taken up? (Nor did he have a clue that political slogans like this had been scrapped.)

Something was not right.

Most likely that pimply bookkeeper in the village had used the letter to wipe his ass with one day when he was delirious from dysentery. He'd seen him having a smoke, looking just like you would if you were having a smoke after hiding a notification letter. He'd seen him having a meal, looking just like you would if you were having a meal after hiding an official notice. And when he saw the bookkeeper spanking his son, there could be no question that he had the craftiness to hide a notice—talk about sleight of hand, just look at how high he brought his arm up, for it only to come down so slowly!

The mail carrier always delivered letters to the home of the book-keeper. He couldn't resist stopping by himself, but the pimply bookkeeper said he hadn't received anything, that there had been no notification let-ter. He even said: "Mad Yin, you have to face the facts. You have bold ears and eyebrows, exquisite and astonishing, but your eyes are small, so you're running against all the principles of numerology, which means you shouldn't do anything but stay up in Bianshan Cavern sniffing ox butt."

Sniffing ox butt meant raising cattle.

He wiped his face and went wordlessly back home.

In autumn, something unexpected happened. He was setting a con-trolled swailing burn with his son in the foothills when his son was stung by a carpenter bee. Like a dog, Old Yin shot into the woods in hot pursuit of the perpetrator of so heinous a crime, determined to make it pay—as they'd say in Bianshan Cavern, to drain that bee of its fluids, till its blood ran poison, if he wanted the swelling to cease. He chased it panting into a hollow, where he came upon a large hive. A swarm of carpenter bees thundered out of a hole in the cliff face, a bucket-thick bolt of black lightning, spiraling upward as it spread into a dark canopy, turning day into night as it covered the sky. Buzzing bees flew all around him, fast and slow, upward and downward, with the force of a tidal wave crashing against the shore, making even the grass blades tremble. He had never heard such a roar, and it sent him into such a daze that he forgot all about the fire he'd set.

He didn't hear his son screaming. Only later did he learn that a patch of the swail fire had been picked up by the wind, turning into a blaze, sparks caught in the shrubs by the road, with no way for his son to manage it other than to sit down and cry. When Old Yin made it back, the flames had ridden the wind and were crackling up the hill, billows of tumbling thick smoke, birds shrieking for their lives in all directions, burning bam-boo stalks popping in the depths of the fire, shaking the hill with their noise, and his legs went weak, his mind emptied, and he couldn't budge.

Fortunately the villagers spotted the fire and rushed up the hill to save them. And fortunately it started to rain just in time, so the fire didn't spread too far. Black mud spilled over the ground as the thunderstorm tangled with the smoke.

An officer from the forestry security department arrived and reprimanded him for destroying the forest. He clapped a set of handcuffs on his wrists, scaring Old Yin's wife so badly that she burst into tears, wailing and clutching at his shirt to keep him from going.

He hadn't had a chance to wash the soot from his face, his teeth were still chattering from fear, and he had to be propped up by the people around him before he could be dumped into the wagon, like a pile of mud himself. "Help! Help!" he screamed nonstop in terror.

He sat for more than half a month in the holding cell. Destruction of over three hundred acres of forest was a felony, enough to get a hearing at the sentencing court. By then, he figured in his madness that it wasn't worth getting overly worked up about—he was, after all, a master folk musician and a composer famous far and wide, so the police could fine him by way of punishment, say, maybe a thousand kuai or so, along with an order to replant two hundred trees, so they could be seen to have treated the matter magnanimously. In fact, the greater incentive was that each day he was in the holding cell was a day he sent the police department into turmoil, until no one could handle it much longer.

Without anything to do, he filled his self-criticism notebook with songs, scribbling words that looked like tadpoles into a tiresome aria of confession. Still bored, he picked up the *Forest Protection* manual and turned it into lyrics, densely writing down the notes. *Guang guang guang, beng beng beng*! After the orchestral prelude, a trill of *the forest is our nation's most treasured natural resource*, a harmony of *unauthorized tree felling is strictly forbidden*, a full baritone solo of *transgressors will be punished to the full extent of the law*, continuing on for quite some time, extending *law* until it cracked its shell and brought the suspended suspense crashing down on the ground. Probably for emphasis, he repeated *the first line, the first line, the first line* in a virtuosic range of high and low. *The second line, the second line, the second line* was likewise repeated, weaving a mellifluous floridity before turning back into the rhythm's clear staccato: *every sector of government, must vigilantly stand guard, against and furthermore, implement each element, of fire and theft protection and deterrence . . .* in the end, he had sung a veritable marathon of rules and regulations covering various principalities, a lingering decrescendo in the phrase *presented for promulgation and practice*, infinite emotion rounded off and sent into the distance.

At first the officers just thought he was insane, learning only later that it was a recitative. When the foreigners sang them they were never clear, like they were singing with hot turnips in their mouths.

Next door to the station was the supply and marketing cooperative slaughterhouse, as well as the town's veterinary office, a pesticide store-room, and a tailor's shop. For several days, the mellifluous tones of for-est protection law provided neither comfort nor suasion to the people of the town, but rather induced a bone-chilling fear and its resultant goose bumps. Even as hot as it was, the windows of all the homes slammed shut.

The police officers going to the slaughterhouse for meat were met with a stern refusal. "With those ghastly noises coming out of the station, I haven't been able to sleep. Keep that in mind when you get hungry for meat." Butcher Wang chopped his cleaver into the block. "So come back after I've had enough rest."

The butcher's wife came out, as well: "You cops say you're here to serve and protect, but you're keeping us all awake—how are we supposed to live?"

Finally the police figured they had no choice but to let Old Yin out.

Not that Old Yin was in any kind of a hurry, lingering and rubbing his eyes as he walked out of the cell, saying, "Nothing but peace and quiet here, a real egg of a place—finally I've been able to catch up on my rest. Excuse me!"

"You can stay for three more years if you're not ready to leave."

"No, I'll go. Better let you guys get back to what you were doing!"

"Hurry up and pay your fine, hear?"

"Of course, of course. You're so understanding, charging me so little, I should be understanding and not keep you from your work. Right?"

The police returned the suspect's belongings from when he had been taken into custody. He verified his shoes, his drinking gourd, and his ration coupons (which he always had with him, never mind that they were no longer in use), and said, laughing, "You're really too, too nice. Here you are providing me with food and tea each day, and you won't take my cou-pons. And then you send me abroad for tourism every other day—you really shouldn't have!" By "tourism" he meant the foreign shows he'd seen on their television. With a "Thank you" and "Goodbye" after every other breath, he shook their hands more like a leader offering condolences than a prisoner being released. The hands of three officers who didn't manage to hide themselves were shaken individually, as were those of a young man delivering firewood whom Old Yin had mistaken for a cop.

"Hurry up and get out of here," said one of the officers, finding him too strange.

"You don't want to shake my hand? Such an unceremonious departure! When armies meet in battle, should they not treat each other with respect?"

He looked each officer in the eye, and they could not help nodding, satisfaction indeed. He shouldn't be rushed, shouldn't be pressured along, the rituals of departure must be observed to their proper completion, the gateway of the office courtyard stepped through correctly.

A scattering of people in the courtyard, mostly there out of curiosity to see the crazy person, as well as some others Old Yin knew in passing, gave their requisite greetings. Obviously mocking Old Yin's vibrato from the past few days, one young man sang out, "The implementation is hereby promulgated—" which got a lot of laughs, a dozen sets of teeth exposing themselves. The madman knew they were there to see a monkey show, but he coughed, pretended he hadn't heard, and went on his way.

7

A year or two or maybe even three years after the fact (sorry, he often gets our memories messed up), Old Yin decided he had to go into town to ask how things had turned out.

He cut his hair, put on the military uniform with two yellow ribbons at the cuff that his nephew had given him, and slung four thin-reed straw mats over his shoulder to head down the road. The minute he stepped off the bus, his vision went blurry and his head began to spin. Only after asking several people and pinching his wrist until it hurt was he certain that he hadn't gotten off at the wrong stop. The streets of the town were narrower, more congested and muddled, with what had been wall after wall of cold and solitary enclosures now a tangle of cluttered storefronts. The shops were filled with electronics and furniture and apparel and liquor and tobacco and the like, which oozed out onto the sidewalk and pushed pedestrians into the street, blocking automobiles and motorcycles coughing black smoke. The street was shrouded in electric music—if you could call it music, its violent noises beating passersby black and blue, threatening them with lumbar strains and stress fractures. Looking at the singers on the television screens, the men weren't men and the women weren't women, and if one minute they were bowing their heads intoning some psychotic sutra, the next they were screaming to the sky from their intestines (not their throats), then bending over again (as if suffering from stomach pain) or squatting on their heels (like they had urinary retention). Their eyebrows and mouths twisted into every sort of contortion, like they'd lost their parents and were in so much pain they wanted to end it all . . . so sad, so, so sad. Old Yin was dumbstruck: no one was going hungry anymore, so what was all the fuss about?

Lost, he wandered through the streets until midafternoon before, in a moment of alertness, scouting out the cultural center. Not that the cultural center was a boat on the move; it was in the same spot it had always been, only swallowed up now by the visual cacophony, it was no longer easy to spot. And the entryway now opened into a video-recording room with a floor covered in scrap paper and tangerine peels. The room he'd lived in was now connected to another room, and was a photographic enlargement center in which two people were working whom he'd never seen before, who asked him if he wanted to take a series of wedding photos in Kodachrome. He didn't find Director He, who he learned had retired. Nor did he find Mr. Liu. A younger Mr. Liu sat staring at robots fighting on a television screen, and said his dad had gone to the provincial capital to buy tables and chairs and whatnot for the restaurant, which would be opening soon. He'd be back in a couple of days.

In the drama troupe dormitory, Old Yin recognized a familiar face peeking out of a doorway, but out of fear of getting the name wrong, he merely let out an enthusiastic "Hey, oh hey!"

"Professor Mao!"

"Yes, it's me—Old Yin."

"I heard you were rotting in prison, or raising trouble somewhere?"

"In their wisdom and lenience, the government decided I should continue to serve the people."

"You haven't paid us a visit in so long—to what do we owe the pleasure of your gracing us with your presence?"

"I missed you, you devil!"

"Ah ha ha, I've missed you, too! Almost died of heartbreak, even. Come, let's celebrate your safe arrival—give us a kiss!"

Old Yin was sure he had misheard. He certainly hadn't expected that Miss Qin not only wouldn't mind his having forgotten her name, but would actually throw her pudgy arms around his neck and pucker her cold lips against his face, where he choked on her perfume.

The room filled with laughter.

Old Yin pinched his nose and discovered several other men in the room. Two of the faces were unfamiliar, with their neckties and hair oil. The other two were actors from the troupe, whom he remembered from the stage back in the day, though by now they'd had full makeovers and looked as if they'd just popped out of the TV, stomach pain and urinary retention not yet resolved and hair down to their shoulders, their faces pale, and gold chains hanging around their necks, eyes agog. Not that they weren't obliging, offering Old Yin a seat and raising their beer glasses. Miss Qin snatched up his glass and traded the beer for something stronger, with a knowing, kindhearted look. It was only because of the contents of this glass that Old Yin could hear what anyone was saying: they were praising Miss Qin's voice, saying that it was beyond compare, better by far than anything you'd hear in any of the clubs or dance halls. They approved of Miss Qin's vocal dependence on conventional singing styles, as folk music really couldn't be compared with what had been coming out of Taiwan or Hong Kong. They recommended that she have more bird's nest soup, since singing was mental labor and required a different sort of nourishment than that required for plowing fields. Then they joked about the girls in Flower-Bridge Town, how they didn't understand that their dark skin didn't go with light-colored fabrics, or that if your knees are bowlegged you really can't go around wearing blue jeans, or that girls with deep dimples should cover their mouths when they smile . . . and yet they still try to make eyes at you, ha ha ha!

They shuffled the mahjong tiles on the table and tabulated their winnings and losses with the bills in their hands.

Missy Qin shuffled between them, patting this one on the head and laying her hand on that one's shoulder. She would scrunch her eyebrows together feigning anger, fully aware that she looked sexy when she was stern. "I oughta punch you!" she'd say, issuing a coquettish threat, regardless of the topic.

Nor did she leave Old Yin out in the cold, calling him "Professor Mao" and squeezing up next to him and whispering in his ear when she dug something or other out of the cabinet. One whisper informed him that Mr. Liu had gone through two divorces, with the next candidate for new wife already lined up, could you believe it? Another reminded him to button his pants properly, which, while it put him on the spot, still heightened his emotional position with its singular secrecy, not to mention the rush of memories it stirred—Missy Qin used to have to remind Old Yin to do this all the time.

Old Yin almost got excited, but as he gulped down another drink, he figured out that he was more like a duck in a flock of chickens; better to sit off in the corner sucking on a cigarette than say anything. He stretched his arms dramatically and pretended to look at the drawings and photographs hanging on the wall, but then decided such actions weren't quite appropriate, or even useful, since he had nothing to follow up with. He looked at a porcelain vase awhile, but he still came up with nothing.

He waited for his hostess to bring up more serious matters. When she said that she couldn't sing anything but Professor Mao's songs back in the day, he figured she'd follow with something about the score, but she veered off and starting talking about tofu in fish stew. He was sure she'd segue into serious matters when she brought up troupe reformation, but again she careened off into talking about sofas and chairs. Old Yin even forced a couple of dry coughs, but in the end he had to broach the topic himself:

"Missy, could I inquire about something?"

"Which something?"

"Something of mine."

"Oh, do you mean your tuning fork?"

"No."

His hostess smacked herself gently on the forehead, cursing her muddled memory.

Ultimately, after Old Yin's prompting, she did *ooh, right right right* and recall something, something called *Heaven and Earth Are Great*, was it not? Was it *Heaven and Earth Are Great*, or *Between Heaven and Earth*? Or *Above Heaven and Underground*? "Well, it's like this," she said. "The score is great and all, but we just don't have the funds to put it on, and it made the rounds with a bunch of people, finally ending up with Mr. Wei of the Provincial Opera Theater, but then we didn't hear anything after that, so I don't think anything is really going to come of it at this point. Last I heard, Mr. Wei was out of the country . . ."

Old Yin's face darkened.

"Mr. Wei really did leave the country. He went to New Zealand, or, wait, was it Canada? Anywhere, somewhere in Europe, we can be sure of that . . ." She asked the men beside her, "Canada's in Europe, right?"

Old Yin didn't know much about geography, either, so he couldn't say why this question caused so much laughter. "It doesn't matter, so long as the thing itself is still around. Even if it's far away, we can still find it one way or another. Canada can't be any farther than India, right? If the Monkey King could make his journey to the west, then so can I."

Again, he didn't know why everyone was laughing. They said it would be absolutely impossible to go to Canada, that even if Mr. Wei had gone, there was no way Professor Mao could go—and not because of the mountains or rivers he'd have to cross, or not knowing whether to go north or south, or even because of money. Only then did panic show in his eyes: "Then . . . then when will he be back?"

"Professor Mao, I blame myself. I've been so absentminded recently."

"He's gonna have to come back sooner or later, right? Is he planning to die over there? If he doesn't come back for the moon festival, he'll be back for New Year's, right? When friends or family get married, won't he come back to join in the festivities?"

"He's emigrated, Professor Mao."

"I don't care if he's living on the moon. If he's holding on to something that's not his, he's got to give it back. I'm not talking about a burp or a fart here, but a stack of honest-to-goodness material pages!"

"Professor Mao, is it really that important?"

"How could it not be? I birthed an egg—an egg this big." He held up his hands as if they were holding something bigger than his face.

"Then maybe I should compensate you?"

"No, I don't want money."

"To be really honest, there's no point in tracking him down, since, actually, it wouldn't mean crap . . ." The hostess didn't want to be too direct, so she changed tack: "Look, don't be so uptight—I have money right here. It's like I'm buying it from you, all right? Doesn't matter to who, right, so long as it's sold?"

"Right! Like you said, it's not a burp or a fart, so have her pay for it!" Some people chimed in mischievously. "Let her buy it! She's made an ocean of money in the dance halls!"

Seeing that Old Yin was silent, and before he had a chance to say anything, a few of them adopted the stance of speaking for peasant music, coming up with reasons he should name higher and higher prices—joint performances and tours, record albums and cassette tapes, not to mention the possibility of actually being released into the world of best-selling instructional material—each one raising the sales figure until it stretched credulity.

"All right, all right, you're pushing it," Miss Qin laughed, pounding the table. "Sold at a hundred thousand to the man in the military suit! What else do you need? I surrender! If Professor Mao killed me, bull-dozed my home, and forced me into slavery, I'd take it all!"

"Be his slave? You mean be his concubine—"

Yes, his concubine! His concubine! The room erupted in laughter and applause, some of them slapping their hands on the tabletop. Caught up in the moment, even Old Yin cracked his lips open—not to smile, but enough to suggest that he'd given in to the laughter, and now needed a way out. What else could he say? The punishment had been meted out, so what else was left? They had moved a round tabletop onto the rectangular table frame and were setting it for dinner. Bottles were on the table already, so the talk naturally turned to anti-counterfeiting strategies in the liquor industry. No one noticed Old Yin's silence, or that he hadn't touched his cup. At some point, while everyone else's glasses were raised, he came to, opened his eyes wide, stood up shakily, stuck out his wizened gut, and pressed himself against the table. He wasn't going to make a toast (as two people expected), or inspecting the contents of all the glasses in case anyone was verging on impropriety (as even more of his companions figured); rather, he was going to release a long howl to the ceiling, scaring those around him—not knowing where the sound was coming from, they looked around to figure out what the noise was before they realized it was him.

His gaze was completely vacant, his body in a shock that was almost electrical: "Break it up, everyone—" He straightened his neck again like a rooster crowing at dawn, and without waiting for those around him to understand, *wham*, the round tabletop flipped up, sending dishes and plates whooshing, hanging in midair for a moment, then crashing down onto the slanting tabletop, where they fell again in a cascade of clonks and clangs. Fish tangoed with braised pork, soy sauce flew with sweet-and-sour soup, and something tumbled into the corner, thumping as it went.

He was a mad rooster. Fortunately everyone had moved away in time, so no one got covered in oil or anything, but a couple of vegetables did land on Miss Qin's hand.

"What's this all about?" Miss Qin blanked: "Have you eaten fresh dog shit? Y-y-you really are insane!"

"Pay me back another meal. How's that?" The rooster laughed, clapped his hands, and exited the room.

"Your old mother's—" Miss Qin stamped her foot, uttered a vulgarity, looked at the mess, then screwed up her face and ran into the next room, wailing.

Tears streaming down her face, she brought out two straw mats and ran to the front entrance, where she threw them outside: "Take your rotten mats! Lay them under your corpse, for all I care! Lay them under your dad's old corpse! Damn crazy person, what do you think you are, you aren't even dog shit, you hear me!" She shut her eyes and continued cursing, cursing his ancestors and descendants, until someone tugged at her sleeve and reminded her he was already gone. She opened her eyes, craned her neck to take a look, and saw nothing but the empty street before her.

8

Walking out of the city, Old Yin had the notion that he'd accomplished something great. Finding that his material pages had become no more than a burp or a fart, and that in the city he himself was but an unnoticed burst of indeterminate air, ended up being a relief, and with nothing holding him down, he felt unburdened.

Not wanting to hurry back to the mountains, he headed to the nearby river, where he'd heard that for flood prevention a dam had been constructed that stretched on for miles, and he wanted to see if the cement embankment was really so mighty and magnificent after all. Ever since he was a kid, he'd liked big things: great big pumpkins, gargantuan trees, super-sized trucks, colossal mountain peaks or dams—everything large gave him uncontainable, hand-rubbing, time-forgetting delight, triumphant elation, even, as if the heavens split open and he himself grew at the sight of it. He needed to see bigness like most people needed to eat.

People who knew him also knew, probably from the same desire for bigness, that his most common curse was "Go die in a matchbox": belittling became besmalling, as small as a matchbox.

But he didn't make it to the cement embankment, since by the time the liquor had worn off he was lost, a sober kind of lost, as if the world were all out of order. A tree kicked him, a car horn tickled him, and two red brick smokestacks ganged up on him, swaggering and throwing their weight around, refusing to let him pass, and tripping him up for quite some time. Stubborn by nature, he had never been afraid of ghosts and didn't believe in spirits, so he refused to give them an inch. In the end, a road rolled over on him, making it hard for him to breathe. When he woke up, brightness was peeking over the horizon.

He found himself in a dry ditch beneath a stone bridge, clothes moist with dew and mouth covered in sand. And the only thing nearby was a hound tilting its head at him.

He tried to move his legs, but he felt a tremendous pain in his right knee, and found that it was covered in dried blood.

Down to the river to wash her silk she goes
But tears stream down each time she washes her clothes
The club in her hand is so big, she knows,
But her husband, he's as small as a nose

Cackling, he limped along, singing as he made his way home, who knows how many days on the road, taking who knows which way back. One of his rubber sandals was lost, but somehow he had on a leather shoe.

The shirt of the military uniform he'd been wearing had been replaced by a big red soccer jersey. He couldn't say if he'd picked it up or if it had been given to him.

He slept when he needed to sleep, walked when he felt like walking, and rested on moonlight and snored beneath a blanket of dew. People who knew him all said the alcohol content of his blood had been so high for so long, it had strengthened his resilience and hardened his muscles into metal, so cold had little power over him. Nor was he ever bothered by ants, mosquitoes, or leeches, since wherever they happened to fall on his body, his murderous vigor would simply burn them off. As for why, well, just think of the disinfectant effects of alcohol in the system, not to mention the fact that they use hard liquor as a pesticide in the country, and you'll get the idea.

Mosquitoes never entered his home, and on summer nights his boys would huddle up against him so as not to get bitten. This didn't surprise him, since one time he told the herbalist that his blood type wasn't O or A or B, but C_2H_5OH. The herbalist, who didn't know much about Western medicine, just nodded.

With one rubber sandal and one leather shoe, he returned to Bianshan Cavern. The following days didn't give him much reason to head back down, so mentions of him gradually diminished. There were always newer marvels to talk about, and eventually he stopped coming up in conversation. And aside from poachers and hawkers of lumber or bamboo, not many people went over to his side of the mountain. If he never came around, or if he got too old to move, townspeople figured, he'd be like a kite with a broken string, forever falling into the depths of the mountains and finally disappearing. Boars and muntjacs lurked in the woods, and from time to time a forest fire would turn all the green to black, or cicadas would come and turn everything yellow, but the disappearance of one lone man never caused a stir.

His music remained, but it would never again become sound. Yet how ordinary it was to hear a resounding symphony in the suppressed sight of rumpled mountaintops, or an instrumental solo in the mists of the wavering woods, or a duet between harp and piano in the fallen flowers stippling the ground beside a brook. Looking back in confusion, you might feel that some secret was hidden in the silence.

The mountains were too quiet, yet could song perhaps be born of such silence? When some white or red squiggle appeared opposite, the people on the mountain could only ask after it with a confused shout. As the red or white squiggle gradually vanished, the words that the people on the mountain had not uttered, and would never have the chance to utter, metamorphosed into solitary intonation. The audience was too small, they knew, and indeed too far away, but the song would contain a piercing endurance, rising into the sky beyond the clouds, to be cast upon the mountains with something like a simultaneous presence and an absence. It was when three professors from Beijing followed such songs into the mountains that year that they came across the young cowherd Old Yin. Hearing him play his suona, as well as his erhu, they decided to take the barefoot boy back with them to the capital—one of the professors even paid for a pair of shoes for the boy out of his own pocket, teaching him to tie the laces.

Who knows why, but in those years Bianshan Cavern was surrounded by singing, and on top of their history songs, love songs, funeral songs, and salacious songs, the people on the mountain even resolved conflicts by singing. Out of respect for an eons-old custom, their conflicts never found their way into official reports. Even if someone was killed, they still felt that singing was more effective than reporting it to an official. Plaintiff and defendant would each send forward an "envoy," who then sat upon the ground facing each other. The first envoy would sing a measure, making knots in a length of hemp rope as a way of recordkeeping. Once ten knots had been tied, the rope would be passed across. The other envoy would then sing a measure, untying the knots, also as a way of recordkeeping. If the ten knots were untied successfully, the trial was over, the hatchet buried, scores settled. If one side lost, that side would slaughter a pig to cook a pot of "face-wash pork," from which anyone and everyone could eat, washing not only faces clean but hearts as well.

But after radios and televisions came along, the folksongs in the mountains diminished, with the noises of modern popular music like an antibiotic that locked down throats and tongues. When singing did happen, it was no more than a line or two for condolence calls during vigils, when the old people were around, and under cover of night, never during daylight. By then the one-time barefoot youth had failed the expectations of the professors from Beijing, failed to write any new *Sister Liu* or *Swan Lake*. On the contrary, he was white-haired and wrinkled, his fingers were so stiff he couldn't hold a pen, and his musical staffs were always poked through with holes. And his songs, well, happy or sad, leisurely or fierce, what was the point anymore? Published or unpublished, who'd end up singing them? These songs could never end up onstage—certainly Miss Qin didn't need them—so they were superfluous, best bundled up and tossed into the storehouse to be munched on by mice. And instruments like the erhu were only fodder for mold or maggots, to be tossed into the cesspit.

Whenever he was asked about these things later on, Old Yin would mimic a line from an old Soviet movie as dubbed into Mandarin: "As Comrade Stalin has put it, the art of the bourgeoisie must be sent to the trash heap of history!"

Then he would cackle with laughter.

His wife had left him not long before, leaving the older son with him but taking the younger one with her. Four years his elder and half a head taller, she would willingly tangle with cattle thieves, so she never let her husband be taken advantage of; under the light of an oil lamp, she had drawn out the musical staffs he'd fill in, sincere in her desire for her man to achieve greatness. Afraid he would lose things, she embroidered his name into all his clothes, writing Mao Sanyin Mao Sanyin Mao Sanyin Mao Sanyin Mao Sanyin in various sizes over practically half her world. Her marks covered twenty years, in which time she had lived in a leaky, uninsulated shack, unable to afford a visit to the doctor or any medicine he might prescribe, even buying their tofu on an installment plan, and in the end it all became too much. Old Yin said, "If you don't leave me, there's no justice under heaven. Here, take whatever you want. Go ahead and take it all."

Only later did he realize his miscalculation, that there was nothing left for her to take, that all the useful items could fit into one wicker basket slung over her shoulder.

His wife took nothing when she left, just stitched Mao Sanyin into another sleeve and on the heels of another pair of shoes, filling in the last blanks she could find.

He cried awhile, recalling her final exhortations as she departed, that he not go crazy again, at least for the boy's sake. His wife was Stalin, her directives Stalin's directives: the nightmare must end, the music must be thrown into the cesspit behind the shack, to be mixed with ammonium bicarbonate and spread in the field to fertilize the crops. That rotten music must be covered in maggots, moss, and froth, to sicken people on sight. So what if *Heaven and Earth Are Great* had emptied him out, squeezed him dry, and left him in the sun, never to recover—he couldn't go back. On this point, at least, his loss came not a moment too soon, and he shouldn't have been angry or gone into town for a fight (though his memories of this were not exactly precise).

He took to raising sheep and ducks, planting grain and pumpkins, weaving bamboo mats and mending his clumsy son's clothes. The fields and cattle of the collective had been disbursed to the households, meaning there were no cows for him to look after, so this was all he could do. As his son said, it wasn't be easy for him to turn over a new leaf, and for a while his old habits would bubble up again, sending him halfway back to his rotting music, jotting down notes in the blank spaces in his son's textbooks. All the distributed teaching material, from *Agriculture and Pesticides, Language Arts, Junior High Chemistry 2, Electronics Maintenance, Planned Procreation—All You Need to Know,* and even *Youth Times Magazine,* was covered in the lumpy traces of his pen, until his son tracked down the perpetrator and gave him a serious scolding. If his son hadn't caught him, he'd never have been able to send those books to the cesspit.

It was his son who actually encouraged him to play violin at the acting school, if for no other reason than to put some change in his pocket. He heard his son out and did end up making his way over there. The way he saw it, violin wasn't really music, since it didn't actually take any more use of his brain than sawing up some wood. But then again, how long had it been since he'd been any good with a saw? His wrist was weak, the bow flittered, and nothing clean or clear or crisp came out of the instrument. With fingers as clumsy as his feet and calloused from working his hoe, he couldn't hit the strings right, always ending up either flat or sharp. Even the simplest West Lake ditty came out jittery and pitchy, like a soundtrack of killing chickens. His fingers might as well have been chopped off, chewed up, and swallowed.

He couldn't see more than a blur, but he felt the performers off to the side wrinkling their brows, and a couple of younger musicians behind him who weren't trying hard to stifle their laughter. "What a clown!" He put down his bow, embarrassed.

"No, old ginger is the hottest," someone explained. "Old Yin has seen so much, even his drawing of the bow is a method beyond methods, like you'd get from the immortals."

"Old Yin's just being modest," someone else added. "Skill like his can't be copied."

"A true artist never reveals his hand," another voice chimed in, "and never quits till the game is over."

He wanted to bore down into the earth.

"Your eyes are small, but your ears and eyebrows are crazy, quite outside the ordinary, overall a very prosperous mien." They were evaluating the reasons for his success. Probably because of the reputation he'd gained in Beijing, a number of students were sawing their violins like him, flighty and obscure, non-methodological, buzzing like a swarm of mosquitoes, and instead of sitting there anxiously, he excused himself to make a trip to the washroom.

"Don't run off," said the carpenter from the next village, catching up with him. He handed him a cigarette and stuffed the whole pack into his shirt pocket. "Don't be like that—hey, you gotta show off some of your technique, at least a little bit. The whole village is like family—your dad's sister is my mother-in-law, don't you know, and my kid's in the same class as your oldest nephew. Last time you came by to hang out, I gave you some watermelon."

"Is this a funeral procession? Why are you following me so close?"

"Forgive me, these smokes are no good. My fingers are stiff today, but I'll shake them out next time—I won't eat my words."

"And you stink, too! Has that sweat been stored up for three months or something? I can barely keep my eyes open without getting an infection. Say what you need to say, but stand back, all right, you son of a pig?"

"Hey, if you don't want to teach me, then don't teach me, but do you have to be so insulting?" The man blanched, his face drooping.

"So what if I insult you? The shoes you gave your mother-in-law were fakes—they were all pulp, did you think they were real? Why should I teach you anything? You're disloyal and unfilial—you should be swatted with a flyswatter and buried in a matchbox."

"No, you should be buried in a peanut shell." The carpenter didn't take things lightly, and snatched back the pack of cigarettes. "What's so big about you, anyway? Putting on all kinds of rotten airs. So you can write songs and play an instrument or two. You're just selling your little skills for money, and you think you're so high and mighty. If you could build an airplane, would you piss in our rice pots? If you made an atom bomb, would you cut off our heads to play soccer with?"

The two squared off in attack positions, and even their ancestors three generations back couldn't have made peace between them—until they each pulled up a bench ready to unknot a fishing net. Only later did Old Yin realize that his eyes hadn't been getting an infection, and the man he'd been talking to hadn't had any stench at all—it had all been his own inflammatory anger.

He never went back to the acting school.

He just listened in from a distance.

Later on, if the drama troupe came by, he didn't even listen, just walked in the opposite direction from where the music was, regardless of where it might take him, regardless of whether he got lost in the moonlight. One day he walked to a hollow where the moon was so bright, trees far and near cast clear black shadows from the incandescence in which they were bathing. Frogs hiding off somewhere chirped like roosters crowing for the break of day. Time seemed completely out of whack.

He spotted something that looked like water damage on an earthen wall, but when he walked up to it, he discovered it wasn't water damage at all, but rather the splash of something living: a stretch of leather nailed on the wall, nailed and pulled into several sharp angles. He knew all the cows in the village, especially those he'd tended. When he reached out to touch it, his hand landing upon a familiar whorl, he felt a pang of sadness: Could this have been his reincarnated Mozart? Wasn't this the dun bull that would wag its tail and wiggle its ears in time to the blowing of his bamboo flute?

And its eyes? Its wet nose? Its broken left horn? Oh God, what was he doing in here lazing on the wall instead of out there plowing the fields? He hit his hand against the bull's rump, but it didn't budge, stuck there dead against the wall.

He was sure he heard the lowing of a bull, a long wail coming from the patch of leather. His heart on the verge of bursting, he pounded his forehead against the leather, against the hard and dried polygon on the wall, as his own tears flowed from the pungent odor of the dried cow's blood. He held it in a long while, but in the end he let out a scream, a shriek like a lady's, not so much a cry as a cough, a dry, hacking cough.

He jumped up, cursing the bull's owner: "Go eat a bullet! Eat a lightning bolt! You murdered a bull! Murdered what you were charged to care for! Malicious, heartless . . . go get struck by lightning! I'm gonna tear off your head and dip my tofu down your neck!"

He had focused so much energy on his cursing that he'd forgotten about his diarrhea—but his warm, wet pants reminded him, and he bunched his waistband up into his right hand and stumbled awkwardly back home.

9

When Mr. Liu came to the mountain looking for antique furniture, he stopped by Old Yin's. Hearing that an engraved bedframe or dining table set could fetch a good price with the dealers abroad, Old Liu got excited, because he had already made his first purchase. His business was growing, and if Old Yin was interested in helping out, he'd set up a purchasing center in Flower-Bridge Town, so as not to be beat out by the competition.

He examined the hen roost behind where Old Yin lived, figuring he could have a lunch of free-range chicken, but spotting the dozen or so pumpkins stashed under Old Yin's bed and the empty cabinet whose door had fallen off its hinges, he felt less inclined to impose, instead dragging Old Yin to the inn by the market, where he bought a couple of bottles. At least twice he made a point of emphasizing that these were the finest lang spirits from Guizhou, running ¥52 a bottle. If he mentioned his wristwatch, he'd remark that it had set him back ¥5,300, and his leather shoes ¥2,100, and his mobile phone and surround-sound were ¥2,800 and ¥14,000—and his company, well, just to register it required an investment of ¥800,000 . . . he was always rattling off numbers, as if he were some kind of pricing bureau.

As might be imagined, he lived in numbers: he woke up in a ¥3,500 bed, brushed his teeth with a ¥52 toothbrush, onto which he squeezed ¥48 tooth gel, ¥1.30 or ¥1.50 of which he'd spit out, before he put on a ¥3,800 suit, tying his necktie looking in a ¥320 mirror. He was comfortable. But here he was, walking on limestone steps that couldn't be worth more than ten kuai each, stepping over a threshold that wouldn't go for eight, to sit in a chair that would top out at three kuai, opposite a man wearing a shirt whose value approached absolute zero, yet who didn't seem uncomfortable in the slightest. He snapped his fingers—they, at least, were hard to put a price on.

As ¥5.40 or ¥5.30 worth of alcohol poured into his mouth, behind his red eyes he truly and sincerely wanted to do something for Old Yin. He told him that he had to strike while the iron was hot, that he should take as much time as he needed to think it through, but that lightning wouldn't strike twice, because time waits for no man. He got impatient with his hemming and hawing and felt like reaching over and opening up Old Yin's skull, dumping out all the yam residue and squeezing out all the yam juice, and stuffing it instead with some basic arithmetic from the pricing bureau. Thirty was thirty, three hundred was three hundred, three thousand was three thousand—is that so hard to comprehend?

"Everything's blurry—how can you see the engravings?" Old Yin sighed.

"How about, here's another idea, you come over to my training center and teach something—piano, synthesizer, whatever you want. Just get up there and say anything; these days kids and their parents are a bunch of pushovers."

"Is this a hand? It's more like a pig foot—better keep it away from anything that looks too much like a piano."

"So you're not gonna do anything but grow and eat pumpkins?"

"You've been all over—you see anywhere they're looking for someone to lay a foundation?"

Mr. Liu shook his head, sympathy and pain appearing on his face. "Old Yin, oh, Old Yin, I really had no idea. Oh, Old Yin, your life is so narrow. Think back to before, all *heh heh heh* on the surface, but your eyes were up on your forehead—where could I ever fit in? You probably forgot everything you said. You said I had the ears of a pig, that you could have written all my songs with your feet . . . you think I didn't know? No, I knew everything, and it all rotted right here in my heart. You know that? All those words, they all rotted in my heart!" He contorted his face as tears formed in his eyes.

"Drink up, brother—drink."

"But I will leave you with this: I hated you so much back then, I wanted to kill you. The reason you didn't make it into the troupe? Me. Didn't know that, did you? Let that fester in your heart. Don't hate me. I'm not as bad as you think, I just have a touch more foresight, which keeps me from having to worry. But I'll tell you something else: back then when someone wanted to criticize you for having bourgeois views on music, I orchestrated your protection. Did I ever tell you that? You owed the canteen so much money and so many coupons, but I paid it all for you, out of my own pocket. Did I ever tell you that? You had such an appetite, and then when you had diarrhea and shit your pants, I drove you to the hospital on my bike, but I couldn't find it because it was the middle of the night, and there was nowhere to get any water to wash you down with, and there we were, shouting all over the place to no avail, and, well . . ." Liu's face got even more contorted, his eyes even more red.

"My brother, I apologize—I've been as useless as livestock since the day I was born . . ."

"You gotta admit, even if I'm talentless, and average, and narrow-minded, I am your friend, I do understand you. Go into any town or village and ask whether there's anybody who's heard of you. Who knows that you're a genius? Who knows that Mao Sanyin is a diamond in the rough? Let me tell you, only me, only me! Do you admit it? Even now, with all the provincial officials in the county, who's taking you out for drinks?"

Suddenly Old Yin stared into that flat face of his with a look of utter astonishment: "My brother, why do you look like that bus in Linye station . . ." He didn't finish his sentence, so Mr. Liu couldn't figure out what he meant.

A hero loves a heroic atmosphere, but with the bus at Linye station having turned the scene farcical, Mr. Liu got angry: "Stop talking. Stop acting crazy. Quit giving me that."

"Sorry, my mind always goes off on its own like that." Old Yin smacked himself.

"What's wrong with you? You're some kind of a genius, an honest-to-goodness king of music, no, a demon of music, but so what? Is that castrated chicken-head of yours really trying to climb to heaven or something? Lemme tell you, your game is up, you're completely behind the times—completely! At least I've taken my share of girls to bed, and made a bit of money, like an official or entrepreneur, and I can eat what I want to eat and play the way I want to play . . ." He paused, then emptied his glass in one gulp, letting out a sigh that came from the pit of his stomach: "Here's to the good old days, oh, the good days . . ."

He didn't continue, as if he were feeling self-conscious about his vacuity.

He stood up to buy a pack of cigarettes, which was when he lifted his eyes and looked around, focusing first on an old tree across the road, and then further on, past the wall behind the tree, and further and further—approaching the obverse side of life that will remain forever out of sight.

Who is he who plows the fields?
To plow well, one must plow deep.
Tell me not about the three-inch plow,
This is how we must plow now—
Not just four or five inches, even six inches is too shallow . . .

A noise trickled out from the back of his throat, hummed with shocking precision and completeness, mellowness piercing through to the marrow. Who knows where such an old song could have come from. But even after so many years, its effects were still stunning—and before he could finish singing, Mr. Liu let out a sigh.

Old Yin's squinting eyelids flickered, but his face was still expressionless. He evidently was uninterested in continuing the song, and not curious in the least how his old friend had remembered his lyrics so clearly. He had no interest in the past. He yawned, looked at the old tree himself, and asked out of nowhere about Mr. Liu's kids. Seeing his friend give no reply, he spoke of his own: "You'll think I'm joking, but that little prince of mine sure knows how to piss you off—he can't rake or plow, and he'd spend all day every day just riding his motorbike up and down the street, like a parasite. He follows that Director Liu around all day. Who's that guy supposed to be? He's in debt to all the restaurants, so he's a parasite, too. All the people of Flower-Bridge say those revolutionary bugs aren't to be messed with. That's the way to put it. We're all bugs, but some are parasites, some are fireflies, and some are those slugs that look like snot. Am I right?"

Old Yin was probably trying to get a laugh, but it wasn't that funny, and he was the only one who laughed a little bit.

They didn't say anything after that.

They had never truly had a proper conversation, and they weren't actually communicating now, just pushing and pulling past each other as they drank. Maybe they both understood: understood that they had nothing really to say to each other, even as they understood that they couldn't very well not talk, either. They had to talk in order to sit across from each other, to breathe the same air. This air was their past: it wasn't very pleasant, but it incited an eternal nostalgia nevertheless.

"To tell the truth, you're an idiot," Liu said.

"To tell the truth, you're a creep," said Mao Sanyin.

"Never mind. We're both just pig-fucked assholes!" Droplets formed in Liu's eyes, tears of laughter.

Tell me not about the three-inch plow, as the sun wiped its blood-red rays across their faces, and not just four or five inches, even six inches is too shallow, with the wind blowing a chill like the sound of mallards returning home. By the time they said their goodbyes, a pile of tissues wet with tears had amassed at Mr. Liu's feet, but he still managed a bit of a smile as he wiped his eyes. He excused himself, saying that something must be wrong with him, that he'd been bursting into tears for no apparent reason for two years, and it was probably time to see a doctor, like maybe that eighty-year-old professor with the clinic in the city.

Old Yin remained sitting for some time after he watched him disappear, finishing off the last few peanuts in the bowl, even snatching up the shells.

The manager came over and asked if he was going to take the bowl home with him, too.

He stayed silent for a minute, took a few deep breaths, then finally got up.

———

10

———

One day Miss Qin came to Bianshan Cavern, bringing important news—or more precisely, a development—about the case: it seemed the good lord had been looking out for Old Yin, as his *Heaven and Earth Are Great* had been located, albeit in someone else's score, and was being played in the concert halls of several cities around the world. Which cities, and in which countries, exactly, she couldn't remember, and she smacked herself on the forehead to try to recall if it was England or Japan.

The composer taking credit for the symphony was none other than Mr. Wei, who had taken it from her all those years ago. Miss Qin couldn't figure out how a refined and scrupulous teacher like him could have taken a big old dump like that, let alone how that dump could have ended up stuck on her. She felt like she had witnessed a child being kidnapped, and all of a sudden she'd become an accomplice. Had any accomplice ever been so dimwitted and so easily taken advantage of? Over something so malicious? Like an idiot, she'd treated him to dinner, even drinks, and loaded him up with souvenirs and local gifts for the bus ride back—she'd even paid for the tickets for both him and his two companions—only to end up delivering the child right into the hands of the kidnapper.

She hadn't expected Old Yin's reaction. Not only had he totally forgotten anything having to do with a score or a script, but when he saw her he cried in glee, "Tailor Yang, you've come back!"

When she finally calmed down, she said, "Professor Mao, don't scare me—don't you remember me?"

"Aren't you Yang, the tailor?"

"Take a closer look—how could someone like me be a tailor? Or did you think I was a pig butcher?"

"Oh, right, I know, you're not Tailor Yang—you're Miss Qiu from the credit union. I got it this time, right?"

"Professor Mao, don't you remember Miss Qin from the drama troupe in town?"

"You're Miss Qin?"

"I sure am! Remember, the big superstar without an education? I sang all your songs, remember? You owe half of your medal of military merit to me, just like I owe you half of mine! We were in cahoots back then, practically joined at the hip—how could you forget?"

Old Yin's eyes brightened as he looked more carefully at his visitor. "Missy Qin? No, Missy Qin was never so fair-skinned, and she didn't have eyes as pretty as yours. You're not Missy Qin. More like Missed Qin." He chuckled, "Don't go thinking my head's full of gravel unless I'm drinking. Just the other day I was looking at this plot of land, and said it must be a quarter of an acre . . . The boy didn't believe it—but in the end, who was wrong, him or me?"

"I *am* Miss Qin . . ." She stamped her foot emphatically, on the verge of crying.

The old man brought his guest, whoever she might be, indoors, stepping over the wicker mat on which snap beans lay drying, over the lazy hound under the eaves, and over the wooden threshold that was nearly worn through, muttering to himself the whole way. "Missy Qin . . . Missy Qin was a good and proper girl, even met me when I went into town that one time, so thoughtful. She wanted to take me to see some park or other, heh heh, on one of those buses, scared me half to death. She remembered I like pig feet, too, meat falling off the bone, stewed up with fennel. And my favorite, amaranth stalks fried up with peppers, she made me two bowls of the stuff to make sure I wouldn't leave hungry.

And my life depended on the bottle, which she was happy to provide. Too bad I can't enjoy things like that anymore, with my blood pressure, been sober for almost eight years now, not so much as a drop . . ."

He didn't forget to pass her a cup of tea—or rather a bowl with a chipped rim and the bottom charred black, with some kind of insect floating in it, which nauseated his guest. He hadn't noticed it, any more than he'd noticed the spider web overhead, the open sores on his hand, or the glistening white in his whiskers. Carried away by the brightness of the sky outside, he opened his mouth, half full of teeth, as if somehow in the depths of the sunlight could be found the taste of pepper-fried amaranth stalks.

The woman bit her lip and rushed to put on her sunglasses, but it was too late. A tear spilled down from behind the dark lenses.

"Professor Mao, how could you? Is this what you've become? Are you really insane? You take such poor care of yourself, you can't even remember anyone else, either? Do you have dementia? How could you be so cruel? You're worse than a pig—at least they can squeal. And a dog could find its way back home. Don't you remember Miss Qin? There'll be no one to bury you when you die, do you understand me?" Her insults were getting mean, and her fist waved in his face as if she were about to knock him out.

Old Yin cleared his throat, evidently still not comprehending, his jaw and its crooked teeth locked in position, threatening to drool.

She cooked him a meal and washed his clothes in the creek until her hands were so sore she could barely lift them. Catching her reflection, she noticed that she'd gotten older, but since she'd had a couple of lifts done, how could he not recognize her? Crazy old man, of course he'd forgotten all her transgressions, like the time she made a fool of herself onstage when her skirt slipped down, or the time she got in a fight and had to apologize in that shop, or all those words of hers that could drive men wild—but then again that wasn't so bad, was it? She had no idea who this Miss Qiu from the credit union might be. The old man had asked for some money for grain, which was obviously intended for Miss Qiu, though she muttered some sort of reply. He'd also asked about someone named Huang, which was also something Miss Qiu could probably answer, though again she managed a noncommittal reply. She basically put herself in charge when she tossed into the forest his two pairs of trousers with the most holes in them, which were just too embarrassing to look at.

"Anyway, we'll just agree that Miss Qiu threw them away." She abdicated any responsibility.

She realized that other than the pumpkins under the bed, and the vaguely sour odor of pig feed and pig shit, she would find nothing else, not even a scrap of paper. A friend had said to her there'd be no hope of apprehending the liar unless you had the originals, just like you need a DNA sample for a paternity test.

"Professor Mao, you really are killing me. Think back carefully—don't you remember an opera you wrote called *Heaven and Earth Are Great*? You wrote it, can't you recall anything at all?"

"I remember it." The old man smiled. "Didn't it end up being published in the provincial journal? They were so nice, sending me royalties—fifty cents, and I got to claim it at the Flower-Bridge post office. Is that an honor or what? It took some time getting there, and then back, but it just sounds so nice: *royalties*."

Miss Qin cried out sharply like she had received a jolt of electricity, but she didn't let it drop. "Then do you remember a piece you wrote called *Sister Liu*? You used to beam with pride at the mere mention of it. Scratch your head and see if you can recollect anything."

"*Sister Liu*? You mean from the movie?" The old man rubbed his face. "The great model worker, now, that's not easy. Just a girl, and she's leading the team in building a highway, only to get yelled at by her husband when she comes home. But what could be done? Her husband was like an opium fiend."

"No, no, you really are demented. People used to call you Brother Liu, and here you are, having forgotten all about *Sister Liu*."

The old man didn't say anything else. She saw his eyelids drooping and realized he was too exhausted to reply. His head nodded over as he fell sleep with a slight smile stuck on his face.

The woman rolled her eyes, let out a sigh, and understood that circumstances would never be right. She released all her pent-up frustrations on the village secretary and the village chieftain—who had once been her fans. She cursed them something fierce, shouting for the tax collector to come and levy a fine, or for the judge to issue a verdict over the maltreatment of intellectuals and master culture workers. But the cursing brought no recourse. Then she tried to stuff two bills in the receptionist's hand as she was about to leave, so that he could buy a pair of pants and a bag of rice for the old man. She even had tips on how his home should be renovated, and how he could exterminate the mosquitoes.

Soon afterward, Miss Qin came back, bringing a portable stereo and a cassette tape, as well as a master of witchcraft and sorcery to dispel Old Yin's demons and restore his memory and his cognitive faculties. They arrived late, having understood the afflicted to be at the hospital, and when she finally showed up, out of breath, she was greeted not by Old Yin but by the detritus of popcorn and sweet potatoes waiting to be swept up. A plow stuck out of the ground, yearning to be shouldered and guided through the field. Thorn bushes lined the road, apparently to keep the boars away, so they wouldn't come in and steal all the popcorn. And at the edge of the field a scarecrow was trying to keep sparrows from eating the vegetable seeds. A wash of sunlight shone through, casting a flapping scarlet glow around the scarecrow's red shirt—a woman's blouse, made from an old undershirt, which looked almost fetching. If Miss Qin wasn't mistaken, under its straw hat two rope braids hung down, with half a plastic bag as a scarf to catch the wind behind its neck. Though its color had faded from the sun and the rain, she thought she could make out a trace of lipstick on the scarecrow's mouth.

If the scarecrow's eyes hadn't been drawn to look so much like coal lumps, and if it had maybe had a pair of earrings, it would have been quite a beauty, enough to convince people they'd seen her somewhere before.

In the background behind the scarecrow, a dense forest rose up the mountainside, murky and thick beneath the cumulonimbus clouds, yet with a rain-washed crispness, as if each and every leaf were visible even in the distance. But precisely in its clarity, the forest evoked the sensation of something about to happen, faintly, yet distinctly, as if the earth itself were preparing to stand up, push forth, and swallow the scarecrow whole.

Someone was approaching. She heard the rustle of footsteps and turned around in surprise, but saw no one. There was only a mountain breeze, cool, damp, sweet, spiced with newly cut grass. A black hound with a magnificent beard was following her, licking at her heels as if it knew her.

"Did you hear something?" The other woman noticed her anxiety.

"I was sure I just heard footsteps."

"I didn't hear anything."

"Am I hearing things?"

They lit offerings around the perimeter of Old Yin's home, recited a spell, sprinkled chicken blood in a spot that was suspicious and inauspicious, and smashed a porcelain bowl in a spot that was even more suspicious and inauspicious. In the middle of the ritual, Miss Qin heard once again the rustle of someone approaching, but when she turned around, there was still no one on the road behind her—not even a trace of that dog that had been licking at her heels.

11

Miss Qin spent several days in a kind of inarticulate haze. When the clothes in her closet had gotten too small for her to wear, and a new crop of singers had emerged, wilder and more unfettered than she had ever been, her halcyon days in the concert halls had come to an end. She spent a while at Mr. Liu's, but then the business world ceased to interest her, and before long she took off. At least that's how she put it; another version had it that Mr. Liu's new wife cursed her out for being a home wrecker, threatening her with pair of scissors if she didn't leave this instant. She subbed at a high school, too, before she decided that life there was inflexible and management had no appreciation for the arts, even though they wanted to make her full-time, but since it would mean giving up the stage, which was her true love, she thought better of it. At least, that's how she put it; another version had it that since she couldn't read sheet music, she wasn't qualified to teach, and on the cultural knowledge exam she flubbed the question about the difference between the court and the police department—and she wrote that "Clinton" referred to a brand of home appliances that made refrigerators. Even if she hadn't taken certain of her students out for drinks and to steal flowers, the school wouldn't have made any plans to retain her.

She had lain low for almost two years, so where she had gone and what she had been doing—for instance, whether she'd really gone to the province for further professional development—no one could say. Or they could say it, and did, but never with full certainty. She could hold her liquor and outdrink just about anyone, and when she got to the table, she'd get everyone to try touching the tips of their tongues to their noses, or to do headstands against the wall, and if they couldn't, then, *Drink! Come on, you lost—drink!*

Officially she was still a troupe member. The troupe still existed, too, but it was nothing like it had been, and some of the actresses had to take risks to make sure the troupe could keep paying their salaries, such as wearing less, putting on more perfume, and wiggling their way into the offices of the officials and bosses to see if they could wring out a bit more financial support. In the end, there wasn't any money left for the wringing, and the sign over the troupe's door changed to Kindergarten of the Arts, which was then overlaid with a sign reading "Artistic Funerary Arrangements Services, Inc., Ltd." It was so inauspicious that everyone entering or exiting had to look away and pretend not to see it, or else act as if it were a banner honoring revolutionary martyrs so that its associations with death wouldn't feel inglorious. Everyone's got to die sooner or later, right? There's nothing improper about death, is there? There have to be funerals, anyway, and there shouldn't be anything improper about that, at least—or at least if people are going to cry, they should be crying about the right things. That's the way to see it.

Didn't catch that? These days, nothing in heaven or on earth is greater than money, and just as there are more and more people bickering over money, there are fewer and fewer tears at funerals, so actors step in to fill the emotional gap, sprinkling tears everywhere they tread, taking over mourning duties for thousands of households. They not only have a crystal coffin for rent, as well as theatrical props, musical instruments, and a speaker hook-up, but most importantly they've got their professional knowledge and the finely honed ability to perfect a performance in short order, from weeping to crying to wailing. In the time it takes to switch from singing "The Asian Wind" to "Come and Meet Us, Our Young Friends" and change from tenor to soprano, it's ready, set, go—and the tears start flowing, right on cue with the music, more dutiful than even the truly filial sons and daughters. Even if sometimes, out of carelessness or because they're working too much, they drop some of their lines or go off script while crying, when it counts they're right on target, punctually and precisely stirring the heavens with their sniffles and cries. As the tenors and sopranos rise, and then rise again, the tears are real, the sniffling is real, as real as if the departed were their own mother or father, a truly surprising and satisfying feat. Quite often the women cry so hard their noses get red, and even the cats and the dogs in the corner start to worry.

Better to cry this way! As they say in town, better these shows than the old rites performed by half-assed Buddhists or Daoists who only became monks and priests so they wouldn't have to work—and this way, we can all be much more modern.

Who else would be able to cry like this? Everyone agrees it's money well spent.

Miss Qin takes part in these performances from time to time as a crier, though sometimes she's nowhere to be found. She's basically Old Xu's wife at this point, but as soon as she starts to sing, when her stage makeup is on right and her handkerchiefs describe their perfect arcs in the air, she can still stir hearts. Dirges are her specialty, and she can sing them for blocks on end. "In an instant the sky turned dark and the earth went black, oh father father father you have died and left us . . ." She can sometimes even extemporize on the tearful plaints of the opera *White-Haired Lass*, with a free encore when the mood strikes. As she's crying these songs, burying her face in her handkerchief, her sobs encapsulate every note, so that each one makes eight or nine runs, up and down the scale, gut-wrenching and heartstring-tugging, till the whole street is drenched in tears, a whole new style of crying, actually, setting the emotions of filiality to music of her own creation—and with no fear either of people not showing up to watch, or of other funeral companies competing with her work.

So for this reason, she enjoys a certain preferential treatment. Their service menu is clearly priced: for every order, an actor agrees to cry for forty minutes; she cries for half that. Other actors will dress in full mourning attire and kneel on the ground, but she only has to wear a black veil and sit while she cries. This is the prestige she enjoys as a star crier.

She has a few other particularities, too, such as absolutely never making an appearance if the portrait of the deceased is hideous and repulsive, and accompanying the dead but never the living, since it is her tears and not her smiles that are for sale—not like some who'd drop anything for a bit of cash. One time, a particularly tactless foreman for a bridge and road construction crew, on the pretense that he was Miss Qin's biggest fan and armed with the fact that he'd donated money to her troupe once, lifted his chin so high to drain his libations that he didn't even wait until the funeral was over before trying to drag her off to a "karry-okie" parlor. She pretended she hadn't heard him. Later, still all smiles, he stroked her hand as he invited her into a VIP room at the restaurant to get to know each other. Miss Qin could have played the fool and feigned surprise or passed the whole thing off, but some might have even said why not give it a shot—after all, if she had asked for a hundred a glass, this old guy would certainly have been good for at least ten.

But this time she was particularly bothered. She yanked off the man's toupee and rubbed his bald scalp. He was stunned.

"If you can rub my arm, why can't I rub your head?" she asked innocently.

"Y-y-you . . . what do you think you're doing?"

"What? You like to stroke arms, I like to stroke scalps."

The whole room laughed, and the guy's face swelled up like a pig liver. It wasn't like he was trying to cop a feel or anything, and here she was exposing his bald head before he'd even had a chance to escape—who knew what this bitch might do next? Grab his ears and start steering him around like a mule right there in front of everybody?

"Drink! Drink!" She wouldn't let him escape, having made up her mind to molest him further. "Go ahead and show me your hundred kuai—is it real or counterfeit?"

Probably out of a sense of responsibility to his customers, a manager of some kind appeared, saying, "Miss Qin, here I was thinking you were a shrinking violet with a face that could launch a thousand ships, and that all you performing types were proficient in the art of elocution . . ."

"Stop it, stop it." She raised a finger. "Let me correct you: I'm not a culture worker—I make money off dead people."

"No wonder—you're around dead people so much, it smells like a coffin the second you open your mouth, and you can't tell right from wrong."

"Yeah, and everywhere I look I see dead people, which must be why you look half-dead yourself."

"Hear that? She opens her mouth, and all you can hear is the toilet."

"Not just a toilet, a bottle of poison, too." She twisted her waist and squeezed out a smile: "Have they figured out if you have cancer or a myowhatsit infarction, lover-boy? Or is it cirrhosis of the liver or a brain aneurysm? You'd better get it checked out quick, before it's too late. I sure can't wait!" She saw his face go from red to white, and said, "I know you work hard, lover-boy, but you've got to think about the future. Why don't you scam old boss Qi here out of some money, or else he won't mourn you when you die. But don't go spending your money on all those girls, or when you go your wife'll find your checkbook, and she won't mourn you, either. But whatever you do, don't insult those guys who work for you, since after all, you'll need someone to carry your coffin. And someone's gonna have to dig your grave." She took a swig, saw that his white face had begun to go green and hard and frozen like a slab of meat fresh out of the freezer, and said, "If you don't hire someone like me to come fake a few tears for you when the time comes, you'll be in big trouble, lemme tell ya."

Each word drew blood, and in one breath she had left him sputtering and stuttering. The frozen slab of meat stared blankly, struggling to stand, and it looked like he might make a move, but he fell over with a creak and an *oh, oh*. He scrambled to find his mobile phone, which had also fallen onto the floor.

Witnessing the tumult, she cursed him—how? *Shit, you haven't even learned how to whine right, and you think you want to fight an old lady?*

Holding her head high, she walked out the door and into the cold wind, with a sense of satisfaction tinged with knowing she'd been wronged. She had been too vicious today, spreading manure as soon as she opened her mouth, and if you start wagging your finger and put your hand on your hip at every occasion, are you anything but a shrew? This wasn't how she had wanted to behave. No matter how much she hated men, she'd still been willing to flirt, but for some time it had been clear that she was distancing herself. She still had some grace left in the way she moved her arms and legs, and she could still make herself attractive, but her looks had gotten coarse, her face harder; her body smelled of the candles and firecrackers from the mourning halls, and she carried a black armband around with her in her purse. Once she put on that armband, the electricity went out in her whole body.

Without electricity, her fake smile—well, try robbing a bank with a toy gun or buying something with counterfeit cash; maybe others could make it work, but she couldn't, and every time she felt like that, she'd have to up and leave.

One of her coworkers chased after her to convince her to take a bus to the other side of town for another gig, so they huddled under their umbrellas, gulped down some instant noodles, bounced around for a while on the bus, and made it to the other mourning hall just in time, where she caught sight of the portrait of the deceased just as it was being put up for display: a former colleague of hers, in fact, who had died in a car accident. Her mind started racing, carrying her back to all the moments onstage or with the troupe, all the steps the departed had made onstage, and she couldn't help but cry real tears of sadness and sorrow. She cried for having descended to the depths of depravity for crying for others' losses, cried for her husband's unwillingness to either agree to a divorce or stop incurring new gambling debts, and cried for her daughter for being both so short of temper and short of stature . . . once her tears began to flow, there was no stopping them. Her handkerchief was soaked through.

The family of the deceased didn't notice that she had flubbed her lines from crying so hard, or care why she seemed so devastated, but they were especially grateful, stuffing an extra red envelope full of cash into her pocket.

Red envelopes. They're fine things. She'd been paid with hundreds of them, and used their contents to go wild on replenishing her life with joy. If she got a facial, she'd do two rounds; if she went for ice cream, she'd have two cones; and when it came to shoes, she'd bring home three pair. A hundred kuai on a dress, that's nothing. Sixty on a silk scarf, what's this, a gift? Most dangerously, haunted by the thick black frames on all the portraits, she saw shadows around everyone, and if she ever let her eyes go out of focus, deathly black frames would fill her sight. She'd rub her eyes, only to find the face of every stranger looking just like a portrait greeting death from inside its black frame: the ice cream-seller might be about to die in a car crash, the woman doing her facial could die from food poisoning, and this man sneezing and talking about fine leather could be on the verge of dying from a stroke. What would their eulogies sound like? Would they pass away at just twenty years of age? Thirty? Or fifty or sixty-eight? Whenever this happened, she'd end up giving these people either a lot more money than they'd asked for or else considerably less.

One day as she was flipping through a translated comic book, her daughter surprised her by saying, "Are you some kind of witch, seeing into the future?"

As she blinked her eyes, a big black frame appeared above her daughter's shoulders.

She screamed and covered her eyes. If she'd had the resolve, she would have gouged them out right then and there and thrown them into the river.

Her daughter didn't understand how such a simple question could scare her so badly, leaving her shaken the whole afternoon. Nor did the girl understand why her mother wouldn't make eye contact with her and turned sideways every time she wanted to talk to her.

The girl's grades in school were poor. As her mother had been looking over tutoring options for her, she happened to notice that the symphony *Haunted Mountain* was playing on the TV screen. No, not *Haunted Mountain*—it was *Heaven and Earth Are Great*, about which she knew too much. She had been curious at first, finding the tune catchy and familiar, but by the time she saw the name of the composer, everything was clear. A bamboo flute half-asleep, a suona transcendent yet otherworldly, suddenly collapsing into or else unexpectedly bursting with drums and cymbals . . . she recalled it all. A headless mountain ghost, eyes where its nipples would be and its mouth for a stomach, was locked in battle with a celestial army . . . she even knew the lyrics. The only difference was that *Haunted Mountain* had added something to its repertoire, a troupe of white-haired Chinese musicians and extravagant gongs and chimes, to please the foreigners in the audience. Afterward, haloed by flashing halogen bulbs in a half-circle of interview requests and gift bouquets, renowned conductors and members of the royal family shook hands with Mr. Wei.

As the following events would prove, her shock and anger were futile. Who'd have believed that an internationally renowned composer, with credentials and degrees from universities and institutions around the world, would have plagiarized his most famous work from some peasant in the hills? And why would some peasant in the hills have composed anything in the first place? Who was this peasant? . . . Even Old Yin had forgotten everything about the incident, even forgotten who he was himself. Who was left to clear things up?

She contacted a few friends, and friends of friends, but nobody could come up with any proof of plagiarism, or for that matter believe that she wasn't suffering from delirium, and the more she spoke the worse it got, jumbling weather and fashion and music and snack food and the law and heart disease and modernization into one mess of a story. No wonder people wondered whether she was delirious.

There was one kid in town in particular, who was probably suffering from hyperactivity disorder, his eyes bouncing all over the place like a racquetball and his mouth incapable of remaining on the same topic for more than five minutes—and in any five minutes his cell phone would interrupt his conversation seven or eight times. Like the previous kid, he was a local reporter on the entertainment beat, and at the sound of Mr. Wei's name his eyes went wide, as if the very name required an endless echo of Mr. Wei Mr. Wei Mr. Wei Wei Wei ei ei, reverberating in a vestibule of sanctity and historicity, never to be uttered in vain—despite the fact that he had never actually heard any of Mr. Wei's works. He had no interest in the countryside; at most he had a passing curiosity about what could have so upset a particular actress. When did you meet Mr. Wei? Tell me, what kind of relationship did you really have? Did he hurt you? Tell me, since obviously whatever he did has been hard to get over . . . He could just see the headline in bold black characters: *Star-Crossed Stars.*

The kid turned on his tape recorder to capture her laughter.

"Don't overdo it, miss. The past is the past—don't you know that expression? Pain and joy—everything in the past is pain, but it's joy, too, since it's the treasure house of all our memories . . ."

"I guess all you need to be a reporter is a good vocabulary and the ability to turn one simple sentence into ten big ones."

"Am I saying anything other than what you're already thinking? If we only face the past but bravely, the stars will still be stars, the moon will still be the moon, but the water under the bridge will soothe us with the sound of its ripples . . ."

"Your words are so moving, I'm about to cry."

"Thank you for your kind encouragement, miss. I don't know you very well, but I believe you to be a brave woman, with a heart represented by the moon, and wild swans that carry your emotions away. I even envy you a little, to tell you the truth. Just think of all the stories you could tell about our little town, like the secret happenings that took place between you and Mr. Wei—what an amazing intangible resource . . ." Maybe because he noticed her face going pale, he interrupted himself. "Are you feeling unwell? Should I call an ambulance . . . ?"

She took a sip of water, patted the kid on the shoulder, and left him with a word of advice: "Brother, I think your nose hair needs trimming."

She strode off, on the verge of angry tears, unwilling to put up with the song lyrics he'd been spewing, but at the same time unsure if she wasn't suffering from some sort of neurosis. No? Every reporter she saw she ended up insulting; she'd burn a pot of soup and then forget to turn the gas off, ended up at the bureau chief's office when she'd gone out for groceries, had an urge to call the police every time her neighbors killed a chicken, and even got lost at the intersection closest to her home: the street turned completely strange to her all of a sudden, unfamiliar buildings in front and in back and to the left and the right, cars front and back and left and right, and people front and back and left and right, and she couldn't figure out which way to turn or why it should be this way and not that way, or why she should be walking at all and not just lying down right there in the street . . . After dark her husband called a few people together, bound her with a rope, and checked her into the hospital.

The doctor gave her a shot, if for nothing else than to help her get some much-needed rest. Later on he admitted that it had just been distilled water, since placebos were sufficient treatment for hysteria.

Mr. Liu came to visit her, to tell her not to be so hard on herself. *Everything that has happened in the past, let it be past. Now is the time to look to the future. That was how Professor Mao was, anyway, and if the king isn't worried, then why should the footmen be?* Mr. Liu spoke with gravitas about tennis courts and the exercise room, and when he laughed, it resounded with an academic baritone: "Come play tennis with me—it's a good way to keep in shape. Tennis is much better for you than badminton, and a far sight superior to ping-pong. They're not even on the same level! If you can't play tennis, how can you even begin to call yourself modern? Have you seen the way Pete Sampras angles the ball? And Steffi Graf's elegance . . . ? Oh, she must be worth over a hundred million deutschmarks by now!"

"Mr. Liu, you're really not going to look into this matter?"

"Where would I find the time? You know, Mr. Wei is an old classmate of mine, too, and these days I'm overwhelmed with business. I have to get to the gym after work, since that's 600 kuai a month to keep up my membership. And tennis in the mornings, which is 800 a month to keep the court. You know how it is, I just can't find the time. You know . . . right?"

"Why don't you sell some cocaine for me, or maybe some ecstasy, and we'll split the profit fifty-fifty?"

"What are you talking about?"

"I thought you were in business! Let's help each other out."

"But . . . cocaine?"

"Guns, too. I'm getting a shipment tomorrow if you're interested."

"You're joking, right?"

Mr. Liu was so shocked it sounded like his tongue had been cut off, and he stammered as he backed out of the room.

After she had a good laugh about scaring Mr. Liu away, the house returned to quiet, except for the sounds of *Haunted Mountain* emanating from the radio.

The familiarity of the music engulfed her, subsumed her. After so many years, the rising and falling semitones made sense to her in her bones, made sense to her in her heartache, made sense to her wherever she might ache. The ghost with its unruly irregular singing, eyes where its nipples should be and a mouth for a stomach, this mountain ghost beheaded by a celestial army and which no one could save, it was her. She was this ghost, and no good end would come to her. She understood that now.

Mr. Liu returned and promised to testify on behalf of Miss Qin, to take part in the class-action suit against the party named Wei. He dared not do otherwise, since before he came back, his wife had demanded from him a written record in duplicate of all his correspondence with Miss Qin, in all its gory detail. How could he withstand that? If he didn't want to face his wife's tears and wails, he could do nothing but take his bruised and battered face back to Miss Qin and offer his assistance.

———

12

———

After the highway into the mountains was built, building buildings was all the rage, and new villages of concrete and ceramic tile and aluminum alloy appeared. Most of the new buildings had a storefront with little more than a shelf's worth of merchandise, but while it might look empty to the untrained eye, it brought the potential for an entire populace to conduct business, for which no amount of preparation could be spared. But Old Yin said the highway was too far from his fields, and too far from the mountain, so he didn't follow his brothers over there. His neighbors left him a silent valley and their hollowed-out homes.

The mud huts had been emptied of any human presence, like a stage set from which the actors had exited, leaving an unreal quality behind. It was on such a set that Old Yin stood guard night and day in the valley, buried more and more by the grandeur of the days and nights of the past, and up to ten days might pass before another human being passed by. Footprints faded from the road and the sounds in his ears disappeared, and when he walked through any door that had once been his neighbors', he saw dust-covered bowls on dust-covered tables beside dust-covered chairs. An old winnow under one of their eaves, lousy with picotee blossoms, had become a warren for mice. When had so many mice come to the valley? His bearded hound used to catch mice, but after it got old it could no longer keep up with them, and now if a mouse was ever spotted peeking its head out, it would only bark.

On this day, with his hound in a trance, a mouse scampering across Old Yin's bed got turned around trying to evade Old Yin's frantic swipes, and ended up running up his pant leg and biting his thigh. The small wound didn't bother him at first, but he hadn't expected that it would swell and get redder, then harden and turn black, reeking with a pus-filled stench, *eww*, like something giftwrapped by a demon . . .

Once they heard his hound barking wildly on the highway, people began to put things together and started making their way up the hill to see what had happened.

But by that point the situation had worsened. His thigh had swollen so much he could no longer pull his pants off, so they had to snip them off with shears. The herbalist took one look and declared that he had to go to the clinic. The doctor at the clinic took one look and declared that he had to go to the hospital. The people from Bianshan Cavern had little faith in hospitals, not because they didn't treat their ailments but because they didn't like to make too big a deal out of things. Particularly the elderly, who didn't want to raise a fuss over a few years of life one direction or the other. Life lasts a lifetime, just like flowers last a springtime, and every leaf has to fall sooner or later. The rich can spend thousands on their intestines or to bypass something or other, but that's just keeping the leaves up on the trees for a few more days—is it really so necessary?

At any rate, they don't have the money to run to the hospital every time they get sick. Even if some relatives offered to pool their money, or if, say, Missy Qin came up with her bankbook, how many days in the hospital would that really cover? So they carried Old Yin back to the Cavern and into the home of his brother Old Yi. Brother Yi filled him with meat, and even got him off the wagon and poured some drink down his throat—it wouldn't be long now, so there wasn't much point in worrying about blood pressure, was there? Old Yin's nephew's cell phone became his new toy.

Now, that was something incredible—poke it a couple times and you could hear everything, even tell people far away to come over for a visit. With the numbers he got from his nephew, he started calling friends and relatives. Once he got the hang of it, he couldn't resist making calls every day, though he didn't have anything new to say. "Little Fu, is that you? Yes, it's you." And then he'd hang up. "Are you there, Pimply Wang? Yes, you are." And he'd hang up again.

He went on joyfully like this, a pleasant surprise for the people he'd called at first, but eventually they began to worry about all the charges on their accounts. They took it out on Old Yin's nephew, ringing him up again and again for a scolding. Nephew implored uncle not to make any more calls except in an emergency, and Old Yin seemed to understand, *yes*sing and *uh-huh*ing, saying that no, he wouldn't place any more calls, what would he make any more calls for, anyway, but then as he lay convalescing in bed, he couldn't keep from poking at the thing. He made sure to heed his nephew's warning and talk only about important matters: "Pimply Wang, have you eaten? What did you eat? What, did you steal a tree, you old goat? Or steal camellia seeds? Who's going to keep an eye on a reprobate like you after I'm dead and gone?" Or: "Little Fu, did you dry the peppers? The sun is strong today, so why aren't you drying them? Why don't you come and make an offering of white peppers before I'm dead and gone? Come on, hurry up!"

He even thought about calling Premier Zhu Rongji, and asked his nephew for the number. He didn't understand why his nephew would say he didn't have it: "A toy like this, how could the premier not have one of his own?"

"Who do you think you are, that he should take your call?"

"I see him every two or three days!"

His rationale, in which he had every confidence, was that the premier visited him—visited him on the television, that is—all the time, and since Old Yin had always been a gracious host, by now they surely counted as old friends. At the very least they could talk over a few matters of importance together.

"You want to ask him what he's eaten today, too?"

"All the bamboo in Hunan is about to be eaten away by locusts, and since he's in Beijing, I want to make sure that someone tells him."

"What the hell does that have to do with anything?"

"Did that witch Zhao Feifei bury herself in the cesspit yet?"

Zhao Feifei was the hostess of one of the entertainment programs on one of the local stations, and her name had been buzzing recently because the kids liked her, but as far as Old Yin could tell, she was poison, couldn't sing, couldn't dance, just went nuts and shook her rump, shaking all proper thought and action away in the process—she should be the first to face the firing squad. And as long as he was on the topic, he wanted to vent his anger about that martial arts picture *Legend of a Fighter* he'd seen a few years ago—word was that there had been no corrupt party officials before they saw this movie. That cop, didn't he say he wasn't in it for the money, and then the next second he's opening up his pockets for you to stuff cash into while he looks the other way? Aren't Director Liu and Chief Wang doing the same thing? Do you think they didn't learn that trick from *Legend of a Fighter*?

He didn't get a chance to finish, since his nephew had to cart the rest of the manure away and had no interest in hearing denunciations. And the neighbors were little better than pigs, barely able to read and write, so there was no point in talking to them. Only the premier could really understand his concerns about the state of the nation, he figured. He should talk to the premier and ask him what happened to the Petersburg Cheka. Shouldn't they be called in to do something about a wreck like Zhao Feifei?—somehow he still had the presence of mind to recall the name of the commission for combating counterrevolution and sabotage.

He let out a sigh, drank the grain alcohol to which he had formerly bid farewell, found it utterly flavorless, and said to himself that he'd drunk too much in this life, so his son shouldn't use alcohol for his libations after he was gone, just pour a pot of tea instead.

Old Yi nodded, sure, sure.

He said his son would need to look after his ma and his little brother, send them glutinous rice after autumn harvest and catch a hen for each of them, and it would be his duty as uncle to remind him.

Old Yi nodded, sure, sure.

Old Yi in fact envied his younger brother a little, since Old Yin should have been satisfied with what he had, getting to go off to Beijing, then to Guangxi and Yunnan and those other countries, unlike himself, who'd only been to town once, to deliver some limestone. Now, well, smack his butt and shout *giddy-up*, and he'd go plow your quarter-acre plot, dig your yams, and still look after the people offering you libations after you're dead. Enough to get you steamed.

Old Yin disagreed. "I went to other countries? When was that?"

Sometimes they'd argue over spiritual matters. "You've still got those moldy ration coupons in your cupboard," Old Yi said. "Are you gonna take them to the grave with you? You're so funny—why don't you bring a pair of shoes, at least, since your feet have barcly known them while alive."

"You think there's been reform and opening up in the afterlife, too, so they don't use ration coupons?"

"Who can say that the ruler of the underworld won't take a liking to you, give you training and a promotion, make you a cadre, and feed you with all the grains of the nation? Maybe you'll be director of the Cultural Bureau."

"A cadre for the ruler of the underworld, is that supposed to be some swanky assignment? Saw off this guy's head today, sever that guy's tendons tomorrow . . ."

Old Yi thought about it and said, "You're not asking for a shrine or for anyone to burn joss paper for you, so long as you get your ration coupons? We've covered everything in Flower-Bridge—these shrines have TV sets, motorcycles, fully furnished homes, all to make things comfortable after you go. What else do you need?

Old Yin's eyes widened: "Maybe a power generator?" He took a breath and added, "And a gas station?"

His point was well taken, because if you don't have electricity in your paper shrine, what good is a TV set? If there were no gas stations down there, what good would all those motorcycles be?

"Well, in that case," Old Yi said, "what's the point of all the ration coupons? Will there be a grain dispensary? A Grain Ration Bureau? Trains and vessels to transport all the grain? If you can buy rice, do you need to bring your own basket? Or a bag? Will you need a bowl and chopsticks when you eat? What about a steamer for vegetables? You'd have to put a whole department store in that shrine just to eat."

Bested by his brother, he laughed out loud, and happily brought over cups for tea.

At that very moment the festering sore started to hurt again. Old Yin's face scrunched up as he clenched his teeth and moaned. His body went limp, and he meekly let out a breath and passed out. It was the final release and departure of his body temperature. His body, curled into a ball, had left very calmly, even peacefully and happily, smiling bug-eyes staring at the wall. His son and nephew tried to rouse him, his brother and sister-in-law tried to wake him, but he didn't move, still staring bug-eyed at the wall, as if he were staring at the last remaining piece on a chessboard, or the last exit in the world—perhaps on the other side of the bug-eyes a new beginning could be found? A multicolor universe lighted by a thousand rays of rising sunshine?

In the mountains the people say animals are like this: no fear or panic once they know the end is coming; they just go silently off in search of that secret corner, go off into the distance leaving no more than an errant shadow. We never find their bodies, never know where or when they took their final step, never comprehend their particular love for the order of the universe. Some people say they only hide themselves so as not to be eaten by other wildlife. Ultimately, death is death, so does it matter how they go about it?

No, they love the order of the universe.

Once the news of Old Yin's death had spread, all his transgressions, like not repaying the money he'd borrowed or how his stench had driven people away, were forgiven, as the people from the village turned magnanimous and noble in their sorrow at his passing. A retired manager of the county marketing cooperative, an admirer and former classmate of Old Yin's, got his friends together to write poems in the old style for his eulogy, and determined to turn his funeral into a proper celebration with hired criers and mourners from the acting troupe in town drumming their parade up into Bianshan Cavern. Thanks to his eager fundraising, some money was able to go toward ordering proper funerary ornaments. An enormous paper rice bowl, as big as a table. A huge paper chili pepper, which it took two men to carry. A pair of extra-large paper shoes, each as big as a small boat. And two big paper eyeballs, like two great rolling lanterns . . . they said it took two whole bags of flour to make the glue, as well as several reams of construction paper. And when it came down to it, the items were so big they couldn't fit through the doorway, so seven or eight of the guys stacked tables and chairs on top of each other so they could get over the courtyard wall and into the mourning hall. Needless to say, everyone who took part in delivering the funerary ornaments was doing it for Old Yin—didn't he want things big?

Under the frighteningly large rice bowl and chili pepper and the shoes and eyeballs, the funeral felt like it was being attended by Lilliputians. The deceased lay in a crystal coffin and had shriveled a little bit, making the Western-style suit he was dressed in look very odd indeed, like a grammar school student wearing adult clothes. The overzealous makeup artist had applied enough rouge and lipstick to give him rosy cheeks and a mouth as red as carnations, and his whole face glistened, the image of a child playing dress-up.

Of course, people could imagine that the crystal coffin was a bullet-proof glass case, and the one to be buried in it the most worthy and heroic of dignitaries, his red face the majestic visage with which he would greet the salutations of ten million visitors paying their respects—only there had been no victory ceremony, just the scattered stars in the heights above the mountain ridges.

At that moment, the corners of his mouth seemed to pull upward, stiffening into a familiar smile.

Let me see you one more time
Who knows when I will see you again?

Let me see you one more time
So I can remember you, my friend . . .

The candle flickered, the streamers and banners swayed, and a popular tune began to play through the speakers. According to the theater troupe's routine, this was task number one—to get people to cry, it was necessary to lay an emotional foundation. With a snap of the director's fingers, the sound mixer turned the music low, a man and a woman buried their faces in their handkerchiefs, and a shudder descended from the sky as the actors began to get everyone to cry, to draw tears from those on the verge of crying and dig into the hearts of those on the verge of emptying their emotions. Seeing two filial sons sobbing already, the other relatives of the deceased began to weep as well, as the remaining reserve of the friends and attendants crumbled, and wailing arose from all corners. With the climax of mourning approaching and the director mostly satisfied, he waved to the band, and the dirge resounded through the speakers, drums and trumpets forming into a new assault, as if the whole world's pain were crashing down, the whole world's sorrow pressing down, everyone present fallen into the bewilderment of mournfulness.

Then Miss Qin appeared. She had come to the front of the mourning hall, looked at the overly rosy-cheeked child playing dress-up in the coffin, knelt down unexpectedly, and kowtowed three times. She beat her breast, but she did not cry; she held up her handkerchief and described with it an arc in the air, but she did not cry. In the end, she covered her mouth with her handkerchief and cast herself into the darkness, and though everyone thought she would cry, she had nothing.

She let out a few wails like lines from a song, but everyone found the song unfamiliar—not "Three Cups" or "Seven Fathers," but something straight and dry, and her voice was hoarse, and nothing sounded right, far from her usual delicate vigor. Her eyes were dry, not the slightest hint of tears. Her body was shaking, but no one understood why. Ordinarily she couldn't make her hands tremble like that, but now she couldn't hold on to the handkerchief, or the microphone, and as she wrung her hands until she felt like they were going to snap, she started to bleed.

"Your hands are so cold, they're like the hands of the dead!" A colleague went up to the front in consternation.

"It's so cold."

"Let me give you my coat."

"I can't cry . . ."

"So just sing, then. Everyone's waiting."

"I can't sing, either . . . I can barely . . . catch . . . my breath."

"You must have come down with something. You shouldn't have come in today." Her colleague turned around and said to the director, "Miss Qin is sick—find someone else, hurry."

"How could that be?" The director's forehead wrinkled, and he called another woman onto the stage, stuffing a sheet of paper into her hands with the words she should wail on it.

Miss Qin came off the stage and collapsed into a thick quilted coat being held up by her colleague, off in a corner where the stage lights didn't reach. Her performance had been a disappointment, frustrating and alarming. From her hair, with not a strand out of place, to her black dress, which had been expertly tailored, to her meticulously matched shawl, earrings, bracelet, and silk scarf, she had been the image of perfection, ready for an impassioned performance, a note amidst silence, simultaneously absent and present, crumbling and dissolving everyone in its exquisiteness. But now her hand was wrapped in gauze, she was clutching a borrowed hot-water bag, and she'd just gulped down two bottles so her exhalations were muddled with alcohol fumes. Her fingers were still rapping on her knees, unable to stop, as if she were tapping out a long telegraph.

Later, when a woman with a mourning shawl covering her head came to distribute the red envelopes, she glanced at the telegraph operator but passed her over, handing the envelopes to the people around her.

In another twenty years, when we meet again,
How great this grand land of ours will be then,
Heaven will be great, the earth will be great,
and the light of the spring will radiate . . .

When the time came for the director to call for the finale, he had as usual prepared a medley of popular songs, upbeat and bold, for the audience to dry their tears to before they withdrew from the sorrow of the funeral. Relatives and well-wishers even managed to crack a joke or two. Tables were set up for mahjong and card games, while engines ignited in a motorcade of exhaust fumes and headlights as people got on their motorcycles or tractors to make their way to Old Yi's place and then back to the bustle of their daily lives. One last string of firecrackers exploded with a crackle.

As she was getting in her car, Miss Qin took out a tuning fork that had once belonged to the deceased and requested that it be buried with him. In her hand she also held a prescription—the old doctor had been one of the attendants at the funeral, and many of his patients had been members of the troupe who saw him at the hospital in town. He took her pulse, looked at her tongue, and said it was nothing serious, just an occupational illness. As for the reason, well, it was simple: do too much fake crying, and at some point real crying will prove difficult. The doctor also said, "In the future, whenever you feel upset, you may suffer some residual shivers."

Such a sickness constituted no serious threat, so she didn't need to worry, just make sure to get some rest. Her prescription was for nothing more than vitamins and a sedative.

As she took the prescription, she said, "This stuff won't kill me, will it?"

Her coworker nudged her: "How can you talk like that?"

"What did I say?" she blinked.

"He treats you out of the goodness of his heart, and you bite the hand that feeds you?"

"Oh, damn it, I always say the wrong thing. I only meant, what I meant was, I'm going to die soon enough anyway, nothing can cure me now anyway."

The color of her face changed once more with her awareness that she had misspoken yet again, cursing herself in such a way. But she had said it, and she could never unsay it. She looked around at her coworkers, not knowing what to do, and smacked herself on the forehead, laughing stupidly.

A Flurry of Blessings

Chi Zijian

TRANSLATED BY ELEANOR GOODMAN

Mrs. Chai woke before the sun. She didn't want to rouse her husband, so she grabbed her padded cotton jacket and pants from beneath the quilt and climbed out of the brick-heated bed. She found her shoes, then carried everything into the west side of the house to get dressed. The stove had gone out early during the night, and the room was chilly. Mrs. Chai felt as though she were walking on frost crossing the cement floor barefoot. Her nostrils felt tight and ticklish, and she knew a sneeze was building. She covered her nose and mouth with her jacket and hurried to the west side of the house, waiting until she had crossed over the threshold before sneezing into the cotton batting.

Chai Wang was still sound asleep. He had reason to sleep well, since the night before he had enjoyed two good meals.

The first meal came to the table in a pot filled with pork and pickled cabbage soup with thin rice noodles. Their neighbors had butchered a pig, and Mrs. Chai had opened the small box where she kept their money and ran her trembling fingers over the bright shiny notes. She thought about their son in prison and snapped the box shut. But then, picturing her husband's sallow, emaciated face, she opened the lid again and pulled out a ten-kuai note to buy a narrow strip of nicely marbled meat. She sliced it thinly and threw it into a pot to stew with Sichuan peppercorns, aniseed, garlic cloves, and scallions. She didn't fry the meat beforehand, in part to save a little oil, and in part because the meat was already fatty. As it slowly cooked, little droplets of fat as shiny as stars oozed out and floated to the surface. When the broth was studded like a starlit sky, Mrs. Chai scooped a chunk of cabbage out of the pickling crock, chopped it into strips, and threw it in. The slices of meat and pale cabbage were aroused by the fire until they began to kiss. A delicious aroma rose, and when the broth had thickened, she threw in a skein of whiskery rice noodles. She watched them soften until they were as translucent as rays of light, and then she took the pot off the fire.

Each day Chai Wang went out looking for work and came home after dark. For men who made their living doing manual labor, it was a sign of weakness or laziness to come back before sunset. Whether or not he'd found work that day or made any money, as soon as her husband set foot in the house, Mrs. Chai's heart would swell with tenderness, and she would hurry to bring him a pan of warm water to wash the day's dust from his face. Then she would put dinner on the table, driving the winter cold or summer heat from his body. Occasionally they would embrace each other and sing "Mandarin Ducks Playing in Water" together in the dark before contentedly going to sleep. When he wanted to make love, he'd tell her, "I'd like a little taste of that."

After Chai Wang had pedaled his pedicab home the night before, he'd come in to find his wife setting a pot of pork and pickled cabbage soup on the table. He felt like a man seeing the sun after days of rain and mist, and his face broke into a rare smile. They sat in front of the pot, happily eating bowl after bowl, and when they could finally see the bottom, he felt another kind of energy rising. As his wife was washing the bowls and chopsticks, he said, "I'd like a little taste of that." His wife admonished him, saying, "I knew if I gave you a taste of this, you'd want 'a taste of that'!" He laughed and said, "Well, weren't you the one who got my appetite going?"

The fire was dying down as she washed the dishes, but she didn't throw on more kindling. She didn't want to waste firewood, and anyway, whenever they had "a little taste of that," it was nice for the room to be a bit cooler so they could hold each other even tighter. Sure enough, when Chai Wang had his second "dinner," he held her tightly under his body, tender and passionate.

Aside from these two ways of taking care of her man, Chai's wife also did a third thing, which was to take her husband's name. Her name was Wang Lianhua, but after she married, she made everyone call her "Mrs. Chai." Her glib-tongued older sister Wang Lianrong once said to her, "You're really too much, giving up your own name after marriage!" "When a woman lives in a man's house, she belongs to him," Wang Lianhua told her sister with a smile. "If she takes his name, he'll treasure her like a precious jewel. He'll do everything he can to treat her right." Wang Lianrong sniffed and said, "What do you mean, a jewel? No matter what kind of man he is, even the best woman is a only a jewel for the first three years. The next three years she's grass, and for the rest of her life she's just chaff." But Wang Lianhua didn't pay attention to her sister's ridicule and threw herself wholeheartedly into being Mrs. Chai. And for twenty years, although their lives weren't everything they'd hoped for, she was happy to be his wife. As for her sister, she was almost fifty, but she still made her husband call her by her nickname, "Rongrong." Although they didn't have to worry much about money, their relationship was distant, and her husband was so apathetic she might as well have been living alone.

Mrs. Chai got dressed and went outside. A northerly wind was blowing, and although the stars were sparse just before dawn, the ones that remained shone brightly. She liked to imagine the stars as a burst of sparks. If only she could collect a few to put into the hearth, they'd have eternal fire, and she wouldn't have to worry about firewood ever again.

Teacher Liu's dog heard her coming and growled softly. As she crossed the courtyard, she called to him, "Diabolo, I'm going to North Mountain to gather bark. You stay here and watch over the courtyard." The dog yapped a few times in response. She took two burlap sacks from the shed, folded them, and clipped them onto the back seat of her bicycle. Then she stuck a rake in the front basket and pushed her bicycle through the gate.

It was midwinter, and cold as a knife, though the wind felt more like a whip. It stirred the snow on the roofs, making the flakes swirl so high that it seemed to be snowing again. The potholed alley was deserted, and Mrs. Chai made her way along unevenly, her bicycle clanking with each step. Once she got onto the paved road, she started to ride. It wasn't easy. There was a strong headwind, and the bicycle chain had frozen stiff, so it was hard to pedal. She might as well get off the bicycle and walk, since it wasn't even dawn and she had plenty of time to get back to make breakfast. Walking was a lot warmer.

Chai Wang and his wife lived on the west side of town. Their small town of about fifty thousand residents was roughly divided into four sections: downtown, uptown, the east side, and the west side. Most of the high-rises and government offices and the two large shopping malls were downtown. There were high-rises uptown, too, but fewer government offices and more small shops. Where there were lots of shops, there were lots of people, so uptown was also the busiest part of town. On the east side, high-rises were interspersed with smaller buildings. The county's best high schools were there, so the area was a bit chaotic and full of vitality. The west side was the only section where there were large swaths of single-story buildings, one right after another. It had been the home of two large factories, a machine repair shop, and a paper mill. But the paper mill had closed down, and the machine repair shop had reduced its employees by half. It was hard to do business in such a poor area, so there were only a few small grocery stores and restaurants, which hadn't even bothered to put up a sign.

The Chais had lived on the west side for thirty years. Chai Wang had once worked a lathe in the machine repair shop, when he was still living with his mother. After his mother died, he married Wang Lianhua and brought her home, where she bore him a son named Chai Gao. Wang Lianhua liked that Chai Wang was honest and dependable, and she liked even more that he was strong. In fact, she had fallen in love with him because of a rock. That fall, her family had pickled an extra crock of cabbage and needed a large rock to place on top to help it ferment, so Wang Lianhua rode her bicycle to the Wuji River on the west side to find one. The machine repair factory was on the riverbank, and during the summer the workers liked to come down to the river after lunch to wash and sun themselves and play cards. In the fall they liked to play a game called "beat the river rat." A few men would form a circle and draw lots for the one who was going to play the rat. They'd make him stand in the middle and give him three minutes to break out. If he succeeded, everyone had to give him a cigarette, and if he failed, they would throw him into the clutches of the icy river.

When Wang Lianhua got to the river that day, she happened to see a few men playing "beat the river rat." The man in the middle was Chai Wang. The weather had already cooled, but he was bare-chested, and his muscles were moving as furiously as a machine. He wasn't tall, but he could jump well, and he hadn't been in the circle for more than a minute when he leapt out as smoothly as a horse. Wang Lianhua crossed in front of him as his coworkers were handing over cigarettes. She laid her bicycle down on the bank and quickly spotted an oval chunk of granite about a meter out in the shallow water. She rolled up her pants and waded in. But it's easy to misjudge things from a distance, and the rock she'd thought was small was actually quite hefty. The rippling water was like a beautician, making it seem thinner than it actually was. She made a few attempts to lift it, and each time it would just sway as though nodding. But she was young and energetic at twenty-two, so she told the rock stubbornly, "I chose you and I'm going to take you home." Gathering all of her strength, she finally managed to lift it from the water. She gritted her teeth and took two trembling steps before it launched itself from her arms and landed with a splash that sent up a colorful spray.

The men on the bank laughed. Chai Wang laughed as well, but unlike the others, he clambered down into the river and helped Wang Lianhua. The rock that she could barely lift rested like a docile baby in his arms. He gently set it down on the back of her bicycle, but fearing that it would fall off along the way, he grabbed a few handfuls of grass and within a few minutes had fashioned a rope to tie down the rock. As she walked her bicycle away, she said to him, "I'm Wang Lianhua. If you need anything washed, I'll do it for you!" Chai Wang laughed and said, "I have a canvas jumpsuit that I can never get clean." She said, "I'll come back tomorrow at noon with some soap. Bring it then."

The next day Chai Wang brought the jumpsuit, and Wang Lianhua washed it in the river for him. And that was how they fell in love. When they married, Wang Lianhua brought the rock with her to Chai Wang's house. She treated that hunk of granite like a treasure. Each spring when she cleaned the pickling crock, she would ask Chai Wang to pull the wet rock from the pickling liquid, and she would scrub it until it shone. Then she would place it below the window to use as a little stool. In the summer she liked to sit on it as she did her mending and washing. In the autumn she would clean the rock once more, and then with great care they would put it back into the pickling crock. So the rock had two baths each year, and even as Mrs. Chai's face had grown wrinkled, the rock's edges had been worn smooth.

Mrs. Chai gave birth to Chai Gao in the second year of their marriage. Chai Wang liked to spoil his son. Whenever no one was around in the factory, he would make toys for him on the lathe: a little iron-wheeled car, an iron man with raised arms, an iron rooster that could open and close its mouth. Chai Gao was mischievous. When he was six years old, he took a ladder up to the roof, saying that his blanket was heavy and dirty, and he wanted to pull down a nice soft cloud to use as a quilt. At eight he had a fight with a goat, which gored him in the nostril, so his nose grew crooked. He didn't like school, and half the time he would play hooky. More than once, Mrs. Chai had to teach him a lesson with a broomstick. But each time Chai Wang heard his son cry, he would come running and grab the broomstick out of his wife's hand. He'd tell her that young bones are soft, and if she injured one, their son wouldn't grow up strong enough to make a living. Mrs. Chai would say, "Spare the rod and spoil the child. The way he is, he's going to grow up to be a big troublemaker!" Sure enough, three days after his eighteenth birthday and a year before he was supposed to start training to be a mechanic, Chai Gao got into a fight on behalf of a friend who worked for the railway. He beat the man badly, and was sentenced to three years in prison. Chai Wang borrowed money from everyone he could think of to pay compensation to the injured man. Only then did he admit to his wife, "The father suffers for everything he doesn't teach his son." Mrs. Chai knew that her husband's father had died when he was young. He had never felt a father's love, and that was why he doted so much on Chai Gao. She wiped away her tears and said, "It's not too late to teach him. He'll only be twenty-one when he gets out."

When Chai Wang retired, he chose to receive his retirement in a lump sum, as many did. He was given thirty thousand kuai and kicked out on the street. He looked at the money and cried. If someone in the family got sick or something bad happened to them, the money wouldn't go very far. He decided that they couldn't live on his retirement alone, and that he'd have to keep relying on his strength to make money. First he bought a pedicab, and after a year he had earned two thousand kuai. Then he lucked into a cushy job, working the boilers for a tobacco company's housing complex. Although it was seasonal work, the income was considerable, and he could bring home three thousand kuai in a single winter. He also saved a lot in firewood for his house.

His coworker was a man nicknamed Heitou. Heitou had once worked as a driver for the county Party members, but he had an accident and lost his job. Since he'd lost that job, his wife had refused to be intimate with him, so he liked to work the nightshift to avoid the whole situation. Chai Wang enjoyed his "little taste of that" with his wife at night, so he gladly took the day shift. He often went to work at six in the morning when the sky was still dusky. He noticed that when Heitou left work, he often wrapped up some coal in a piece of canvas and took it home on the back of his bike. But wasn't that stealing? Chai Wang said nothing until one day Heitou got drunk and pointed his finger in Chai's face, saying, "You're so fucking stupid, you really want to go rat on me? Don't you know enough to take some coal home for yourself?" Chai Wang said, "That's public property. What if someone sees? You'll be taken in as a thief, and is that worth it?" Heitou spat at Chai Wang and said, "If you're going to live in the mountains, you have to live off of them. If you live in water, live off of the water. I drove for those officials, do you think they have me fooled? In this day and age, the high officials are highly corrupt, and the little officials are a little corrupt. Who isn't going to use his job to help out a family member? If we take home a bit of coal, it's like shaving a sliver off somebody's fingernail—it doesn't even count! You're telling me you've never taken advantage of any position before?" Chai Wang said haltingly, "Well, I did . . . when I worked for the machine repair shop, I used the scrap metal to make toys for my son." Heitou sneered and said, "You think that's even worth mentioning?" From then on, Chai Wang started to do as Heitou did, waiting until after dark to bring a bag of coal home every few days. At first he was terrified, and Mrs. Chai was, too. But he soon grew accustomed to it, and when he thought about how he was no better than a weed to some people, he felt even more justified. So not only did he make money, but he could also feed that ravenous stove. Of course, good luck always runs out, and after he'd worked the job for three years, a project was begun to put in central heating, and small boiler rooms were banned. That spring, all the men looking for work had to dig ditches for a living. Then that summer, when the initial stages of the project had been finished, the county Party head was arrested by the anti-corruption office. He'd taken advantage of his position, not only receiving bribes in exchange for promotions, but also tampering with the bidding process for the central heating project and interfering with the organization of workers, for which he'd received huge kickbacks. After it got out, the city fell into an uproar, and construction on the project was halted. Come fall, all the boiler rooms urgently needed to be inspected and repaired and stocked with coal.

So Chai Wang and Heitou returned to their old jobs. To celebrate, they bought two pounds of head cheese, a bag of peanuts, and two bottles of erguotou liquor, which they jubilantly finished in one sitting. But the following spring, the project was started up again. It was said that although the county Party head had broken the law, his projects were still good for ordinary folks. Putting in central heating not only would conserve resources, it would also reduce coal pollution. So Chai Wang and Heitou were sent home. Before they went their separate ways, they went to a bar and drank until dusk became midnight and their tongues had turned numb. As they left the bar, Heitou pointed at the stars and said, "I . . . I wanna . . . turn into . . . black smoke . . . and float up there . . . till I suff . . . suffocate you!" Wang Chai pointed to the stars and complained, "You . . . you all . . . peeing on the ground . . . with your light . . . isn't it . . . polluting us?" Heitou swayed on his feet and said, "Polluting?" Chai Wang swayed, too, and said, "Polluting!" So the two of them joined hands and happily shouted *polluting!* until they parted ways. Heitou soon left town and went to Nanjing to live with his uncle, where he took a job as a chef in a northeastern-style restaurant. As for Chai Wang, he started to take his pedicab out again to look for work each day from dawn until after dark. He would take passengers or transport things, and he could make thirty or forty kuai in a day. But when winter came, he would often make less than ten kuai, and it wasn't all that rare for him to go home at night empty-handed.

During the winter, Mrs. Chai liked to think of her husband whenever she was out walking. As soon as he came to mind, she would feel warmed. The northerly wind wouldn't seem so northerly, and instead would feel as warm as a kitten licking her cheeks. After her son got into trouble, the forty thousand kuai they had saved seemed to disappear like a puff of cotton on a fire, until soon nothing was left. They even borrowed twenty thousand kuai before the matter was settled. Being in debt left a bad taste in their mouths, and they didn't dare buy new clothing, or meat or fish or fresh fruit to eat. Over the summer Mrs. Chai grew her own vegetables, and their only fruits were cucumbers and tomatoes. In the colder months their fruit was the young radishes they stored in the cellar. They always bought soy sauce and cooking vinegar in bulk, along with the cheapest peppercorns and aniseed. She even replaced sanitary pads with the cheapest toilet paper that was sold by the pound. For a little fish or meat, sometimes Mrs. Chai would go to the fish market to gather discarded organs. She would come home, wash the organs and intestines, and make fish broth with noodles. To save money on coal, every few days she would go to the mountains to gather twigs, or to the willow grove at the bend in the river to cut down withered saplings. She would saw the trees into sections and use a sled to pull them home.

Then a year ago she had discovered a good place to find kindling. The lumberyard by North Mountain was far, almost ten li from home, but there she didn't have to go searching. They mostly brought in larch trees twenty centimeters in diameter, larger than a soup bowl but smaller than a basin. This wood came from deep in the mountains and had suffered many years of wind and rain, so its reddish-brown bark had grown thick. As the logs were loaded and unloaded, some of that bark would drop like rose petals in the autumn wind. It was as though the logs wanted to fully disrobe before settling down for a long sleep. The bark was natural tinder, but people weren't allowed to gather it, since the lumber mill could process it into the raw material for paper and sell it. The security guard at the lumberyard was an old man named Wang Dian, and he was still quite strong at sixty. Each day he would eat an entire stack of flatbread. The first time Mrs. Chai sneaked in to gather bark, he caught her and yelled at her. She told him the story of her family's misfortune, but he just blinked at her. If somebody saw him let her in, he'd be fired. And besides, if he let her do it, others would do it, too, and wouldn't the lumberyard just become a public firewood stack? Mrs. Chai promised Wang Dian that she would come early in the morning and be gone by daylight, before anyone was around to see her. And even if someone did see her, the bark would be hidden in her tightly closed burlap sacks.

Wang Dian felt sorry for her. Soon he started to gather the thickest pieces of bark and pile them up so she could just throw them in her sacks and leave. Once in a while he would hold the sacks open for her so she could fill them faster. Or he would prop up her bicycle as she tied the sacks onto the back. Mrs. Chai was grateful to him, so she unraveled one of her own sweaters and knitted four thick pairs of woolen socks. One pair she gave to her husband, one pair she mailed to her son in prison, and the remaining two she gave to Wang Dian. He took the socks and knocked them together like wooden clappers, then asked her very politely, "May I know your name, ma'am?" "My name is Mrs. Chai," she said. "I wanted to know your own name," he said. She straightened a bit. Thinking of her own name felt strange, and she said shyly, "I'm called Lianhua." Saying it was even stranger. He said, "You're the first woman I've ever known who forgot her own name when she got married!"

Mrs. Chai had been walking her bicycle for half an hour, and the stars were disappearing as the ship of dawn arrived. Like secret reefs, they knew they couldn't hold the golden ship back and went to hide. The northerly wind had died down a bit, so she got on her bicycle. She'd already walked a third of the distance, but once she was pedaling, the road seemed to disappear like a noodle being sucked into a mouth. In the city there were cars, and people who swept the walks, so the snow didn't have a chance to accumulate. Outside the city limits, however, with fewer cars and people and no one to take care of the streets, every surface was covered with a solid layer of snow. Her bicycle tires squeaked as they went over the hardened crust. The smooth fields out to either side of the road were untouched, covered with an undisturbed swath of white. There were places where sparrows had left their tracks, as though to them the snowy surface was a large quilt and they were spreading the cotton out evenly with their feet.

North Mountain appeared before her, and the sky was beginning to show faint signs of light. When she reached the lumberyard, she realized that Wang Dian was waiting for her. White bulbs hung on electrical poles set twenty meters apart on the perimeter flooded the yard with bright light, so she could see Wang Dian there. He was holding a dead rabbit.

"Where have you been?" he said. "I haven't seen you for days. I thought you might be sick."

Mrs. Chai took off her gloves and rubbed her frostbitten fingers. "It's almost the New Year," she said, "so I've been painting the walls. They're filthy from all the flies this year, and I want to get them clean before the holiday."

"The holidays are going to busy, then," he said.

"Well, we can't do everything perfect like rich people do. We just make pork and radish dumplings for dinner, and along with some fire-works, that's the New Year."

"You don't buy yourself any new clothes? I went into the city the other day, and they're selling cloth in the market for only forty-five kuai. Red flowers on a green background; it's nice."

"I'm a middle-aged married woman. Even in new clothing, who's going to look?"

"Your husband will. Besides, you don't look old. You're very pretty."

Mrs. Chai laughed and said, "When my husband eats dumplings, he doesn't like to eat the wrapper. When he looks at people, he doesn't see the outside, either. Even if I wore a gown made of gold, he wouldn't give me a second glance!"

"So he likes to eat the filling," Wang Dian mumbled.

His words made her think of a tender scene the night before, and she laughed bashfully. Wang Dian realized that what he'd said was funny, and he laughed along with her. He held the rabbit out to her and said, "Take it for your New Year's dinner. I trapped it up on North Mountain."

"No, no, no, I couldn't possibly take it," Mrs. Chai protested. "You let me collect bark for free. I already owe you so much. You should keep it for yourself."

"I caught two and I'm already keeping one. Go on, take it."

With that, Mrs. Chai could hardly keep on refusing. As she took the rabbit from him, she was thinking that it would be a shame to eat such good game. She would tell Chai Wang to hawk it to a restaurant. They would keep half the money, and she'd buy some nice food for old Mr. Wang with the other half.

Wang Dian had made a pile of bark for her, so she didn't need to use her rake. She quickly filled the two sacks with bark and hung them over the back of her bicycle. Her rear tire was squeezed between the bags on either side, which threw off the balance so much it felt like it had lost a wheel. Wang Dian put the rabbit in the blue basket, and she was still thanking him profusely as she left.

The sky brightened like it had let out a good sneeze. The stars were gone, and the snowy road was no longer dark. Mrs. Chai was in a good mood, and she wanted to take advantage of the weather to gather more bark. That way she could sleep in for the next month. The meandering rural road was full of bumps and holes, so she held on to the handlebars and watched the road carefully. As her warm breath mixed with the cold air, a thin layer of frost gathered on her bangs and eyelashes. It accumulated until she couldn't see the road and had to stop. As she brushed the frost away, she asked it, "Are you sad to be reborn to such a short life on my eyelashes? You should have landed on the tree branches. At least then you could have lived for half the winter." Perhaps because of her cheery joke, she felt more energetic when she climbed back on the bicycle. She pedaled quickly back to town, where there was already smoke coming from the kitchens of the low buildings.

The sun hadn't yet risen, and she'd already finished a major chore. She felt pleased as she walked her bicycle through the courtyard gate. She heard Teacher Liu's dog growl, and she knew it was greeting her. "Diabolo, I'm back," she called. "Thank you for guarding the gate for me. I'll give you a pork bun at the New Year."

Mrs. Chai dumped the bark by the courtyard wall and put the sacks back in the shed. She brushed the sawdust from her clothes and went inside with the rabbit. Chai Wang rose from the bed and drowsily put on his quilted pants. He was startled at the sight of the rabbit. "Where did you get that?"

"Brother Dian from the lumberyard gave it to us for New Year's," she said.

"You went to North Mountain again for bark?" Then he said tenderly, "Your face is all red; it must be freezing out."

"Of course it's cold," she said, "it's already the twenty-ninth. Listen, when you leave, take the rabbit and sell it to a restaurant."

"That rabbit is wild game. If we sell it, we'll get fined."

"You mean it's illegal for Brother Dian to trap rabbits?"

He buckled his belt and said, "Of course!"

Mrs. Chai clicked her tongue. "Then we've really put him in a tough spot!"

"You took apart your sweater to make him a pair of wool socks, and now you're calling him Brother Dian? I'm not going to let you go back to that lumberyard again!"

"Didn't I make a pair of socks for you, too?" she said, laughing. "And haven't I told you he's over sixty, the poor old man?"

Chai Wang put on his socks and stamped his feet. "So sixty-year-old men can't 'have a little taste of that,' too?"

"I see you've been learning from bad examples!" She gave him a little kick in the rear.

With the kick, he let off a fart like a firecracker, which sent them into gales of laughter. Finally he said, "Rabbits are rare this year. I bet I can sell it for at least a hundred kuai. With the money we make, you can buy Wang Dian a few bottles of liquor and some walnuts and dates for the New Year to thank him."

"I was thinking the same thing," she told him happily.

The sun had started to come up, and when Mrs. Chai went into the kitchen to light the stove, the window was flooded with the orange glow of dawn. Behind her Chai Wang said, "You know, this time of year is the best time for New Year's scrolls." He thought about how the scrolls were made—they were printed, and the characters were written in silver, not even gold, on red paper. They were all pretty much the same. And suddenly he had the idea of writing some himself. If everyone in town bought just one, he would definitely turn a profit! It wouldn't take much of an investment to get started, just some red paper and ink. Mrs. Chai said, "Your calligraphy looks like the scuttling of a cockroach. And you don't know how to make up the sayings. Quit dreaming!" He said, "I don't know how to do it myself, but I could collaborate with someone. Teacher Liu makes his own scrolls each year, and his calligraphy is pretty good. I'll buy the paper and ink, and he can do the writing. I will sell the scrolls, and whatever we make, we'll split in half. That way he won't just be spending all day every day alone at home."

"I guess you haven't been totally wasting your time," Mrs. Chai told him. "You do have a bit of business sense!"

The Lius had moved there from the east side seven years before. They were both teachers, and they had twin girls. They also happened to share a surname: his name was Liu Jiawen, and hers was Liu Ying. Their daughters were Liu Hehe and Liu Shunshun. Liu Jiawen had been a language teacher, but since a car accident in which he had lost both of his legs, he couldn't go out except in a wheelchair, so he'd had to retire. His wife was an English teacher. She was tall and pale with an oval face, a crescent mouth, and delicate eyes and eyebrows. She never spoke in a loud voice. A pretty girl who'd grown up on the east side, she made her own living and could speak a foreign language fluently, so everyone knew who she was. They used to live in a teachers' dormitory, but since Liu Jiawen had lost his legs, their income had dropped, and they'd sold that place and bought a cheaper house on the west side. The house had three small rooms, a bedroom for the two girls and one for the parents, plus a kitchen. Like the other houses, theirs had a small courtyard in front, but instead of vegetables they planted flowers. Roses, lilies, cornflowers, lantern flowers, chrysanthemums, ivy, yam blossoms, sunflowers—anything Liu Ying could find seeds for. In the summer, the fragrance from her garden filled air. Their courtyard made their alley the prettiest on the west side, and the butterflies and birds loved to visit it.

When they moved there, Hehe and Shunshun were twelve or thirteen, about the same age as Chai Gao. They were in the same grade as him, but not the same school. The girls didn't go out much. After school, they would come home to do chores and homework, unlike Chai Gao, who ran wild all day long. In the summertime, they liked to sit among the flowers reading schoolbooks or reciting English vocabulary. When Chai Gao heard them, he would stand in the courtyard and call sarcastically, "Hey, what kind of bird is making that noise?" And the voices from the garden would fade. Occasionally he would bump into the twins at the gate, and since they looked and dressed the same, he could never tell which was which. He'd just shout at them, "How come you don't wear different colors so we can tell you apart?" The girls would just cover their mouths and laugh. One time in the courtyard, Chai Gao unexpectedly sighed and said to his father, "If I ever married one of Teacher Liu's daughters, I might end up sleeping with the wrong one! They look exactly the same, so how would I know which one I took to bed at night?" He just happened to be overheard by Liu Jiawen, who was sunbathing in the flower garden. He laughed and said, "My boy, those are big words!"

It was at that moment that the Lius and the Chais began talking. Liu Jiawen wasn't very mobile, so when there was work that needed to be done, he would call across the courtyard to ask for Chai Wang's help to fix the gate or install a pane of glass or fish out the embers from the flues in the walls or move a crock of pickled vegetables. To repay them, Mrs. Liu offered to tutor Chai Gao. But when Chai Gao went to their house for a lesson, he would listen to about two sentences before dozing off. When he fell asleep, the naughty Shunshun would tap him with her fan as though brushing away a butterfly. Chai Gao would awake with a start to find her laughing at him, and he would fly into a fury. Perhaps his words had an effect, because the two girls started to wear different-colored clothing. The older girl, Hehe, wore red, and Shunshun wore green. That way Chai Gao could tell them apart, and he even started to call them "Red Hehe" and "Green Shunshun." Hehe was quieter and more studious than Shunshun, and so although they were both in the top high school, Hehe was put on the faster track. As for Chai Gao, he only tested into the regular high school. He developed a crush on Shunshun, and would make her willow flutes and flower wreaths and gather wild fruit for her. Shunshun once told him with a heavy heart that a boy in her class had written a love letter inviting her to meet him at the Wuji River. If she didn't go, he would leave a suicide note on the bank and drown himself, and everyone in town would know that he had died for her. Chai Gao said, "He's got some balls to threaten you like that!" So Chai Gao went with her to the river, and indeed the boy was waiting for her. He hadn't expected Shunshun to bring someone else with her. Chai Gao had come prepared. When he saw the other boy, he wordlessly unzipped his jacket with a loud rasp. The boy took a step back in fear, and Shunshun flinched away as well. Chai Gao had revealed a veritable arsenal: around his naked chest was a web of hemp cord from which hung several lengths of knives, a hammer, pliers, an adz, and a hatchet. Basically anything that could be used as a weapon he'd hung on himself like a suit of armor. He extended the sides of the jacket like eagle wings, and with his mouth open, he advanced on the boy, forcing him backward all the way to the water. Only when the boy started to cry did he relent.

From then on, the boy didn't dare harass Shunshun, but Shunshun also began to fear Chai Gao. He was too savage, and she started to avoid him, which infuriated him. He would point at her and say, "You're heartless, Green Shunshun!" When they graduated from high school, the sisters tested into college, with Red Hehe going off to Beijing and Green Shunshun going off to the provincial capital. Chai Gao was left behind to attend a vocational school. He likely realized that Green Shunshun was flying as high as a kingfisher, so whenever he saw her, he would hang his head. Shunshun said to him, "You should study for another year and get my parents to tutor you. Next year you can take the entrance exam again. Otherwise you'll be stuck here for the rest of your life!" Chai Gao pretended not to care and said, "It'd be a waste of time. I was never meant to go to college. I was meant for manual labor. I know you like flowers and want to study horticulture, so maybe I'll become a gardener. You like to eat, so I could study cooking, but I'm afraid of grease smoke. Or how about I learn to be a hairdresser, so I can cut your hair into long jagged layers?" Despite his cynical words, his heart was writhing in his chest. Shunshun started to cry. She pointed at him and said, "My hair's so nice and smooth, how can you even say that? Do you want it to look like snakes hanging from my head?" She ran away crying, and he followed behind her, shouting, "Green Shunshun, Green Shunshun, I was only kidding!"

After Hehe and Shunshun went to college, the Lius had even less money. The girls' school fees and living expenses took up more than half their household budget. Liu Jiawen had been housebound for some time and was bored. Over the past few years, his temper had gotten more and more explosive. He'd developed heart trouble and had to take medicine every day. Every so often, Chai Wang would hear him fighting with his wife from across the courtyard wall. If it happened in the morning, Mrs. Chai would say to her husband, "They didn't sleep well last night. If people don't get enough sleep, they get short-tempered." And if they fought at night, Chai Wang would say to his wife, "Maybe he wants 'a little taste of that,' and Mrs. Liu won't let him?" Mrs. Chai would say, "His legs were cut off; how can he have 'a little taste of that'?" Mr. Chai would answer, "You don't get it. His legs might've been cut off, but his thing is still there, and when it's hungry it needs to eat!" She knew she was fighting a losing battle, so she just tickled his armpits until he giggled and writhed.

To save money and earn a bit of cash over her break so as to lessen the burden on her father, Shunshun hadn't come back for the holidays the year before. Instead, Hehe had returned, still wearing the same red shirt she'd worn in high school. On the third day of the new year, she'd gone back to school so she could work as a tutor. After Chai Gao got in trouble, Shunshun called home and asked for the address of the prison where he'd been sent. Liu Jiawen asked Chai Wang, but he just shook his head and said, "Why is Shunshun bothering with that bad egg? Let him figure things out for himself in prison, that worthless brat!" Liu Jiawen said, "Shunshun wrote to him to encourage him, and it might help him change for the better." Chai Wang debated for a moment, then told him the address. He knew his son was in love with Shunshun. He had even started to like the color green. Every T-shirt, every pair of pants or sneakers he bought had to be green. He liked to eat green vegetables. He'd also added green to the house—the walls of his room were yellowish brown, but he said that was the color of shit, and it made him sick to look at it. He pestered Chai Wang into buying some green paint, and brushed it thickly onto the walls. It was a child's trick and didn't fool anyone. But Chai Wang knew his son wasn't good enough for Shunshun, like a sparrow would never be good enough for a peahen, and that was the real reason he didn't want to give her the prison's address.

Liu Jiawen did whatever he could around the house, wiping the table and sweeping the floor, lighting the stove and cooking a few simple dishes. In the busy time around the New Year, he would tie the broom to a pole and clean each of the rooms one by one. What an ordinary person could finish in a day, he needed three or four days to do from his wobbly wheelchair. He also liked to paste together a red lantern to hang from a crabapple tree in the courtyard on New Year's Eve. What Chai Wang admired most was that Liu would write his own New Year's scrolls to hang on the gate. Each year, Chai Wang would go home and say enviously to his wife, "See, he's really got culture. His calligraphy is nicer than the stuff they sell in the shops. The characters are perfect." Mrs. Chai would say, "When you put up a scroll like that, it's to let everyone know that your family isn't like everyone else's. It's an educated household." Chai Wang said, "It's too bad I can't really read it." And his wife said, "Even their dog's name has to do with religion, so of course their scrolls are meaningful!" Her husband thought of the name "Diabolo" and laughed.

When Chai Wang finished breakfast, he went over to Teacher Liu's house. Diabolo heard the gate opening and rushed joyously out of his shed. He nipped affectionately at the hem of Chai Wang's trousers. Liu Ying had already left for work, but Liu Jiawen was there reading by the window, wearing thick glasses and draped in a quilted cotton jacket. When he saw Chai Wang coming, he put down his book and called out, "Brother Chai," then asked him if business was good. Chai Wang said, "Good enough. I can make one kuai eighty in a day, and that buys two pieces of tofu for dinner." He noticed that the window was patterned with frost and the room was freezing, so he asked, "Why is it so cold in here? Why don't you throw something on the fire?" Liu Jiawen laughed bitterly and said, "To save coal, of course. Coal gets more expensive every year, and I'd feel like I was burning my own bones to keep it warm in here. As soon as Liu Ying goes to work, I put out the stove, and then late in the afternoon I light it again so the house is warm when she comes home." Chai Wang said, "Ah, you're so good to your wife." Liu Jiawen said dejectedly, "With a crippled husband like me, how much is that worth? It doesn't do her any good." Chai Wang thought of how he often heard them fighting, and, fearing Liu's temper, he didn't dare respond.

Liu Jiawen prepared some tea as Chai protested, saying, "Please don't trouble yourself." He had to chuckle at his own words. Ordinarily he'd say, "Forget it," but since he was in a literate and cultured household, he found himself being more genteel. Finally, he explained to Liu why he'd come. At his words, Liu's gloomy eyes began to sparkle. He kept saying, "You're right, New Year's scrolls are all the same now. If it's not 'A good year, a good present, a good future; may your desires sail to you on wind and water,' then it's 'May the four seas send wealth to this treasured place; may everything bring good luck to your auspicious space.' They couldn't be more common. I could write new ones! Besides, it's printed on the computer, and it's all the same flavorless stuff. If you hang those saggy old scrolls on your door, it's like boiling up quack medicine—all it does is make the place stink." Liu's words made Chai Wang think about the scroll he had on his own door. Each year he liked to paste up one that said "Smooth sailing into future years; may your wishes come true without tears." Did Liu Jiawen think that scroll was "quack medicine"? He felt a bit put out, but then he thought about Liu's disability, and he forgave him any grumpiness. "Let's do it," Liu said. "I have a hundred kuai here, so you can go out and buy red paper and a container of 'Good Idea Pavilion' ink." "What about brushes?" Chai Wang asked. Liu said, "I have plenty of good brushes already." "You just worry about the work itself," Chai told him. "You don't need to put in any money. This afternoon I'll go out and get the red paper and ink for you. Any money we make we'll divide evenly, okay?" Liu Jiawen answered in pleased surprise, "Of course, of course! If we really manage to make some money, I'm going to buy a cervical brace for Liu Ying. She's buried in her lessons and grading all day long, and her spine is compressing so much it makes her dizzy. If she doesn't do something about it soon, she'll be as immobile as I am, and then how will Hehe and Shunshun cope?" Chai Wang said, "Can that really paralyze someone? Is it that serious?" Like a real doctor, Liu started to explain cervical spine problems in great detail, while Chai clicked his tongue and said, "Well, there's no time to waste. How much does the thing cost?" Liu told him, "I called a medical company, and even after a discount, it'll cost seven hundred sixty kuai." Chai Wang clicked again, thinking that it would be hard to make that much money selling New Year's scrolls. But he didn't want to say that, since doing business was a lot like fishing: you never knew which net would catch something and which would come up empty. Then Liu said, "Selling scrolls is mostly just for fun, and whatever we make is fine. Don't worry too much about the money." At that, Chai Wang felt relieved, and he asked if Hehe and Shunshun were coming home for the New Year. Liu said, "We've decided that to save money, each year just one of the girls will come back. Anyway, they look so similar, seeing one is like seeing the other! Last year Hehe came home, so this year it's Shunshun's turn." Chai Wang sighed and said, "They're really grown up, not like our family failure." Liu said consolingly, "There's nothing like the return of a prodigal son. Don't give up on him yet!"

With their business settled, Chai Wang hurried back home to tell his wife. Mrs. Chai lifted the lid of their money box and asked, "How much will it cost to buy paper and ink?" He went over and shut the box. "Don't we have that rabbit?" he said. "I'll sell it and use the money to buy paper and ink." She laughed and said, "We have been lucky lately. I brought home two bags of kindling and a rabbit, and now someone's going to help us write New Year's scrolls. It's a good omen! I just want to put these hungry years behind us."

"Just wait until our good-for-nothing son comes back," Wang Chai said. "He's going to have to come work with me to make up for the hungry times he brought us. How else will he know how hard it is to be an adult?"

His wife agreed and said, "Let that old wolf hunger follow him around for a while, and he won't dare behave badly. He'll have no choice but to be good!"

Chai Wang wrapped the rabbit in brown paper and clamped it under his arm. On the street he bumped into some old friends, and when they saw that he wasn't riding his pedicab, they called to him, "Hey, Chai

Wang, are you taking the day off?" He answered cheerfully, "Yup, I'm off today."

The little restaurants on the west side offered potatoes and cabbage, rice noodles with peanuts, and tofu stuffed with shrimp paste. Usually when Chai Wang passed by such places, it was as sweet as seeing his wife's smile. But because the rabbit could only go to a fancy establishment, today he had to make his way up in the world, and he hurried by with only a sideways squint.

The fancy restaurants and bars in the city center soon began to appear one after another. Their busiest times were noon and evening, so many of the restaurants hadn't yet raised their metal security grates, and their signs hadn't been placed out front. Chai Wang knocked on three doors and was sent away each time. Finally he knocked on a door that opened. The restaurant owner was brushing his teeth, and his mouth was filled with white foam. Chai carefully set the rabbit down on the ground and opened the brown paper as though presenting a princess to her subjects. He said, "Look how fat and beautiful it is. It's enough to make at least four or five dishes. Somebody else would sell it for two hundred kuai, but since I need the money now, I'll give it to you for a hundred fifty, ok?" The owner brushed vigorously and shook his head. Chai was undaunted. He continued to sing the rabbit's praises until the proprietor finally clamped his toothbrush between his teeth and leaned down to pick it up. He weighed the rabbit in his hands and even stroked its belly a few times as though it were a woman's breast. That made Chai Wang uncomfortable. The owner laid the rabbit on the ground and spat out, "Too thin." He opened his fingers in the symbol for five. "Fifty kuai is way too little!" Chai cried. He wrapped the rabbit back up, planning to take his chances with the next restaurant. But the owner wanted to do business, and he waved his hand at Chai to tell him not to leave. He went back into the kitchen and quickly finished brushing his teeth. Then he came back and said, "How about sixty?" Chai said, "Sixty would be about right for half a rabbit!" "Okay, seventy, then," the owner said, "but that's my limit!" "I won't go less than a hundred!" Chai cried. The owner said, "Well, then, you'd better get out of here." In fact, Chai had already accepted the price, but he'd wanted to see if he could get a little more. Who would've thought that bargaining would lead to a dead end? He was disheartened, but he could only pretend that he didn't care at all. He picked up the rabbit to leave. But unexpectedly, as soon as he turned around to go, the owner called out, "This is my first deal this morning, and I want to get off to a good start. I'll give you eighty, just leave the rabbit here." Chai Wang silently recited a little mantra of thanks, and went back to give the rabbit to the owner with shaking hands. He pulled out a wad of cash from his pocket and counted out eighty kuai. Chai felt as though he'd been given a miracle, and he said thank you over and over again. He practically floated to a department store and went straight up to the stationery section to buy red paper and ink. He put the ink in his pocket, slung the roll of paper over his shoulder, and whistled all the way home.

In the meantime, Liu Jiawen had copied out two pages with more than twenty scroll couplets. He'd taken out his *Han Folk Ballads and Poetry and Verses for Children* and had copied lines about springtime, like "From the branches and water, spring returns anew / Long willows brush the ground and peach blossoms fly." He also picked out lines rich in familial moral lessons, such as "When yin and yang combine, a lustrous rain falls / When a man and wife collaborate, their family succeeds." In addition, he also composed a few of his own couplets: "The heavenly lights bring warmth and the moon is bright / Spring breezes blow the snow until the days turn light." Of course, there was also ancient poetry that drew from ordinary experience that he could revise slightly, as in "Seeing the spring light on the Wuji / I hear the music rising like clouds," in which he replaced the original "footpaths" with a reference to the Wuji River.

After Chai Wang dropped the paper and ink off at Teacher Liu's house, he hurried home to give the remaining forty or so kuai to his wife. She had never thought that her husband would sell the rabbit so quickly, and she praised with him a simple "Well done." He straightened his back and said, "With you at my side, how could I not do well?" She laughed and joked, "Since I'm with you, even doing bad will still have to do!"

Chai Wang returned to Teacher Liu's house with a happy heart, and found Liu making a fire. He couldn't stint on the coal today, since he had to keep his hands and feet warm as he wrote; otherwise the characters wouldn't be smooth. Chai Wang chimed in, "If you write with cold hands, the characters will be as stiff as a piece of old cornbread!"

The fire slowly grew, and the room filled with warmth. Chai Wang acted as Liu's assistant, cutting paper, arranging the inkstone, rinsing the brushes. Cutting paper took skill: if it wasn't cut exactly along the folds, the knife would leave jagged edges. New Year's scrolls tended to have lines of seven or nine characters each, so the paper had to be cut to different dimensions, some long, some short. But the length of the horizontal blessing banners was set, since they were all in lines of four characters. In half an hour, Chai had cut thirty or forty sections of paper. Before Liu Jiawen began to write on them, he practiced a few characters on an old scrap of paper, and only when he felt comfortable did he start to write on the red paper. Watching each of those ink-scented characters leap onto the paper with vigor or grace, Chai Wang felt as though he were watching a flock of songbirds descending. He clicked his tongue in approval, saying, "Look at that character, it has such presence and energy!" Teacher Liu started laughing and told him, not without some pride, that he had wooed Liu Ying with his calligraphy. That year he and a chemistry teacher were both pursuing her, and they each sent her a love letter at the same time. When Liu Ying compared Liu Jiawen's unique, bold calligraphy to the chemistry teacher's dense, miserly, frowning characters, she agreed to go out with him. "You teachers are so romantic, using letters to express your affections," Chai Wang said enviously. "As for me, I got my wife into bed with a big old rock!" He told Liu the story of helping Wang Lianhua pull the heavy stone from the Wuji River. Liu Jiawen said, "What a marvelous rock! It's what made the two of you fall in love, so it was given to you by the gods." Chai grimaced and said, "There's nothing special about a rock. Right now it's out there in our pickling crock."

When Liu Jiawen finished a scroll, Chai Wang would take it off the desk and spread it out carefully on the floor. He waited until each one was completely dry before draping it on top of the others. It was noon before they knew it, and the frost on the window had melted into droplets that dripped off like nostalgic tears. Diabolo began to yap softly, which was the way he welcomed people he knew, and in a moment Mrs. Chai came through the gate carrying a porcelain bowl. She wasn't wearing gloves, and her fingers were bright red from the cold. In the bowl was drop dumpling soup, and when she took off the lid, a delicious fragrance rose with the steam. The broth was neither too thin nor too thick, not oily and perfectly seasoned. The drop noodles were distributed evenly among the cracked wheat and succulent strips of cabbage and white turnip. "This soup's so beautifully made, it's like a painting!" Liu cried. "Yours is much tastier than the way Liu Ying makes it." Mrs. Chai laughed and said, "I'm in the kitchen all day, I can't help but get better at cooking. Liu Ying goes to work every day, and with everything that she does, putting together a meal isn't easy!"

As the two men ate happily, Mrs. Chai bent down to look at the scrolls. She said to her husband, "Wow, each of these characters is like a young man, so energetic!" Chai Wang wiped his mouth and said, "How come when I look at them, they all seem like pretty young girls?" She joked, "Does that mean you two are actually selling young wives?" They laughed together. Then she said, "Why are they all in couplets, instead of having some blessings also? I like the blessings the best, and I always buy one. I think they sell the most, too." With those words, Chai Wang was reminded that families all had to put up a blessing banner each year, and he said, "That's right, no matter what, you have to put up a blessing!" So Mrs. Chai began to help them cut red paper for blessings. Since she had a careful, feminine hand and was so practical, after she cut out the sections she trimmed the paper left over from Chai Wang's cuttings into small blessing squares. As Liu Jiawen set down his bowl, he said to Chai, "Your wife is a very good wife." Chai Wang laughed and said, "She's only good at this kind of work." Mrs. Chai pouted at her husband, then laughed pointedly, and Chai knew exactly what she meant. He thought of the pleasure they found together at night and couldn't help but blush.

Everyone who sold New Year's scrolls would peddle their wares in front of a few large vegetable markets and malls. Chai Wang decided on the New World Mall, since it was large and popular. As the end of the year approached, everyone was busy getting ready for the celebrations. The peanut and watermelon seed sellers and the haw candy and steamed sweet bun peddlers were all doing a brisk business. Six or seven people were already selling scrolls in the square in front of the New World Mall. Chai Wang was new, and he worried that he wouldn't be welcome. So he apologized to the other vendors for coming onto their turf and bought a few bags of seeds to give to them, apologizing for the inconvenience. The vendors might love to haggle over every cent, but once they felt the proper respect had been paid, they became quite friendly. Those who knew Chai told him, "You can only sell these for a few months out of the year, but it'll make more than what you earn pedaling around in that pedicab of yours." Those who didn't know him said, "Go ahead and try to sell your scrolls; maybe you can make a bit of money at it. Who can get rich these days, anyway? No one has it easy." And so Chai Wang's business began amid the sound of seeds being cracked open between teeth.

Like the other peddlers, Chai Wang spread his wares out on the ground and anchored the scrolls with chunks of brick so they wouldn't be blown away. His spot was near the main road, so as soon as his scrolls appeared, they caught the eyes of the passersby. Many cried out in surprise, "Hey, that's real calligraphy!" Printed characters didn't seem like real characters at all, while the characters in ink were as vivid as flesh and blood. But although a lot of people came and looked, few of them bought one of the scrolls, since most couldn't read them properly. For example, in the phrase "Virtue is the treasure of the country / Confucian values are the jewel of the banquet," many of them read "Confucian" as "confusion" and said, "What's it saying about confusion? Are we supposed to be confused about not being invited to the table?" One of the other scroll sellers added, "No, it's a word for a food, but is it meat from a flying, running, or swimming animal?" Even Chai Wang himself had only a vague idea of what "Confucian" meant, so he said, "It's written with a 'person' part in it, which means it has to do with people, so I'd say running." Hearing that, the other seller began to laugh.

That first day, Chai Wang sold only five scrolls, but the blessing banners of both sizes sold quite well. When it came time to wrap up for the day, he'd made twenty kuai. Figuring in the costs, it was less than ideal, but he wasn't upset. The sky was dark as he went home, but he first dropped by Liu Jiawen's house. Liu Ying was making dinner, and when she saw him, she welcomed him warmly. Liu Jiawen asked anxiously, "How did it go?" Chai Wang said, "Everyone loved your calligraphy. They all said the characters were written well, but they didn't know what the words meant. So I sold more of the blessings than I did of the scrolls." Liu Jiawen let out a sigh and said, "What can you do in this backward age. There are so few people with culture!" Chai Wang said, "You mean they think you wrote your characters backward?" Liu Jiawen laughed and said, "A backward age and a backward character are two different things!" Chai Wang said, "There's a lot I don't know, but I do think that whatever it is people like, that's what we should sell them. Stuff with 'happiness' and 'wealth' and 'money' and 'treasures'—those will definitely sell well." Liu Jiawen answered angrily, "Then I'll just write scrolls like 'More happiness, more wealth, more peace, *hehe*, more prosperity, *shunshun!*' and 'More money, more treasures, everything where it should be!' And then on the horizontal scrolls I'll write, 'Lovely and complete.'" Chai Wang was startled and said, "What a great couplet, and you've even worked in your two daughters' names! If you write that kind of scroll, they will definitely sell!" Liu Jiawen sighed and said, "Today nobody recognizes things of true value." Chai Wang said, "That couplet you just composed has real value. I know it, and other people will know it! Tonight you can work late and write a few of those scrolls, and tomorrow we'll turn a profit." As he spoke, he took out the money they had earned that day and gave Liu Jiawen half. Liu refused it again and again until Chai cried, "If you don't take it, I won't sell any more!" Liu Jiawen finally took the money, and looked at it with the same joy as when he'd read Hehe and Shunshun's admissions notices.

That night Chai Wang tossed and turned, thinking about the scrolls. He finally got out of bed and dressed. He washed his face and brushed his teeth, then went over to his neighbors' house. Liu Jiawen had been up late writing; he had bags under his eyes, and his face was pale. He was sitting on his bed eating rice porridge, and the hand holding the bowl was shaking as though he'd hurt himself holding the brush so long. In all the times Chai had seen him in his wheelchair, he had always had his legs covered, with a green blanket in winter and a square of white linen in summer. When Chai suddenly saw the two withered stumps, his heart thumped in his chest. Although they were covered with thin cotton pants, he felt as if he could see the scars spidering out like the black streaks left by a lightning strike. He felt heartsick. Not having expected Chai to come over so early, Liu Jiawen was flustered. He put his bowl down to pull a blanket over his legs, but it was too late. Chai Wang quickly grabbed an armful of scrolls and went back outside. Before he could close the door, Liu Ying said, "You're working too hard, Brother Chai." "Not at all, not at all," he said quickly. Then he remembered what Liu Jiawen had said about her spine, and he turned around to take a peek. When he saw her throat, he wondered how such a straight white neck could have a problem. It was only when he'd gone out through the gate that he suddenly remembered that the spine was in the back of the neck, and he let out a bark of laughter at himself.

Around the end of the year, the market was busier than the spring festival and a temple holiday combined. Customers flooded into the New World Mall as soon as it opened. More people were buying scrolls as well, so Liu Jiawen's efforts had not been in vain. The new scrolls sold like hotcakes, once more than twenty in a single afternoon. There were a few people who complained that the handwritten characters were ugly and that the plain red paper wasn't edged with silver or gold. Chai Wang never argued with them. He just said, "If you don't like it, you don't have to buy it." In between customers, he liked to watch the shoppers. The women were mostly carrying bags of clothing. Knitwear always sold well at New Year's, since everyone with money wanted new clothes from top to bottom. Even families who were less well off would purchase cotton underwear or vests, as though it wouldn't be the New Year if they didn't have something new to wear. Seeing those women in their crisp outfits, Chai Wang would sigh and wonder when he'd have the chance to buy his wife a present like that. Men mostly bought cigarettes and liquor and expensive snacks. Chai looked at them enviously and thought to himself that when his son was out of prison and had paid off his debts to them, they would at least have one comfortable year. He'd buy a few bottles of good liquor, a few five-spice smoked pigs' feet, some chicken wings, and dried fish, and they would eat their fill. He'd buy his wife some wool pants, a soft silk jacket, leather gloves, and good leather shoes lined with cotton, so she could dress in style. Chai Wang also liked to look at the two cream-colored buildings across the street. They had been built the year before, and he'd heard that the apartments all had heated floors, sort of like how their old-fashioned bed was heated with warm air piped in from the stove. People could sit on the floor and drink tea and watch TV, and that filled Chai Wang with envy. The other peddlers felt the same way, and they would cross their arms and gaze up at the buildings between sales. The apartments were so warm that people had to open their windows, and some even propped open their balcony doors. Chai Wang wished their excess heat would flow into his house, so his wife wouldn't have to get up early and go to the North Mountain lumberyard for bark. Among the scroll peddlers was a man they called Old Pi. He was always smoking, and with each puff he would cough up a glob of phlegm that he spat out onto the sidewalk. His spitting was so disgusting that people avoided his stall. He had a lot of time to just stand there, and his eyes and mouth were always moving. Once he spotted a woman in a pink sweater standing on a balcony, and he shouted, "Look how pretty she is!" As everyone looked, he suddenly smacked his lips and said, "With those heated floors, her man doesn't even need to use the bed to screw her." The passersby burst into laughter.

Chai Wang had earned sixty kuai that day, but as he pedaled his pedicab home, he kept an eye out for someone to pick up. He passed by a woman standing in front of a rice and oil shop. She waved at him. At her feet were two sacks of flour, and she was annoyed that no cabs would stop for her. "Pedicab man," she cried to him, "I'll give you three kuai to take me and my flour to the water company apartments, okay?" He stopped his cab to help her with the bags of flour. Worried that she might step on his scrolls, he collected them and tied them to the top of the pedicab. As soon as she had settled herself, she started to complain about cabdrivers. "Around New Year's," she said, "business is good and they get arrogant." Chai learned from her long tirade that one cab that had come by already had a passenger, and because her destination wasn't on the way, the driver had refused to take her. Another driver had wanted an additional two kuai, saying that her bags of flour added up to another person. She'd sent him packing. Another had agreed to take her, but said that her flour had to go in the trunk. He said he'd just cleaned it, but when they put the two bags in, a bloom of dust rose, dirtying the bags. She'd yelled at him over the noise of the market, "Didn't you say your trunk's like an old maid— so clean it's like nothing's ever been put in it? What an idiot!" Chai Wang laughed at that, thinking that when he got home, he'd have a good story to tell his wife.

By the time he dropped the woman off, it was dark, and the streetlamps had come on. After standing all day and pedaling the pedicab, his legs were sore and his back was covered in sweat. Nearing the west side, his legs started to go numb and wouldn't be able to pedal much longer. He passed by a few small stores, and suddenly glimpsed Liu Ying by the side of the road. He thought she must be buying soy sauce or cooking vinegar, and he said, "Out to get a few things?" She called his name and gestured him over, then asked quietly, "Did anyone buy your scrolls today?" He told her, "We sold a lot more than yesterday, more than sixty kuai worth!" She exhaled audibly and said, "Then I don't have to worry. He was up all night making those scrolls. I was even thinking that if you didn't sell any today, I'd give you some money to give to him, just to make him feel like it was worth it. You have no idea, Brother Chai. This is the first time I've seen him happy since we moved to the west side. He's exhausted, but he's whistling again. I haven't heard him whistle since before he got injured. And these past few days he hasn't even argued with me. Before, he'd lose his temper at the drop of a hat." Chai Wang said, "People like having something to do. It's too bad New Year's only comes once a year; otherwise I'd help him sell scrolls every single day!" Liu Ying laughed, a clear, lovely sound. It gave him a strange sensation. She surreptitiously slipped Chai Wang a hundred-kuai bill and said, "On slow days, give him a few kuai from this." Chai Wang tried to push the money away, and their hands got tangled together. Although they were both wearing gloves, he blushed like they were holding hands.

Chai Wang finally accepted the money, since he didn't want to be seen on the street talking to another woman. But he vowed to find a way to return it within a few days. He wanted to tell Liu Jiawen how much his wife cared for him and how lucky he was to have her, and that he had nothing to complain about. But he knew that what had happened had to stay secret. He'd always had a good impression of Liu Ying, but now he felt she was even more wonderful, and as he opened the door to his own home, his ears still rang with her sweet laughter.

Each day Chai Wang left early and came back late, regardless of how much he sold. And no matter what, he always told Liu Jiawen that business was good. Mrs. Chai visited the lumberyard at North Mountain a few more times, and piled the bark into a small brown hill in their courtyard. She used part of the money from selling the rabbit to buy Wang Dian two bottles of erguotou liquor, some marinated beef, three jin of peanuts, and a jin of sesame candy. When she gave it to him, he exclaimed, "What a good woman you are! When someone's nice to you, you remember it for a lifetime." She said, "I like to return anything I'm given tenfold. It's just a shame we're so poor!"

Early New Year's morning, Mrs. Chai rose to burn incense for the kitchen god. By the time her husband got up, the sweet buns were already steaming. He dipped them in sugar and ate six, one right after another.

Worried that he would eat himself sick, she brought him some pickled vegetables to counteract all the sugar.

"It's New Year's Day," she told him, "so come home early whether you sell anything or not. I'll have the dumplings ready to boil when you get back."

He deposited a few tidbits of pickled vegetables into his mouth with his chopsticks and said, "Once we've had our dumplings, if you'll let me 'have a little taste of that,' I'll definitely come home early."

She laughed and said, "You think you can have so many good things all at once? If you don't come home early, I'll just have to eat by myself!"

"There's nothing good to taste on your own," he teased her.

"Well, maybe not the way you eat!" She grabbed hold of his chopsticks and said, "Why are you pecking like a chicken?"

He pouted and said, "It's so salty, I can only eat a little at a time."

"Naughty boy!" she said, pretending to scold him.

"Well, this naughty boy has to go to work," he said. He pinched her bottom, put on his cotton hat and gloves, and went off to set up his stall.

Because it was New Year's Day, the New World Mall was busier than ever, and a constant stream of customers came to buy scrolls. One peddler kept shouting, "Scrolls for sale, scrolls for sale! Buy one for a tranquil life, buy two to get rich, buy three for eternal happiness!" Everyone likes to hear about good luck, so his stall was busy. Not wanting to get left behind, Chai Wang started his own patter: "Scrolls for sale, scrolls for sale! All handmade! Sincerity brings good luck!" And his stall didn't lack for customers, either.

At noon he bought two flatbreads for lunch as usual and ate them in the cold winter wind. He was brushing crumbs from his coat when he heard a familiar voice calling to him. He followed the voice, and to his surprise he found Heitou, the man he had once worked the boilers with. Heitou was wearing ironed trousers, a cotton-lined leather jacket, and shiny black shoes. His hair was combed smooth, and his skin was white and soft. He looked years younger than before.

Chai Wang started to extend his hand to shake, but pulled it back. Heitou slapped him on the shoulder with an easy air and said, "Old Chai, I think of you often! Those were good years."

"You . . . you've done well for yourself," Chai Wang said haltingly. "You're not a cook anymore, are you?"

"I finally had a run of good luck," Heitou said. "Back when I was a cook, a TV crew used our restaurant to film a few scenes for a show. They needed someone to play a cook, so I did it, and they said I was a natural. So I threw away my ladle and started acting!"

"You're on TV?" Chai said. "I'd never have imagined it."

"I just play a bit part; you wouldn't notice me."

"But if you play a bit part long enough, doesn't that mean you're a star?"

Heitou told Chai Wang that he had come back to town to get divorced. For many years, his wife had complained that he was useless and said she wanted a divorce. Back then he'd resisted, but now that he wanted the divorce, she refused. She said her feelings for him ran deep and it wouldn't be that easy. Heitou said, "Goddamn it, she used to curse me like a dog. But now that I've made something of myself, she won't let me go. In the morning she fries eggs, for lunch she makes spareribs, and at night she draws me up a footbath. Who could live with such a conniving woman?" As he was pouring out his resentments, his cell phone rang. He pulled it out of his breast pocket and said to Chai, "I've got to go buy some smokes and liquor for the relatives. You get on with your business, and we'll find another time to talk." Chai Wang laughed uneasily and said, "Come over to our place for a chat whenever you're free."

Chai felt sad and envious as he watched Heitou leave. Back when he had repaired boilers, he could hold his head up high, but since then he'd accomplished nothing, and now he had to work outside in the cold winter wind like the nobody he really was. Listless, he didn't join in the peddlers' loud calls to potential customers. When someone came over to ask the price of his scrolls, he didn't bother to answer. It was as though he didn't care if he sold a single thing. For a few hours he felt numb. But Chai Wang was still Chai Wang, and after he'd turned the matter over in his head for a while, he thought about his wife telling him to come home early to eat dumplings with her, and his mood brightened. On the surface, Heitou seemed to have it made, but he was actually very unhappy. And while Chai Wang's life seemed to be in shambles, his heart was warm and cheerful. Only when a man was happy could his life be truly good.

So Chai Wang threw himself back into selling scrolls. The wind picked up that afternoon, sending the scrolls flapping like flames that licked at the New World Mall doors. Around three o'clock the sky turned gray, and a lot of the peddlers packed up to go home for their New Year's celebrations. More people came out of the mall than went in. At four o'clock, the sun had already dropped down to the mountains. It had been tossed around by the wind all day, and it looked pale and tired and ready for a rest. The market had closed its doors, and the other peddlers had packed up and gone home, but Chai Wang was still at it. Old Pi told him as he left, "Old Chai, it's getting dark, and everyone's gone home for New Year's. Don't waste your time. Who's going to buy anything now?" But

Chai Wang said, "I'm going to stay another half-hour or so. Somebody might still come by."

The mall was different from his own neighborhood: when it was busy, it was absolutely packed, but when it was empty, it was desolate. As soon as the stores closed, only the sparrows remained. Chai Wang brought his pedicab over to the side of the road and loaded up the scrolls. He was near the sidewalk, and there were plenty of cars, too, but no one stopped. He thought, people probably like to buy good luck scrolls on bright sunny days so their whole year will be bright and sunny. With that thought, he decided to go home. But just then an old man happened by and wanted to buy three sets of scrolls. He said one was to paste up on the outer gate to his courtyard, the second was for the door to his house, and the third was for the storage shed. Chai Wang was secretly delighted because he'd made Liu Jiawen write a few sayings that had to do with sheds. Storage sheds were filled with grain and dried fish, and although no one lived in them, older people considered them even more important than houses, so they liked to paste up a New Year's scroll by the door. The couplets had to have the words "shed full of fish" and "bins full of grain," and the blessing banners had to have the old cliché "Every year filled with plenty." In addition to buying the scrolls, the old man also bought two large banners plus six small ones. Chai Wang took the money, rolled up the scrolls and banners, and handed them over, saying, "Have a very happy New Year, sir." And the old man answered in a thin, quavering voice, "Happy New Year to you, too."

The sale dispelled any idea he might have had of going home. The sun had gone down behind the mountains, and it was getting darker and colder. Chai marched in place and wiggled his fingers and toes to keep them from freezing. Although he used bricks to keep his scrolls from blowing around, their edges riffled in the wind like they also felt the cold. "Go ahead and blow," he said to the wind. "Before too long, spring will come, and you'll be nowhere to be found!" As though in response, the wind suddenly started howling, whipping up a gale that nearly knocked him off his feet. The scrolls in his pedicab flapped wildly until two blessing banners were snatched up and fluttered away. He chased them about, trying to grab them back. He caught one of the banners, but the other one was taken by a gust and tossed across the street to the cream-colored buildings. He watched anxiously as it dipped and then rose toward the western building. It paused for a moment in a balcony alcove on the third floor before floating right in through the open door. At least it was a blessing banner, he thought. If he were selling paper money for the dead and some of it floated into someone's house, they'd come after him for sending a bad omen!

The wind raged for a few minutes, then gradually lessened. As it died down, the streetlamps came on. Chai Wang saw that there were hardly any cars or pedestrians on the street. There was no business to be had, so he packed up his scrolls again to go home. Just as he had climbed into his pedicab and started to pedal, he heard someone calling from across the street: "Hey, scroll peddler, wait!" Chai stopped and watched a man huffing and puffing across the street toward him. "How many scrolls do you want?" Chai asked.

The short, plump man was around thirty, with a round face, small eyes, and a flat nose. His forehead was crisscrossed with scars. He wore no hat or gloves, just a short sable jacket as if he had dashed out of the house. His jacket buttons were undone, and he had a gray cashmere sweater on underneath. He said, "Are you the only one selling scrolls here?" "It's already dark," Chai said. "I'm the only one left." The man asked, "Did you just lose a blessing banner?" "Yes," Chai cried, "one of mine was swept away in the wind!" "Did you write it yourself?" the man asked. "I had my neighbor write it," Chai answered. "His calligraphy is better than mine." The man grinned, "Well, that banner flew into my house! Here, I want to pay for it." He reached into his pocket and pulled out a hundred-kuai bill. He slapped it into Chai's hand forcefully, knocking him a bit off balance. "Today is New Year's Day, and God sent me a blessing!" the man cried. Chai Wang clutched the bill and said, "This is too much, I feel bad taking it." The man said, "What's there to feel bad about? It's just a little show of appreciation. You don't know who I am, do you? I'm Scarface Hua—have you heard of me?" Chai Wang's hand with the money trembled, and he said, "Of course I've heard of you. You're the owner of the Five Happinesses Restaurant and the Four Pleasures Spa." The man said, "So, what do you say?" And Chai Wang said quickly, "Thank you, I'll take the money."

Scarface Hua waved his hand and walked back across the street. Chai Wang stood there as though he were just waking from a dream. Scarface Hua was famous in their small town. He depended on a group of determined lackeys who weren't afraid to brandish a gun or a club in order to force a supermarket to sell a prime locale so that he could open a restaurant. If the restaurant didn't have enough business, his lackeys would go to important businesses around town with their knives and ask, "Why haven't we seen you around the Five Happinesses Restaurant lately? Can't you afford it? If you can't afford it, borrow the money!" Most bosses didn't want to incur the wrath of the local hoodlums, so they would find an excuse to eat a few meals there, figuring it would buy them peace and quiet for a while. Rumor had it that Hua had used the girls at the spa to involve the police in collusion, so within the limits of their town, his arrogance knew no bounds. Scarface Hua had originally been called Scarface Hu, since his last name was Hu and his forehead was covered with scars. But then a fortuneteller had looked at his scars and said that they were shaped like hua flowers and had brought him good fortune and money. So he'd changed his name to Hua. Scarface Hua owned a lot of property and kept several women, so Chai Wang figured that one of his mistresses lived in that cream-colored building.

Money was a useful thing. But since he had received it from a man like Scarface Hua instead of earning it himself, Chai felt like it was dirty. He counted up what he'd made, and it came to eight hundred kuai. That was more than he could normally make in a month, and that was a true blessing. He sighed, pondering what he should do with it. He thought and thought, and then he suddenly thought of Liu Ying. He remembered Liu Jiawen saying that if he had enough money, he'd buy her a cervical brace, though it cost more than seven hundred kuai. If she didn't treat the problem soon, she might actually become disabled, and what would they do then? Chai Wang didn't want to imagine such a good woman suffering that kind of fate. He decided that he should spend the money on her, and once he'd decided that, he felt much better. But he couldn't tell his wife about it. She would be suspicious. And he couldn't tell Liu Jiawen, either, because a man who'd been sick a long time was even more distrustful. Liu would think, how come you're worrying about my wife while you dress your own wife in rags?

Firecrackers were being set off all around as he headed home, and he could tell that a lot of households had started to boil their dumplings. From a distance, he saw his wife on the doorstep waiting for him. As soon as she saw him, she called out, "The water boiled a long time ago. I was so worried, I was just about to go out and look for you."

"What were you worried about?" he said. "I'm just fine."

He washed his hands and face as his wife built up the fire and dropped the dumplings into the boiling water. He cut up a strand of firecrackers and spread half around the courtyard. As they went off, Diabolo started to yowl along with them, his clear voice matching their tone. Chai Wang laughed and said to the dog, "So you know it's the New Year, do you?"

After he'd eaten his dumplings, he went over to Liu Jiawen's house. Liu was wearing a purple V-necked sweater, and his hair was carefully brushed. He was helping his wife make dumplings. Chai said, "You're eating late!" Liu Jiawen answered, "The firecrackers told me you've already eaten." Chai Wang gave Liu half the money they'd made that day, and Liu gave him the new scrolls he'd written. As Chai left, he said, "Your calligraphy is famous now. I'm guessing at least a few hundred families will put up your scrolls this year." For the first time, Chai saw Liu Jiawen really laugh.

The next morning, Chai Wang hurried to the medical supplies store in his pedicab. He wanted to buy the cervical brace for Liu Ying before he went to the market with his scrolls. He was the first customer in the store, so when he complained that the brace was as soft as a pillow and how could it possibly cost that much, the salesperson said, "It's good luck to give the first customer of the year a break, so I'll tell you what, I'll give it to you for seven hundred." Chai Wang thought, since his price is like sugarcane, I can shave a bit more off the top. He said, "Six hundred sixty, or no deal." The salesperson balked, so Chai made as though to leave, thinking, if you're going to treat me like a fish, you're going to have to reel me in. The salesperson stamped his foot and said to Chai's back, "Okay, okay, six hundred sixty. The two sixes are good luck anyway. But I can't give you a receipt, or I'll take a real loss!"

Chai Wang carefully placed the brace in his pedicab and started to pedal toward the Number Two Middle School on the east side. The sky was very dark and the barometric pressure was low, and his chest felt tight. There were a lot of cars and people on the road, and peddlers sell-ing paper money had appeared. He thought about buying the customary paper money to burn at his parents' graves.

Once he'd passed the commercial center and was on the road to the east side, there were fewer cars and pedestrians, and the road seemed tidy and clear. The schools there were the best in the city, the kind of schools his son hadn't tested into, so Chai Wang rarely had reason to see them. The thought of his son spending New Year's Day alone in a prison cell depressed him. It had begun to snow, the kind of thick, insistent flakes that fell at this time of year, and in the blink of an eye the world turned white. He felt the snow's gentle caress, and suddenly he felt happy again.

The old guard outside the Number Two Middle School blocked his way and asked who he was. He said he was looking for an English teacher named Liu Ying. The guard asked him for ID and said that strangers who wanted to go inside had to sign in. Chai Wang said he hadn't brought an ID. The guard shook his head and said, "Well, you can't go in, then." Chai Wang said urgently, "Brother, I'm her neighbor, and there's been an emergency. Can't you help me call her out here?" Taking in Chai's pitiful appearance, the guard thought that maybe there really was an emergency. He squinted at a list of phone numbers pasted to the wall, then made a call. "This is the outside guard," he said. "Can you let English teacher Liu Ying know that there's been an emergency and someone is looking for her?" After a moment, the guard turned to Chai and asked, "What's your name?" Chai told him, and the guard repeated it. The guard clapped the phone down and said, "Just a minute, Teacher Liu is coming."

Chai Wang watched Liu Ying come staggering through the blowing snow, and to him, she was an early breath of spring in her dark green quilted jacket. His heart began to pound, and he pulled his bike outside the gate to avoid being overheard by the guard.

Liu Ying saw him and said, "Brother Chai, what's happened to Jiawen? Did he fall? Did he have a heart attack?"

Chai Wang laughed. He pulled out the cervical brace and said, "Teacher Liu said that you hurt your spine, and he wanted to buy this for you with the money we made selling scrolls. I had a little windfall yesterday, and I worried he wouldn't let me buy it if he knew, so I went and got it on my own. You can just tell him your school bought it for you."

Liu Ying let out a deep breath. Her body grew weak as she listened to him tell the story of the gust of wind blowing the blessing banner that Liu Jiawen had written through someone's balcony door. Chai said, "It's lucky that their central heating drew the banner in; otherwise it would've just floated away." Then he said that it was really a gift from Liu Jiawen, and she had no choice but to accept it.

With gratitude shining on her face, Liu Ying took the brace and said, "I know you and your wife don't even have enough to eat. You should keep the money for yourself. You can return the brace."

He said, "If I returned it, I would be too embarrassed to remain your neighbor. I'd have to move!"

"Then I'll just have to accept it," she said in a trembling voice. "Thank you, Brother Chai!"

Though they were separated by the falling snow, he could feel the tears blossoming in her eyes, and they were the most beautiful flowers he had ever seen.

By the time he finally got to the New World Mall, the snow had slowed to a few flakes here and there. Old Pi saw him and yelled, "I thought you weren't coming with all this snow! They say an early snow makes for a good harvest, so there should be a lot of people buying scrolls today. You would've lost out big if you hadn't shown up."

Chai quickly parked his pedicab and spread the scrolls out on his spot. Against the snowy background, the red paper was as resplendent as a tamarisk tree by a river. Customers began to come as soon as he was set up, and before he knew it he'd sold half of his blessing banners. In the breaks between sales, he couldn't help but look up at the balcony where the banner had flown in. Today the door was shut; perhaps one banner was enough.

He quickly made a hundred kuai. He thought about the money he'd saved by bargaining down the medical supplies salesman, and he abruptly asked Old Pi to watch his stall for him. He went into the mall, and after picking through lots of clothes, he finally bought his wife a jacket for fifty-two kuai. He had wanted to buy a green one, but that would only make his wife's skin look darker. He considered a red one, but it would make her look even plumper. So in the end he chose a blue one instead. The jacket had large flat buttons and old-fashioned embroidery in snowy white thread. He liked it immediately.

When he took the jacket home to his wife that night, she told him, "I already have enough to wear. We're not children, I don't have to have anything new. You really shouldn't waste money like that." That was what she said, but in her heart she dearly wanted to keep it. She hurried to the washbowl and washed her hands before carefully bringing the jacket over to the mirror to try it on. "Come take a peek," she called out. "How does it look?" Chai saw his wife standing there in the soft light, wearing the little blue jacket with white stitching, her posture delicate and her head lifted slightly as she gazed at him. She looked just like a new bride, and he had to give her a kiss. "You look beautiful," he said. "What do you mean, beautiful?" she said. "You're the only one who's interested in this fat old wrinkly body." "Well, if someone else liked it, I'd be mad," he said, and she laughed. That night, Chai Wang had two good meals. During the second "meal," he thought about Liu Ying's liquid eyes as she stood there in the flying snow, and he felt confused. Suddenly he was no longer in the mood. His wife thought he was simply tired and gently stroked his hair, saying, "You've been working all day, you should get some sleep."

By the fifth or sixth day after the New Year, sales had slowed considerably. Everyone who wanted a scroll had already bought one. On the twenty-seventh day of the lunar calendar, Chai Wang went to the mountain to pay his respects to his parents, and when he came home that afternoon, his head felt heavy. Mrs. Chai boiled some ginger tea and made him stay in bed instead of going to work. He felt awful and slept away the whole afternoon. He woke at dusk, and his wife heated some washing water for him. She worried he would get chilled, so she filled the bathtub with pot after pot of hot water, testing the temperature with her hand. "Take a nice bath and let yourself sweat a little," she told him. "You'll feel better right away." He climbed in like an obedient child, squawking about the hot water. He said it was too hot, but she told him to try it for a few minutes. He slowly eased himself in, and the water rose until it nearly overflowed the tub. She splashed water over his shoulders and gently wiped the grime from his body. He stayed in for more than an hour, until the sky was dark and his body was bright red. He felt clean and refreshed when he got out.

He ate a bowl of noodles for dinner, then helped his wife make a date cake. She worked the dough while he pressed dates into the cake one by one, layer after layer. When he found a date riddled with insect holes, he popped the good part in his mouth. He didn't want the New Year's cake to have any imperfections. As they were heating water to steam the cake, they heard an argument coming from next door. They could tell it was a terrible fight even through the walls. Mrs. Chai stopped kneading and said, "They haven't fought for a long time, how can they start again at the New Year?" Chai Wang said, "They'll stop in a minute, don't worry about it." They slid the cake into the steamer and built up the fire. The arguing grew louder, with a man roaring and a woman crying and things crashing to the ground. Mrs. Chai said, "You didn't go to work today. Could he think that you made off with the money? Go tell him you were sick." But Chai said, "Neither of them would be that petty." Then he heard the woman's crying rise to a wail, and Diabolo joined in. "If she's crying like that," he said, "maybe something bad has happened. You should go over and see. I can stay and watch the steamer." Mrs. Chai said, "If we want to check on them, we should go together. If there's nothing wrong, we'll just forget about it. The cake won't be ready for half an hour anyway, and the fire's fine without us." So they locked the door and went over to Teacher Liu's house.

As soon as they went in through the gate, they saw Diabolo up on his hind legs, scratching at the door. He barked mournfully at them until they opened it.

What they found inside didn't look like a house at all. There were shards of broken cups and a shattered teapot strewn all over the floor. In some places, everything was dripping wet. Liu Jiawen sat panting in his wheelchair, his face ashen and his lips pale. Liu Ying was huddled by the desk, sobbing so hard she couldn't get up. Mrs. Chai went over to help her, while Chai Wang said to Liu Jiawen, "You two are educated teachers; what's going on? What could be so bad between a husband and wife?"

Liu Jiawen cried for a moment before he choked out, "Brother Chai, we've been neighbors for many years. You've seen it yourself, do you think I have it easy? I'm a cripple, but am I totally useless around the house? I'll even do women's work, but see what things have come to anyway? She's been running around behind my back!"

Liu Ying had quieted, but her husband's words roused her, and she waved her arms and defended herself in a hoarse whisper. "It's not true! I haven't done anything. How can you not trust me? I've been with you for more than twenty years! I raised two good daughters for you—"

Liu Jiawen broke in, saying that two days ago Liu Ying had come home with a cervical brace and said that her work unit had given it to her. At first he had believed her. But given how expensive the brace was, and that the school was so poor that sometimes they didn't even pay her salary on time, how could they possibly have bought it for her? So today he had given the school a call, and they'd told him that this year's bonus was a box of apples and two bags of sweet dumplings. Then he had known for sure that Liu Ying was lying. Liu Jiawen said, "I know it's from that man who used to pursue her. He's made money these past few years as the director of the Education Bureau. He even bought himself a car, and he can write off anything as a work expense!" He pointed a finger at his wife and yelled, "You think I'm useless, and you've been going behind my back with that man with cockroach calligraphy! And you still deny it! I'm telling you, Liu Ying, I'm not a parasite, and I'm not some mangy dog. You can have your freedom. Tomorrow I'm going to roll myself down to the courthouse and get a divorce!"

Liu Ying was looking helplessly at Chai Wang. Sweat rolled down his back like rain. He'd never felt so trapped in his life. It felt as though someone had framed him by stuffing some stolen item into his pocket so that he couldn't claim innocence. He looked at his wife, then at Liu Ying, then at Liu Jiawen. Then he looked at the glass and ceramic shards all over the floor, and he realized that if he didn't tell the truth, the Lius' marriage would be shattered. But if he did tell the truth, his own marriage might be smashed instead.

As the sweat poured from his body, he managed to open his mouth and tell them all the truth.

Liu Jiawen and his wife fell silent. Mrs. Chai let go of Liu Ying's hand and stood up unsteadily. She walked across the broken glass and out the door. Liu Jiawen asked, "How much did you spend on the thing?" "Six hundred sixty kuai," Chai answered. Then he went to find his wife.

Mrs. Chai went home, and the first thing she did was open the steamer. A section of the steaming cake was already cooked through, gleaming and fragrant as a lotus flower. She carefully pulled it out and put it on the cutting board. She wiped the pot down and put the lid back on. The stove was about to go out, and she squatted to examine the last few embers. She went to the back of the room where the unsold scrolls and banners were. One by one, she stuffed them into the stove. They flared up like bolts of lightning as soon as they hit the fire. Lighting brings rain, but those flares brought a blazing fire, and the pot soon began to boil loudly. Mrs. Chai beat the fire back, then went to grab the blue jacket her husband had bought her. She wadded it up and threw it onto the fire. It was quickly engulfed and let off a puff of smoke as foul as gas.

Chai Wang didn't dare speak a word to his wife. He didn't know how to explain himself. That night as he arranged his quilt to go to sleep, his wife took her blankets into their son's room to sleep. She even closed the door. He heard her crying from the other room, and he felt his heart breaking. He was worried about her, so he kept his eyes open and listened for any movement. Finally, around three in the morning, he heard snores, and he fell asleep himself.

Not long after, Mrs. Chai woke again. She rose and got dressed. She could hear her husband snoring, and she cursed him, thinking, you have no conscience at all, sleeping like that! She was so upset she didn't want to stay in the house, so she went outside for a bit of air. The sky was as dark as her mood. Diabolo growled softly at her in greeting from across the courtyard wall, and she responded irritably, "What are you growling about over there?" Then she thought about old Wang Dian on North Mountain, and suddenly she wanted to see him. She got out her bicycle, strapped on the two sacks as usual, and set out.

The street was deserted. There was barely any wind, but the air was unusually cold. Around the New Year, the sky was very dark. The moon was only a sliver, and to her it looked like a sardonic smile. She pedaled her bicycle slowly. Her eyes and legs had never felt so useless. Her legs were numb and her eyesight was blurry. Once she even slipped off the road and slid into a pile of snow on the shoulder. By the time she made it to the lumberyard, her body ached from falling so much. She found a pile of thick bark and stuffed it piece by piece into the sacks. She tied the sacks to the back of her bicycle, then brushed the bits of wood from her clothes. Dawn was breaking, and she made her way to Wang Dian's lit cabin. If a night guard wanted to sleep, he would often turn on a lamp and let the light do his guarding for him. Mrs. Chai knocked on the door. Wang Dian thought there was something wrong and pulled the door open quickly. A draft of warm air burst out. He was wearing black long underwear and a blue undershirt, and his arms were bronze and muscular.

"Mrs. Chai," he said in surprise, "didn't you say you had enough kindling for the holiday?" "Brother Wang," she said in a small voice, then flung herself against his chest and started to cry. He held her and let her weep without saying a word. At first he held her loosely, but then he tightened his embrace. Mrs. Chai felt something hard rising against her stomach, and she felt as shocked as if she'd seen a ghost. She stopped crying and ran.

She left with her loaded bicycle. She'd never thought that a sixty-year-old man could still be like that. No wonder he had to eat a stack of flatbread a day. I'll never be able to come back, she told herself drearily. My stove's had its last good meal. When she made it out of the lumberyard, she propped her bicycle by the side of the road and sat down in the snow to cry. She startled two crows into cawing. She cried until the sun came up and she had no tears left. Then she climbed back onto her bicycle and pedaled down the cement road. When she got to her alley, she saw Liu Ying bicycling toward her, probably going to work. Liu Ying stopped to wave, calling timidly, "Mrs. Chai—"

"My name isn't Mrs. Chai," she said coldly. "My name is Wang Lianhua."

Chai Wang was squatting by the stove starting the fire. He saw her come in covered with bits of wood, her hair coated with snow, and he covered his face and cried.

The lunar New Year was coming quickly, and neither the Chais nor the Lius had put up scrolls. Liu Jiawen called a Korean restaurant and sold Diabolo for a hundred and eighty kuai. The dog was trussed up, and as he was taken out of the courtyard, he cried like he knew he was facing death. Chai Wang watched from his courtyard, his heart thumping wildly in his chest.

When Liu Jiawen had managed to scrape together six hundred sixty kuai, he rolled his wheelchair over to Chai Wang's place and gave it to him. Chai Wang said shakily, "Please don't do this."

On the eve of the lunar New Year, Mrs. Chai made dumplings. As she was about to boil them, Chai Wang brought out a strand of firecrackers. She stopped him and said, "Today I want to set them off." She found the big dusty lantern in the shed, lit it, and hung it in the courtyard so it illuminated the entryway. Then she rolled up her sleeves and took the lid off their pickling crock. She wrestled the large blue stone out and carried it outside. Her arms were red from the cold pickling liquid, and the stone splattered sour water like tears. She dropped it in the courtyard with a thump and began to beat it with a sledgehammer. But the stone had already undergone a thousand hammerings and was impervious, just sending up sparks. Mrs. Chai redoubled her efforts, and finally the stone started to send chips off in every direction. Finally, with one last smash, it collapsed into a pile of pebbles. Chai Wang stood there watching, stupefied. That crushed smelly rock was his heart. If his wife could destroy that stone, it meant she would never forgive him.

On the first day of the lunar New Year, Mrs. Chai seemed to return to normal. She warmed the date cake, cut it into pieces and arranged it on a platter, and brought it to the table. She put a bit of sugar onto a small plate and set it beside the cake, and without a word began to eat. Chai Wang sat to one side and took a piece of cake. He dipped it into the sugar and took a bite. His mouth was filled with a bitter taste. The past few torturous days had turned his eyes red and his tongue dry. He put the cake down and said to his wife, "You're the one I love, don't you know that?"

She glanced sideways at him and let out a grunt.

"I can't take the way you're treating me," he said.

She grunted again.

Chai Wang couldn't take it anymore, and he felt the world dim. His body dipped to one side, and his head whacked against the table as he lost consciousness.

When he woke up, it was the next morning. He was lying in bed and felt as light as a ball of cotton. He could smell the familiar scent of mugwort, and he managed to turn his head to see his wife sitting beside the bed watching over him. As a new bride, she'd often burned mugwort to freshen the air. He loved the smell, a sort of sweetness carried by bitterness. In the summer she liked to pick mugwort and dry it in the sun. But over the long years of hardship, she had gradually stopped gathering it.

"That mugwort smells nice," he told her weakly.

She was about to reply when the door opened and Liu Ying and Shunshun came in. Shunshun was wearing a green quilted jacket, and her face was flushed. She carried a green and white bag. Liu Ying said, "Shunshun's just off the train. She couldn't make it back for the lunar New Year because she went to visit Chai Gao."

Shunshun wished Mrs. Chai a happy New Year, and then, as if everything were fine, she told them that Chai Gao had gotten taller and had acne. In prison, he had learned to play the accordion and was a member of an arts club. He had asked her to bring back a present he'd made for the family.

Chai Wang struggled to sit up and said eagerly, "Let's see it."

Shunshun took the present out of her bag. It was a square straw mat. Chai Wang was just about to say, "What's so good about that thing?" when Shunshun turned it over, and woven into the straw was the outline of the character for "blessing." It wasn't written on top, but rather had been woven into the mat with strips of green cloth. The character looked like a willow branch reaching toward water, full of vitality.

Chai Wang looked at his wife and said, "It's very good."

She said, "He has prospects as a craftsman."

Shunshun didn't know what had happened between them, and she said exuberantly, "Chai Gao made two, one for my family, too!"

Chai Wang said nothing, but Mrs. Chai mumbled to herself, "Like father, like son."

Liu Ying lowered her chin and brushed at the front of her jacket, though there was no dust on it.

Shunshun's stomach suddenly growled as loudly as a cuckoo's cry. She laughed and said, "I'm so hungry, my stomach's eaten itself! I think Dad's already boiled up some frozen dumplings. I'm going back to eat." And she was gone like a wisp of smoke.

Liu Ying lifted her head and said, "You two probably haven't had breakfast yet. I'd better get back, too."

Chai Wang implored his wife with his eyes, hoping she would show Liu Ying out.

Mrs. Chai pursed her lips tightly, but she walked Liu Ying to the door.

As she left, Liu Ying said, "Sister Wang, I'm just your old neighbor, and you still were kind enough to escort me out. Thank you."

Liu Ying saw that Mrs. Chai was frowning, and she thought she must not like to be called by her last name, so she said quickly, "Sister Lianhua, come over for a chat when you have time."

Mrs. Chai couldn't stand it any longer and cried out, "My name is Mrs. Chai!"

Liu Ying let out a breath and said gently, "Mrs. Chai, I'm off, then."

After the Chais had breakfast together, Chai Wang took the mat his son had made and put it beside the door. He wasn't sure where to hang it. As for Mrs. Chai, she was thinking that the day was sunny and there wasn't much wind, and it was a shame to stay inside. So she grabbed her bags and rake and rode her bicycle out through the gates to go gather kindling. When she got to the cement road, she turned by habit toward North Mountain. Not far from the lumberyard, she saw a sparrow hopping on top of an enormous snowdrift. The snowdrift was so familiar, she suddenly remembered that she'd sat on it herself once, that time when she had stopped to cry. And then she remembered that she couldn't go to the lumberyard anymore.

Dejected, she turned her bicycle around and rode over to the Wuji River. There was no bark to be had there, just withered willow branches and blackened tree stumps. To break them down, she would need an axe and a saw. She regretted that she hadn't brought them with her.

Love and Its Lack
Are Emblazoned on the Heart

Fang Fang

TRANSLATED BY ELEANOR GOODMAN

1

As the bird flew directly overhead, Yao Qin watched a white glob drop through the sunlight onto Xin Rong's hair. Her gasp was a sharp pin that pierced the tense assembly hall, and it started a disturbance like a distended balloon releasing air. Startled, she covered her mouth with her hand. The general manager of the factory was onstage reading out names. He paused. His gaze fell on Yao Qin, and he announced her name. She stiffened as the others turned to look at her. She had never thought this round of layoffs would affect her.

Yao Qin believed herself to be good-looking. Whenever one of the factory managers saw her, he would smile, and Xin Rong would pinch her arm and say, "Look, the manager's smiling at you again." She noticed it, too. *Everyone likes a pretty face*, she thought to herself. And wasn't hers just as pretty as a picture? So she'd assumed she would never be laid off, and she hadn't thought about what she would do if she were. But today as she half-listened to them announcing the names, she heard her own. Everyone else heard it as well. She recoiled as though she'd been clubbed with a stick, split open with a knife, and fallen against a floor covered with spikes. Pain engulfed her body.

Xin Rong, who had long since prepared to be laid off, hadn't been called. Yao Qin couldn't help looking over at her, and saw that her face was flushed with excitement. Yao Qin had never thought Xin Rong was pretty, but now she appeared to be. And Yao Qin suddenly understood why she'd been fired: Xin Rong was the pretty picture now, while her own scenery had faded. She had thought the managers were smiling at her, but actually they'd been smiling at Xin Rong. She felt terrible, and a bit angry. She had once liked their managers, but now she hated them. She thought, *They looked at me so much it aged me, and now they're going to throw me away like an old rag?*

She had a good cry when she got home. She cried hopelessly through the dinner hour. The room was silent; no one was there to hear her. The phone rang, and she wiped her tears before she answered. The person on the other line said nothing and instead just started crying. She could tell it was Xin Rong. *What do you have to cry about*, Yao Qin thought. As though she'd heard her thoughts, Xin Rong said, "Yao Qin, I know you're going to say *what does she have to cry about . . .* but I just need to cry. I feel terrible. I thought I was the one who was going to be laid off. I didn't try to talk to the managers, I just got ready for it to happen . . ." Yao Qin hung up on her. She had stopped weeping. She thought, *Xin Rong is crying harder than I was.* She wanted to call her back, but her hand hesitated, and in the end she didn't.

The room was so quiet she could hear the air move. Moonlight flowed onto the windowsill like water. She sat for a while, then pulled out a photo of Yang Jingguo. Last month she had finally put all of his photos away, after they'd kept her company on her thirty-eighth birthday. She'd looked at them as she got drunk alone, crying and drinking. Through a haze of tears, she suddenly thought that Yang Jingguo was staring at her fiercely, displeased with her. He'd never looked at her that way before, and she felt worried and didn't know what she'd done wrong. That night, as she held his photo against her chest while she slept, he emerged from a river mist. He stood on the opposite bank and told her that he was unhappy on the other side. He was unhappy because he had promised to bring Yao Qin a lifetime of joy, and he hadn't done it. His clothes were damp and clammy, and they never dried. Yao Qin had been crying for ten years, and every tear had landed on him. He begged her to let him wear dry clothes. When she heard that, she started to cry again and saw that raindrops had begun to fall on his head. His clothes were already so wet that they clung to his body. "Look at that," he said. "Can't you smile for a while and give me some sunshine?" The rain followed him as he left. She woke up and saw that Yang Jingguo's photo was stained with water-marks. That day, she gathered up all of his photos and put them away. She had to give him dry clothes and sunshine. She had to be happy.

But now she had been laid off, and that meant she no longer had an income. It meant that the company she had given twenty years of her life to had just thrown her out on the street. It meant that they didn't want her, that she was useless. She felt wronged, and as she wiped away her tears, she said to Yang Jingguo, "I'm sorry I'm getting your clothes wet. I'm sorry, I'll get them dry again."

———

The love story between Yang Jingguo and Yao Qin was famous in their factory. It was the first story new workers heard when they arrived. The story started like this: Ten years ago . . .

Ten years ago, Yang Jingguo had been sent to work at the factory after college. On his first day, bowl in hand, he had to ask for directions to the cafeteria. The person he asked was Yao Qin, either by chance or because she was beautiful. At that time, Yao Qin had a boyfriend named Zhang Sanyong. Zhang's biggest fear was that she would run off with another man, and when he saw her talking to an elegant man in glasses, he exploded. Without saying a word, he ran over and punched Yang Jiangguo. Before poor Yang had met a single person there, he met someone's fist. One of Yang's eyes turned black and blue, and on the other side his glasses were totally shattered. Yao Qin was furious and screamed at Zhang. She felt responsible, and apologized to Yang three separate times. She took him to the hospital and bought him new glasses. After that, every time she encountered him she felt guilty. Yang Jingguo was a technician, and when she saw him in the workshop, she would try to help him out. Over the course of things, they started to fall in love. The other factory workers laughed at Zhang Sanyong, saying that with one jealous punch he had pushed his girlfriend into another man's embrace.

Yang Jingguo was from the countryside, and his parents hadn't had much time for him as they worked from dawn until dusk. He felt like he had raised himself. He'd grown up with the hearth and the trees beside the village and lonely old foreman Chen's ox. In college, because he was so poor and felt inferior, he hadn't dared look for a girlfriend. His life was rough, and it seemed to him that it wouldn't matter to anyone in the world if he lived or died. He was terribly lonely. But then Zhang Sanyong's fist had brought him Yao Qin's attentions. It wasn't much at first, but suddenly his heart felt warm, and he fell in love with her. For a man like Yang, who had never loved before, the emotions were uncontrollable. He wanted to be with her every second. Because of this, Zhang Sanyong had hit him a few more times and destroyed several pairs of glasses, but that didn't stop the love that burst forth from his chest. Yao Qin had dated Zhang Sanyong only because they were part of the same work unit. They had never talked about love and didn't really know what it was. They thought that if their ages were appropriate and neither of them was too hard to look at, they would just get the right papers and settle down. That seemed like love. But then Yang Jingguo appeared, and Yao Qin suddenly felt differently. She didn't understand the new longing in her heart. She only knew that when Yang stared dumbly at her, she felt flustered and her heart beat wildly, and she wanted to pour out her feelings to him. One day she fought with Zhang Sanyong and decided to break up with him. It rained that night, but Yang Jingguo still came to find her. He waited outside her door for hours, getting soaked. When Yao Qin came home upset, she found Yang standing there like a bedraggled rooster. Her pulse raced, and without saying anything, they embraced. She wanted to cry, but before she had a chance to, he started to weep. They both cried and cried and decided that they never wanted to be separated again. In the face of that kind of love, Zhang Sanyong could only resentfully withdraw.

It was true love, the kind that many women long for. They met every day, and in the evenings they went for long walks along the river, holding hands and returning late. At lunchtime they would ignore the stares and sit together in the cafeteria. Like actors in a TV show, they would feed each other from their own bowls. Yao Qin didn't eat fatty meat, so Yang Jingguo would remove it from her bowl and give her the lean bits from his bowl. She liked to eat vegetable leaves but not stems, so he would give her all of his leaves and take all of her stems. Each time they ate, he busied himself with these tasks, and sometimes his earnestness brought tears to her eyes. She knew she could be happy with that kind of man. How had she been so lucky? And she became even gentler and more considerate toward him. At the New Year, Yang Jingguo always went home to see his parents, but after he met Yao Qin he didn't want to go. She told him to go back home, but he said he couldn't leave her. He told her he couldn't bear to be away from her for even a day. The whole world would turn dark, and he wouldn't know what to do. So Yao Qin wept and told him not to go. She told the girls in her work unit what Yang had said, and they all wept, too, and said a man like that was worth dying for. Only Zhang Sanyong said, "Would a real man talk like that?" She paid no attention to him, but rallied her friends to ask Zhang, "Why wouldn't a man talk like that? Why wouldn't he say things that make his girl happy? How could saying things like that make him less of a man?"

Her life before she met Yang Jingguo was completely different from the one she had now. Over the years they were together, she only grew more beautiful. The other workers said in surprise, "Who knew that a man's love could make a woman even prettier?" Although Yang was clever and good at his job, he hadn't become known at the factory for his skills;

rather, it was because he'd begun dating Yao Qin that nearly everyone knew who he was. One year the factory had put on a Labor Day celebration, and as a joke the emcee asked the women workers who the most popular male worker was. Before he even finished speaking, they began to shout, "Yang Jingguo!" The assistant secretary of the factory was a woman, and even she shouted his name. The other men were shocked. When they'd recovered, they started to yell at Yang Jingguo, saying that he'd ruined the atmosphere at the factory and was causing trouble in a lot of marriages. Yao Qin once asked Yang if he minded that people made fun of him. He only laughed and said that the others didn't understand. Happiness was being able to truly love a woman.

Yang Jingguo wanted to get married right away, but the factory hadn't given him his own apartment. A few times when the others had gone off to watch a soccer game, he and Yao Qin were secretly together in his dormitory. Once she wasn't careful and got pregnant. He took her to the countryside to get an abortion. After that, he tried to control himself as much as possible. He said, "Qin Qin, I can't hurt you like that again. I want to get married as soon as possible." After they had dated for three years and eight months, he was finally given an apartment. That day after work, they went together to look at the place. It was a spring evening with a mist of rain, so Yao Qin held an umbrella open over them as she rode on the back of his bicycle. All of a sudden, a large truck barreled past them. She hadn't seen it coming. She heard Yang yell, "Jump for it!" She didn't know what was happening, but she jumped off, feeling a car brush past her before she caught her balance. Yang Jingguo and his bicycle were struck and pushed all the way to the other side of the road. A woman was struck at the same time, while Yang's head smashed against a rock on the highway shoulder. There was blood everywhere, pooling together. Yao Qin screamed as she ran to Yang's side. Wailing, she cradled him to her. He opened his eyes and said with a faint smile, "Don't cry, give me a smile." She whimpered and forced herself to smile. He said, "Now I feel better." That was the last thing he said to her. Yao Qin grieved until she wanted to throw herself against the same rock and return to Yang's side. But Xin Rong watched her like a hawk, and each time she saw Yao Qin about to collapse, she would shout for someone to restrain her. After a while, Yao Qin pulled herself together. She knew that Yang Jingguo wouldn't want her to die. Everyone at the factory pitied her, and although apartments were in very short supply, no one wanted to take back the one meant for her and Yang. And so she had lived there ever since, absently passing the years.

—

Her tears had dried. She wiped Yang Jingguo's photograph with a towel. The frame was shiny, and Yang was smiling. She stroked his lips with her index finger, then wrapped the picture in his sweater and set it back inside the trunk. She thought, *The weather's getting colder, I can't let his clothes get damp anymore.*

She still felt uneasy, perhaps because she knew she'd gotten his clothing wet again. So she went into the bathroom and carefully washed her face and put on makeup. She smiled in the mirror for him. He would definitely see her, and she felt as though the sun had burst out over the riverbank and was shining down on him. But that didn't change the fact that she'd been laid off from work.

2

Yao Qin's mother was an elementary school teacher who had long since retired. Those who took early retirement might have more relaxed lives, but they didn't get as nice a pension as those who retired later. Her father had worked away from home for many years as a geologist. When he came back, he was too restless to just hang around the house, so he opened a small bookstore. Business was bad at first, and he could barely make ends meet. Her mother started to work there, too, and added an awning in the front to rent videos. The polytechnic school was nearby, and once students started to come and rent movies, business gradually improved. Her mother moved the videos into the main store and divided the space under the awning into three small sections the size of chicken hutches, into which she put a television and a video player. Each space was just big enough to seat two people, and she hung up a piece of blue cloth to keep out the sunlight. That way, in addition to renting videos, people could rent a place to watch them. That was very popular with the students, and nearly every night pairs of students or young couples would come to watch a movie. Business took off. People would even come during the day to watch movies for ten kuai a pop. It was cheap entertainment, and so many customers came that the video players ran nonstop. In just a few years, two of the machines had to be replaced.

The day after she was laid off, Yao Qin called her mother. Her mother told her to come home, saying, "The factory might not need you, but we do." She felt better hearing that, and she carried that feeling as she went to the eastern suburbs to visit Yang Jingguo's grave on Pine Hill. This time she didn't cry; she simply cleared the weeds from his grave and arranged the flowers she'd brought in the cement vase. Then she crouched down and asked him softly, "What am I supposed to do now?" She didn't hear his answer, only the sound of the wind. The weather had grown cold, so she knew she couldn't cry.

Yao Qin's mother wanted her to work at the store, but she refused. She didn't say why. She knew she could do almost anything, but not that. Once she had gone into the bookstore to grab something and had brushed against the curtain to the video rooms. She saw a young couple holding each other and kissing as they half-watched the video. She stared at them, shaking as though in a storm. Suddenly the feeling of Yang Jingguo's embraces overtook her. She ended up leaving without the thing she'd wanted, and went back into the house to cry.

Ten years had gone by, the time passing in dribs and drabs. She was thirty-eight and could see forty approaching. Wrinkles had climbed up from her heart onto her forehead. But those four years she'd spent with Yang Jingguo were the longest she'd had, tucked away deep inside her heart.

Yao Qin continued to refuse to work in the bookstore. Her father sensed what the problem was, and told her mother, "Don't force her. Let her do what she wants to do." Then he said to Yao Qin, "Go find a good man to marry you. Jingguo would have wanted you to have a family. You think you can go through life alone? If you never find someone, do you think Jingguo will be able to rest in peace?"

Yao Qin didn't respond. Her father had said this all before, and she hadn't wanted to listen. But this time she heard him. She'd known that the issue would come up sooner or later, and now that she was unemployed, she might as well face it.

Her mother saw the expression on her face, and knew that a little crack had opened in her heart. Over the past ten years, if someone mentioned to Yao Qin that she should find another man, her face would harden and she would lash out like someone had come to steal her husband away. After that happened, no one would dare mention it. But her mother knew that once a heart cracked open a little bit, some fresh air could flow in. Perhaps it was just a tiny breeze, but it could still dry up the mold and help the heart's greenery grow again. And for the first time in the ten years since Yang Jingguo's death, Yao Qin's mother let out a sigh of relief.

Yao Qin was much calmer returning to her apartment after her visit home. What she felt wasn't a happy, contented calm; it was more like smooth water, a kind of letting go. The next morning, she went to the factory office to settle her affairs. She initially thought she would go to the general manager's office to say goodbye, but when she went to his door and saw him and his secretary chatting about emigrating and laughing loudly, she grew cold. She left and went to the workshop to turn in her toolbox. The workshop director wanted her to say goodbye to everyone, but she thought about the general manager and his secretary laughing together and told him to forget it. She had worked there for twenty years, but when she left, she didn't say goodbye to anyone. She was completely at a loss, floating in the middle of a vast ocean as the sounds of the workers and machines dissolved in the mist rising off the water.

In fact, her fellow workers had seen her and wanted to call out to her, but the look on her face stopped them. They watched helplessly as she left the workshop, her footsteps leaden, her silhouette wavering with exhaustion and sorrow. Everyone who saw her felt a jolt of sadness, and it was under those gazes that Yao Qin disappeared.

Yao Qin didn't leave the house for three days. She used that time to rearrange every piece of furniture she owned. She didn't know why, but she knew that if she did nothing, she'd suffocate. On the fourth day, she had done everything she could in the house. At loose ends, she lay down in bed. Everything was so still that she felt as though the air had solidified and fossilized her room.

She thought, *I'm just going to lie here and not think about a single thing, not even Yang Jingguo.*

3

That night, Yao Qin's mother knocked on the door, and she dragged herself out of bed. Her hair was messy, and she looked exhausted. Her mother cried, "For heaven's sake, child, what's the matter?" Yao Qin said, "Nothing, I'm just tired from napping." Her mother told her, "Well, you should get up and rest for a while."

Her mother drank a glass of water as she watched Yao Qin brush her hair and wash her face. A friend of hers, the retired principal of Fangshuo's Middle School No. 5, had just had his birthday, and he had invited a few other retired principals to come to his house for a little party. The principal had told her about a nice chemistry teacher named Chen who taught at his school. Chen had patiently nursed his bedridden paralyzed wife for nine years. The local television station had even done a report on him. Six months ago his wife had died, and everyone had started to introduce him to new women. The principal said that these days a goodhearted man was a rare find. Yao Qin's mother said that her daughter was loyal and could love a man wholeheartedly, and that was a rare find, too. The other principals all agreed that they should introduce Yao Qin and Teacher

Chen, since they seemed like a perfect match. Yao Qin's mother told her, "Teacher Chen doesn't have children. He just turned forty-two, which means he's four years older than you, which is perfect." After lunch, the principal had gone to find Teacher Chen, and Chen said he'd like to meet Yao Qin.

Yao Qin's heart beat loudly. Perhaps her heart had opened up a crack, but in truth Yang Jingguo's shadow was still in her mind's eye. That shadow pressed down upon her, permeating her body through her every pore. It infiltrated her heart, streaming into all the empty corners until even the crack was blocked. "Forget it, Mom," Yao Qin said. "I don't feel like dating." Her mother said anxiously, "Haven't we been through this already? It won't be easy for you to find someone at this age. Teacher Chen is a college graduate, and handsome to boot. Perhaps he was sent down from heaven just for you." Yao Qin was silent. Teacher Chen seemed wonderful in many ways, better than any of the other men she'd been introduced to, but her heart still resisted. She said, "I'm just not ready yet. He had a wife and took care of her for almost ten years without complaining, so he must have really loved her. I don't want to get in the middle of that, and I wouldn't be with a man like that anyway, and besides, he could never replace Yang Jingguo." Her words flew out in a quick stream.

Her mother muttered recriminations until she was so agitated she leapt from her chair. Yao Qin couldn't hear exactly what she was saying. She silently asked Yang Jingguo, who was standing on the opposite bank, *Do you want me to go out with that other man?*

Her mother went on and on, but when she saw Yao Qin sitting there as though mesmerized, she finally stopped. She sighed and said, "Well, I wasted my efforts on you. I really thought you would agree to meet him. Since his wife was hurt in a car accident just like Jingguo, I thought you two would have a lot in common."

Yao Qin stared blankly, then asked, "His wife also died in a car accident?" Her mother said, "She was paralyzed by a car, so all she could do was eat and shit. She couldn't move or speak, so tell me, what has that poor man been through? He's even unluckier than you. He deserves a woman who'll give him a nice, comfortable life."

Yao Qin suddenly thought about the woman who'd been struck by the truck just after Yang Jingguo. She remembered that as she'd cradled Yang and cried, there was also a man holding a woman and wailing. She relived the brutal scene in her head, then said quietly to her mother, "Okay, I'll meet him."

—

The principal of Middle School No. 5 arranged for them to meet at a bar. The place was called "Sculpting in Time." The principal said young people liked to go there to drink and soak up the atmosphere. Yao Qin's mother said that Chen and her daughter weren't young anymore. The principal said that in order for them to fall in love, they had to feel young again. So she agreed.

Yao Qin wore a long dress and a white cashmere sweater on the date. She wasn't sure she wanted to meet him, but she dressed well anyway. She didn't put on any makeup, but she did go to the local beauty shop to have her face exfoliated, her eyebrows plucked, and her nails done. So although she wasn't exactly decked out for an imperial audience, she looked radiant.

She followed her mother into Sculpting in Time. The principal and the man beside him both stood up. When Yao Qin noticed the name of the place, she thought, *Can time be sculpted? If it can, do we use our own tangled lives to shape it?* As she was thinking, she heard the principal say with surprise, "I had no idea Yao Qin was so young. She doesn't even look thirty." She heard her mother answer, "She's been pretty since she was a little girl. She's never shown her age."

After the principal and Yao Qin's mother had exchanged a few pleasantries, they excused themselves, saying that they weren't used to bars and would go to the teahouse just across the way, and Yao Qin and Teacher Chen should talk together. They were gone before anyone had time to agree or disagree.

The bar was playing sentimental music. Sometimes you go to a bar to get sentimental; after savoring the feeling, your frazzled heart can find peace for a while. The music surrounded Yao Qin and seeped into her heart like seawater leaking into a ship's hold, rising drop by drop. It irritated her and made her feel tired. She sat down and lowered her chin, not looking at Teacher Chen. Her silent unhappiness was written all over her pale face. She still hadn't gotten a good look at him. All she recalled were the thin voices of her mother and the principal, like the last bit of toothpaste being squeezed out of a tube. It was totally different from Yang Jingguo's voice. His voice was simple and gentle, and he could move her just by opening his mouth. He sang beautiful songs at karaoke. But Teacher Chen's voice was low and weak, and she didn't like it. The more she thought about it, the worse she felt. But she didn't know how she could make an exit, so she just sat there.

The low voice across from her suddenly spoke. He said, "My name is Chen Fumin." She nodded her head slightly. He said, "I didn't know you were so young and pretty. If I'd known, I would never have had the courage to meet you." She forced herself to smile. He said, "It's okay if you don't think I'm good enough. If you want to leave right now, you can. I won't mind. This kind of thing has to do with fate, and it's no good for anybody to try to force it."

Yao Qin suddenly felt like the low voice wasn't quite as awful as she'd thought. She lifted her head and smiled at him. "Thank you," she said. Then she stood up and left. She had taken a few steps before she felt that she'd been terribly rude. She turned around and waved to him. As she did, she caught an impression of him. Thin body, white face, long hair. His eyes were large, and he looked stunned. She thought, So this is Chen Fumin.

She left the bar and let out a long sigh. The sun was shining brightly on the street, and everything looked lovely. Advertising banners flapped in the wind. The men and women walking by were all smiling. Someone called across the street. Loud music flowed out of the decorated door of a boutique, making the whole street sing.

The world was truly wonderful. She stood there waiting to cross the street. The cars flowed steadily by like water, and she couldn't get across. She watched the cars and the street scene, and realized that she was lonely. Lonely down to her bones. She was so empty inside that any sound would echo and reverberate painfully against her bones, and that pain would spread through her whole body.

She felt very tired and leaned against an electrical pole. Someone asked her if she was all right. The voice was thin, and she realized it was Chen Fumin. She said, "I'm fine. I just have to cross the street to catch the bus." Chen said, "I'm going that way, too." She wasn't sure how to answer, so she just stared unblinkingly at the cars passing tight on each other's bumpers. Her neck felt stiff. He said, "This part of the road is always busy, but there's a pedestrian overpass up ahead. It's safer to cross there." She glanced at him, and he said, "I'll show you."

Without thinking, she went with him to the bridge a few meters ahead. They didn't speak to each other until they were crossing over the street. Chen said, "If I biked and took the shortcut, it would only take me a few minutes to get home. But since the accident, I haven't dared to get on a bike." Yao Qin's heart thumped, and she said, "Me neither." He said, "It's better to be careful. Always take the pedestrian bridge if there is one. Don't jaywalk just to save a little time. There's no need." She said, "I feel the same way."

A few children came running past, and Yao Qin's shoulder brushed against Chen's arm as she moved aside to let them by. It had been a long time since she'd walked beside a man, or even talked to one, and her heartbeat quickened.

Yao Qin got to her bus stop first. Chen Fumin said, "Will you give me your phone number?" She hesitated, then nodded. She was thinking that the milk deliveryman and water deliveryman and coal deliveryman all had her number, so why couldn't she give it to him? She wrote her number in the notebook Chen held out, and he tore off a piece of paper with his. She didn't want his number, but it would be rude to refuse, so she took it. She glanced at it and saw that not only had he written his office and home number, he had added his cellphone as well.

Yao Qin's bus rumbled up, and she politely said goodbye and got on. He stood there watching her until the bus pulled away. As she looked at him, she suddenly felt a familiar warmth. She thought, *How come he looks so much like Yang Jingguo?*

That night as she got ready to take a shower, she discovered the note with Chen's phone numbers in her pocket. An image of him standing at the bus stop and the sound of his low voice came into her head. She laughed, crumpled the paper up, and threw it into the toilet. It floated there until she flushed, and with a gurgle it was sucked away. She thought, *So that's that, then.*

———

4

———

The next day, Yao Qin's mother called her to come home so she could feed her spare ribs and scold her soundly. Her father sat nearby sighing. They both felt that Yao Qin was a victim of bad fate. She had met a good man, but he died. She was introduced to another good man, but she cast him aside. Her father said, "Teacher Chen would make an even better husband than Yang Jingguo. He's responsible and was so good to his wife. You're not going to find anyone else like him." Yao Qin let them talk without comment.

The news was over, so Yao Qin's mother sat down to watch soap operas. *Deep Emotions in Drizzling Rain* was on. As she watched, she twisted a handkerchief in her hands, and every time someone onscreen cried, she sobbed along. She even proclaimed, "If I were a few decades younger, I would have an earth-shattering, heart-stopping love affair." Her father glanced over, shocked, and said that since she'd retired, she had gone soft in the head.

Yao Qin never watched soap operas and thought that her mother's earnest words were silly. She'd already had a love affair like that with Yang

Jingguo. It had been heart-stopping, but that was over. The earth had shattered, and it hadn't come back together. What was so great about that? It was fine to watch that kind of love, but what point was there to feeling it oneself? The pain was endless. And after that kind of pain, she wanted nothing to do with love ever again.

And so loveless Yao Qin quietly left as her mother watched her soap opera.

It was dark by the time she got back to her building. The moonlight dissolved on the ground in the light from the streetlamps. There was a small flowerbed just beyond the door where red roses were in bloom. Someone was sitting beside the garden smoking. The smoke swirled up in front of his face, and he seemed lonely, with the single glow of the cigarette as his only companion. As she walked past, he stood up and asked in a low voice, "Yao Qin, is that you?"

She was surprised to hear Chen Fumin's voice, and her heart skipped a beat. He was embarrassed that he'd startled her. He said he had asked the retired principal for her address. He didn't know why, but he wanted to see her. Though he'd only met her once, he felt close to her, and he hadn't felt that way with other women. He quickly explained that for a while a lot of people had introduced him to possible girlfriends, and each time it had felt awkward. But this time, she hadn't made him feel awkward at all; instead he'd been excited. He didn't know where the excitement came from, he just wanted to see her again. Yao Qin said nothing as Chen talked and talked.

People from the apartment complex kept walking past. They were from the factory and knew Yao Qin's story. When they saw her there with another man, they had to take a good look. She couldn't stand being stared at, so she interrupted Chen and said, "Let's go inside."

Chen immediately shut up and followed her inside. His eyes lit up, then darkened again. For a single woman, her financial situation was decent, and her living room was nicely decorated, with not a speck of dust on the windowsills or chairs. He thought how comfortable it would be to live in such a nice house. When she gestured for him to sit down on the couch, he couldn't help but let out a sigh.

She said, "Why are you sighing? You don't like my house?" He said, "How could I not? I was sighing because I was thinking of my own place. Yours is a heaven and mine is a hell." "You're exaggerating," she said. He said, "Maybe a bit. I'll say it another way. Your place is a flower garden, mine is a garbage dump." "That's still an exaggeration," she said. "You don't believe it?" he asked. "You'll know when you see it." She didn't answer, thinking, *That'll be the day.*

They were quiet for a few moments, so she turned on the TV. The music show *The Same Old Song* was on. The veteran singer Zhang Xingzheng was singing a well-known piece, "Passing by Springtime, Passing by Myself." Chen began to whistle along. He whistled very well, blending in with the tune. Zhang Xingzheng sang with great vigor and filled the whole auditorium, and there on her couch Chen's whistle sounded forlorn. She sat quietly listening to him instead of to the singer on TV. She thought, *What's wrong with me? Why did I let him in, and why am I sitting here listening to him whistle?*

When the song was over, she said, "I didn't know you had such talent." He said, "I only have that one talent. Besides, that song is the best to whistle along with, so it gave me a chance to shine." She laughed and said, "Isn't that lucky." Chen Fumin said, "Sometimes things are so lucky that you can't believe they're happening." "Really?" she said. "I've never experienced that." He laughed and said, "I haven't either, but that's the way it happens in books." She said, "I never did a lot of reading. That's how I ended up a factory worker." He said, "It doesn't really make a difference how much you read, it's what you do with it." She said, "How could it not make a difference? If I'd gone to college, I wouldn't have been laid off." He said, "I went to college, and I haven't been laid off, but isn't my life still a complete mess? So like I said, it's all what you do with it. In the end it doesn't really matter how much education you have." Yao Qin thought that made no sense, but she didn't want to argue with him. He continued, "Every person is different. A country kid like me has to go to college if he wants to change his fate." She had just been thinking about Yang Jingguo, and it occurred to her that it hadn't necessarily been good that he'd changed his fate. If he had stayed in the countryside, he would definitely still be alive. But then she thought that was wrong: if he had lived in the countryside, he'd have seen nothing of the world, and wasn't that just like never really living? It was worse than dying young. So it was a good thing he had changed his fate. These thoughts went around and around in her head until she felt completely confused.

Chen Fumin saw her daydreaming, and he worried that she was unhappy. He thought that maybe he'd been a bit out of line. He needed to take things slowly, otherwise she'd soon get sick of him. So he stood up and said somewhat guiltily, "I'm sorry for turning up in front of your house so rudely. I'm just lonely, and I needed someone to talk to. I have trouble talking to other people, but for some reason I feel close to you. Maybe because our lives have been so similar." As he spoke, he walked toward the door.

She stood up, thinking that although his voice was low and weak, he sounded completely sincere. She felt moved and warm inside. The fact was that she, too, was lonely and needed someone to talk to. He didn't bother her, and his whistling made her house seem more like a home.

She followed him out to the door. She hadn't invited him to stay longer, but as he went to open the door, he suddenly turned around and asked her, "Would you mind if I called you sometime?" She was following him closely, and when he turned, it brought them face-to-face, so close that she could feel his breath. He smelled masculine, and she felt so dizzy that she didn't really hear what he said.

He hadn't expected to be so close to her, either, and he was suddenly taken in by her sweet perfume. Before he could stop himself, he pulled her into his arms. Frightened, she struggled for a moment, but soon she was intoxicated by his embrace, and her whole body relaxed. She buried her head in his chest. Overcome with joy, he held her tightly, stroking her hair and shoulders. Their cheeks were pressed together as they both trembled. They had embraced for a long time before he sought out her lips. Her lips were as red and hot as embers, and when he felt them, his body caught fire.

At that moment, Yao Qin understood that although she might not need love, she still needed something. That something was lying latent in her body, and she couldn't control it. It was an animal that had been locked up for ten years, hidden, and now it took her over with a vengeance. *Go ahead*, she thought, *run free*.

It was midnight by the time Chen Fumin left. He had class the next day and had to hurry back to the school. He asked her, "Can I visit you again?" She said, "What do you think?"

He knew exactly what she meant.

5

It was a cloudy day, with a dark sky that threatened rain. Yao Qin thought about what she and Chen Fumin had done, and she felt ashamed and also wronged. So despite the terrible weather, she rose early to go to Pine Hill. It wasn't a grave-visiting holiday, but she brought flowers anyway. She purchased some incense at the foot of the hill, and just as she lit it by the grave, the sky began to drizzle. She had an umbrella, and, worried that the rain would extinguish the incense, she knelt and held the umbrella over it. The sweet smoke hovered there as the rain soaked her back.

Only when the incense had burned down did she say, "Jingguo, I'm lonely. His name is Chen Fumin. Is it okay if I date him? If you have any thoughts about it, you can tell me in a dream. I will do whatever you want me to do."

She began sneezing before she had even made it home. As soon as she was inside, she made herself some ginger tea. She knew she couldn't afford to get sick, since the hospital was corrupt, and even if there was nothing really wrong, they would charge her half a month's salary if she went to see a doctor. She didn't want her money to turn into a doctor's bonus. When she'd had her tea, she went to lie down. It was just a short rest, but she dreamt that Yang Jingguo was smiling at her in the river mist. His smile was wide and bright. She was so happy, she called to him, and promptly woke up. She thought, *Does that mean he approves of my being with Chen Fumin?*

It rained harder and harder until nightfall. The rain pounding on her windows made her house seem even quieter. She lay in bed, not wanting to get up. After all, she'd be alone if she got up, though she was just as alone lying there. She hadn't moved all afternoon and wasn't even hungry. She wasn't sleepy, and she didn't want to get up. She watched the room as the light outside slowly faded, and then as it approached dark, an orangish light appeared, and she knew the streetlamps had come on.

A sudden knock at her door surprised her. No one had knocked at her door at night for many years. "Who is it?" she called. "It's me," said the low, weak voice. She hesitated, thinking she could tell him that she was already asleep, but then she thought of Yang Jingguo's bright smile, and she said, "Just a minute." She quickly pulled a V-neck sweater out of her dresser. Then she ran into the bathroom and pulled her hair up into a messy bun, strands escaping everywhere. There wasn't enough time to wash her face and put on makeup, so she just wiped her skin with a wet washcloth and rubbed in a bit of lotion before going to open the door.

Chen Fumin was holding a bunch of vegetables in one hand and an umbrella in the other. He came in and set the umbrella down, saying, "Sorry to burst in on you like this. I saw it was raining today, and I thought you probably hadn't gone out. And if you didn't go out, what would you eat? So I thought I'd come over." She said, "Actually, I did go out." He looked at the vegetables and said, "I guess I assumed wrong, then." She said, "Not really. I went out, but I didn't buy groceries." He brightened and said, "Great!" "But I've already gone to bed," she said. "This early?" he asked, surprised. She said, "Sometimes I go to bed after lunch and sleep right through until the next morning." He said, "That's the first time I've heard anyone say they do that. I don't know if that's the way the rich would sleep or the way the poor would sleep." "It's the way the unemployed sleep," she said. He said, "In any case, most people wouldn't enjoy sleeping that way." She wanted to say something, but he stopped her and said, "Whether you enjoy it or not, you haven't eaten." She laughed and said she hadn't. As he went into the kitchen, he said, "Just give me a chance." He put the vegetables on the cutting board and told her, "Go watch TV, and I'll have something ready in an hour."

She was silent for a second, then did as he said. She turned on the TV, took off her slippers, and curled up on the sofa. Chen Fumin poked his head out of the kitchen to look at her and said, "That's exactly what I wanted to see. How can the world be so beautiful? In life, simplicity and tranquility are the most beautiful things. Such beauty is a kind of warmth and peace. It's what I like best." Yao Qin was moved by his words, though she didn't let on.

Chen was a good cook. In short order, he had stir-fried three dishes and made a soup. It was a nice variety of meats and vegetables, and all different colors. He made them just the way she liked. He asked her whether the food was good, and she said yes, and that she hadn't had a home-cooked meal in a long time. "How did you learn to cook like this?" she asked. His face darkened, but he still spoke clearly. "Nearly ten years. I got a Ph.D. in that time, too." She saw his expression and asked, "Was it terrible?" He smiled and said, "It was okay. After that kind of thing is over, an ordinary comfortable life seems like heaven." "Really?" she said. "I haven't felt that way."

After they ate, Chen insisted on doing the dishes. She thought that after he'd cleaned up, he might sit down on her couch again like the night before, and would take advantage of it to kiss her. It made her feel uncomfortable. She saw Chen drying his hands, and she planned out how she would turn him down. *Aren't you getting just what you asked for?* she thought.

He turned off the light and came into the living room, but he didn't sit down. He seemed a bit embarrassed as he said, "Yao Qin, I need to go home. The students turned in tests today, and I'm going to be up all night grading so I can return them in the morning. I will come back tomorrow, all right? You seemed to like what I cooked, so I'll make you dinner again, okay?"

It wasn't at all what she had expected, and she had no need to say what she'd been planning to say. "Okay," she said. "You don't need to bring anything; I'll go out and get something." "Great," he said, "that way I can come a bit earlier." He went to the door, and she followed behind him. He opened the door, and this time he didn't turn around until he was outside. "Sweet dreams, Yao Qin," he said. Then he disappeared down the stairs, and the sound of his footsteps faded.

She leaned against the door, watching him leave. She was just a little bit disappointed.

<hr/>

6

<hr/>

That was how Yao Qin and Chen Fumin started dating.

He came to her house almost every day. Their life was very simple. She would buy groceries, and he would cook. After dinner he liked to drink a bit, and every so often she would buy a few bottles. At first he did the dishes, but soon she felt embarrassed by that and insisted on doing the washing up. When she was done, they would sit together and watch TV. He liked to watch sports, so she watched with him. She didn't much care what they watched, as long as someone was talking and something was happening onscreen. That came from living alone. The TV stayed on so long that sometimes he would turn to stare at her helplessly, and she would know that he wanted to go to bed. She wanted it, too, so they would. At ten-thirty, he would get up and hurry to catch the last bus back to the school dormitory. Because they lived so far apart, he didn't dare try to leave in the morning. He said that for a teacher to be late was just as bad as for a factory worker to have an accident. She knew about accidents, so she didn't ask him to spend the night. He even went back on Saturdays. He was teaching the graduating seniors, and that meant neither the teacher nor the students got any breaks.

A few times, when the weather was cool and comfortable, Chen Fumin wanted to take Yao Qin for a walk along the river. She never wanted to go, saying she feared that they'd be seen by someone who knew them. He said that they would be seen sooner or later, and she said she'd rather it be later. He wasn't happy with that and said, "Is it that you don't want to be seen with me?" She laughed and said, "Of course not." But she refused to go out, and he couldn't force her. He couldn't understand it; he thought they should do something romantic together, otherwise what kind of memories would they have?

One day Chen had a meeting, and he called Yao Qin to say that he couldn't come over. For some reason, she felt relieved. That day she didn't make dinner, and instead peeled an apple and had some yogurt. An uncooked dinner had once made her feel sad, but now it made her nostalgic, and she realized that Chen had been coming over to cook her dinner every night for three months.

It felt completely different with no one there at dusk. She thought, *I'm going to give this evening to Yang Jingguo.* She put on a pair of sneakers and went alone to the riverbank. She hadn't been there in quite some time. There was a large stone that Yang Jingguo would tell her to rest on for a moment during their walks. He would spread his handkerchief out for her to sit on.

When she saw the rock, she wanted to sit down for a bit, but how could she sit on it without Yang Jingguo's handkerchief? Ten years had passed, and the stone was exactly the same, but Yang and his handkerchief were gone. She felt her old grief rising again.

The stars spread brightly through the sky, and the river and the darkness flowed together silently. The path along the bank had been fixed up and was nice and smooth. The flowers along the path were blooming, and their colors looked strange under the lamplight. She couldn't imagine coming out here to walk with Chen Fumin. She would lose what she'd had with Yang Jingguo. As she thought about it, she felt a little bit resentful.

She went to bed as soon as she got back home. She thought she would dream of Yang Jingguo, but she didn't. She stood by the riverbank in her dream calling out to him, "Why aren't you here?"

———

When Chen Fumin's summer break started, he took Yao Qin to Lu Mountain for a few days. He had wanted to go to Mt. Huangshan, but she refused because she'd gone there before with Yang Jingguo. She wanted to go to Zhangjiajie, but he refused. He didn't give her a reason, and she didn't ask because she thought he had probably taken his wife there. So in the end they decided to stay at an old villa on Lu Mountain. One of the attendants there told them that the place had once belonged to Sun Yat-sen's ally Wang Jingwei. Chen laughed and said under his breath, "Are we really going to stay in a traitor's house?"

Lu Mountain was a romantic place. In the evenings, the valley was so quiet that all they could hear was the sound of the wind and the river. Chen feared nothing, and he took her out late at night to wander through the west side of the valley. He liked to look at the old winding corridors and crosshatched windows of the villas. There were a lot of trees and a lot of mosquitoes. Chen didn't like the mosquitoes, but he also really wanted to kiss Yao Qin out in the open air. So when they came to a bridge or a streetlamp beside the road, he would suddenly attack, grabbing hold of her and kissing her uninhibitedly. He was passionate, but she wasn't. She felt she had already gone through that stage of life. She'd spent ten years undisturbed, and it wasn't easy to open up again. She didn't understand how he could be so passionate, either. She even wondered if he'd really had a wife who had died. If he had, how could he be so happy now? Wouldn't he think about her? She had a lot of questions, but she suppressed them. That only distilled them into small rocks. Each day as Chen caressed her body, he never managed to touch those rocks inside her heart.

In that old villa, Yao Qin sometimes woke up in the middle of the night and couldn't get back to sleep. She would hear the sound of the wind and the river outside and Chen breathing next to her ear, and suddenly she would start to cry. She knew why. The man sleeping beside her, who held her and kissed her and caressed her each day, whose breath brushed her face—he wasn't the one she wanted most. And the one she did want was gone. That was the way it was destined to be. She tossed and turned on her damp pillow. She could no longer fight her fate. Yang Jingguo would never return, and she had to accept that. But it wasn't easy.

When they got back from Lu Mountain, Chen still had some time off, so he thought he might as well stay with her. She wasn't used to living with him. Her father also disapproved; it was the kind of immoral thing young people did, and they were approaching middle age. So her mother and father joined forces and insisted that Yao Qin and Chen Fumin get married. Chen said he was willing, but it was up to Yao Qin. She felt uncertain. It seemed proper to get a marriage license, but each time she thought about it, her heart quailed. She had decided to marry Yang Jingguo, so how could she now become the wife of someone named Chen Fumin?

Yao Qin's parents saw that they hadn't convinced her, and they called her shameless and said she was an embarrassment to them. Their words made her feel terrible. Her mother said, "If you don't want to be told that, you should go apply for a marriage license. Once you do, everything will be legal and proper, and it's up to you whether or not you have a wedding banquet."

She asked Chen what he thought, and he said he didn't care either way. He said, "It's totally up to you. If we love each other, I don't care what papers we have." "Do we love each other?" she asked. "Do you think we don't?" he asked. She said nothing, but she thought, *If I loved you, where would I keep Yang Jingguo?* Chen said, "If you don't love me, why are you letting me stay with you?" She looked out the window and didn't answer. She thought, *I don't need love. I'm letting you stay here because I need someone around, I need someone to help out. Why else would I want you? Otherwise, Yang Jingguo is enough.* When Chen didn't hear an answer from her, his face fell.

He said, "Maybe you don't need love, but I do." He got up, and Yao Qin heard the sound of the door and then his footsteps descending the stairs.

They were angry sounds, and after that she lay awake the whole night.

The next morning she went back to Pine Hill. Yang Jingguo's grave was the same as always. He was there with all the others and wouldn't be lonely. She silently knelt and stared at the inscription she knew so well. "What do you think?" she asked him. "Should I get married?" Her legs started to hurt, so she stood up. The rows and rows of graves and thick grass along the little paths spread out before her. She sighed and carefully trimmed the weeds around his grave. She thought, *Let's just leave it at that.*

7

They decided they would apply for a marriage license before National Day in November and use the holiday to take a honeymoon. When her mother heard the news, she broke into a smile as bright as a flower in full bloom. Her daughter wasn't young anymore, but she was still a new bride. And after so many years of loneliness and difficulty, she would finally have a real home. She would need to have a big wedding banquet, which Chen would have to pay for. Chen said that if she wanted to redo the house and buy new furniture, he wouldn't have enough money left for a banquet. Yao Qin's mother waved her hand as though to say, "Forget it." She would come up with the money herself.

He started teaching freshmen in September, which was much easier than teaching seniors. He gave Yao Qin the good news that he could now spend Friday and Saturday nights with her. But she felt no happiness at that, and simply told him he could do as he pleased.

On the first day of class, the sky had darkened and Yao Qin had washed all the vegetables, but Chen still hadn't come back. She cooked the rice, but Chen still wasn't there when it was done. She was hungry, but she didn't want to cook. Chen's cooking was better, and besides, she had just washed her hair and didn't want to get oily smoke in it. So she told herself to be patient and sat down on the sofa to wait.

It was pitch-black outside when someone knocked on the door. Finally, she thought. She hurried to the door and pulled it open, ready to complain to him. But it turned out to be Xin Rong.

She took a moment, then stuttered, "What are you doing here?" Xin Rong said, "Who else would it be? Are you waiting for someone? Like Zhang Sanyong?" She was afraid and said, "Why would Zhang Sanyong come here?" Xin Rong snorted. Yao Qin said, "Did you want something?" Xin Rong said, "Yes, can you let me in?" Yao Qin didn't want to let her in and felt uneasy, worried that Chen Fumin would come back while she was still there.

Xin Rong said, "It's been way too long. I was worried you didn't want to see me, so I didn't come around." Yao Qin said, "Why wouldn't I want to see you? I was laid off and haven't been working, so I've just been staying home." Xin Rong said, "Don't say that." Yao Qin said, "Didn't you say you were going to get laid off?" She said, "It should have been me, but my mother . . . one day she realized that my uncle and the factory manager are old schoolmates, so she made my uncle . . . anyway, some money changed hands." Yao Qin said, "So that's what happened." There was contempt in her voice. "Don't be like that," Xin Rong said. "You know my father's been laid up sick for a long time, so what could we do? I only told you because we're old friends." She looked so pitiful that Yao Qin softened. It was true, they were old friends. When Yang Jingguo died, it was Xin Rong who took care of her and even cried with her. She'd been laid off and Xin Rong hadn't, but how could she blame that on her? So her frown disappeared, and she said, "I've been mean, but don't be mad at me." Xin Rong smiled tentatively and said, "How could I be mad at you?"

Yao Qin suddenly felt their old familiarity return. She tugged at Xin Rong's skirt and said, "This is nice. Are you buying nice things now?" Xin Rong said, "Everyone likes it. Do you know how I got it? One day I ran into Zhang Sanyong, and we chatted for a while in front of a boutique. He pointed to the skirt on a mannequin in the window and said, 'That's the kind of thing Yao Qin likes to wear.' I didn't have any money on me at the time, but the next day I went back and bought it. Zhang Sanyong was right." As Yao Qin listened to Xin Rong going on and on, she thought back to her first boyfriend. She said, "How is Zhang Sanyong? His son is already in school, right?" "Second grade," Xin Rong said. "And Zhang . . . is divorced." Yao Qin was surprised. Xin Rong said, "His wife has custody. She's terrible. When she was laid off, she opened a little store and started an affair with the shop owner next door. There was nothing Zhang Sanyong feared more than being cheated on, and then he was. He was so angry that he went in and made a mess of their two shops, and then he laid the other guy out on the ground. Within a month, he divorced her." Yao Qin let out a little breath. She was picturing Zhang destroying the shops and punching the other man, and she thought, *He's just the same as ever.*

Xin Rong was looking at Yao Qin as though she expected her to say something, and when she didn't, Xin Rong looked disappointed. She said, "Don't you want to know how he's doing?" Yao Qin said, "What difference does it make to me?" Xin Rong said, "But Zhang Sanyong still cares a lot about you." Yao Qin said, "That doesn't matter to me." Xin Rong said, "He wants to come see you." Once she'd said this, she felt as though she were doing something wrong, and she glanced apprehensively at Yao Qin before dropping her eyes. Yao Qin was surprised and said, "Did you come here today just because you wanted to see me?" Xin Rong dropped her head and said, "Zhang Sanyong begged me for days to come. He wants to get back together with you, but he doesn't know whether you're still free."

An image that had come to her head many times returned: it was Zhang Sanyong punching Yang Jingguo and shattering his glasses, and Yang's eye turning black and his face bleeding. She said, "There's no way. Doesn't he remember what he did to Yang Jingguo?" She said it as though it had all happened yesterday.

Xin Rong looked around the room and said, "The room has changed, but you haven't. It's a shame." Yao Qin said, "You think it's a shame?" Xin Rong said, "Do you still miss Yang Jingguo?" Surprised, Yao Qin said, "How could I not?"

Xin Rong stood up to leave and said, "Zhang Sanyong said if you were still missing Yang Jingguo, you should go straight to the mental hospital." And then she walked out the door. When Yao Qin heard Xin Rong close the door, she got up. She thought, *Mental hospital? What do they say behind my back?*

She sat back down and thought for a long while. She was really hungry, and Chen Fumin still hadn't come home. The rice had been ready for a long time, but the vegetables weren't cooked. She had no interest in food, but she had to eat something, so she made a packet of instant noodles.

She was in the middle of eating when Chen called. His voice was a bit rough and uncertain, like a borrower begging a creditor to clear his debts. He said that the beginning of the semester was very busy, that there were a few troublesome students and there would be a lot of meetings, and then he said that he might not be able to come see her for a while. She was surprised, and she felt that something was a bit off. But she merely reminded him to get proof of employment from the school so they could apply for a marriage visa sometime soon. He laughed and said, "How come you're more eager than I am now? If it takes a few months longer, what difference does it make?" And she thought, *What exactly does he mean by that?*

8

Yao Qin's mother nagged her every day about the wedding, saying she only had one life to live and she should live it well. She should experience everything once, otherwise what was the point? Yao Qin said that some people murder, commit arson, take drugs, visit prostitutes, go to prison, and decapitate other people, and was that something everyone should experience? Her mother sat down angrily on the side of the bed and was quiet for a while.

Without anyone else there in the evenings, the room returned to its old silence. Thinking about the wedding bored her. Chen Fumin was fine, but she still felt unenthusiastic about the whole thing. Then she thought about her mother saying that she only had one life and should live it well. But didn't everyone have to live by their own fate? People's fates were also connected, though, and if one didn't act according to other people's hopes, too, then the other person couldn't live well. So it wasn't totally up to her. One couldn't just live for oneself. Everyone's fate was mixed up with everyone else's, like a company in which one held only part of the stock in one's own life.

When she thought that way, she felt better. It wasn't only her getting married; she was getting married for her company. Her mother was a stockholder, as was her father. Chen Fumin was a stockholder, and so was Xin Rong. Everyone who cared about her was involved in the company. As the chairman of the board, she had to do well by all of the company's shareholders.

The next day, Yao Qin went out to buy a few new things for her house. She bought a new blanket, sheets, and duvet cover. Then she bought clothes to get married in.

With her many packages, she got onto the bus. Before she got to her stop, she desperately had to pee. When she got off the bus, she ran home, dashed through the door without even taking off her shoes, and went straight into the bathroom. As she peed, it suddenly felt like her whole body hurt. When she was done, she still felt bad. *Is this what it feels like to be pregnant?* she wondered. *At this age, could it still be that easy to get pregnant?* She started to worry.

When Chen called that evening, after a bit of chitchat, she told him that she wasn't feeling well. His end was silent. Surprised, she said, "Why aren't you saying anything?" After a long moment he said, "You'd better go get checked tomorrow." She said, "Do you think I'm sick? What could be wrong with me?" He said, "You'll feel better when you see the doctor and know what's going on." She said, "But what should I tell them? What department should I go to? Gynecology?" He paused again, then said, "Maybe you should see a urologist." She said, "I don't want to go alone." He said, "You really should go. If there's something wrong, you don't want it to get worse. I have class tomorrow, so I can't take you. If I didn't, of course I'd go with you." She thought for a moment, then said, "Fine, I'll go tomorrow."

As she hung up the phone, she thought that Chen Fumin was acting strangely. His tone of voice and those silences weren't like him. Her heart started beating faster, and she thought, *Please don't let something happen just when I'm ready to get married.*

She went to the hospital early the next morning. The doctor told her with all certainty that she had contracted a venereal disease. There was contempt in his voice and eyes. A nurse who had come in to get the doctor to sign a prescription asked Yao Qin, "Are you out of work?" Then she said, "There's a song about a woman who gets fired, and instead of crying she goes out to a nightclub and eats and drinks and sleeps with men . . . at first I thought that was really insulting to us women, but now that I've seen what I saw here, I don't think so anymore." Yao Qin gasped, and for a while could barely breathe. She told the doctor three times that it was impossible. She had never been to that kind of place in her life. The doctor's eyes softened, and he said quietly, "Go home and ask your husband if he's been going to brothels."

Her head started to buzz, and she suddenly knew what had happened.

She called Chen Fumin's office. It was the first time she had ever called him, and she had trouble finding the number. She had to ask the directory service. When she got hold of him, the first thing she said was, "Please, just tell me this: how could I have a sexually transmitted disease?" He didn't answer. She started to scream, and her voice pierced him like needles. He moved the receiver a few inches away from his ear. When she started to calm down, he said, "Go home; I'll come over this afternoon." Then he dropped the phone like it was on fire.

Chen took the afternoon off. He found Yao Qin curled up on the couch. She was despondent, but seemed not to have been crying. He tried to sit down beside her, but she recoiled like he carried the plague, so he sat at the other end of the couch. He pulled out an envelope with two thousand kuai and said, "This is for the hospital and medicine. The shot should only cost a thousand, and the rest is for you." She stared at him and said, "What is that supposed to mean?" He said, "I had no idea what was going on, but I infected you." She said, "You could always come here and be with me, so why did you have to sleep around?"

He was quiet for a long time. Then he said, "It wasn't like that. I'm not like that. My wife was sick for nine years, and during that time she was more dead than alive. It was terrible, but she was my wife, and I never once had an affair. When she died, my students took me to a sauna to steam the odor of sickness out of me. It was the first time I'd ever been to that kind of place. There was a masseuse. She was wearing practically nothing, and she seduced me. I just lost control. Of course, even if she hadn't tried to seduce me, someone who'd been through what I had would have lost control anyway."

She said, "Is it that simple?" He said, "That's not everything. Her name is Qingzhi, and she's from the countryside. I liked her. But it wasn't exactly because I liked her, it was because she was the first woman I had touched in almost ten years. So I went to see her again." Yao Qin said, "Did you continue to see her after we met?" He said, "Of course not. I realized she'd given me a disease, so I stopped seeing her. I got treatment, and I was fine when we met." She said, "You were fine when we met? Then how did you give it to me?" He said, "After we met, Qingzhi came to see me. She said she didn't want to keep doing what she was doing, but her boss wouldn't let her quit and sent someone to watch her. She had escaped, but she had nowhere to go, and she wanted to stay with me for a night. She said her brother would come for her the next morning. So I agreed. And because . . . because . . . I don't know if it's because I like her or because I pitied her. I don't know what I was thinking. We spent the night together, and since she said she'd been cured, too, I wasn't careful. So before school started, I found out . . ." Yao Qin interrupted, "There's no need to go on. Get out. I never even knew you."

He stared at her, not moving. She said, "Are you refusing to go?" "No," he said, "I just can't believe that we're going to end it this way." She said, "How else should we do it? Do you want me to publish it in the paper?" He said, "I thought you would understand." She said, "Of course I understand. But that doesn't mean I can accept it." He said, "I don't want to break up. I love you." She said, "When you say those words, it's like three centipedes crawling out of your mouth." He said, "Don't be so cruel. It's not easy for you to find a man like me. Nothing like this will ever happen again. Can't you forgive me?" She said, "If you don't leave right now, I'll scream for help." He said, "You're being childish. You live alone; who are you going to call?" She immediately started to yell at the wall, "Yang Jingguo! Yang Jingguo! Where are you? Come here and get rid of this man for me! What are you waiting for? Throw him out! Don't you hear me?" Her voice sounded bizarre, and it terrified Chen Fumin. He stood up and hurried to the door, saying, "I'm leaving, I'm leaving."

He was as flustered as if a man named Yang Jingguo really were going to throw him out.

That night, the moon flowed into the room as gently as before. She stayed curled up on the couch all night, feeling that Yang Jingguo was finally there, watching over her.

9

The days as silent as a dried-up well came back. There were more and more days when she slept from noon until the next morning. Her mother scolded her over and over, and her father's long sighs had returned. The principal of Middle School No. 5 came over, wanting to make peace, but he was as silent as a log in front of Yao Qin. Her mother kept exclaiming, "What are you thinking? What are you thinking?" And Yao Qin said, "I'm not thinking anything at all."

Before she knew it, it was the anniversary of Yang Jingguo's death again. And yet again it rained. She went to the hills and lit incense and left a plate of fruit for him. She held her umbrella over the incense, and the slowly rising smoke encircled her face. She didn't cry. The rain replaced her tears.

It was still early when she came down the hill, and there was nowhere she needed to be. She walked to where the accident had happened and found that the rock was still there, though the blood wasn't. She thought that while the incense was burning, she should go to the job market. If she was going to stay single, she would need to find a job, something that she could support herself with.

As she was thinking that, a low, thin voice said with surprise, "Yao Qin? Is that you?" She lifted her umbrella and saw Chen Fumin. She asked what he was doing there. Seeing the incense burning in her hand, he stuttered, "That . . . that . . . man who died here . . . was it Yang Jing-guo?" She looked at him without speaking. She suddenly understood. He pointed across the street and said, "The woman who was hit was my wife." Yao Qin felt the blood rushing through her body.

The misting rain. The spinning scenery. The sound of cars. Yang Jing-guo's voice. The bicycle sent flying. The man and woman knocked to the ground. Brains on the rock. The screams of passersby and the sounds of wailing. Everything came back to her in a blur. It was their most painful moment. It had smashed their lives to pieces and changed their fate. She started to cry silently. The old unbearable pain wrapped itself around her like a rope. Chen saw her crying and took her in his arms. He tried to control himself, but before he knew it, ten years of pain rose in him like nausea, and he began to cry, too. His tears wet her hair and dripped onto her cheeks, mixing with her own.

Pedestrians turned to look at them and whispered or laughed behind their hands. They didn't know the bloody past. They could never understand other people's pain. They were merely passersby, whereas Chen Fumin and Yao Qin had a history there. That was the place their pain had begun.

They took the bus back and got off at the same stop, planning to transfer to separate buses to go home. At the same time, they noticed the "Sculpting in Time" sign. Chen thought about the first time he had ever seen Yao Qin, and she thought about the moment she had first heard his thin, low voice in the bar. Chen said, "Do you want to sit together for a while?" She didn't object, so he began to walk over to the bar, and after a moment's hesitation she followed.

Sad music seeped out of the bar. Yao Qin was soaked through from the drizzle, and she ordered a glass of orange juice while he ordered a beer. He took a sip and said, "See, aren't we fated to be together?" She thought for a moment and nodded. He said, "I had no idea. How come I have absolutely no memory of you being there?" "I don't remember you, either," she said. "I just heard you crying."

They had never talked about the accident with each other, since it was painful just to bring it up. But seeing that rock had made them cry together, and it had brought them closer. Only they could truly understand what the other was going through, and they weren't alone in their pain. That warmed and calmed them both. So they began to go over the details of what had happened. She talked about Yang Jingguo's last breath, and how they had made the funeral arrangements. His family had insisted that he be buried in their hometown, but she had fought to have him buried near her. Chen Fumin told her how he had stopped a passing car to take his wife to the hospital, and how he'd spent many nights in the hospital hallway, not eating but smoking pack after pack. After his wife had been stabilized, he wanted to vomit if he even smelled cigarette smoke.

They finished their drinks and ordered another round.

"Life is so fragile," Yao Qin sighed. "A few seconds and a single blow, and a person can be gone just like that. Yang Jingguo was always so healthy. I never even knew him to catch a cold."

Chen Fumin laughed and said, "I've always thought people were incredibly resilient. A person can be practically dead, not able to speak or think or move, and can still linger on and on. You know what I realized most deeply over those nine years? I realized why it's right that people should be the rulers of the animal kingdom. It's because they're so tenacious."

She stared at him doubtfully. Was Yang Jingguo the weak one, dead in an instant? And was the strong one Chen's wife, hanging on for so long?

She sighed and said, "You're luckier than I am. You took care of her for nine years, had all of that love for her. But me? He just up and died without caring about how I would feel. Two people who spend all their time together, and suddenly one is gone. You have no idea what that feels like."

At her words, his face took on an odd expression, and before she had a chance to ask him what was wrong, he said, "Love? You think I still loved her? I'm not afraid to tell you what I really felt. By the end, I felt nothing but hatred. I lived up to my responsibilities, but inside I was filling up with hate. I had no life at all. Every morning I'd get up and wipe down her body, then clean the sheets and clothes she had dirtied, feed her some milk, get her medicine ready. I'd barely have time to get that done before I had to go to class. On my way, I'd pick up something to eat. At noon I'd hurry back home and do it all again, then eat something I'd gotten from the cafeteria. I wouldn't even have the time or energy to heat it up. It was even worse at night. I worked like a machine. My whole salary went toward buying medicine. I felt like I was suffocating. We were so poor, and the whole house was filled with the odor of sickness. I didn't have enough money to hire a nurse, and her family didn't want to help. They'd occasionally come to see her, and then as they were leaving they'd say, *'Just as long as she's alive.'* Maybe that was enough for them, but for me? Nine and a half years, every day, the same steel needle stabbing me until I turned black and blue. Every night I would curse her for not dying, for torturing me like that. So many times I thought of strangling her to death, but I couldn't do it. You tell me, with that kind of life, could I still love her? Am I stronger than you? You have pain, but you still have all those cherished memories. But me, all I have is pain. You don't know what that's like. Thank goodness she finally had the decency to die. Otherwise I never would have met you, and I'd be more dead than she was."

His voice was loud and urgent, and his glass shook in his hand. Yao Qin had never seen him like that, and she felt sorry for him.

She took his hand and held it tightly. At the touch of her warm palm, he calmed down and his trembling stopped.

He said, "You know, I really just want to live simply. A woman that I love, who isn't a burden to me, just like you. Someone who can just be beside me, who will give me a good life. I really want us to start over. Can we? I never forgot about you. I want to try again, okay?"

That was a certainty. Because she had cried with him, because they had shared the same tragedy, because they had both endured a decade of lonely years.

She said, "Let's have dinner at my place tonight. I'll buy the groceries, you cook."

———

10

———

So Yao Qin and Chen Fumin got back together. Their collective tragedy suddenly gave them even more passion. Yao Qin thought, *Let Chen Fumin take over the place Yang Jingguo used to have.*

The autumn passed and winter came.

Chen Fumin came over every day. With his late classes and long commute, he'd arrive after nightfall, so gradually Yao Qin took over the cooking. After Chen had eaten, he'd sit in front of the television picking his teeth, and when he was feeling particularly satisfied, he'd announce, "This is how it should be." Each night at ten o'clock, he would hurry back to his apartment to grade and prepare for class. Sometimes a few other teachers would see his light on and come over to play mahjong. They all said he was so free, that he could do whatever he liked. They had forgotten his past troubles. He would play mahjong with them until two or three in the morning, then send them off and sleep until seven-thirty. He didn't have to be at work until eight o'clock, so he had plenty of time. Especially compared to before, he couldn't imagine things getting any better.

Chen got paid on the tenth of every month, but he never gave the money to Yao Qin. She'd been laid off, but her house was still quite nice, and his meager salary wouldn't make a difference to her. Yao Qin couldn't ask for anything since they weren't married, but it was her money that went toward buying food every day. The small severance she'd been given hadn't lasted two months, and she had started to use her savings. Her mother found out and scolded her harshly, saying, "If he isn't taking care of you, then why do you stay with him? You've got to talk to him about it." Yao Qin felt conflicted and said, "If he hasn't offered, who am I to demand it from him?" Angry, her mother said carelessly, "He's nothing compared to Yang Jingguo. You and Yang Jingguo hadn't been together for more than a few days, and he was already handing his salary over to you." Her words left Yao Qin with a sour taste in her mouth, and she thought, *You just figured that out? Who could compare to Yang Jingguo?* But what she said was, "You all wanted me to forget Yang Jingguo, so why are you bringing him up?" Her mother knew that she had spoken out of turn, and she clapped a hand over her mouth.

Yao Qin's mother had a former student who had opened a large bookstore. She set aside her old status as a principal and went in person to beg the student to give Yao Qin a job. The student had seen Yao Qin years before; he had heard about her story and had felt deeply for her. So when her mother came asking about a job, he immediately fired one of his workers and hired Yao Qin.

And so Yao Qin went back to the working woman's life.

Chen Fumin asked her, "Why did you take this job? You have enough money." She said, "You think my tiny severance is enough to live on?" "What about your parents?" he said. "What else do they have to spend money on aside from you?" She said, "That's ridiculous. I have hands and feet, so why would I want to take money from them now that they're getting on? How can you even say that?" He said, "If you're at work until late, who's going to make dinner?" "Whoever comes home first," she said.

After that, Chen started to come home even later. She usually got home at six-thirty, and he started to come home around seven-thirty, which was an hour later than before. In that time, Yao Qin could just about finish making dinner, and he could come in and sit straight down at the table. He explained himself by saying that he'd been tutoring a few of the slower students and could make quite a bit of money doing it. Though he mentioned money, he never offered her any. She felt uncomfortable about it but said nothing, thinking, *Men are like that.*

One day the bookstore had a sale, and everyone worked late. She didn't get home until after eight. When she opened the door, she found Chen sitting unhappily on the couch watching TV. He said nothing when she came in. "Have you eaten?" she asked him. "Yes," he said. "Did you cook when you got home?" she asked. He said, "I'm always totally worn out when I get home; who would have the energy to cook?" She said, "So what did you eat?" He said, "I heated some leftovers and made some fried rice, and it was just enough." She said, "And what about me?" He said, "It's bad enough I had to take care of myself. Why did you come home so late?" That made her angry, but she still said nothing and just made a bowl of instant noodles for herself.

That evening, she fell into a dark mood. Chen acted as though nothing were wrong, made out with her for a while, and then went back to his apartment at ten-thirty. As he was leaving, she suddenly said, "I have a job now, too, so it's not that convenient for me to cook for you. If you want to come over, you should eat first. Or maybe you should just come over on Fridays." He stared at her, frozen beside the door as though thinking something over. Then he said, "Are you mad about something?" She said, "I'm not mad, I'm just worn out." He said, "If you're worn out, just say so, and I'll make dinner. That's simple, right?"

After he left, she lay down but couldn't sleep. She felt that passion was like paper, burning hot at the beginning but easy to extinguish. The ordinary passage of days dribbled water onto the paper and put out the fire.

The next day when she came home, Chen wasn't there. She made dinner anyway, and just as it was almost ready, Chen came in. He said, "Didn't I say I would make dinner?" She said, "I got home first; was I just supposed to sit there and wait for you?" He said, "Well, then, it was your decision to cook, so don't blame me." She said, "Would it make a difference if I blamed you?"

She had lost her appetite completely, so she set the table and went into the bedroom. She felt anxious and restless, as though fire were running through her veins instead of blood. She wanted to stomp her feet and yell at someone, tear out her hair, throw something. She didn't know why she was so angry, and she didn't know how to calm herself down. She paced the small room like a cornered animal. She thought about Yang Jingguo and how he used to hug her, soothe her, counsel her when she would get upset. She found his picture in the drawer and pressed it against her chest as though she were trying to feel his embrace again. "Jingguo," she begged him, "come help me."

A chill touched her skin, seeping slowly through her chest and dripping onto her heart. It was as though a tiny mouth were eating the flames that raged through her body. She sat down and felt calmer. She saw the tree out the window, but she couldn't see the color of its leaves in the darkness. Other spots were washed out by the moonlight. Bright lights shone in the windows of the building opposite, and the red windowsills shone like inlay. A woman was leaning out of a window to speak to someone a story below. It was like a painting. She thought, *Actually, there's nothing wrong. I'm totally fine. I shouldn't have bothered you, Jingguo.*

Chen Fumin put the food on the table and came to the bedroom door. "Let's eat," he said. "Where'd you disappear to?" He saw that she was holding a photo, and he came over to her. He took the photo from her and asked, "Is this Yang Jingguo?" She said yes. He looked at it again, as if to stop himself from saying something. After a while, he tossed it on the bed and went out. Then he turned his head and said, "If you don't forget about him, we're never going to work."

Chen didn't speak as they ate, just sighed unhappily a few times. Instead of watching TV after the meal, he left without saying a word. She heard the door shut and knew that while she had moved toward him earlier, now she was moving away, back toward Yang Jingguo, where she had a feeling of home. She thought, *I haven't seen Jingguo for too long.*

The next morning she asked her boss if she could leave early to take care of a few things. Her boss, her mother's former student, asked her, "Do you need to go somewhere? Do you want me to give you a ride?" She said, "There's no need. I'm just going to the suburbs. I have to go alone." Her boss said, "Are you going to Pine Hill, to see your . . . ?" She nodded. He was silent for a long while, then said, "You still go to see him? How many years has it been?" "Ten years," she said. "If I don't go to see him, I feel bad." He said, "Do you go every month?" "Yes," she said. He said, "Then every month I'll schedule you for a day off so you can have the whole day to go." She was grateful and thanked him. He said, "Your boyfriend's dead, but he's still a lucky man." She laughed bitterly and said, "I'd rather he be a little less lucky and still be alive." He said, "But you know, when someone you love betrays you, you'd rather be dead than alive." "Really?" she said.

As she walked to the bus stop, she heard a familiar voice call to her. The name Zhang Sanyong leapt into her head, and indeed it was him. He said, "I was just thinking of visiting you, and here you are. Isn't that a coincidence? Where are you headed?" She said, "I'm going to the suburbs." He opened his mouth wide. "Are you going to see Yang Jingguo?" he asked. "How could I not go see him?" she said. He reached out and touched her forehead. She jumped and pushed his hand away. He said, "I just wanted to see if you're a real person." "Nonsense," she said. He said, "If you were going somewhere else, I'd go with you. But if you're going there, I won't go. I hate him." She said, "I wouldn't let you come anyway. But you know, he didn't hate you. He said that if it hadn't been for you, he and I never would have gotten together." Zhang Sanyong said, "It's all my fault. That punch hurt a lot of people. Otherwise we would've gotten married, and you wouldn't be living a lonely life in your empty house. I wouldn't have married the first woman I found, then gotten divorced and become a lonely bachelor. And if Yang Jingguo hadn't been with you, he wouldn't be up on Pine Hill, either. I regret it. And I can tell from your face that you regret it, too. If only . . ." "The bus is here," she said. "I'm going."

She climbed heavily onto the bus. She didn't want to talk to Zhang anymore. His words made her feel hopeless—there was no "if only." Could it really be that if she'd married Zhang, all three of their lives would have been better? Who could say whether they wouldn't have gotten divorced, too, and she'd have ended up alone in an empty house. Who could say whether Yang Jingguo, living in this "if only" world, wouldn't have died in some other "if only" situation. It was useless to talk of "if only." The world was big and complex and constantly changing, and everyone could only see their tiny part of it, like a blind man touching an elephant: whatever he touched was what existed to him.

It was barely spring, and the trees on the hill hadn't yet turned green. The grass lay yellow against the ground. There were footprints across the patches of old snow, and dried mud covered the bare spots. She squatted in front of Yang Jingguo's grave, feeling that she could see him there. He was waiting attentively for her to come and tell him all of her problems, all of her joys and sadness and frustrations. He was the best listener. He never interrupted her, and her worries all dissolved under his patient eyes. When she was sad, her pain would melt like snow. When she was happy, she would glow. Who else could do that for her? She spoke aloud to the early spring dusk. She said that she was a terrible person. She had almost let someone replace him. She had even tried to forget him. She wanted to bury him in a deep place in her memory, and in the silence of night she could think about him forever. But right now she understood that no one could ever replace him. She could never love anyone else. She said, "Today, here, I want to say this clearly. I want to say it to you. Can you hear me? If you can, let me know."

Nothing moved on the wide, motionless hill. Her words made a small breeze that rippled among the plants as though moving them and making their branches dance, and in that dance was a voice, a voice of nature, and that was Yang Jingguo's answer.

She got home much later than usual, and this time Chen Fumin had made dinner. He stared at her as she came in and said, "Did you go to the west suburbs?" She said, "No, I had to stay late at work." As soon as she said it, she thought to herself, Why on earth would I lie?

11

Yao Qin's mother came to talk to her about the wedding. She said that the principal of Middle School No. 5 had come to see her, and it was Chen Fumin who'd sent him. Chen wanted to get married, but he was worried that Yao Qin had given up on him and wasn't interested anymore. He was too timid to seek her out himself, so he'd sent the older generation. "Do you really want to behave like a couple of teenagers?" her mother asked. "You've already fought and made up. You practically live together. Why don't you just get married? What's the point of putting it off?" "There is no point," Yao Qin said. "What's the point of getting married?" Her mother said, "Being married and not being married are about the same. So why not just do it? Your father and I can't take it anymore. Are you really going to live like this? What is there to think about? If everyone took forever to think about things, and everyone needed everything to be exactly like they wanted, then life would be so dull. Even if you choose the wrong person, you've still got your whole life to live, right? Out of a hundred women who get married, ninety-nine and a half of them suspect that they've chosen the wrong person. But if you don't pick this one, you'll pick that one, and that would be a mistake, too. So just pick the one in front of your face and stop wasting time. If everyone worried night and day about the decision like you are, the apes never would've managed to evolve into people."

Her mother nagged for quite some time before she left. Once she was gone, Yao Qin thought carefully about what her mother had said, and felt that a lot of it made sense. Although getting married was about the same as not getting married, and although one could marry the wrong person and still live one's life, and although two people could still be lonely together, the single life was just as lonely, so why not just do it and forget about it.

That night when Chen Fumin came over, Yao Qin studied him carefully. "Why are you staring at me?" he asked her. "You're making me nervous." She said, "Did you send somebody to talk to my mother?" He said, "Did your mom come over? What do you think?" So she described what her mother had said.

As she was talking, his eyes wandered, as though she were describing something as unimportant as washing the dishes. She said, "What's wrong with you? You're the one who sent her here, and now you don't even want to listen?" He said, "I want to hear what you think, not what your mother said." She nearly choked. What did she think? She thought she still hadn't figured things out. But then she thought, if she did manage to figure things out, what conclusion would she come to? And would it satisfy her mother and father and Chen Fumin?

He seemed to sense what she was thinking and said, "You're not sure yet, are you? You're still thinking about that dead man, aren't you?" She said, "Why do you always say such stupid things? If you want to get married, then let's do it. I don't care." He said, "Don't underestimate me." "What does that mean?" she said. He said, "I want to get married, but not without love. I don't want a loveless marriage." "Oh?" she said. He said, "And I still don't know if you actually love me. I'm not sure whether your heart is still with Yang Jingguo even if your body is with me. I'm a greedy man; I want both your body and your heart. If you just give me one of them, it's not any better than waiting hand and foot on a paralyzed vegetable and then going to see a prostitute to let off steam." She said, "Two people who don't love each other can still have a fine life together. Isn't that enough?" "Maybe," he said, "but I already spent ten years in misery, and now I need at least ten years of happiness to make up for it. Is that silly?" She said, "Is that how it is?" He said, "Marry me and love me for ten years, okay? After ten years, if you still don't actually love me, you can do whatever you want." She laughed and said, "Ten years? If we get married, we'll have at least thirty years. How about I love you the last ten years, since all you want is ten." He looked surprised, then laughed and said, "I didn't know you could be so clever." She said, "I didn't really want to get married before. But now I think it wouldn't make much of a difference, so we might as well do it." He said, "Is it because you feel like nothing matters at all?" She thought for a moment and said, "Maybe a little, but that isn't entirely it."

He fell silent. Then he said, "Since that's the way you feel, maybe we should wait a bit longer, until you love me desperately and can't bear to be apart from me. Then we can get married." "Okay," she said. But she thought, *Love you desperately? Can't be apart? Do you think I'm some naïve eighteen-year-old?*

Later as they were lying together, he said into her ear, "What I mean when I say 'love' is that I want you to forget about Yang Jingguo. I don't want to smell him while I'm holding you." "What are you talking about?" she said. "I'm not kidding," he said. "I can smell something damp on you, like something coming out of a mist. It's not your smell, it's his. I know it."

Her heart was thumping in her chest. That night as she slept, she saw Yang Jingguo coming out of the thick mist onto the riverbank.

———

So for a while they put aside the whole idea of marriage, and life became dull.

Some evenings Chen Fumin came over, and some evenings he didn't. When he didn't come, he would call and say he was tutoring a student or playing mahjong with a friend. But he had to come over on the weekends. He said that if he wasn't with her on the weekends, he felt as lonely as if he were the last person on earth. So come Friday, Yao Qin would buy some groceries and wait for him to come over to make dinner. Now that she had an income again, Chen never brought up money, and she didn't raise the issue, thinking, *After all, it's only a meal.*

Sometimes he wanted to do something romantic, like go dancing or see a movie. She always refused. "Are you still twenty?" she would ask. "Aren't forty-year-olds people?" he would say. "Of course they're people, but they're also adults, and adults don't need that kind of childish stuff." He said, "Maybe there's more to an adult life than the kitchen and the bedroom." "Of course there is," she said. "Adults are separated into the rich and the poor. If you're rich, you can fly all over the country enjoying yourself. Today you're on some ocean island, and tomorrow you're way up in the mountains. If you're poor, I'm sorry; if you have a kitchen and a bedroom, that's already doing well." He said, "That makes no sense. Rich people have rich people's enjoyments, and poor people have poor people's enjoyments." She said, "Fine, then, poor people go out dancing and to the movies. It costs thirty kuai for a ticket to get into the dance hall; that's sixty for two people. A movie ticket is twenty-five kuai each, so fifty for two. Are you paying or am I?" Chen fell silent. *You're this stingy*, she sneered silently, *and you call it romantic? Who wants that kind of romance?* He said, "If that's how it's going to be, let's just stay home and talk."

But they didn't have much in common to talk about. Chen liked to talk about his classes, mostly stories about his students misbehaving. He even told her about three girls who he said had secret crushes on him. Yao Qin talked about the books that had come in recently, and which ones had ugly covers, which sold well, and which were obviously excellent but still weren't selling.

The clock ticked away on the wall as they chatted awkwardly. Sometimes it sounded quick and sometimes slow. When their TV programs came on, they watched together. She curled up on the couch beside him. He would reach out and touch her arm, or pull her into his embrace as though they were sweethearts in the throes of love. She wasn't used to it, but she didn't resist.

As she leaned against him, she felt as though her heart were seeking something. Her mouth spoke to Chen and her eyes looked at the television, but inside of her something was sending out feelers in all directions like a sea anemone. Though Chen's breath was right beside her ear, each time a feeler reached out, it came back disappointed. It made her feel empty inside. It was totally different from the way it had been with Yang Jingguo. Chen noticed her expression a few times, and he asked her with a touch of jealousy, "What is it? Are you thinking about Yang Jingguo again? Can't you be a little more practical?"

One evening, Chen called and said he couldn't come over. Yao Qin made dinner for herself, and as she was finishing, someone knocked on the door. She thought maybe Chen had finished his business and come over late, so as she opened the door she said, "Why didn't you tell me you were coming over?" But the man she saw on the doorstep was Zhang Sanyong. She stared at him in surprise.

He said, "What, did you think I was somebody else?" "Yes," she said. "Why on earth would I think it was you?" He walked in past her without her an invitation, and sat down on the couch. He found an ashtray beneath her side table and lit a cigarette. It was as though he were still her boyfriend.

"Did you have some kind of business with me?" she asked. He said, "Do I need a reason to come see you? I don't have any business at all today, and I knew you didn't, either." She said, "You think you're so smart. You don't know anything." He said, "Not long ago I saw you going to Yang Jingguo, and I knew your life was the same as before. I thought, God gave me a chance. He knows we're destined to be together." She said, "I'm warning you, Zhang Sanyong, don't give me that crap. We can see each other as old colleagues, and I'll let you sit here nicely and smoke your cigarette, and then you have to go." He said, "Yao Qin, why are you being so unfriendly to me? We were a couple for a long time. We've hugged and kissed before, and practically went to bed together. Can't you just relax a little? I didn't plan to come here and rape you." She said, "If you're going to talk like that, I'm leaving." He said, "Okay, okay, I just came to see you. I was worried about you. I thought you might be lonely." She said, "I'm not lonely at all." He said, "You're as stiff as a dead duck." She said, "I don't want to talk to you anymore. When that cigarette's gone, I want you to leave." She went into the kitchen to wash dishes. It was raining, and she could see the tree outside shaking as the raindrops beat against it. She said, "It's raining, you'd better get home." He said, "If I leave, you'll be alone and I'll be alone. If I don't leave, we can chat for a while. The only reason I'd go home now is to see whether my tropical fish have died or not."

As he spoke, someone knocked at the door. Yao Qin didn't hear it in the kitchen, but Zhang Sanyong heard it. He opened the door, and in came Chen Fumin. Zhang said, "Who are you looking for?" Chen said, "Who are you?" Zhang said, "I live here." Chen said, "What the hell are you talking about?"

Yao Qin came out of the kitchen. "What's going on?" Chen asked her. Yao Qin said, "Oh, we used to work together at the machinery factory, and he came to see me today." Chen said, "Is it that simple?" Zhang said, "It's not that simple. Before Yang Jingguo, Yao Qin and I were deeply in love. We almost got married, but that bastard Yang broke us up. Fortunately he's not around anymore. Otherwise I'd come and get rid of him."

Yao Qin said, "Stop spouting rubbish. Here, I'll lend you an umbrella." Zhang said, "You still haven't told me who this guy is." Chen said, "I live here. Yao Qin and I are deeply in love, and none of that has anything to do with you." Zhang started to yell, "You found someone else? What the hell were you doing going to see Yang Jingguo practically every day?" She said, "You really need to go. Get out!"

After Zhang Sanyong left, Chen Fumin sat where Zhang had been. The ashtray still held Zhang's cigarette. Chen started smoking, depressed, sighing out the smoke. She said, "Doesn't the smoke make you sick?" He didn't answer.

After he'd smoked the cigarette down to a stub, he said, "I've had to deal with Yang Jingguo, and now another one's crawled out of some hole, and his claim on you is even older than Yang's. Not to mention that he's still alive. How am I supposed to deal with this? What's his name?" She said, "Zhang Sanyong." He said, "He really just came to see you? What was he doing treating this like his own home?" She said, "That's the kind of jerk he is. What was I supposed to do?" He said, "Why did he come here?" She said, "He's divorced. I guess he wanted to pick up where we left off. But there's no way that's going to happen." "Why not?" he asked. "You were together before. It's so familiar, it could definitely happen." She said, "Do you want me to get back with him?" He said, "It's none of my business. If you want to get back with him, I can't stop you. This whole time you've been thinking of Yang Jingguo, and have I been able to stop you?" She said, "Zhang Sanyong and Yang Jingguo are completely different. As far as I'm concerned, Zhang Sanyong is nothing more than an asshole." Chen said, "Good women can still be caught by assholes." She said, "Just like you caught me?" He thought for a moment, then laughed. Then he said, "Yeah, I guess I pretty much count as an asshole." The way he said it made Yao Qin laugh, too.

Chen said, "Zhang said you went to see Yang Jingguo nearly every day." She said, "Of course I didn't." He said, "But did you go often?" She said, "It was just a habit. If something came up, I'd go there and sit for a while." "To tell him your troubles?" he asked. "Or to cry? Or to tell him you miss him?" She said, "I just felt better when I went there and sat for a while." He said, "So you have to go? You can't keep doing this." She was silent. He said, "When are you going to understand? He's dead. You're still alive. You have no way of actually talking to him. You need to turn that emotion toward someone who's alive like you." She said, "You can go cry at your wife's grave, and then we'll be even." "How can you say that?" he exclaimed. "Why would I want to cry over her? I haven't cried over her for a long time. Back then, any tears I cried were for myself."

Yao Qin tried to remember what the woman who'd fallen beside Yang Jingguo looked like, but she couldn't picture anything. All she remembered was that she was lying there covered in blood and there was a man wailing. At that moment, the only thing in the world she had cared about was Yang Jingguo, listening to his last words, seeing his last smile. She hadn't cared about the woman next to him. That woman was just a rough sketch in her mind. She'd been hit by a truck. She'd become a vegetable. She'd begun to torture the man who loved her and whom she had loved. And so the man who had loved her had begun to hate her.

Chen said, "Don't say I didn't warn you: you're not going to go again, otherwise . . ." She said, "Otherwise what?" He said, "I don't know, but I think I might . . . bulldoze his grave." She was frightened and said, "You're crazy!" He said, "Then don't let me go crazy. If you don't go there, I won't, either."

The next two nights, she dreamt about Yang Jingguo. He was standing beside a sunken hole, shrugging his shoulders and staring at her like a hanged ghost. She was terrified, crying out, "What's wrong, what's wrong?" Yang was silent, his face anxious. She thought, *Could his grave really have been disturbed?*

On the third day, she asked for time off and nervously hurried to Pine Hill. She thought, *What if Chen Fumin really did bulldoze Yang Jingguo's grave? Would he really dare to do such a horrible thing? If he did, what would I do?* She felt both worried and indignant.

The hill was quiet, and the dew hadn't yet fallen from the grass. Yang Jingguo's grave was the same as always, peaceful. She circled it, then stood there for a moment. She didn't light incense, but merely said, "From now on, you'll have to take care of yourself. I'm afraid I'm not going to be able to come back very often." Then she started down the hill, feeling bereft. She looked back every few steps, as if she were leaving herself behind.

That evening she told Chen that she had gone to Yang's grave to break things off. She'd told him that she wouldn't be back to see him and that he'd have to take care of himself. As she spoke, she started to cry, though she didn't know why. She tried to control her tears, but they fell unbidden. Chen took her into his arms, and she felt his warmth. It was a different warmth from Yang Jingguo's, and she started to cry even harder. Finally he said, "Let's get married. I don't care if you love me or not."

12

So that was decided.

She thought that sometimes decisions were very simple. It might not be what you really wanted, but didn't you have to be incredibly lucky to get that?

When Xin Rong heard that Yao Qin was planning to get married, she came over to her house. She said, "When Zhang Sanyong heard about it, he was so mad he chugged a whole bottle of liquor. But I'm happy for you. Do you want me to be your bridesmaid?" Yao Qin said, "Do you think I'm going to get married in some big ceremony like a girl?" "Why not?" said Xin Rong. "You only have one life to live, and you're not like other people. It's taken you a lot to get here. Everyone at the factory wants to come and give you presents." "Tell them there's no need," Yao Qin said. "If I were marrying Yang Jingguo, I'd want it all. But I'm not. I'm not that happy about the marriage, and I don't want a wedding ceremony, either." Xin Rong said, "What's the matter? Is it that you still only want Yang Jingguo? Well, then just pretend it's him you're marrying. Pretend he was gone for ten years, and now he's coming back to marry you. If you think that way, you'll be happy. Of course, you should keep that to yourself. Don't tell anyone else."

Yao Qin was struck by the thought. Could she really just pretend she was marrying Yang Jingguo?

So she tried imagining that she was marrying Yang Jingguo, and after a bit she began to feel something. Years ago, she and Yang had run around looking at things for their new apartment. They had decided what they wanted, and as soon as they'd gotten the keys to their new place, they would have started buying things to go in it. Now she could finish what they'd started.

At first Chen Fumin wanted them to move into his place. But Yao Qin thought about his wife, who had lived there for nine and a half years. She could practically see her lying like a skeleton on her sickbed, and it made her shudder. She wouldn't even dare go in the door, let alone live there. She told Chen that since neither of them was well-off, and since her place was already furnished, they could save a lot of money if they lived there. He thought about it and admitted that she had a point. Besides, if he kept his old place, he would have someplace to retreat to, and that would be even better. Once he'd thought that, he felt like getting married was going to be simpler than he'd thought. No matter where they lived, Yao Qin would set it up the way she liked. Nothing he said would make any difference, so he might as well just hand the decisions over to her and not worry about it.

So each day after work, Yao Qin went to the shops, and when she saw something she wanted, she brought it home. Her mother had given her thirty thousand kuai and told her to buy new things for their house, and that she should get things she really liked. Yao Qin told Chen that, and he said, "Let's be reasonable about it, though. We don't have to be fashionable or anything." She said, "You buy the new TV and refrigerator, okay?" He said, "So I have to get the most expensive things? I'll just move the ones from my place over to your place." She said, "There's no way I'm using the stuff your old wife used. I'll just buy new things myself." He said, "If you want to buy it, go right ahead. Your mother gave you thirty thousand kuai; that should be enough." She said nothing. "Are you mad?" he asked. "If you're mad, I'll go buy them." She said, "I'm not mad."

She thought to herself, *Why should I be mad? Xin Rong told me to imagine that I'm marrying Yang Jingguo, and since I'm not marrying you, what you buy and don't buy is no business of mine.*

She also didn't want to argue with him about what to get. So she just made all the decisions herself. She was so busy that all the depression of the past ten years burned off as she bustled about. Her whole face glowed, and when she came into her apartment building, those who knew her would laugh and say, "Yao Qin, you look like someone who's about to get married. You're getting prettier by the day." She would laugh, and they'd say, "It's been a long time since we've seen you laugh like that. You're just as happy as you used to be with Yang Jingguo."

Chen Fumin came over to help on the weekends.

She decided to replace the old wallpaper in her bedroom with a cream-colored paper. She said, "When I went wallpaper shopping with Yang Jingguo, this is the kind we liked." The curtains she bought were thick, with flowers on a yellow background. She said, "Yang Jingguo said these curtains went perfectly with the wallpaper, and when I compared a few others, I discovered he was absolutely right." She even changed the overhead light to an antique one, saying, "When I first saw this lamp, I thought it was too Western, but Yang Jingguo liked it. And his taste was always better than mine." The bedspread was from Shanghai, because Yang Jingguo liked things from Shanghai. He loved to buy things from Shanghai because the Shanghainese were very particular, unlike people from Guangdong, who cared only about the latest fashion and not about quality.

At first Chen liked the way she was redoing the house. But when he heard her talk about Yang Jingguo this and Yang Jingguo that, as though it were completely natural for her to bring him up all the time, his mood immediately darkened. Finally he couldn't take it anymore, and he said, "Are you somehow under the impression that you're marrying Yang Jingguo?"

She was startled and suddenly realized that she had inadvertently revealed what she'd been thinking in her heart of hearts.

That night Chen left without eating dinner, and for a few days he was nowhere to be found; nor did he call. She thought, *So is this the way it's going to be?*

Finally, she called him. She said, "What's going on?" He said, "Nothing. I'm just thinking about things." "What are you thinking?" she said. "Are you thinking about whether you want to marry me?" He said, "Why would I? Of course I want to marry you. I told you, whether you love me or not, I want to marry you." She said, "Then what are you thinking about?" He said, "I've been thinking about what kind of man Yang Jingguo must have been for you not to be able to forget him after all these years." She said, "Don't think about that." "I can't help it," he said. "He's standing in the way of my happiness." She said, "Then I'll tell you. He was the best man in creation." "Really," he said. "It makes me uncomfortable to hear you say that." She said, "Even so, it's the truth. But he's dead, so why does it matter to you?" He said, "What I don't get is that he's been dead for ten years, but he still makes me uncomfortable. Zhang Sanyong is alive, but do you see me caring at all about him?" She cried, "You're sick!" And she hung up the phone.

That night, she sat up thinking. There was so much in the world that was mysterious; did he have to understand every little thing? And wasn't having to worry about a dead man better than worrying about a living one?

13

They decided not to choose a holiday as their wedding day. Instead they thought they would get married on the first day of Chen's summer vacation and go on a honeymoon to Yunnan. They'd heard that Yunnan's scenery was beautiful. Chen said, "We'll go and cleanse our spirits, and then we can start again." He always knew how to say nice things. That was something Yang Jingguo didn't have, but he could do nice things that Chen never did. Yao Qin was forever comparing the two in her heart.

As their wedding day approached, Chen suddenly was busy and didn't see her for several days in a row. He called a few times, but his conversation was odd. Once he called to say he was at a teahouse, and he wanted her to guess who was there with him. She didn't know, so he told her he was with Zhang Sanyong. She had no idea why Chen would want to have tea with him. Another time he called to say he was having a chat with Wu Wangyuan. The name was familiar to her, but she couldn't remember who he was. Several days later, she remembered that Wu was one of Yang Jingguo's friends from college. Then Chen called to say he was in the countryside, and it was very windy there. He held the receiver out for her to hear the howling, then said, "Can you hear the wind?" She didn't know what he was up to, but she decided it wasn't any of her business.

Chen finally came over on a Saturday, carrying a chicken and a rolling pin. She said, "It's like the sun is rising in the west—what are you doing with that chicken?" He said, "It's for my wife." She said, "Why did you get such a big rolling pin?" Chen said, "The guard at the school gave it to us. He said the heavier the rolling pin, the better it is for making noodles. He's a northerner." She said, "You could kill somebody with that thing." He said, "If you want to run a household, you have to have practical things."

They had agreed that they would go get their wedding photos taken the next day. Yao Qin's mother insisted that she buy a wedding gown. Yao Qin thought that since she was only going to wear it once in her life, she might as well just rent it. And a qipao would be good enough. Her mother said, "Just because you'll only wear it once, you want to put on some dirty old thing that a million other people have worn?" Yao Qin thought about it. Maybe it would be a dress that Chen's wife herself had worn before her death ten years ago. So she called Xin Rong, and they went together to a dress shop. They went through dress after dress until they found one they both liked. "It's *killer*," Xin Rong said. Then she said that that was the adjective all the young people were using. But Chen wasn't happy. He said, "I don't get why you're spending money like water." She said, "It's not like you bought it. It's my mother's money, anyway." He said, "You should be saving the money your mother gave you. As the old adage goes, 'Save the best steel for the sharpest knife.'" She said, "What are you talking about? Marriage isn't a knife." He said, "What if you get sick one day? You don't have insurance." She said, "You really have a way with words." He answered, "My words are like that big rolling pin: eminently practical."

The wedding photo shoot was going to cost a thousand kuai, which was more expensive than they'd thought it would be. Yao Qin asked Chen, "Should we do it anyway?" He said, "Whatever you want." She said, "I didn't bring enough money." He said, "Neither did I." She thought to herself, *Up until now, I haven't spent any of your money.* Annoyed, she said, "Let's just forget it." "Okay, but you're the one who decided," he said. "Don't blame me." Yao Qin said, "When have I ever blamed you?"

They had planned to go see a movie after the photo shoot, but she wasn't in the mood. "It costs fifty kuai to see a movie," she said mockingly. "We should save that money so we can go see the doctor if we have to." He said, "I'll pay for the movie, okay? I don't want you to think I'm a cheapskate." She said, "Let's just forget it. Being a cheapskate isn't a big deal."

So they went back home without accomplishing anything, and they both felt depressed. Yao Qin went to lie down for a while. As soon as she lay down, Yang Jingguo's face floated above her on the ceiling. He looked at her gloomily and said, "Don't worry about anything. You just concentrate on being a bride, and I'll take care of everything else. My money is your money. I'll be your servant and housekeeper." All the things he had said to her those many years ago came back in a rush.

Chen Fumin started to make dinner. He called out, "Getting married is exhausting; you need to take care of yourself. I'll make spicy chicken and egg custard with pork for you. This is free-range chicken, which is a lot more expensive than regular chicken. I bought it just for you."

Silently, she sat up. The wedding gown she'd bought was still wrapped in plastic. She thought, *It's for the best that we didn't take any photos.* If it had been with Yang Jingguo, she would have paid for the photos whatever the cost. It was just too bad that if she didn't wear the dress on the day they were supposed to get married, she would never get to wear it. She thought about whether she should wear the dress or wear a qipao. After a lot of consideration, she decided that it would be better to wear a qipao. She wasn't young anymore, she had wrinkles, and it would look ridiculous if she wore a big white dress. The wedding dress would just be a memento for her: having it meant that she was a married woman.

With that decided, she unwrapped the gown to put it in her trunk. As she opened the lid, she saw Yang Jingguo's photo. She didn't know how the sweater she'd wrapped around it had come undone, but his face was right there in front of her. His eyes were sad, staring at her through his glasses and the picture frame glass. She stroked his face with a finger. She said softly, "Are you okay?" Then she set his photo down on top of the dress. *That's right*, she thought, *the dress should be with you. That way, you'll know we're married.*

With that thought, she suddenly felt happy. But then she heard a voice behind her, low and weak but severe, saying, "Just what are you doing?"

She closed the trunk, but she was too late. Chen was at his wits' end.

"Why do you always let him come between us?" he said. "Why can't you just let the past be the past? I . . . I . . . I . . . ," she stuttered. He said, "Don't say a word. I'm going to tell you exactly what kind of person Yang Jingguo was." She was surprised and said, "What do you mean?" He said, "You don't even know him. I understand him much better than you ever did. You revere him like a treasure or an idol, as though he were perfect in every way. But he's worse than dog shit." "Why are you spewing such bullshit?" she said. He said, "It's not bullshit. I want to save you, so I've spent a lot of time figuring out exactly what kind of man Yang Jingguo was. I went to see a lot of people. I went to his hometown and his school. I was afraid you wouldn't believe me, so each time I went somewhere or met with someone he knew, I'd call you. And now I want to tell you about the man who's given you no rest for the last ten years." Yao Qin felt nervous, and she didn't want to listen. It was enough to know who Yang Jingguo was in her heart. "I don't want to hear it," she said. "I'm not interested."

Chen said, "You're afraid, aren't you? You're afraid of what I'm going to tell you. Well, someone in his village told me that he was a really evil kid. One day his five-year-old sister stole some of his food, and he threw her into a pond and drowned her."

"He'd never do that!" she cried.

Chen said, "When he was in school, he stole some oil from the principal and got caught. They kept him under lock and key for a year."

Yao Qin's voice rose. "That never happened!"

Chen continued, "So he was put in the same grade with his younger brother. His brother was a much better student, and the principal hoped to send him to Peking University. But his family could only afford to send one son to college. Yang insisted that they send him. He told his mother that if they didn't send him to college, he'd jump into the river and drown himself. His brother gave up on school so Yang could have his shot at college."

"You're making this up!" Yao Qin said loudly.

"He was a very dark person, and he hated himself. He was too jumpy to find a girlfriend, so he would spy on the showers in the girls' dormitory. Once he even snuck in and stole a girl's underwear. He was notorious at that college. He was always failing his exams, and he was at the bottom of his class. Why didn't he ever find a girlfriend in college? Because everyone there thought he was a loser."

"Bullshit!" she shouted. "You're horrible!"

"Yang Jingguo was the horrible one," Chen said. "He had his eye on you from the moment he went to work for the factory. He would purposely follow you to ask for directions or strike up a conversation. He pretended he was as deep as the ocean so he could get you interested in him. He was lucky that he died before he did anything bad to you. If you two had ended up married, I don't know what terrible thing he'd have ended up doing to make you lose face."

She leapt up and slapped him, shouting, "He's dead, so why are you insulting him like this?" Chen said, "Because he still lives in this house. It used to be that he was only torturing you, but now he's torturing me, too. I want to make you realize the truth. I want you to be very clear about the fact that the perfect lover you've been idolizing was actually a total failure of a man."

She began to cry. "Do you think I believe you? Maybe to other people he was a loser or a failure or shameless. But that's what other people thought. To me he was the perfect man. I'm not going to change my mind about him, no matter what you say." Chen felt hopeless. "How can you be so confused?" he said. "He isn't worth it." She was still sobbing as she said, "Even if you were the best person in the world, to me you'd still have nothing on him."

Chen was panting so hard he thought he might suffocate. There was nothing more he could say. He felt that she was so stupid that he had no hope of saving her. He said, "You need to finish things with him today. I don't want to see any of his things in this house ever again." He opened the trunk and took Yang's picture from its place on her wedding gown. Without thinking, he threw it on the ground, and when the glass shattered, he pulled out the photo and ripped it up. He tore his finger open on the glass, and blood dripped down onto the shredded photograph. He had moved so quickly that Yao Qin had no time to react. Her heart had been ripped apart with the photograph, and the blood dripping onto the photo was hers.

Chen said, "Is that bedspread the one that Yang Jingguo would have liked? Get rid of it tomorrow. Those curtains were the ones he liked, right? Get rid of them. He liked that lamp, didn't he? I'm going to smash it to pieces right now. That wallpaper has to go, too. Everything that has anything to do with him, I want gone. I don't want a trace of him left in this house."

"What about me?" she said. "I'm his fiancée. I've been intimate with him. I had an abortion because of him. Do you want to get rid of me?" With that, Chen started to cry. "I love you," he said. "I don't want him to ruin our happiness. But I can't stand it anymore." "Do you think I can?" she said.

She went into the kitchen. The chicken was already chopped up, and the ground pork was sitting ready in a bowl. Two eggs had been broken, and their yolks were two yellow rounds. She began beating the eggs and mixed the pork in. The water in the steamer was boiling, so she turned the burner off. She picked up a knife, but it was oily with chicken grease, so she set it back down. As she went to the door, she spotted the rolling pin and grabbed it.

The house was very quiet. Now that he had calmed down, Chen realized that it had all been no use. He sighed and bent over to pick up the shredded photograph.

Yao Qin stood in the doorway. She thought, *Am I going to let this anger out for Yang Jingguo? Only when I release the anger will it be over with him.* She raised the rolling pin. Concentrating all of her power in her arms, she brought it down on Chen's back.

Chen knew that she was in the doorway, and he wanted to stand up to tell her something. He wanted to say, "If you really can't forget him, then don't forget him. Give me some time to compete with him." But as he was starting to get up, Yao Qin was already bringing the rolling pin down, and it smashed into his skull. Before his brain had time to react, his body fell with a crash. His blood poured out onto the glass–covered floor. Yao Qin stood there frozen.

Chen's face was covered in blood, and he was lying on the ground just as Yang Jingguo had lain against that rock.

14

Xin Rong tried everything. In the end, she went through her older cousin, who was a policeman, and finally got in to see Yao Qin. Xin Rong started to cry. "Yao Qin," she said, "how could you be so stupid? Why did you do it?" Yao Qin's face was white. She said, "How is he?" Xin Rong said, "He's unconscious. He's still in the hospital. What are you going to do?" Yao Qin said, "Find me a lawyer who can get me out of here, and I'll take care of him." Xin Rong said, "Why do that to yourself?" Yao Qin told her, "I need to get out of here. It doesn't matter how much money it takes, just get me out."

Xin Rong found her a good lawyer. In court, the lawyer described Yao Qin and Yang Jingguo's story. He described her endless love and longing for him. As he spoke, Yao Qin burst into tears. Her past rose up before her and gradually faded. The lawyer said, "I've described their story to explain why a poor woman like Yao Qin would commit this violent act. It was because Chen Fumin destroyed the photograph of the person she loved most. Just imagine, a photograph that she had lived and slept with for ten long years. You must understand her rage. Only when the injured party hurt her in this way did she lose control of her senses. With that in mind, she had every reason to do what she did. I hope the court will show leniency on her."

There were many people in court that day, and they were all nodding their heads. The feeling in the courtroom was one of sympathy toward Yao Qin. Her parents were both crying. Everyone else, whether they knew them or not, also had tears in their eyes.

Finally the judgment came down. Yao Qin was given a three-year suspended sentence for her crime. When they let her out, she went straight to the hospital.

Chen Fumin lay in his hospital bed, his head wrapped in white gauze. His eyes and mouth were tightly shut. "I'm here," Yao Qin said. "I will take care of you. If you don't wake up, I'll take care of you for ten years. If you do wake up, I'll love you for ten years." Tears were streaming down her face as she spoke. And she knew that she had begun a second life.

From that day on, she didn't dream about Yang Jingguo. The man who came out of the mist on the other riverbank was Chen Fumin. She could see him clearly.

No one went to tend Yang Jingguo's grave on Pine Hill. The weeds grew tall around it.

Then, one very cold day, Chen Fumin suddenly opened his eyes. He saw Yao Qin, and he seemed to think for a moment. Then he asked her, "Is it over with him?"

"Yes," Yao Qin said. "It's over."

Safety Bulletin

Li Tie

TRANSLATED BY CHARLES A. LAUGHLIN

I

Safety Bulletin (No. ■)
[Date omitted]

Safety Office, Zhangjin Electrical Power

Our company planned to generate 5852.002 megawatts, but it actually generated 5031.7 megawatts. There were 3 accidents recorded, 4 malfunctions, and 2 minor injuries (none of which affected the safety record), so that by the end of the month, we achieved our 293rd day of safe production.

However, there have been many instances of safety breaches. On [date omitted], the No. 1 boiler was undergoing maintenance. The No. 1 mill had its internal steel plates replaced, and in the attempt to use the capstan to rotate the drum, the capstan suddenly lost power. When Wang Zhanyuan, chief of the First Milling Squad, climbed into the drum to check, he neglected to shut off the power switch for the capstan starter. When he entered the drum, the capstan suddenly started to rotate, causing the steel cable to snap; fortunately, no one was hurt. The responsible party: the operator himself . . .

I couldn't say whether the incident was an omen, but I can say that to me it was certainly an extraordinary beginning. Looking at this face I thought about day and night, I didn't even know what to think. I stared at that pair of familiar yet unknown eyes, and my nose strained to receive the slightest scent emanating from her body, while my lips kept flapping, using continuous conversation to conceal my nervousness and doubts. The lazy sunbeams of Sunday afternoon blended with the suggestive lighting, making my feelings blend with fantasies, and I had no way to keep myself from doubting their reality.

—

The young woman sitting opposite me was named Qu Li. Before this incredible afternoon, I could only observe her coming in and out of the company courtyard, watch her talk, laugh, and goof around with coworkers. Initially I, too, had the chance to chat and joke with her, but ever since I declared my love to her, she's been completely cold to me. To use coldness in response to a declaration of love is common enough. Although that coldness was enough to make me get the message and go my own way, the idea that she might go off and start a legendary factory romance with another guy at the company actually hurt my feelings deeply. The guy was named Liu Hongli, and he had come to the factory with me in the same group of vocational school graduates. After we came in, he left our team to become a worker. I say "legendary factory romance" because their relationship shocked everyone in the company. Qu Li was beautiful, and she had no shortage of admirers both inside and outside the power station. Perhaps it was to put an end to our advances that she officially announced her relationship with Liu Hongli at a company youth league dance. That night, some guy asked Qu Li to dance, but she shook her head and said, "I want to dance with my boyfriend." The guy stared at her, stunned, and asked, "Who is your boyfriend?" Qu Li said, "Liu Hongli," and in the midst of a roomful of shocked gazes, she and Liu Hongli began to dance gracefully around the room. I was there at the time, and I could see that only Qu Li and Liu Hongli were dancing, gazing radiantly at each other, devoted and tender.

"What would you like to drink?" I asked.

"I'll have some red wine," Qu Li said.

"Red wine is like a soft drink; it doesn't count as alcohol," I said.

"I want wine because I don't want to get drunk."

I wasn't about to keep pressing her, so I ordered a bottle of red wine. Everyone in the Western restaurant was speaking in hushed tones; even the music they were playing was very quiet with slow rhythms, as if it were whispering a story. To tell the truth, I hate eating Western food. But when I invite women to dinner, I usually take them to Western restaurants. I think the atmosphere is better for conversation between a man and woman. Even loudmouthed people lower their voices in a place like this. And when you're across from someone of the opposite sex speaking in hushed tones, it feels like a date even when it isn't.

I said, "I'm surprised you were willing to have dinner with me."

"What's the big deal? Having dinner isn't against the law."

"Nevertheless, I feel it's kind of unusual."

"You think so? I'd say there is plenty that is unusual going on nowadays."

I clicked my tongue a couple times, but said nothing. In fact, the opportunity for this visit had come both randomly and simply. I ran into Qu Li on the street, and when we exchanged greetings, I said that I'd like to invite her to dinner. I thought for sure she would refuse, but she actually accepted, and for a long moment I didn't know what to do next. The Western restaurant put us in an unexpectedly lyrical mood, and it softened the hard-edged memory I had of Qu Li.

I asked, "Are you in a bad mood?"

"You could say that. I have been in a bad mood lately."

"Why?"

"No reason, I'm just always feeling annoyed."

"Is that why we're sitting here together?"

"I couldn't say, although now that I've had a glass of wine, I'm feeling better already."

"Are you two having an argument?"

Qu Li's eyebrows arched a bit; of course she knew whom I was referring to with "you two." The only reason I asked was that I couldn't think of any other reason why a girl in love would be annoyed all the time.

She said, "No, we aren't, we get along just fine. You should know that Hongli throws himself completely into his work, and he's been working overtime a lot lately. I haven't seen him for at least a week."

I said, "And that's why you're annoyed?"

"Not really. Even though we see each other less, we call each other all the time. Whenever he gets a few minutes free, he gives me a call."

As she spoke, Qu Li unconsciously glanced at her cellphone on the table, and my gaze followed hers to that compact little phone. It was quite ordinary, and somewhat out of date, but it was testimony to the love between a man and a woman: how many sweet nothings were conveyed through it? At that thought, my heart began to ache, and I started to become suspicious of my state of mind at the time. What was I thinking? Was I still after Qu Li, or was I spending money to rub salt into my own wounds? I'm a stubborn man; even if a beautiful flower is spoken for, that doesn't mean I can get my mind off her. I had compared myself to Liu Hongli countless times; when it comes to natural attributes, I am taller than he was: Liu Hongli was less than 5'7" tall. The lines on my face are masculine, and my body and features are well proportioned, harmonious, and handsome. Liu Hongli was more effeminate, which combined with his diminutive stature made him come across as petty and vulgar. In terms of family background, both of my parents are well-educated, so you could say I was born into a household redolent with the fragrance of books. Liu Hongli's family is from the countryside, and he only became an urbanite by dint of his efforts in school and being assigned to the power station. Another attribute was our current status, mine being an inspector in the company's Safety Office, while Liu Hongli was just a welder in the production line. True, he was a model worker, but nowadays people don't pay much attention to model workers. What people care about now is the distinction between blue-collar and white-collar. The gap in salary between blue- and white-collar employees has gotten wider, so they are practically like two different social classes.

"You're a pretty unusual couple," I said. "There aren't many cases of someone on the office staff falling in love with a worker."

"Hongli is no ordinary worker."

"But he *is* still a worker," I said.

Qu Li rolled her eyes, and I could tell she found my words offensive, yet she didn't contradict me. She was an administrator in the Training Department, so her status was not equal to Liu Hongli's, though it was equal to mine. I know I shouldn't think this way; it's silly, but what can I do? I can't help the way I think.

I changed the subject: "The company has made it to two hundred and ninety-three straight days of safe operation."

"Really?" Qu Li answered as she absentmindedly glanced at the cellphone on the table.

"If we can get to three hundred days of safe operation, we can all collect a big bonus," I said. "Ordinary workers only get a thousand yuan, but cadres like us can get three thousand!"

"Are you satisfied with that?" Qu Li's mouth slanted down on one side. She said, "From what I've heard, department supervisors can get eight thousand yuan, and the guys at the top might get tens of thousands."

I got onto this topic to poke at Qu Li's pride by referring to the different bonus levels and give her a sense of the gap between herself and Liu Hongli. I didn't expect her to use the same method to get back at me. I felt awkward, and gulped down a mouthful of wine.

—

Above the table hung a chandelier with three columns, and it gave off a dark blue light that shone on Qu Li's hair like a fuzzy blue halo. Those fibrous beams of light made me feel like I was dreaming, because I had been drinking. After a while, a cellphone started ringing. Qu Li absently picked up the phone on the table, but it wasn't hers that was ringing, it was mine. I pulled it out and answered. It was Old Cao, my boss in the Safety Office. In a strange voice, he told me that there had been a serious accident at the power station and I should get right to the scene.

"But . . ." I looked at Qu Li sitting across from me and hesitated.

But what? I had to get there fast. Director Cao hung up as soon as he finished talking. I knew this wasn't something I could talk my way out of. The "but" I had blurted out was mostly for Qu Li's benefit, or as a comfort to myself. Once I had put away my phone, I apologized to Qu Li, and left the restaurant immediately to rush off to the plant.

II

Safety Bulletin (No. ■)
[Date omitted]

Safety Office, Zhangjin Electrical Power

At 3:55 P.M. on [date omitted], the No. 3 generator was undergoing maintenance, and the No. 3 high-pressure heating unit was disassembled for repairs. Liu Hongli, a welder from the Turbine Department, was working inside the heating unit. When his welding gun touched the heating unit wall, he was electrocuted. Gao Gang, the monitor, immediately cut the power and called the police. The cause of the accident is under investigation . . .

When I got to the scene of the accident, it had already been sealed off by the authorities. There was a crowd of employees outside the police tape looking on, and many of the company executives were there, discussing what had happened. The noise inside the generator room sounded like the wheezing of an asthmatic, winding everyone's nerves up tight.

The disassembled heating unit was already empty. I rushed up to Director Cao's side and asked quietly about the injured party, and he said he had already been taken away in an ambulance. I asked if his life was in danger, and Cao gave me a sidelong glance and said, "He's dead." My heart came up into my throat, and I was going to ask who it was, but looking at Director Cao's darkening face, I thought better of it and swallowed my words.

It wasn't until the emergency meeting that I learned that the victim was Liu Hongli. The dormitory of Liu's welding team was converted into a temporary meeting room. The company CEO, Chairman Yin, was there, too. I saw him sitting in the welding team leader's wobbly swivel chair, wearing a cold expression. Someone handed him a cigarette from behind, and he took it, but then tossed it on the floor without looking at it.

"Tell us how the accident happened, from the beginning," Chairman Yin said.

It was the welding team leader, Chen, who went through the series of events. He stood as he spoke, and because he was nervous, his whole body was trembling. He was stuttering a bit, but everyone understood him well enough. What had happened was that afternoon, welder Liu Hongli and Gao Gang reported that the No. 3 high-pressure heating unit had been disassembled for repairs. According to the safety regulations, no one is allowed to go inside it to weld unless it has been disassembled and allowed to dry out for at least forty-eight hours, because the interior of the unit contains steam and water. In other words, if you want to do any welding inside the heating unit, you must make sure that all of the moisture inside has evaporated before you can start. At three o'clock that afternoon, Liu Hongli entered the heating unit under Gao Gang's supervision, but when the welding torch touched the wall of the unit, there was a huge blinding flash. Liu Hongli screamed and collapsed, and a powerful electrical current went through his heart from his left arm. Seeing what had happened, Gao Gang shut off the power switch and called the station police. By the time the ambulance got there, Liu Hongli had already stopped breathing.

"Had the unit really been aired out for forty-eight hours?" Chairman Yin asked.

"Yes," Old Chen said.

"You saw to it personally?" Chairman Yin continued.

"The person responsible was Liu Hongli," Old Chen said.

"Do you mean to say that the only person who knew whether the unit had dried for forty-eight hours is the dead man?" Chairman Yin asked.

"Everyone involved knew it," Old Chen said.

"Only seven days short of three hundred days of safe operation . . . what an honor that would have been for our company! I had already submitted the paperwork to the provincial headquarters, and Accounting had already calculated all the bonuses. Now it's all for nothing," Chairman Yin said.

A rustling sound could be heard in the room.

Everyone began discussing how to deal with the accident. Through it all, I felt dizzy; it was like I couldn't understand what anyone was saying. Liu Hongli's death gave me a feeling I couldn't describe. When I first heard it was him, it was like taking a bullet; I just about passed out. When I began to come to my senses, I experienced a fleeting moment of joy, but it immediately gave way to astonishment. I thought about Qu Li;

I thought about how she would look and feel when she heard about it; I even began to guess what her attitude toward me might be in the future.

"Liu Hongli's death is a tragic loss; he was a Provincial Model Worker, after all!" Chairman Yin said, adding that the appropriate personnel must do their utmost to get to the bottom of the situation, and if anyone was guilty of neglect, he would not let them get away with it.

As Yin spoke, the room was notably silent; the terrifying effect of this statement combined with Yin's powerful charisma sent shivers up our spines. Director Cao gently nudged me with his elbow and whispered, "We have to be careful, or people are going to lose their jobs."

I nodded, stupefied. I knew that Cao was right; if Chairman Yin was unhappy, it could mean that my own meal ticket was in jeopardy. These days state-owned enterprises practice contracting and hiring by the level: the chairman chooses his own subordinates and mid-level managers, and the mid-level managers choose their own subordinates. I was Director Cao's subordinate, and I was always reminding myself that if I wanted to hold on to this position, I had to stand by him no matter what.

The accident response team was organized during this emergency meeting. The team leader would be a vice chairman of the company, Cao was deputy team leader, and I would be the other member. I was very experienced with accident response, but I was in unfamiliar territory with this one. I knew that if we were going to be truly fair and just, I had to resist something inside me. Not only that, but I had to think carefully about how I would deal with Qu Li as well.

I didn't sleep that night; it seemed there were heavy winds. Something kept knocking, noisily and rhythmically, like a percussion instrument accompanying my insomnia. Though my eyes were shut, I kept seeing images of Liu Hongli and Qu Li. Although Liu was already dead, unconsciously I began to doubt whether it had really happened at all. All along, I had pictured Liu Hongli as a powerful romantic rival, so it was hard for me to accept the fact that this formidable adversary could have been annihilated so easily. I also thought about my date that afternoon. I had invited Qu Li out so many times in the past, and she had always turned me down without the slightest hesitation, so why, of all times, had she accepted *this* afternoon? Could it be the workings of fate, that a single lunch out of the ordinary would so accurately predict a man's death?

I also carefully pondered matters related to Qu Li's future—with her fiancé dead, who would her next boyfriend be? I couldn't help but think it would be me, but that was all there was to it; I firmly broke off this line of thought. I knew that this was not a time to indulge in fantasies. I had to adopt a mindset appropriate to my role, and quickly take action.

—

At the first organizational meeting of the response team, Chairman Yin and some other relevant parties joined us. Old Xu, the chairman of the union, made a suggestion. He said that since Liu Hongli had been a model worker in the company for years, couldn't we make something of the fact that he gave his life in the line of duty? Chairman Yin asked him, "Make what of it?" Xu said, "Couldn't we make him into a hero like the Iron-man Wang Jinxi or Kong Fansen? Nowadays there are no worker role models, and if we handle the publicity correctly, we won't have to worry about this role model catching on like wildfire." Xu's recommendation immediately won the support of some at the meeting; they said that if we could successfully create this image, it would do a lot for the company's name recognition, so this was a rare and valuable opportunity. But Director Cao was opposed. He said that if we built him up as a positive model, that meant we would have to redefine the nature of the accident: "I'm afraid we'd have to rule out the victim's own responsibility. If we did that, not only would it subvert our established principles of accident response, but it would also lead to a series of negative consequences."

"What negative consequences?" Old Xu asked.

"First, it would undermine the cautionary effect of the accident. Second, the company would lose the initiative in guiding the final arrangements. Third, some threats to safety would be concealed," Director Cao said.

"Let's let Chairman Yin make the call," Old Xu said.

I noticed that Chairman Yin was carefully listening to the debate, or at least he was showing unusual patience toward it. As everyone waited for him to make a decision, he even leisurely sipped his tea and smoked a whole cigarette before he raised his head to speak. I knew that as he was sipping and smoking, he was struggling with conflicting feelings. His decision not only would affect the dignity of a worker's death, but it would also have an incalculable effect on the company's future. I thought it was patently unfair for such an enormous weight to be placed on a single individual, but what could one do? After all, many matters much more important than this are determined by some person's momentary decision!

Chairman Yin said, "I think it would be best not to make a hero out of him. It would be most prudent to investigate the accident according to our usual procedures, then deal with the result appropriately."

Chairman Yin's voice was not loud, but that did not diminish the tone-setting effect of his words. No one debated any further, and everyone else who spoke dealt only with the details of responding to the accident.

Among these, the most important matter was the question of whether Liu Hongli had entered the heating unit forty-eight hours after it was disassembled. If not, then the situation was much simpler; clearly it was Liu Hongli's failure to heed safety regulations, and the man was responsible for his own death. But if he had started the process more than forty-eight hours after the disassembly, then they would have to look for other explanations.

After the meeting was adjourned, the investigation officially began, and Director Cao put me in charge of gathering evidence on the ground. As everyone was leaving the meeting, Director Cao said into my ear, "You'll have to depend on the others, and make sure the people involved have the right idea about this. Remember, we must not let the situation get out of hand."

I nodded, and as I looked at the serious expression on Director Cao's face, I felt the weight of responsibility on my shoulders grow much heavier.

III

Safety Bulletin (No. ■)
[Date omitted]

Safety Office, Zhangjin Electrical Power

At 11:55 A.M. on [date omitted], there was a positive pressure fault in the No. 6 boiler chamber, and the steam drum water level began to fall. On inspection, the operator detected the sound of a leak coming from the economizer in the boiler's high-temperature section, and submitted a boiler shutoff request to the main dispatcher. The dispatcher gave permission at 3:00 P.M., and at 4:58 the generator was isolated from the production line. After the boiler was shut off, it was discovered that the second pipe in row 42 and the sixth pipe in row 21 on side B of the high-temperature segment's economizer had burst. After the pipes had been replaced, the generator was reconnected at 12 midnight on [date omitted]. Accident unit: Boiler Department.

After lunch, I returned to my office alone to rest. I was surprised to find Qu Li waiting for me at my door. My heart instantly leapt into my mouth; I wasn't ready to deal with her under the circumstances. Flustered, I fumbled for my keys and opened the door, then turned sideways to let her enter.

It was only after she sat down that I was able to observe her face. She had all the telltale signs of a woman who has endured a devastating shock: no makeup, a somber expression, solemn eyes. In the intense rays of sunlight coming in through the window, her face looked quite pale. I poured her a cup of water, and as she took it in her hand, I caught a whiff of that delicate fragrance I often longed for.

"I never imagined that such a thing would happen," I said.

I saw her eyes understandably tear up. Her pretty face was somewhat disfigured from crying so much; in the sunlight I could discern ripple-like streaks on her cheeks and nose. I guessed how miserable her mood must be at this moment, but what could I do? I could only use common words of comfort to try to ease her pain.

"You've got to hang in there."

Qu Li continued to cry, and she pulled out a handkerchief, absently wiping her face. That handkerchief seemed to have some kind of magic power, because her tears stopped falling. Even though there were still wet streaks on her face, I could see that there were no more tears welling up, only more reddening of the whites of her eyes.

"There's something strange about this," Qu Li said.

Finally she had said something, but I didn't have any idea how to respond to it, so all I could do was wait quietly for her to continue.

"It seems to me there were signs; I was inexplicably annoyed the afternoon it happened, and I wasn't myself when I was having lunch with you."

"Perhaps it was an omen," I said.

"A living man, especially one with so much vitality, doesn't just suddenly die like that."

"It was an accident. It's not unheard of in industry, after all."

"I heard that you're in charge of investigating the cause."

Qu Li stared at me, and I could see the meaning in her gaze. I also knew that my attitude now would determine her attitude toward me now and in the future, and naturally I couldn't ease off. I earnestly nodded my head.

Qu Li picked up a safety bulletin from my desk and waved it at me, saying, "Don't these always say that the responsibility for the accident falls on the victim?"

I hesitated, and said nothing.

Qu Li stood up suddenly and dropped to her knees in front of me. It scared the hell out of me. She said, "I beg you, for my sake, you have to do the right thing!" Flustered, I helped her up, saying, "Please don't! Even if it weren't for your sake, I would certainly be fair!" Just then the bell for the afternoon shift sounded. Qu Li said nothing else. She wiped her face again, then turned and walked away.

—

The first person I went to ask was Chu, the manager of the Turbine Department. The accident had occurred in his department, so his views and the materials he provided would be the most important.

When I walked into his office, he was sitting behind his desk in a daze. The machinery could clearly be heard through the walls, making his office seem like a moving train car. It always feels like I'm moving forward in an office like that, and the muted noise of the machines, sounding very much like train wheels, only reinforced the illusion.

"Hello, Old Chu," I said. "Could we talk about some aspects of the accident?"

Chu indicated that I should take a seat, and he pulled out a cigarette to offer to me. I told him I don't smoke, so he stuck it between his own lips and lit it, taking a dramatic drag. Then he said, "The accident was actually very simple. There's not much to tell. Let me begin by talking about Liu Hongli."

I took out a paper and pen and got in position to take notes.

Chief Chu said, "Liu Hongli's death truly hurts and was tragic. He was a rare young man. His spirit of self-improvement, eagerness to learn, and enjoyment of helping others were incomparable. Six years ago, buried in a new group of vocational school graduates assigned to the station, he did not stand out. When I went to Personnel to bring them in, I wasn't even aware of his existence. He was small and skinny, and didn't say much when there were a lot of people around. He was the kind of person who was easy to forget. On the way back he walked behind me, one of my six new employee candidates. Along the way, several young men were scrambling to talk to me, trying their best to give a good impression in a few words. They all knew that our department needed only two employees, and the other four would be assigned to work teams, so my impression of each of them would be crucial. Before this, there had already been someone referred to me through connections, but I rejected him. I would never select someone before I met him in person. When I brought these guys back, I was not in any hurry to make my choices, so I sent all of them to undergo training from a technician in the department to understand how things work. I do this so that I can observe them individually. Nowadays industries are all downsizing; when there's an exception and you can bring new people in, you want to bring in new blood and let some skilled and well-educated young men enrich the team. I was very careful in my selections, and after a week of observation, Liu Hongli gradually rose above the others in my estimation to become one of my favorites. Why? Because I discovered that this young man was both intelligent and reliable. When I went onsite to explain the workings of each kind of equipment, it was always Liu Hongli who picked it up the quickest. Once when we had to go down into a ditch, the others all hesitated because there was a lot of mud in it, but Liu Hongli was the first to jump in there. I also had them all write a report on what they had learned on the worksite, and most of them either just wrote a bunch of flowery language with no content, or they jumbled their words into a meaningless mess. Only Liu Hongli wrote in a clear, fluid style and with substance, making it impossible not to take him seriously.

"I had already decided to keep Liu Hongli in the branch station office, but what I didn't expect was that he would come to my house for a visit the night before I made the announcement. I asked him if he wanted to work in the office with us. He didn't answer my question, but instead replied with a deep and direct question in return: he wanted to know, if someone wants to make great strides in an industry, what path should he follow? I was initially taken aback by his question, and I hesitated for a while, but it was pretty clear to me what he was getting at. I said that if a person wants to make great strides, he must first plant his feet firmly on the ground of reality, then leave a footprint with each step, learning production techniques and mastering every aspect of the company. Having earned the respect of the leadership, you will be on the road to success. My answer energized Liu Hongli, and he said, 'Thank you, sir, for the advice. I came here tonight because I have a favor to ask you. It's not that I want to work in the office, but I want to man a team in the rank and file—inspection and repair, transport, crane operator, welder, I want to do them all. Once I've gotten the hang of being a worker, then you can think about promoting me.' I agreed to his request. I have no right to get in the way of a young, ambitious man. And so Liu Hongli worked the lifter for two years, did transport for two years, and then two years ago I transferred him to the welding team.

"Liu Hongli was the kind of guy who loved whatever he was doing, and what really impressed me was that for him, doing a job was not just doing a job, but learning the ins and outs of all the technology and equipment related to that job. On top of that, he had a heart of gold. His warmth didn't come through in his words so much as in the things he did. He was always a guy who did a lot and said a little. One time I was on the production site directing maintenance on the control console. I had put in several shifts in a row and suddenly fainted because of fatigue. With all those big louts on the site, it was that skinny little Liu Hongli who carried me off on his back. We don't have natural gas in the company residential area; having to replace liquid petroleum bottles was always a pain in the neck for me. But after he came into the station, he was the one who changed our gas bottles. I didn't even have to tell him; every time a bottle was almost empty, he'd be there right on time. My wife likes to eat wild vegetables. He said that all the wild vegetables in the market were actually farmed, and not really organic, so he would go up into the mountains every Sunday during his time off to gather a basketful of herbs for her.

"When he was working the lifter, Liu Hongli qualified as a productivity leader in the department. When he was doing inspection and repair, he was named a productivity leader for the whole plant, and after he took up welding, he was named a Provincial Model Worker for the National Grid. Even Chairman Yin thought very highly of him. Just a few days ago, he talked to me about promoting him, and I recommended that he be made assistant manager of the Turbine Department. Yin agreed . . . but how could such a thing happen to the boy?

"On the question of whether he entered the high-pressure heating unit forty-eight hours after it was disassembled, I can't say for sure at the moment, but I am certain about one thing: even if he went in early, it was surely for the sake of the plant. There can be no suspicion about his motives!"

IV

Safety Bulletin (No. ■)
[Date omitted]

Safety Office, Zhangjin Electrical Power

At 4:30 P.M. on [date omitted], Wang Yuhua and another worker from the Chemical Department, at the direction of their team leader, were constructing a toolshed in front of their team door. When they were about to turn the toolshed, a steel corner of a door on the shed rebounded and struck the metal side of the toolshed, crushing Wang Yuhua's left little finger, breaking a bone. The responsibility lay with the injured worker . . .

I put on my work clothes and safety helmet, required for anyone who enters the plant buildings, and went to look for Chen, the leader of the welding team. To tell you the truth, when I walked into the welding workshop, I was still caught up in Chief Chu's account. Although the things he'd told me seemed not to have any direct relationship to this accident, I was drawn to some of the details in it, which turned my thoughts in many other directions. The welding workshop was poorly lit, and the expressions on the faces of some of the welders who were sitting in there smoking were a corresponding steely gray. I asked them where Chief Chen was, and they said he was probably working onsite. I wanted to chat with them for a while, but they seemed to be deliberately avoiding me, filing out of the workshop with guarded looks on their faces.

Left with an empty smoke-filled room, I was in a daze for a while, then turned and went to the worksite. The sound of machines rolling past me like oppressive thunder made my whole body tense. I asked a number of different workers before someone was able to direct me to Chen. He was straddling a fat pipe welding a narrow tube. I reached out and patted his thigh; the blinding sparks immediately stopped flying, and he looked up at me in surprise, a look of resignation in his eyes.

Once he understood why I was there, Chen had to stop the job he was doing and call someone else over to finish it for him. He walked behind me, slowly, off the site. I knew that no team leader in his situation could be relaxed, but there was no getting around it: the situation had forced him into a position that he very much did not want to be in. Surely he knew that if he wasn't careful, not only would he lose his position as team leader, but even his job could be in danger.

We didn't go to the welders' break room to talk; instead we found a nearby exit and went outside the building. We sat down on the ground, leaning our backs against the wall. As before, I took out my notebook and got ready to take notes.

Old Chen said, "Liu Hongli definitely entered the high-pressure heating unit forty-eight hours after it had been disassembled. The job ticket proves it. As far as we know, it should have been safe for him to go in there. Nobody imagined he would get electrocuted as soon as he started welding. When I carried him away, I could see that half of his arm had been scorched by the current, and his ribs were exposed. As soon as I saw him, I had to look away. People are so fragile; your life can be gone just like that.

"I won't lie to you. Two years ago when Liu Hongli was transferred here to the welding team, I was against it. If Manager Chu hadn't lost his temper and forced him on me, I would not have backed down, and this whole thing would never have happened. But there are no 'ifs' in real life, or if there are, I certainly wouldn't stand up against Chu! He made me team leader, and just as he gave it to me, it would be easy for him to take it away. A team leader's job isn't glorious, but it's everything to me. You know that team leaders get hundreds more than workers in our bonuses. My wife is unemployed, and my son is already in the third year of middle school. You can imagine how much those few hundred mean to our family.

"The reason I didn't want to take Liu Hongli in is that he was a special worker, a productivity leader at the company level, and Chief Chu's wonder boy. If you're a team leader, you don't want a guy like that on your crew. How do you manage him? If I'm hard on him, he'll get offended, and he'll go over my head and say bad things about me. Would you be able to stand that? But I couldn't leave him alone, either; after all, he was working on my crew! So his coming was like a threat to me: if he wanted to, he could arrange to have me replaced at any time. Of course, on the other hand, Liu Hongli was a skillful worker; even if he was a schemer, he was clever and good with his hands. He learned welding in a few months and had great technique. After two years, he was able to do things it takes most people at least five years to master.

"One time our crew went to another affiliated factory to help them on a big project, and we got paid well for it. The guys in the front office didn't know about this money, and I wasn't going to tell them. Instead I divided it up three different ways based on how much work each of the boys did. I was afraid Liu was going to complain, so I gave him extra on purpose. But he wasn't okay with it and gave it back to me. I asked him if it was because I didn't give him enough. He said it wasn't that; he simply didn't want it. I asked him why, and he said, 'I heard that it's not honest money, so I don't want it.' Well, with him refusing, I wasn't sure what to do. Even though he didn't report it upstairs, I told everyone to give the money back anyway, and gave it to the department like I should have.

"I quickly began to realize that Liu Hongli was not a threat to my job; that's not where his ambitions lay. Or to put it another way, his ambitions were on a level I would never dare imagine. What did he want to be? He wanted to be the chairman! He never said as much, but I could see it. Once he answered a phone call and actually called the other person 'Godmother,' and spoke really respectfully. When he hung up, I joked with him, 'When did you get a godmother?' He smiled without answering. I asked him who the godmother was, and he just kept smiling. I bet this godmother was no ordinary woman, and was probably Chairman Yin's wife, or the wife of someone even higher up. It looked to me like he wanted to be the next Chairman Yin!

"As for his job, Liu Hongli was honest and responsible; he did a good job and was hardworking. I heard that in this maintenance project on the

No. 3 generator, there weren't enough hands, so he often went there and put in overtime, and when the accident happened, he had already gone three days without sleeping. You might think the accident had to do with excessive fatigue, but I don't think so. Most of what I said is crap; just keep the first part."

———

After leaving Old Chen, I was overwrought. From Chu and Chen's testimony, Liu Hongli was growing in stature in my eyes. I had underestimated him before, and that was probably why I had failed on the field of love. And Qu Li? I could see that she was a woman who knew a good man when she saw one.

That night I called Qu Li to ask her whether Liu Hongli had a godmother. She was not happy with this question at all, and asked me back, "What does this have to do with your investigation of the accident?" I said, "Nothing, I was just asking." Qu Li was silent for a few seconds, and then she said, "I'm not sure about this one way or the other, and I don't really care. With all that's happened, I'm only concerned with the final arrangements, and I hope the result will be fair."

I said, "Of course it's going to be fair. As long as I'm here, you have nothing to worry about."

"Thank you."

After I put down the phone, I was still feeling unsettled. I was like Old Chen. I was very sensitive to Liu Hongli's having a godmother. It was a habitual sensitivity, because indications pointed to Chairman Yin. Just about everybody in the company knew Chairman Yin's story: he was an ordinary worker who worked his way up to chairman, leaving a footprint at each step along the way. Of course, there were many people who helped him along, the most important among them being the company's previous chairman. At the time he was called factory chief, and not chairman. Chairman Yin took the old factory chief's wife to be his godmother, and so naturally the factory chief by extension became his godfather. And with the guidance of such a godfather, Chairman Yin rose quickly; only because of this had he achieved his present glory. Could it be that Liu Hongli was trying to retrace Chairman Yin's steps?

I struggled to warn myself that these matters were of no consequence to me, and I shouldn't be thinking about them. The important thing was to get to the root cause of the accident, and do right by Liu Hongli and everyone else.

V

Safety Bulletin (No. ■)
[Date omitted]

Safety Office, Zhangjin Electrical Power

Reprint of a report on an electrocution accident from an outside unit.

At 7:35 A.M. on [date omitted], in the Yongsheng Transformer Department of the Baicheng Electrical Bureau, after the person on duty disconnected the 66 kV Yongsheng-Tongyu line according to dispatched instructions and engaged the ground line for repairs, operator Du Guohao was mounting the ground wire at the line outlet, and he accidentally stepped on the live C knife gate of the circuit. Because the 3 megawatt switch and the main transformer were both operational, and the bypass bus was live, it caused Du to fall between the B phase insulated ceramic pillars. Once the main transformer had been shut off, a rescue was initiated. After Du was shocked, he fell to the side where there was no current, so fortunately there was no serious injury. The responsibility lay with the injured party . . .

When I returned to the welding workshop, they were in the middle of a meeting. Chen, who was sitting in the center, looked surprised. He glared at me and said, "I told you everything I know already. If you want me to say it again, I don't think there will be anything new." I forced a smile and said, "This time I'm not here to talk to you; I want to talk with Gao Gang." Every eye in the room turned toward a tall, thin young man. His face was carved with lines, and he had a rather large nose. To look at his face was basically to look at his nose.

Chen smiled awkwardly and apologized. I told him to continue with his meeting, and I would wait outside. Chen said, "You don't have to wait, we're already done here. Gao Gang, you stay behind, and the rest of you go back to the site with me and get back to work."

There was a sound of shuffling feet, and the room emptied out. Gao Gang and I sat facing each other across a large table. The smoke left behind by the group thoroughly engulfed us, taking a while to disperse.

Out came my notebook, and once again I assumed the position.

Gao Gang began, "According to regulations, there has to be at least one monitor when someone goes into the high-pressure heating unit to perform operations. Team Leader Chen assigned me to go along with Liu Hongli, so whether it was Liu Hongli entering the unit and me outside monitoring or the other way around, it was up to us. That afternoon

I was in a good mood, so my face was probably looking good, but Liu Hongli was looking poorly that day; his face had a gray cast, and he had dark circles around his eyes like a panda bear. I knew he had been working continuously and hadn't slept for three days, so I opted to go into the unit and let him monitor. But he pulled me aside and said in a low but determined voice, "Let me go in." You probably know that he pushed himself hard; if the work was heavy, unpleasant, tiring, or dangerous, he was always out in front. I knew it was useless to argue with him, so I didn't pressure him. I had no idea that choice would cost a life. As soon as the welding gun touched the container wall, there was a large arcing spark, and he went down forever.

"Now when I think back on it, I get frightened. If it had been me who went in, if he hadn't insisted, well, then it would be Liu Hongli sitting here talking to you and not me. I really should be grateful to him. He gave his life for me, although he may not have known it at the time. But those are the objective facts: he's dead, and I'm alive.

"Liu Hongli and I were about the same age. We usually got along pretty well. He didn't much like to pal around with the boys on the crew. While they were eating and drinking together, he was always off in a corner reading a book or a newspaper. The guys didn't think much of him, either; they said he was arrogant, and only mixed with the higher-ups. But I know that Liu Hongli wasn't a bad guy. Although he may have been a Provincial Model Worker, he didn't lord it over the people around him. And if he wasn't into goofing around, can you blame him? Once when we were both on the night shift, we were tired and hungry when we got off work. As soon as we were out of the company gate, we slipped into a little tavern. When we paid up, he stubbornly held down my arm, insisting on paying. That night we drank a lot. The alcohol got us spewing our true feelings, and he told me a lot of his inner thoughts. He said that it wasn't the era of the worker anymore; the working class is the poorest and most disrespected. He said that once he went with a vice chairman to the provincial capital for a meeting about model workers. He was taken aback by a conversation between that vice chairman and the chairman of another company. The vice chairman asked how much the workers were making at the other company, and that chairman said, 'Don't you have anything better to worry about than that? These days who cares how much money workers make?' And when he said that, the two of them burst out laughing. Liu Hongli told me us workers were really too miserable; we make so little money, and people look down on us, while our rice bowls are in other people's hands. Only when you can become a boss will people look up to you, and you will have your rice bowl in your own hands. I said that most of his classmates were already working in offices, so why did he go out of his way to be a worker instead? He took a drink, then let out a long breath and said, 'If a little clerk wants to work his way up, it's really slow, so if you really want to go up by leaps and bounds, you have to take a different approach.'

"Everything I just said was off topic, so you shouldn't keep it in the record. The important thing is whether he went into the heating unit forty-eight hours after it was disassembled. Of course he did, but then who would want to go in there anyway? Even if Liu Hongli was greedy for work, he wouldn't play around with his own life. What would be the point of throwing his own life away?"

———

I compiled the interviews I had conducted along with those of the other relevant employees, then submitted the report to Director Cao. Cao read it through and then looked at me with a furrowed brow: "What the hell is this? How could you arrive at such a result?"

I was psychologically prepared for his reaction. If I wanted fairness, I couldn't worry about the consequences. I said, "I was very careful in making this report; I'm certain there is no mistake."

"You must know the company policy regarding how to deal with accidents, right? What good is a result like this to our treatment of the accident?"

I said, "The accident is a fact. This time the victim should not be blamed."

"Liu Hongli really only entered the heating unit forty-eight hours after it was disassembled?"

"Yes," I said, "they were all very clear about it."

"But . . . that . . ." Cao's face was turning red as he stammered, "You're not a newcomer here. What do you expect me to . . . Do you really expect me to take care of this myself?!"

I said, "That's not what I mean."

Of course I was aware that I was in violation of an unwritten practice, and when I thought about how much trust Director Cao usually put in me, I felt pangs of remorse and anxiety in my heart.

After I left Cao's office, I realized that I was drenched with sweat, and the air conditioning in the hallway made me shiver involuntarily. I'd worked in the Safety Office for many years, and I was very familiar with the principles used for investigating accidents: the responsibility must as much as possible be placed on the injured or dead victim. That way the company's responsibility would be lighter, and the final arrangements would be much easier to manage. In the past I had always worked according to this principle, guiding the story in the company's favor when I was gathering evidence from witnesses, and I would always try hard to gather only evidence that was beneficial to the company's interests. If I were to work that way in this case, not only would I easily get back at my former romantic rival, but I would also perfectly fulfill the task assigned to me by Director Cao. But I didn't want to lose my dignity in Qu Li's eyes. After all, I needed her to see me as a good man. This was more important than anything, and it made me almost incapable of changing my story.

Before I knew it, I had made my way to the Training Department, the office where Qu Li worked. At the time there were quite a few people in the office. When Qu Li saw it was me, she took the hint and came out to talk with me in the hallway. "What is it?" she asked.

I looked at her blankly, and for a moment I couldn't think how to answer.

In fact, I didn't have anything to say to her; I seemed to have been driven there unconsciously. When you take a risk to do something right, you have to find someone to tell it to.

Qu Li said, "Well?"

I said, "Rest assured, the result of my investigation is fair to Liu Hongli."

"Thank you."

"You have to hang in there."

"I know."

I said, "Maybe we could have dinner tonight?"

She hesitated for a moment, then shook her head and said she wasn't in the mood, that I should wait a while and ask her again.

VI

Safety Bulletin (No. ■)
[Date omitted]

Safety Office, Zhangjin Electrical Power

On [date omitted], the mill at the No. 1 boiler was undergoing maintenance to replace the lid on the intake. The pulverizing team worked through their second night shift, and when the welder Zhou Jieyong had finished his work, he took the welding gun away, but the power supply wire was sitting in a pool of water with the electricity on. Around 8:00 A.M. a horse was electrocuted when it pulled a garbage cart through the boiler room and stepped on the power supply wire. The company paid damages of 1,000 yuan. The responsibility lay with Zhou Jieyong.

Liu Hongli's family moved into the company guesthouse. They were all farmers, so they made a spectacle of themselves when they moved around the company, and they became a topic of gossip among the employees.

That day, Director Cao said to me as soon as I came to work, "You'd better get to the union and talk to Secretary Xu on behalf of the Safety Department about dealing with Liu Hongli's family." I briefly hesitated, as I had hoped to continue with the accident response report, but although my lips started to move a bit, I kept it to myself. I knew that I had already lost Cao's trust, so nothing I might have to say would be of any use.

When I got to the union office, Old Xu turned out to be just on his way to visit with Liu Hongli's family. When he saw me arrive, he suggested I go with him, and I followed him to the guesthouse.

In a large room in the guesthouse, more than a dozen men and women were scattered about, some sitting, some standing; judging from their faces and clothes, it was clear that they had just come in from the countryside. Because some of the men were chain-smoking, the room had a powerful smell of the northeastern tobacco that makes you choke. When Old Xu and I entered the room, we began by shaking hands with some of the more important men. I noticed that there was a young guy who looked a lot like Liu Hongli, so I casually asked if he was Liu Hongli's brother. He nodded and said, "I'm his little brother, Liu Guangli." I deliberately used a little extra strength when I shook his hand, as an expression of sympathy.

Before we had exchanged the first few sentences, one of the women suddenly started crying, and before we knew it, the crying had spread throughout the room, and a lot of people were crying with gusto. Old Xu said, "Please don't cry, everyone! The company is actively responding to this accident, and we will make sure you get satisfaction."

"What do you mean by satisfaction?" Liu Guangli roared at Old Xu. "Are you going to bring my big brother back to life?"

"People don't come back to life. All we can do is try to do a good job on the final arrangements," Old Xu explained.

"How much are you going to compensate us?" Liu Hongli's father asked bluntly as he wiped tears from his eyes.

"We can't come up with a concrete number until the cause of the accident has been determined," Old Xu said.

"We're country people; we depended on Liu Hongli's pay to get by. Liu Hongli's mom and I were even planning on moving in with him in the city when he got married! Without Hongli's money, how can we treat his mom's illness? His little brother is a senior in high school; who will help us with the expenses?" Liu Hongli's father said.

"We take care of things according to the law," Old Xu said.

"Don't talk to me about the law," Liu Hongli's father said. "I'm an old fool, and I don't know anything about the law. But I do know that a life is priceless, that a life is worth more than anything."

I sensed that Xu was running out of moves, so I broke in. "Uncle, don't get upset. Hongli was our employee, we won't do him wrong. You should all get some rest, everybody. We'll take care of everything as quickly as possible."

After smoothing things over for a while, Old Xu and I made our exit. When we got to the gate of the guesthouse, I suddenly heard someone calling me from behind. When I looked back, I saw that it was Liu Guangli. "Brother, I heard that you were Hongli's good friend," he said.

I stopped in my tracks and asked Liu Guangli, "How did you know I was your older brother's friend?"

"Qu Li told me," he said.

I smiled weakly, thinking how clever Qu Li was. Apart from being Liu Hongli's rival in love, I'd had no relationship with him whatsoever. How did I become his friend? But I could hardly correct him at this point, so I merely nodded. Old Xu glanced back at Liu Guangli and me, and seemed to fear that Liu Guangli would pull him in as well, so he turned and continued to walk away.

"I heard that my brother didn't break any safety regulations when he entered into the unit to work," Liu Guangli said.

I knew what he was implying by "didn't break any safety regulations": it could only mean that Liu Hongli had entered the heating unit a full forty-eight hours after it was disassembled. Obviously it was Qu Li who had leaked this to him as well. I didn't want to conceal anything, and I said, "The matter of whether safety regulations were observed determines liability; it's really important."

"Brother, please do the right thing, and my brother will bless you from above," Liu Guangli said.

"Don't worry, I'll do everything in my power," I said.

———

After I had finished lunch, Qu Li came to my office again. I was the only person there during the lunch hour, and it was extremely quiet. Maybe that's why she picked this time to come looking for me. After I finish my lunch, I never go anywhere else; I just hurry back to my office to await her arrival.

When I was with Qu Li, whom I had admired for so long, it was hard to avert my eyes from the alluring curves of her body. I was afraid my fantasies would spoil the solemn mood of our recent exchanges. Qu Li still looked pale and haggard, and her voice was soft, as if she were afraid of waking something up. So I lowered my voice, too; that made our conversations seem like secret planning sessions—intimate and mysterious.

Qu Li said, "The company is about to start another round of evaluations."

I acknowledged this with a light "mm-hmm."

The evaluation Qu Li was referring to was a company practice; it was a policy instituted after the reforms, the purpose of which was to make every employee feel constant pressure. Specifically, they would do an evaluation on every level every two years; the chairman would hire middle managers, and the middle managers would hire underlings. For example, the chairman would hire the heads of the various departments, while the department heads would hire their team leaders, and the team leaders would hire the workers on their team. If a manager was not rehired, he would have to join a work team as a worker; but workers who didn't make the cut had to pick up and go home.

Qu Li asked, "Aren't you afraid you won't get rehired?"

I answered, "I would be lying if I said I wasn't concerned, but there's no use worrying about it until it happens."

She asked, "Won't the accident investigation negatively affect your chances?"

I said, "Since I've gone ahead and done it, I don't have any regrets."

"Thank you; I know you did it for me."

Qu Li's voice was tender, and it gave me a feeling I had never felt before. This feeling managed to suppress the fear creeping up from the bottom of my heart. I knew I had already offended Director Cao; it would be perfectly natural if Cao did not rehire me, but if in doing this I could win Qu Li's heart, it would all be worth it.

"Maybe I was selfish; for Hongli's sake I didn't think about your situation, your feelings," Qu Li said as she bowed her head. "But what choice did I have? This was all I could do for him."

I said, "Don't talk like that. It's our job to get at the truth behind every accident. Anyway, it feels good to do right by your conscience."

What I was telling her was straight from the heart. Maybe back when Qu Li first asked me to deal fairly in the accident investigation, I felt a little forced inside, but now that I had offended Director Cao, I was feeling a surge of inner power, and that power was already making me feel righteous, so that nothing else mattered.

"Thank you," she said. "You're a hero to their family."

I said, "Please—if you put it that way, I will feel more distance between us."

Qu Li slowly raised her head, and that beautiful sad face once again aroused feelings of tenderness in me. My gaze slid down from her eyes past her nose and lips, and came to rest on her chest. I had never thought I would have the chance to stand so close to her, but when I thought how this chance was brought about by the death of Liu Hongli, it spoiled the mood, and the tender feelings vanished.

My gaze moved upward until I was finally looking into her eyes, and I said, "I want the facts to speak for themselves, and I want to change the habit of always putting the responsibility for accidents on the victim."

Qu Li was staring at me, too, her eyes filled with gratitude, and something else besides.

VII

Safety Bulletin (No. ■)
[Date omitted]

Safety Office, Zhangjin Electrical Power

At 6:27 P.M. on [date omitted], the power switch on the No. 2 coal mill in the No. 5 boiler malfunctioned. The circuit breaker was tripped on A branch switch #251, but not #451; Section 5A lost power. The No. 805 low-voltage transformer plant switch tripped the circuit breaker; backup power switch 905 tripped a circuit breaker after connecting due to branch current overload; and after the water shutoff protection was engaged, the generator shed its load and automatically closed the steam valve. After the No. 2 mill malfunction was investigated and the switch was manually engaged, at 6:29 P.M. backup power switch #551 was implemented. At 10:20 P.M. repairs to switch #451 were completed, all systems returned to normal. Accident unit: Electrical Maintenance Department . . .

The accident response team met in the small conference room in the head office. Chairman Yin was there; he put his great big tea mug down on the table, and the meeting was considered under way.

Director Cao reported the result of the accident investigation; he said it was a classic case of human error, entirely due to Liu Hongli's foolhardy commencement of work in violation of safety regulations. According to regulations, work may be performed on the interior of the high-pressure heating unit only after it has been disassembled for forty-eight hours, but Liu Hongli went in before the forty-eight hours were up, resulting in a tragedy.

"The lessons of blood!" Chairman Yin interjected. "We must learn from the lessons of experience, and all personnel must look upon this event as a warning."

"Yes, we will begin writing the next edition of the safety bulletin very soon," Director Cao said.

My blood was boiling; I felt like my head had suddenly swelled up a whole size. Director Cao's report both shocked and outraged me. In order to curry favor with Chairman Yin, he'd actually had the audacity to alter the facts of the investigation. Didn't my investigation count for anything?

I sprang up from my seat, but Director Cao, who was seated next to me, immediately pulled me back down. I swung my head around to glare at him, and he glared right back at me. In a hushed voice he said, "Calm down; don't do anything stupid."

I thought for a moment, and realized that maybe Cao had a point: if I wanted to overturn this report of his, I would have to check some things first. I swallowed my anger and said nothing.

"How are things with the family members here?" Chairman Yin's gaze turned toward Old Xu.

"They're pretty agitated," said Xu, "especially the younger brother, Liu Guangli. I don't know where he heard this, but he's convinced that his brother entered the heating unit after more than forty-eight hours."

"The family's feelings are understandable; after all, a young man in his prime is suddenly gone." Chairman Yin sipped his tea and paused for a moment before continuing, "However, we can't just do whatever they want us to do. We must not back down where damage to the company's reputation is concerned."

"But . . ." Xu wanted to say something, but he checked himself.

"Of course, on the matter of money, we can make concessions; we're a big company, after all, and must show generosity," Chairman Yin said.

"Since you put it that way, that makes my job a lot easier," Old Xu said. "As long as we pay them more money, I don't think it will be hard to deal with the family."

After that, everyone animatedly discussed things, invariably in accordance with Chairman Yin's words. My thoughts were a mess; all I could think about was getting to the end of the meeting.

When it finally did come to an end, Director Cao asked me to meet him in his office. I guessed it could only be about blaming me and warning me. I didn't go with him; I went to the worksite instead.

———

Being in a hurry, I neglected to put on my safety helmet, and I had not gotten far inside the plant before someone stopped me. A safety inspector from some department waved his finger at my nose, saying, "You're a safety officer—how could you violate the safety regulations by failing to wear your helmet?" I said I had an urgent matter; he said however urgent it was, it certainly wasn't more important than safety, and I roared at him, "If this thing gets messed up because of you, you'd better watch out for your job!" He took that in and backed off. I shoved him aside and rushed toward the welding workshop.

I forcefully pushed open the big iron door to the welding workshop and saw a room full of thick cigarette smoke. There were two people in the midst of it smoking: one was Chief Chen, and the other was a technician from the Turbine Department. Chen came toward me wreathed in smiles. "The department technician is giving our team some guidance."

I said, "I'm sorry for interrupting your work, but my work is more important, it's urgent, and I must talk with Chief Chen immediately."

The technician gave me a lot of slack and said, "You go ahead and talk; I'll be getting back now." After Chen showed him out, he turned and said to me, "All the higher-ups are my superiors and can direct my work, and I must accept it with a smile; if I rub any of them the wrong way, they'll give me 'tight shoes to wear.'" As he said this, he seemed to suddenly realize something, and he immediately smiled again. "I'm not talking about you; you're very easygoing, very approachable, not like those big shots up there, who are so hard to get along with."

I said, "Chief Chen, you already gave your testimony, right? You said that Liu Hongli entered the heating unit forty-eight hours after it was disassembled."

"Yes, that's right. No, but . . ." Old Chen started to stammer, and with a pained expression he said, "but at the time I didn't fully understand the situation and spoke rashly, s-so when Director Cao came to investigate, I corrected myself."

I said, "Did someone put pressure on you?"

Old Chen said, "No, nothing of the kind. *Seek truth from facts* and all that!"

I said, "If he went into the unit before the forty-eight hours were up, as team leader you are also liable."

Chen said, "I'm responsible, and I'm willing to accept the consequences."

"Have you thought about whether doing this is doing right by the dead man?"

"This isn't about doing right by anyone. It's the facts, so I can't do anything about it." Old Chen added, "Actually I'm very sympathetic to Liu Hongli."

My eyes were sore from glaring. I was practically hating him with my eyes. He probably didn't want to offend me, so he held out a cigarette. I waved my hand, and he realized that I don't smoke, so he got up and poured me a cup of tea, saying softly, "I'm in a fix here, too; what kind of rank is team leader, anyway? If one of the higher-ups so much as coughs, it'll knock me to the floor."

Since that was how it was, I knew that anything I might say would be useless; a miserable sense of failure had my head spinning. When you think about it, I had every reason to go with the flow just like Old Chen, but the way things developed put me into a boat going upstream, so if I did not go forward, I was going backward . . . could I back off . . . could I *stand to* back off?

"Where is Gao Gang?" I asked.

"He went to work at the site," Old Chen said.

I left the welding workshop to look for Gao Gang, and it took a while before I finally found him in the noisiest possible place. I patted his shoulder; he turned his head, and when he saw that it was me, a look of panic flashed in his eyes. I yelled out loud that he should come with me. He put on a long face and said, "I'm right in the middle of something, and I can't get away." I yelled right into his ear, "No matter how busy you are, you've got to come with me now. It's work when I call you, too, you know?"

Gao Gang had no choice but to come with me and bring his miserable expression. Outside of the worksite, the loud noises faded away, and I got right to the point: "Why are you flip-flopping? Contradicting your own testimony?"

Gao said nothing.

I said, "Did someone put pressure on you?"

He nodded, then shook his head.

I said, "I'm going to ask you again: Did Liu Hongli go into the heating unit after it had been disassembled for forty-eight hours?"

"Don't force me."

I said, "I'm not forcing anyone, just tell the truth. You have to answer the question."

Gao Gang was silent for some time before he opened his mouth and said in a trembling voice, "I was mistaken last time I talked to you; what I said to Director Cao was the truth."

I said, "You're lying."

He lowered his head and stopped talking.

I really wanted to smack him in the face, but I knew I couldn't get away with something like that, and it wouldn't have done any good anyway. When I thought about my promise to Qu Li, I felt a pain pierce my heart. Apparently I had oversimplified things; this wasn't a situation where you could get justice merely by asking for it, or promising it.

———

VIII

—

Safety Bulletin (No. ■)
[Date omitted]

Safety Office, Zhangjin Electrical Power

On [date omitted], due to voltage increase testing after maintenance on the No. 1 generator, use of the 220 kV southern bus bar of the West Section was interrupted for use in the test. When the operator shut off the knife switch of the bus bar on the south side of the No. 2 line, the static and dynamic contacts of phases B and C were separated, but the A phase did not separate. The monitor, Qiu Lijun, ordered that the operation be stopped immediately. When the phase A knife switch was checked, a ceramic column was found to have broken off under its conductive rod. It was fortunate that the operation was stopped decisively, otherwise it would have caused a major accident. The monitor, Qiu Lijun, was commended . . .

When I got to the Training Department to see Qu Li, she wasn't there. According to her officemate, Chairman Yin had called her out. Why did Yin want to talk to her? Could it have been about the Liu Hongli affair? My thoughts were suddenly running wild.

In the hallway of the office building, I was momentarily uncertain which direction to go, and someone called out to me. I didn't clearly hear what he wanted. I slowly walked a few steps, then fished out my cellphone. I dialed Qu Li's number. A familiar popular song played on the phone for a while before she finally answered. I asked her if she was in Chairman Yin's office, and she very carefully said, "Yes." I was planning to say more, but she said not to bother her right now, and she hung up. Listening to the beeping busy signal, my mind was a complete blank.

On the way home from work that day, my thoughts were still jumbled. I wasn't sure how far I had gone when Qu Li caught up to me. Judging from her face, her mood had improved somewhat; there was now a bit of color in those cheeks that had been sallow for days.

"What were you so anxious to reach me about? Did something happen?" she asked.

I countered by asking, "What did Chairman Yin want with you?"

"Why, the Liu Hongli business," she said. "He told me to be strong."

"Is this something that you can cope with by just saying be strong?" I said.

"Are you going to tell me what you wanted with me or not?" Qu Li asked.

How could I put it? You could say this wasn't a big deal, but then you could say it was. I sighed and said, "I wanted to apologize to you."

She cocked her head and looked at me quizzically.

"The investigation of the accident turned out not to be as fair as I promised, and I feel bad about it."

"You did everything you could."

"The responsible party will very likely still turn out to be the deceased," I said.

"I realize that," she replied.

"But it's not fair . . ." My mood quickly got worse, and my voice rose as I said, "Even his coworkers and partners changed their testimony. Was their conscience eaten by wolves?"

"Don't get too upset about it. If you think about it, it's actually quite normal," Qu Li said.

I was shocked at her calm and rational attitude. The last thing I had imagined was that she would bear up better than I would; only a day before, her mood had been worse than mine. Was Chairman Yin that effective at bringing people around?

"These people are so inhumane," I said.

"Perhaps . . . this is actually humane."

I looked at her in astonishment.

"People's conscience is shaped by their environment. If you look at something from another perspective, you might be able to see it more clearly. For example, if the victim wasn't Hongli, but someone else, and Hongli had to give testimony, how do you think he would do it?" Qu Li stopped and then continued, "He would also say that the guy went in before forty-eight hours were up."

Her example made me gasp. I knew that she was trying to reassure me, to help get me through it. By all rights I should have been grateful to her for this empathy. The smart thing to do would have been to go with the flow and focus my attention on her, to quickly bring myself closer to the object of my ever-hopeless affections. But for the moment I couldn't bring myself to do it.

"Why don't we have dinner?" Qu Li said.

I said I had other things to do, and walked away alone. At a time like this, I knew that I was in no mood to have dinner with her.

———

The next day was Saturday. In the afternoon, Qu Li repeated her invitation and asked me to take a walk with her along the Huofang River. I hesitated, but then relented. The Huofang was the closest river to our Zhangjin Electrical Power. Originally it was as narrow as a rope, but in recent years it had enlarged due to improved management, and the river surface had become much broader, and the current stronger. Because it had rained the night before, moreover, the sky and the water were unusually clear, and the rain-washed trees and grass were almost suspiciously green. After a night of struggle, my mood had become much calmer, and I kept turning my head and looking at Qu Li's face as I walked. The feelings in my heart were complicated.

"What you said yesterday should really have been said by me," Qu Li said.

"What did I say?" I said.

"I should apologize to you. In fact, I involved you and made you offend your superior."

"For your sake, I feel like it was worth it."

"Actually, Liu Hongli and I had not yet married, so I didn't have any legal relationship with him," Qu Li said.

"But you did in fact have a relationship," I said.

We stopped walking, and I could see that Qu Li's eyes seemed to be tearing up. Perhaps it was to keep me from seeing that she kept moving along the slope down to the river's edge, where she squatted and rinsed her hands in the water. After a while, she turned and raised her face to look at me. She was below me, and I could see her silky hair hanging down, with the slanted rays of sunset forming a kind of fuzzy halo around it. Her uplifted face looked large, that kind of exaggerated look of being enlarged, as if to make me see it more clearly; actually she was one of those girls with a relatively small face. From this angle, the lovely contours of her bosom were in evidence, the top halves of her breasts heaving above her low collar. Our gazes interlocked, but I quickly averted mine.

A strange sensation surged and then vanished; I knew this wasn't the time to let that kind of feeling intensify or continue.

I reached out my hand to help Qu Li up, and the contact between our hands felt very calm. We sat on the ground, and she threw a stone into the river. The surface of the water broke into expanding concentric circles, and we stared at them in a daze.

"You're right about that; we'd been dating for three years, so how could I say we had no relationship?"

I cocked my head to the side and looked at her wordlessly.

"Do you want to hear our story?" Qu Li asked.

I nodded. Without looking at me, she began to tell it. Unconsciously I fished in my pocket as if for a pen and paper, but then I realized I didn't have to take notes this time. I quickly returned my hand to where it had been, and assumed an expression of careful listening.

"You know that in the beginning there were lots of guys pursuing me, including you, and they all had good prospects. But to be honest, none of you moved me. I'm an unusual girl; apart from needing a completely new feeling, what I want in a man is extraordinary potential for success. To other people, Liu Hongli was just a worker, with ordinary looks, so he didn't deserve me. I initially felt the same way; the first time he came to talk to me, I didn't treat him well. He said he wanted to be friends, and I coldly told him that I already had a boyfriend. Liu Hongli didn't get discouraged at all; he said if I had a boyfriend already, that wasn't a problem, that he just wanted to be regular friends, and we could chat a while when we had time. I said, 'I'm very busy, and I don't have any spare time to chat,' and Liu Hongli said, 'No problem. I won't disturb you when you're busy; I'll only come when you're free.' Seeing how stubborn he was, I really was afraid he'd come around a lot to harass me, but after several days he hadn't come back looking for me, so I breathed a sigh of relief.

"By the time I had just about forgotten about this Liu Hongli, something unexpected happened. One day when I got off work, my bicycle hit a rock, and I flew over the handlebars. I wrenched my back and scraped a bunch of skin off my shin. The blood seemed to be gushing out, and it got all over my dress. I tried several times to get up but couldn't quite manage, and just when I was so anxious I was about to cry, Liu Hongli showed up. He helped me to my feet, called a taxi, and took me to the hospital. That event brought us closer together, so thereafter when he came to chat, I was too embarrassed to refuse. He often came to my office after lunch. At that time the others in the office had all gone home for lunch, but because I ate in the cafeteria, I had nothing to do when I was finished, so I went back to my office. Of course, he didn't go every day; that definitely would have been annoying. He really knew how to pick his moments—often it was just once or twice a week. Sometimes I would be just starting to feel lonely, and there he was. If he didn't come for more than a week, I would sometimes actually start to miss him a little bit, as if something were missing.

"At first we were just idly chatting, talking about everything under the sun. Later he told me the story of Chairman Yin. We all know a thing or two about Chairman Yin's background, but hearing Liu Hongli tell it was an entirely different matter. He said that initially Chairman Yin was not that well liked by the old factory chief; whenever they ran into each other, the chief was standoffish. But Chairman Yin did not get discouraged: if one road is blocked, you can look for another. Chairman Yin began to deliberately approach the factory chief's wife; he went to the chief's house to do any work he was capable of doing. Once when the factory chief's wife was bedridden with an illness and vomiting a lot, it was Yin who always cleaned up, without being disgusted at all. The chief's wife was quite moved, happily taking him as her godson. It's not easy to be a godson; you have to pamper your godparents as if they were your own. Chairman Yin often went with the old factory chief to the public baths; in those days the bathhouses did not have attendants for rubdowns, pedicures, and all that, so it was up to Chairman Yin to do it all. Later when Chairman Yin became deputy factory chief, he finally had the chance to collect the dirt on the old factory chief, and Chairman Yin wasted no time in getting rid of him by exposing everything. Some people say Chairman Yin was too underhanded, but Hongli didn't think so. He said Chairman Yin was a hero: anything he did for his own advancement and the attainment of a respectable life for his wife and children was justifiable.

"Liu Hongli said he would be a man like Chairman Yin for his future wife and kids. I smiled and said, 'You're only a worker; that goal is a little out of your reach, don't you think?' Liu Hongli said, 'If you dare to imagine it and then do it, no goal is out of your reach.' That comment moved me; I guess you could say the whole speech moved me. I couldn't deny that this ordinary-looking guy was way ahead of other guys in some respects.

"Somewhere along the way, we fell in love. In the process I got to understand him better; to him, being a worker was 'taking the long route to save the nation.' If he had been a common clerk in a department office, he would have been surrounded by competitors; it would have been practically impossible for him to get promoted into the top company leadership. As a worker, he could become a model worker for the company, he was able to become a sensation among the younger staff and workers, and he had opportunities for contact with the company leadership. Every time he had such an opportunity, he made the most of it and demonstrated his abilities. Having worked in the trenches all these years, he was familiar with all of the production equipment, and his broad knowledge would become crucial when it was needed. He introduced many recommendations for rationalizing production, and had already impressed Chairman Yin. You don't know that when the accident happened, he had already been promoted to assistant department chief. And with his godmother's support, his future rise to the top would have gone even faster.

"We dated for three years, and our relationship developed steadily. Liu Hongli had a strange aura about him; it could move you and scare you at the same time. For example, how was it that he used to show up every time I needed him? Unless he was sneaking around following me everywhere for days, he couldn't have achieved this. I believed he would succeed, but our love was too bland; in three years there had been no excitement. Liu Hongli was too devoted to success; the time he spent on his so-called career was far greater than the time he spent on love. At the beginning, when he was pursuing me, he wasn't miserly with his time at all, but once we had established our relationship, his time investment in me got progressively shorter. When I complained about it, he told me to think long-term, that he would eventually be like Chairman Yin, who gave his wife a white Honda sedan for her birthday and sent his kids to England or the U.S. to study.

"It's not that Liu Hongli wasn't good to me; he may not have spent time with me every day, but every few days he would give me little gifts as a token of his affection, like hair clasps, handkerchiefs, stockings, even bras and panties. He never got tired of saying that although now he was just giving me little things, there would come a day when he would give me big things. Looking at these various trinkets, my heart would be filled with a different kind of feeling. I wasn't sure if it was gratitude or helplessness. Sometimes I thought I didn't need these gifts, and not just the small ones; I also didn't need the so-called big ones he talked about. What did I need? Suddenly I felt lost.

"You probably have already sensed that there were some little cracks forming in our relationship. After something that happened, those cracks gradually became clearer. The situation was a company excursion outside the city last year; the trip was organized by the company labor union, and the people who went were all outstanding performers in the various departments. Liu Hongli and I both went. There was a special participant in the group, and that was Chairman Yin's wife. Naturally she got special attention from the organizers; for example, on the bus she sat up in front next to the driver, and during meals she would be seated in the place of honor at the head table. On the trip back, the bus was speeding along the highway at full power when suddenly a great big freight truck turned onto the road from a side road. The bus had to dodge to one side, but the driver turned too hard, and the bus went right into a water-filled ditch next to the road, and came to a stop tilted to one side. Everyone on the bus was screaming in panic. I fell on a glass window, and Liu Hongli shoved his way over to rescue me, but no sooner had his hand touched my arm than he put it back down. I watched as he lunged over several people at an unbelievable speed toward the front of the bus, and pulled Chairman Yin's wife out of the bus before anyone. Afterward, I asked him a low-class question that everyone has heard: 'If your mother and I both fell into the river, and you could only save one of us, which one would you save?' He grimaced, asking, 'How could you ask me to make a ruthless choice like that?' Then I said, 'What if Chairman Yin's wife and I fell into the river at the same time. Which one of us would you save?' He said, 'Of course I would save you.' I disdainfully eyed him and said, 'Actually you don't have to answer that question, because you already answered it with your actions.' He anxiously tried to comfort me: 'You've got me all wrong. I only went over to help her when I discovered that you weren't injured. You have to remember that this was an opportunity I couldn't pass up. How could I let it go?' I didn't say anything more, but when he left, I couldn't hold back the tears. I didn't know whether I was lucky or unlucky to have a boyfriend like that.

"In fact, our relationship had already been on the brink of collapse for days before his accident. Otherwise I never would have agreed to have dinner with you. But even so, his death has been an enormous blow to me. On that first night when my face was drenched with my tears, the differences between us had become blurred, and in effect I have become a widow who has endured a painful tragedy.

"Fortunately it's all over now; dead people can't come back to life, and we have to live on."

IX

Safety Bulletin (No. ■)
[Date omitted]

Safety Office, Zhangjin Electrical Power

At 10:00 A.M. on [date omitted], Liu Yongsheng of the High Voltage Team of the Electronic Maintenance Department was measuring the No. 1 pump motor of Machine 4's DC resistance and insulation resistance. As he was walking past the No. 1 pump motor of Machine 4 on the south side, he slipped on some oil on the ground and fell, and the front of his left lower leg was punctured by a steel wire. The responsibility lay with the injured man . . .

I knocked a few times on Director Cao's office door. My hand wasn't trembling as much as I had thought it would; instead it was steady and decisive, the impact of my knuckles on the hardwood of the door reverberating crisply, reflecting the impatience I was feeling at the time. I was looking for news; according to a leak from a reliable source, the list of rehirings in every office had already been determined. Would I be on the Safety Office list? I had already greatly disappointed Director Cao in the process of the accident investigation, so it was not hard to imagine that I would not be on that list.

I had only knocked a few times before Director Cao said, "Come in." I pushed the door open and entered to find Director Cao gloomily staring at me from behind his desk. I knew there would be no reward in offending the top man in our office, but since it had come to this pass, there wasn't anything to fear, either. The worst that could happen was that I'd have to join a team as a worker. I was psychologically prepared for that, so my back was straight and I was not averting my gaze in the slightest.

"Director Cao," I said, "I heard that the list of hires has already been decided?"

Cao furrowed his brow and nodded.

"Am I on it?"

"Do you think you're on it?"

I remained silent for a moment.

Director Cao said, "You were always a young man who could be relied on, and I trusted you all the way. But your actions on the Liu Hongli business really put me in a fix!"

I said, "I was only acting according to my conscience."

"Do you think you're the only one around here with a conscience? Don't I have a conscience?" Director Cao's face was turning red, and he excitedly continued, "In business today, everything is up to the boss; he's got our rice bowls in his hands. Even if we don't want our own rice bowls, what will our wives and children do when they get hungry?"

I wanted to say, "This is selfish," but before I could get the words out, Director Cao's speech turned a corner. "Of course, you're still young, and some things can be forgiven. Chairman Yin and I both want to give you a break, so your name is still on the list."

I stood there in a daze with my mouth half-open. This was a complete surprise to me, and for a moment I wondered if there was something wrong with my hearing.

"As long as you don't do something stupid again next time, there'll be no problem," Director Cao said.

I don't know how I made it out of Director Cao's office; I felt like I was walking on cotton, staggering. Was it Director Cao's generosity of spirit, or was Chairman Yin giving me special treatment? Why would Chairman Yin give me a break? Had someone gone to him to plead on my behalf? Who could this be, other than Qu Li? A chilly breeze blew through the hallway, and I involuntarily sneezed loudly.

After I got back to my own office, I called Qu Li on the phone. I said, "Did you put in a good word for me?" She didn't say one way or the other, only, "I'm glad you're on the list; otherwise I wouldn't feel right."

—

Liu Guangli came to the company offices by himself. He accused the company of indifference to human life, putting the responsibility for a fatal accident on the dead man. He wouldn't stand for it, and would appeal. His voice resonated through the hallways like rapid fire from a mortar, causing everyone to peer nervously out of their office doors, curious to see what was the matter.

My head was also stuck out of my door, and I saw Old Xu from the labor union trying to reason with Liu Guangli. Xu's voice was very low. I couldn't hear anything he was saying, but I could hear every word that Liu was saying. He said, "Don't try to pull the wool over my eyes; I already know the real story. My brother went into the heating unit forty-eight hours after it was disassembled, not before the forty-eight hours were up like you guys are saying."

I secretly admired Liu Guangli, so courageous at such a young age. I was secretly rooting for him; I thought if he stuck it out to the end, the company might make concessions to avoid trouble, and reassess the accident.

Liu Guangli's voice gradually got quieter; Old Xu was probably worried about repercussions and had pulled him into his office. I retreated into my own office and returned to my desk. The afternoon sun shone so brightly on my face that I couldn't open my eyes. The documents and safety bulletins on my desk faded in the sunlight, the words blurred faintly into a blob that made it impossible to read anything. Not long thereafter, the door opened, and Director Cao walked in.

"You go and reason with Liu Guangli tonight," he said.

"Okay," I said, and obediently nodded. Perhaps it was because my name was on the hiring list, but subtle changes were occurring in my attitude.

"Comforting bereaved families is the labor union's job, but they didn't do a good job with this one. This gives us an opportunity to do our work, and we mustn't miss such an opportunity," Director Cao said.

"I will do the best I can."

I went to the guesthouse as soon as I finished dinner. My feelings were complicated. The cars going back and forth in the evening sun looked like so many moving spots of light, while the pedestrians looked like crawling ants, and amid the light spots and ants, I felt haggard as I walked alone. I knocked on Liu Guangli's door, and was met by a bunch of astonished eyes. These were Liu Guangli's family members, and they were obviously in the middle of a discussion. Once I arrived, they all shut up, and one after another they pushed past me and out the door, leaving only Liu Guangli in the double room, facing me.

I said, "I came to see you."

Liu Guangli said, "Have a seat."

I sat on the edge of the bed, and Liu Guangli sat on the edge of the other bed facing me. I could see that his eyes were red and puffy; obviously he had cried a lot during the past several days. I didn't know where to start, and he beat me to it, saying, "Thanks for your help . . . my brother up there will also thank you."

I smiled weakly and said nothing.

Liu Guangli said, "We'll be leaving tomorrow."

I was taken aback and blurted out, "Aren't you going to appeal?"

Liu Guangli shook his head and said, "No, I've thought it over, and I don't want to appeal."

I should have expressed approval for this decision; it not only saved me a lot of talking, it also completed the mission Director Cao had given me. But for some reason, the suppressed resentment in my subconscious suddenly flared up. I said loudly, "What about justice?"

"Justice?" Liu Guangli shook his head. "Justice doesn't pay the bills; if my brother were still here, he would agree with my decision."

"So you're going to accept the compensation amount offered by the company?"

"The company agreed to pay the amount we asked for," Liu Guangli said.

"Is money that important?" I asked.

"My mom is sick, and I'm still in school. Our family really needs the money," he said.

For a while I couldn't speak.

Liu Guangli was still struggling to say something, but I was not taking it in. I watched his tongue move around in his mouth; it was a light red color, with a white coating on top.

———

X

Safety Bulletin (No. ■)
[Date omitted]

Safety Office, Zhangjin Electrical Power

At 3:55 p.m. on [date omitted] at the maintenance site for the No. 3 generator, welder Liu Hongli of the Turbine Welder Team entered the disassembled high-pressure heating unit on a work task less than forty-eight hours after disassembly, leading to his fatal electrocution. The responsible parties: the deceased, his work monitor, the on-duty team leader, and the department chief all share significant responsibility.

The company calls upon all its employees to learn from this accident, to strictly carry out the production safety protocols in order to prevent similar accidents from occurring again in the future . .

Sitting behind my sun-drenched office desk, I put down the completed draft safety bulletin, and with some effort exhaled at length. The matter was finally coming to a close, and I thought that I, too, should finally be finding my way after having been lost.

I sipped some tea for a pick-me-up, then picked up the phone to call Qu Li to invite her to dinner after work. The sudden fatal accident had given new life to what had been a hopeless love, but I didn't know whether I was happy or sad.

I had just punched in some of the numbers when someone pushed the door open, and in walked Director Cao. I set down the receiver and smiled politely at him. Director Cao was looking pretty good; the successful resolution of the accident case had surely given him a sense of accomplishment, and his face was adorned with a rarely seen joyous smile.

Director Cao asked, "Have you written up the latest edition of the safety bulletin?"

"It's done," I said.

Cao took the draft I handed to him and sat down to read it carefully. I noticed that his face maintained its original expression, which made my unsettled heart calm down a bit.

"Not bad," he said, smiling, "Objective, specific, well-documented, and logical—I can see that the clever and capable young man from before has returned!"

His praise made me feel awkward; I smiled a little sheepishly, not knowing how to reply.

Cao continued, "The company is about to give out the seasonal bonuses, and as you know, the gap between the managers and the workers is bigger than ever."

I was still smiling sheepishly, and still silent.

Director Cao suddenly changed tack. "You're already twenty-nine; you should have a girlfriend."

"No hurry," I said.

Director Cao said, "Age is unforgiving; if you miss the chance, you could come to regret it."

His advice was certainly well-intentioned, but it annoyed me nevertheless. On the other hand, he did have a point. So as soon as Cao walked out the door, I hurriedly dialed Qu Li's number.

I said, "Shall we have dinner tonight?"

Qu Li said, "I can't do it tonight."

I said, "Why?"

"Chairman Yin will be hosting the leaders of the company's provincial headquarters," she replied, "and he said that all of the women in the head office should be present."

I said, "But you're not in the head office."

Qu Li said, "Starting today, I've been transferred to Chairman Yin's office."

I stared blankly for some time after putting down the phone, and then was suddenly gripped by a terror I had never felt before. I had never imagined that Liu Hongli's death could get Qu Li a promotion. How could this have happened? I had no answer, and my heart was in more turmoil than ever.

———

After work, I didn't go straight home as usual; instead I went to a hot pot restaurant by myself. I had originally wanted to go to the Western restaurant with Qu Li, but since I was alone, there was no need to eat Western cuisine. A lone person doesn't need the atmosphere, and the pungent spiciness of hot pot was probably better suited to the mood I was in: hot soup and spicy liquor; break a sweat all over, and maybe I'll feel a lot better.

The restaurant was really crowded, and it took some doing to find a small table off in a corner. A hot pot, a pint of liquor, and in that clamorous atmosphere it didn't take long for me to break out in a sweat, but an uncontrollable urge to rant and rave emerged as quickly as the sweat did. I had a whole bellyful of complaints, but who could I tell them to? And what would I say?

I took a belt of liquor, then had another mouthful of soup. My gaze swept through the dense, hot air over the dozens of purplish-red faces covered in beads of sweat, and I knew that my face was purplish just like theirs. They were all talking loudly in excited voices, full of joy, but my urge to spew ravings could only swirl madly around inside my body, desperately looking for an opening to burst out.

Amid the countless faces of strangers, I finally found a familiar face, and I was overwhelmed with the excitement of grabbing hold of a life preserver. I unhesitatingly stood up and weaved my way through the unfamiliar faces to stand before that familiar one. I roared at him, "Old Chen, what are you doing here?!"

Chen was with a bunch of workers, drinking together, and I could tell by his color and his voice that he'd already had quite a bit. Alcohol had taken away all his surprise and doubt, and he loudly shouted back, "Oh, *you* can be here, so why can't *I* be here?"

"I didn't say you couldn't be here, but Liu Hongli, he can't be here," I said.

I had no sooner said it than I realized it was the liquor talking, but I couldn't control myself.

"Don't bring him up, okay?" Old Chen said.

"Are you afraid that if I bring him up, it means you did wrong by him?" I said, staring into Chen's eyes, "He obviously went into the unit after forty-eight hours, but you testified that he didn't!"

"Who cares if it was forty-eight hours or not?" Chen said, starting to choke up. "Even if it was forty-eight hours when he went in to work, the accident still happened, didn't it?"

He had me there. Or you could say I was suddenly gripped by a realization, and I seemed to sober up by half. I thought to myself clearly, *How could I have overlooked something so obvious, and not only me, but all those clever people—how could we all have overlooked this?*

"All the parts inside the heating unit were low-quality; if they didn't all dry out in forty-eight hours, it was quite normal," Old Chen said.

"Why use parts like that?" I said.

"It was all brought in by Chairman Yin," said Old Chen.

"No one said anything about it?" I said.

"Chairman Yin tells other people what to do; who would dare tell Chairman Yin what to do? And who *can* tell Chairman Yin what to do?" Old Chen said. "Here, bottoms up!"

I took the glass Chen handed over to me and drank it all down in one gulp. It was too much for me, and I started coughing hard.

The Sanctimonious Cobbler

Wang Anyi

TRANSLATED BY ANDREA LINGENFELTER

1

In order to explain how this particular bit of turf ended up belonging to the young cobbler, it's probably a good idea to first look at the history of the city and its development in modern times—which, practically speaking, means certain people and certain events. Originally, the patch of dirt in question had been on the edge of town, part of a larger tract where the city's foreign residents had located their cemetery, which locals called the Foreign Graveyard. The streets nearby were crowded with florists, candle shops, sellers of statuary—crosses, angels, Virgin Marys carved of wood or stone—and other objects suitable for placing on graves. Later on, a Chinese cemetery was established on the farmland adjoining the cemetery, and shops catering to Chinese funerary customs soon proliferated as well, selling things like incense, candles, paper effigies, burial robes, ghost money, and Chinese-style coffins. The graveyard grew larger and larger over time, and the farthest tombs were abandoned and fell into ruin. Things went along in this way until one day the Municipal Council—which oversaw the Foreign Concessions—appropriated the land in order to create a new residential district. The first task was to clear the cemetery—the one known as the Foreign Graveyard. A notice was published in the newspaper, giving Chinese residents seven days to move their ancestors' remains. Any unclaimed bones were then collected and cremated together. This left only the graves of foreign residents, which lay within a boundary wall. The neighboring funerary businesses closed up shop of their own accord.

After plans were drawn up, lanes laid out, and Western-style buildings erected, some of the shopkeepers returned to the neighborhood, only this time they were pursuing new lines of work. Some opened fruit stalls, others sold wontons, and others still worked as watchmen in the newly built longtangs—narrow lanes flanked by row houses. One of the people who came back was a man from Pudong who had formerly sold ghost money. Pedaling a bicycle loaded with baskets full of freshwater fish and shrimp, he went door to door selling his wares. People in the neighborhood gradually got to know him, and he became chummy with a policeman who had come from Shandong. The two of them built a lean-to in one of the lanes, where they sold shrimp wontons that proved to be so popular that they drove the other wonton sellers out of business. The Pudong man's wife came up from the country to join him, and she spent her days sitting at the side of the lane and shelling shrimp. Business was so good that they outgrew their space, and the policeman scouted around for a new location. The lean-to was only big enough to hold a single-burner coal stove and one stockpot, and they turned the spot over to a metalworker. The policeman moved away, and the metalworker gave the spot to a leatherworker from his home village in the countryside near Yancheng in Jiangsu. From then on, this little patch of ground belonged to the leatherworker, his fellow leatherworkers, and their families.

When people in the city said "leatherworker," what they really meant was "cobbler." Life in town was very different from life in in the country. In the countryside, people had livestock and needed bridles, harnesses, and other kinds of tack—but apart from a pair of shoes, what did townsfolk need? The old cobbler eventually passed his skills and his patch of dirt on to his son and returned to his home village, where he lived out his later years. Time passed, and the son grew old in turn, changing from a young cobbler into an old cobbler. The city itself had continued to spread outward, and the neighborhood, once on the outskirts of town, was now in the heart of the city. Nonetheless, it hadn't lost its residential character, and the longtang itself was separated from the hustle and bustle by a side street. The cobbler had moved his business several times, but he had never left these precincts. When the Public Hygiene Committee reorganized the lane, businesses were told to move—but where could they go? The metalworker moved to the little market, the woman who darned socks worked from home, one of the water boilers was shut down, and the fried-dumpling seller joined the local food and beverage company, which was now operating under the moniker emblazoned on its brand-new sign: "Cooperative Canteen." The cobbler gathered up his gear and moved to a spot beside a miniature park facing the larger street. The "park" was nothing more than a greenbelt, two meters wide and ten meters long, backed by the walls of a teachers' college. Most of the students were women, and women's shoes are often in need of repair—buckles break, heels wear down, soles come unglued, and so forth. There was a little folding stool in front of the stall, and it wasn't unusual to find a young woman perched there, one bare foot resting atop the shod one, waiting for the cobbler to finish his work. It was a pleasant and friendly scene, but before long the street was reorganized again, and the cobbler was banished once more. He packed up his things and moved back to his original place under the archway at the mouth of the lane. It was a rather shady spot, but it was relatively quiet, and the archway offered some protection from wind and rain. There was also a low wall where he could put his materials—glue, leather, heels, nails, and laces—and where he could lean back while he waited for customers to drop off or pick up their shoes. Sometimes nobody came by, and sometimes he was besieged with customers—men and women, old and young, bearing all kinds of shoes, but none of them was in a hurry, and they were happy to leave their shoes with him for a day or two before retrieving them. He didn't bother with claim checks, either—not because he was good at remembering faces, but because he never forgot a pair of shoes. And besides, he wasn't worried about people running off with the wrong pair—who in the world would want somebody else's old shoes?

Life continued on peacefully for some time, until yet another government office kicked him out. Just as before, the cobbler quietly packed up his things and moved back out to the main street. This time, rather than setting up shop by the greenbelt, he relocated to the vestibule of a building. The building had fallen into disrepair—paint peeled from the wooden doors, and plaster flaked from the walls and ceiling. The cobbler put his stall at the top of the stairs that led to the entry. It was a good site, and his business blended into the surroundings. Life was good until the day renovations began on the old building, and the cobbler had to move again. So he packed up and went back to his old haunts, sometimes to the lane and sometimes to the greenbelt. And so it went. Although he floated from spot to spot, he never floated out of the neighborhood altogether—not that the long-ago verbal agreement with the policeman from Shandong had any standing; after all, who could possibly know for sure what had happened in the past? Even if you could confirm the agreement, who would be willing to honor it? He was just a humble cobbler, a local fixture; the neighbors were regular customers, and he wasn't about to give up and move on. People were used to his workmanship, and when on occasion he went back to the countryside for a few days' visit, they waited for him to return, rather than take their shoes to someone else—

even though there was a cobbler on every street. What's more, he was able to work unhindered, since the various government offices charged with the task of chasing people like him away didn't make a genuine effort. Instead, each month the tax collector came to collect a fee, and the cobbler was able to settle down at the mouth of the lane. There was now a row of nails in the wall, and below them stood a tool chest and a metal cabinet. Every morning, the cobbler pushed the short end of the chest against the wall, creating a little workspace. He then unlocked the chest and took out the tools of his trade—a machine for stitching shoes, which he set on the ground, and assorted awls, clamps, pliers, and scissors, which he hung from the nails on the wall. He also hung a few strips of rubber on the wall and pulled a little tray out of the chest, stocked with glue, nails, buckles, needles, thread, and shoe polish.

All of this brings us up to the present day. A new generation has come to take the place of the previous one, only the young cobbler isn't the old cobbler's son, but his son-in-law. The old cobbler passed his skills and stall on to his daughter's husband and retired to the countryside. Not long thereafter, he got cancer and died—or, in the words of his son-in-law, he "went to see Karl Marx." Because his father-in-law had given him his trade, the young cobbler was more than a son-in-law; and thus it fell to him to support his aging mother-in-law, who was, after all, also his teacher's wife. The young cobbler had brothers, but they weren't close to their parents, who had given the cobbler a large house with a tile roof, along with a courtyard with two cedar trees. Thus, the responsibility of looking after his own parents also fell to him. Although these three members of the older generation were all able-bodied enough to work, he demonstrated his commitment to caring for them by leaving his wife in the village and living alone in Shanghai. The old cobbler had also bequeathed to him his living quarters—a garret in a ramshackle tenement one bus stop and a few blocks away from where he worked. The owner of the building and the old cobbler had known each other a long time. The sprawling slum had been slated for demolition while the old cobbler was still living there—hand-painted emblems consisting of circles painted around the word "raze" still marked the walls—but as yet nobody had come to tear them down. The real estate market had been weak for quite a while, and by the time it improved, the cost of relocating the residents had become astronomical. The slums were densely populated, and the houses—all privately owned—had been added to again and again, with new stories teetering atop former rooftops. The developers were stalled, and so they remain as of this writing. The young cobbler's landlord had bought another house and moved out, renting the ground floor to three men from Henan who sold roasted nuts. The cobbler wore two hats—not only was he a tenant, he also kept an eye on the property for the landlord. The garret was sixty or seventy meters square, large enough for a double bed, a table, a wardrobe, and a rush mat. From time to time, the cobbler's wife would come for an extended visit. Sometimes his parents came to stay, and he gave them the bed and slept on the floor. At other times his mother-in-law and wife would come together, and the women would sleep on the bed while he took the floor. When his wife was in Shanghai, she didn't go to his stall—she was too shy. His parents didn't visit the stall, either—their feelings about the matter were complicated. It was as if someone else had given their son his livelihood, and they felt ashamed. The only one who would accompany him was his mother-in-law; and she would sit herself down on the little folding stool and watch him work. When her husband was alive, he had plied his trade in this very spot, and both the current customers and their parents had done business with him. The tableau of street life and traffic moving past the lane was the same one her husband had looked out on; the work that her son-in-law did with his hands was the same craft her husband had practiced—her future felt secure. And how did the young cobbler feel? He was clear in his mind, but being from the countryside, he wasn't used to showing his feelings, and in the end both he and the old woman kept their thoughts to themselves. Still, although they each kept their own counsel, their familial closeness and interdependency were apparent to one and all. Thus, from time to time people would have to remind themselves that the elderly woman who sat and watched the cobbler was not his mother, but rather his mother-in-law.

The cobbler's mother-in-law stayed by his side, looking on as he greeted his customers and repaired their shoes. Most of his customers were women, and their interactions were warm and friendly—sometimes too friendly, flirtatious even. The cobbler maintained a formal and proper attitude and never chatted them up—and not because his mother-in-law was there, either; he was always like that: he was a man of integrity. That said, he was an attractive fellow, with a solid build and wide eyes set in a childlike face. Women, including the ones who flirted with him, treated him like a child, calling him Young Cobbler. In fact, he had married young, like most country folk, and he was already the father of two, which was one reason he acted so staid.

The cobbler kept up with the times, and his business expanded. He had a deep reservoir of expertise and was a quick study, and he easily learned how to repair zippers, how to put rivets in blue jeans, and how to wax metal buckles. When it came to his original line of work, there were also many new skills to learn. Take soles, for example. Materials were constantly evolving, and the structures as well. One type had a sort of keel running through the interior. Lifestyle changes created patterns of wear different from the traditional ones. People who drove cars wore out the part of the sole that pressed down on the gas pedal. But the young cobbler took it all in stride; he was profoundly committed to his craft. What did that mean? It meant that as far as he was concerned, shoes were shoes, and they all took a beating, which meant that sturdiness was paramount. He may have spent his days glued to the same spot, but his knowledge was vast. Name any brand of shoe—or handbag, for that matter—and he'd seen them all. At some point, the walls around the teachers' college behind the greenbelt were torn down and replaced by a row of shops. These included a bakery, some boutiques, a stationery store, and a little storefront with a sign that read "Uncle Sam's Machine Shoe Repair." Some people would tease the young cobbler: "Think you can fix this? You'd better do a good job, or I'm going to the competition!" and the cobbler would retort, "Go ahead!" In the end, some of his customers did take their shoes to "Uncle Sam," but do you know what happened? Not only were "Uncle Sam's" prices exorbitant, but no matter what the problem was, their solution never varied: resoling. Faced with less common problems—say the soles were just fine but the insoles had fallen apart from being sweated on, or maybe the soles were good but the uppers were worn out—or perhaps it was something very minor, like an eyelet that was missing its grommet or a seam that needed restitching—in cases like these, "Uncle Sam" was useless. And so it transpired that the shoes that had been taken to "Uncle Sam" came right back to the young cobbler, to the extreme embarrassment of those shoes' owners. But the cobbler never made fun of them. Instead, he acted as if nothing had happened and simply took the shoes and repaired them according to his time-honored methods. Within two months, his competitor had quietly closed up shop and disappeared, and the cobbler continued to ply his trade, as unfazed as ever, even if a customer brought him a pair of thousand-yuan Italian shoes. Not that he didn't notice—he was fully aware of such distinctions, in addition to being careful by nature. He wasn't impressed by how expensive they were—as a matter of fact, he felt that it was deeply wrong to charge so much for a pair of shoes. When someone brought in a pair of designer jeans with a broken zipper, he didn't think twice about tossing out the old zipper and replacing it with a new one. The customer would rescue the broken zipper from the trash, chiding him, "This is a designer zipper!" But the cobbler would reply, "Who cares whose name is on it?

It's broken!" His attitude toward designer goods was a fair measure of his opinion of consumerism and consumer society.

He dealt with shoes all day long, and not brand-new unworn ones. The smell of the leather was overlaid with every imaginable foot odor and sweaty aroma, which combined to become the cobbler's personal scent. Generations of cobblers had borne this scent, and their wives and children grew accustomed to it. It permeated their homes. The young cobbler's wife, who was also the old cobbler's daughter, had grown up with it, and her mother, the young cobbler's mother-in-law, identified the odor with her husband. But the young cobbler was an exception to this rule—unlike his predecessors, he didn't smell that way. He never wore his work clothes home; he always left them in the tool chest he kept at work. Like a real professional, he put on clean office attire before work, typically a Western suit and tie, which he put away during working hours. To ward off the traditional cobbler smell, he never wore anything made out of wool to work, since wool absorbs odors. As dusk was falling, but before it got completely dark out, he packed away his tools and supplies and went to a neighbor's house, where he washed his face and hands with perfumed soap and water and put on his clean clothes. Then he went home.

If he had family up from the countryside, dinner would be waiting for him when he got home, the aroma of the women's wok-frying greeting him long before he reached the threshold. In hot weather, the whole neighborhood would bring their tables outside, and, if I may say so, the cobbler's family boasted the best spread by far. Everything on the table was farm fresh—braised chicken, breaded and fried midsummer crab meat, scrambled eggs with clams, fermented tofu in brine, and ham and cured goose at New Year's, not to mention wine. When his father was there, the two men drank together; and when his father wasn't there, the cobbler drank alone. After a few cups of wine and a few bites of food, his wife would fill his bowl and heat up some chicken soup, even at the height of summer. Where they were from, people served their soup boiling hot, which made them break out in a sweat and flushed out the heat trapped inside the body. Indeed, when the fan blew on one's sweaty skin, it was very refreshing. The moon had risen, and the women cleared the table and wiped it clean. The meal over, the young cobbler felt like reading for a bit.

His taste was broad. He had the complete biography of the Song general Yue Fei and a volume by the famous local Qing Dynasty literatus Wang Shaotang called *Wusong*, along with one or two copies of the eleventh-century medieval history *A Mirror of Governance*. He also had magazines, like *Prosecutorial View*, *Reader*, and the martial arts fiction journal

Timeless Tales. He had picked up some of these at the newsstand, while others had come into his hands by chance. In his opinion, modern books didn't hold a candle to the classics, a category that included used or old books. The classics were repositories of moral teachings and eternal verities, both large and small. The larger moral issues related to society, while the smaller ones were concerned with being a good person. Of course, he thought that modern literature was important, as well—it described the world that was right in front of him, and it had the ability to open his eyes and broaden his mind, provided it wasn't too obscure. Nonetheless, no matter how exciting and filled with novelties the world around him was, it paled in comparison to the eternal truths encapsulated in ancient texts. It was just like the old saying: even though the Monkey King Sun Wukong could make seventy-two different transformations, he could never transform his way out of the Buddha's hand. Current events were straightforward—you could take things at face value, but there were no lessons to be drawn. On the other hand, events in ancient books revealed many layers of meaning, and that's what made reading interesting in the first place. He could measure the people and situations in newer books against the principles in old books; and likewise he could apply the verities found in the classics to the explication of modern life. For these reasons, the young cobbler read with deep concentration, poring over texts by the light of a lamp connected by a long cord to a socket inside the house. All around him were tables filled with people playing cards or mahjong, but the ubiquitous sounds of falling tiles, rustling cards, and argumentative players disputing each other's moves didn't penetrate his consciousness. His wife, mother, and mother-in-law all knew not to speak to him while he was reading, lest they interrupt his thoughts. But if his father was there, the cobbler would show his respect by looking up from time to time and talking about some of what he'd learned from his readings. All of these people depended on him, but it wouldn't do for him to put on airs; although naturally his female relatives were another matter.

The majority of the time, the young cobbler was by himself in Shanghai, and it got a bit lonely. Every day after work, he still had to cook dinner. Not that cooking was hard for him—all the men around there were good cooks; it was just that if you were eating alone, the food tended to be simple. He would wash and chop whatever vegetables he had bought on the way home, and then he'd stir-fry a couple of dishes—one meat and one vegetable. He'd eat half and put the other half in a steel pot, which he took to work the next day for lunch. What with cooking and washing up, taking a sponge bath, and brushing his teeth, the evening hours passed quickly. By the time he finished these chores, there wasn't much time left for reading, but he still sat down and read a couple of pages. To him, reading was also a skill, and if you missed a day, you'd have to work twice as hard the next time just to catch up. After reading his pages, he turned out the light and went to sleep. As he was drifting off, he couldn't help but think about his wife's soft body. This was by far the most difficult aspect of being alone and away from home. Sometimes one of the Henanese men who lived downstairs would bring a girl home from the foot massage parlor—more than once, he'd bumped into them in the entryway. The Henanese shrank from the cobbler's angry expression, but he couldn't help but pity them. The young cobbler was very straitlaced, and he found their behavior disgusting and unclean; what's more, it was his responsibility to keep an eye on things for the landlord. But the cobbler was also a man, and he knew how hard it was to be alone. Back in the days of the People's Communes, there was an old bachelor who lived in his home village. One day the man did something unsavory to an ox that belonged to his work team, and he served time in prison. After his release, he returned to the village, but none of the parents would let their children speak to him, and even his own brothers broke with him, condemning him to a lonely and solitary existence. Ever since he was a little boy, the cobbler had felt sorry for this man, but it was the same kind of pity he would feel for an animal. In his opinion, a person who lacked self-control was no better than an animal. For that reason, he decided not to report the matter to the landlord, but from then on he kept his distance from the men from Henan. Some of the facilities in the house were shared, including the bathroom and the coal-burning stove, and he removed his things and put them in his garret so that he wouldn't have to mingle with them. The landlord had installed a small toilet, but the cobbler stopped using it and instead went to the public toilet across the street. In truth, the men from Henan were kindhearted, and when they cooked something especially good, they would invite him down for a drink. He had joined them on several occasions in the past, and they drank till their tongues got loose and they swore eternal brotherhood. Eventually he would manage to extract himself, and everybody would retire for the night. Nowadays, however, he always made some excuse or other, and the camaraderie they'd once shared was sacrificed.

The young cobbler didn't permit his wife very long visits. This was in no small part due to his concerns about the environment—and not just the immediate environment of his rather spare accommodations, but also the urban environment as a whole. Although he trod the same path between home and work every day—a mere five hundred meters—he nonetheless saw and heard more than enough of the seamier side of the city along the way. One of the streets on his commute was lined with barbershops, and while the signs proclaimed that these businesses were barbershops, there was no sign of any barbering going on inside. What he did see behind those plate-glass doors was long hair covering women's faces, and bare arms and legs, all of which had a dull pallor that had never seen the light of day. The girls looked prepubescent, frail and thin. The cobbler was filled with pity—not for any one person, but rather for the entire society. His wife had widely spaced brows, rosy cheeks, and a mole at the corner of her mouth. When she smiled, the mole winked like a little star, and her eyes sparkled. She hadn't seen or experienced much of the world; and though she hadn't enjoyed great happiness, she hadn't been subjected to bullying, either. He wished he could cover her eyes and ears and spare her the crude talk of those around her. Better that she spend her days at home, waiting on her elders and looking after the children! Of course, unsavory things also happened in the countryside, like the business with the old bachelor—but weren't they always punished? Nobody would go near him after that. Things were different in the city. Everything and everyone mixed together, and there was no escaping it—people called it the "Big Dye Vat" for precisely that reason. "Big Dye Vat" was right!

On solitary nights, it was these thoughts that swirled in his mind and accompanied the young cobbler as he drifted off to sleep.

———

2

———

As we've already related, when the cobbler arrived at his stall at the mouth of the lane, he changed into work clothes. In winter he arrived wearing a parka over his Western suit, and in summer he showed up in a crisply ironed shirt—whatever the season, his clothes were clean and respectable. But what did he do with these clothes while he worked? He kept them at Gendi's. And who was Gendi? She lived in the lane; and not only did he store his clothing at her place, he also heated up his lunch there. Depending on what he'd brought, Gendi might heat it up in her rice steamer, or she might add some rice to make a sort of porridge, or she might serve him some condiments or cook something fresh as an accompaniment. The cobbler wasn't a freeloader—each month he gave her some money to pay for the natural gas, and he repaired her shoes at no charge. That way, everyone was happy.

Originally the cobbler had approached one of the neighborhood grannies. Weather permitting, this particular old lady would sit outside and watch the comings and goings of people on foot and in cars. As a matter of course, she and the cobbler would pass the time of day, and they got to know each other, but she had refused his request. She had no voice at home—it was her daughter-in-law who ran the household. "How can she treat you that way? You're her mother-in-law!" the cobbler had protested, but the old lady simply replied, "Oh, no—she's the boss!" When she said this, her face grew very serious, as if she were arguing with all of society. The cobbler smiled and changed the subject, realizing that if they were to pursue the subject, they would soon be entangled in thorny moral questions. No matter where you were, town or country, this topic was sure to get people riled up. When the old lady had calmed down, she suggested that he warm up his lunches at Gendi's. When he told her he didn't know Gendi, the granny said, "What do you mean you don't know her? She's the one who knocked you over the head." Then the cobbler remembered. One day he was joking around with a few of his women customers, and one of them struck him on the chest with the heel of her shoe. It was sharp as a nail and broke the skin. The cobbler had spent a long time in this lane, and he knew that Shanghai women and village women were very much alike. In the countryside, once they took a shine to someone, they became free and easy, both in what they said and in how they acted—especially if the person they'd taken a shine to was a young man. No matter how much they made fun of him, the cobbler kept his cool and didn't react. After all, they weren't ill-intentioned—on the contrary, they quite liked him, although they didn't give it more than a moment's thought.

The old lady's hunch was right, because Gendi readily agreed. She was a friendly woman, and she had a lot of time on her hands. She was one of the "forty to fifty" set who had found themselves jobless after the government abandoned central planning. Gendi had originally worked at a chemical plant, but when it was bought out by some people from Taiwan, workers like her were sent home. Not yet having reached the legal retirement age of fifty-five, she found herself at the employment office, looking for new work. Like her younger coworkers, she spent those first years working a string of jobs, first as a cleaning woman in an office building, then as a cook in a private company, before training as a supermarket cashier. It seemed that every work unit underwent the same process: the factory or other business defaulted on its loans, the banks repossessed the buildings, the tenants were kicked out, and the workers were terminated. After that, the private companies that replaced them folded, too; and overnight, a shopping center would have sprouted up on the site of the old businesses, dealing a fatal blow to the little mom-and-pop stores. The minimart she worked at also closed its doors. All told, she'd spent three months learning to be a cashier, and less than two months actually working a register. These experiences tempered the rage she'd been feeling toward the employment office and gave her firsthand knowledge of the upheavals that had overtaken the entire society.

She discussed the situation with her husband—like her, he'd been working at a plant that had closed, and he had followed in her footsteps and frequented the employment office. The couple had been classmates in technical school, and their work units had been similar in nature. She told him that she thought it would be safer for them to go into business for themselves, so they decided to sell boxed lunches. The neighbors pitched in to help them out—after all, they had both lost their jobs and still had a child in school. But no sooner had they embarked on this enterprise than their troubles began. They used the common kitchen for wok-frying in the summertime, and the gutters in the back alley became clogged with fish scales and vegetable peelings, causing wastewater to back up. Because customers had to pick up their meals, all sorts of people came and went, filling the lane with unfamiliar faces. The presence of all these interlopers led to disputes. Gendi was originally from a poor and rundown district of Zhabei and had married into this neighborhood. In Zhabei, seventeen or eighteen households shared a single faucet—if you weren't a little bit pushy, you wouldn't be able to get any water. Growing up in a place like that, where she had to fight for everything, had made her scrappy—she wasn't afraid of anything! She was as powerful as ten people—nobody dared take her on, and most people in this lilong in the city center had never heard the sort of earthy curses that regularly issued from her mouth. Neighbors accused her behind her back of killing her mother-in-law with her nasty temper—small wonder Xiaodi was such a weakling! Xiaodi was Gendi's husband, and from the moment he married her, he had barely uttered a peep. Nonetheless, this was a society governed by laws; tough as she was, even Gendi couldn't go outside the law. The neighbors didn't confront her in person—instead they got together and wrote a letter. First they sent it to the neighborhood committee; next it went to the public hygiene team; and after that, they wrote the tax office. In the end, it was the chengguan—not officially police, but the strong arm of the law nonetheless—who came to enforce the regulations, ordering Gendi and her husband to cease and desist. Once again, the couple found themselves unemployed. Xiaodi eventually got a driver's license and became a taxi driver. The more he worked, the more he earned, and while it was grueling work, it enabled him to feed his family and pay their child's school expenses—but Gendi was left idle at home. She'd been living this way for eight years already; in eight more years she'd be fifty-five and could start collecting her pension.

At forty-seven, Gendi was old enough to be a grandmother where the young cobbler came from; but people in Shanghai had a much broader outlook on age. Dressed to the nines and nicely made up, Gendi could easily pass for a young woman. She had attended her niece's wedding banquet in a pale pink outfit, her hair piled high and nary a silver root in sight—she could have been the bride! Now, although Gendi was an attractive and lively woman, Xiaodi had a stooped and shrunken look about him, and a personality to match. When they had first fallen in love, Gendi had taken the lead, of course. There was a popular saying in the lanes—"When a man pursues a woman, he has to move mountains; but when a woman goes after a man, all she has to move is a piece of paper." This was even truer for a man and a woman like Xiaodi and Gendi.

Xiaodi's father had died young, so his mother was the head of the household. As the youngest child, and with two older sisters, he was used to being ordered around by women. This fostered the development of his indolent streak, and he typically let others take the initiative. This extended to matters of great importance as well, which led to conflicts between his family and his wife. His mother and sisters had never approved of Gendi, because she came from the lower-class district of Zhabei and had grown up in an enclave of people from northern Jiangsu. Her father hauled loads on a flatbed tricycle, and her mother worked as a tender in a spinning factory; but what really stuck in their craws was how good-looking she was—for a woman of her ilk to be so attractive was downright dangerous. Who knew what kinds of mischief she might get into? Would she ever be satisfied? Now, the truth of the matter was that Xiaodi's family was quite poor, and they lived in even more straitened circumstances than Gendi's family. After Xiaodi's father died, his mother kept the family afloat by spinning yarn for the neighborhood production team—that, along with handouts from relatives, helped her make ends meet. Xiaodi's sisters had gone down to the countryside during the Cultural Revolution, and for a time the family had to borrow money just to get by. But none of this changed the fact that living on the west side of the Huangpu River—Puxi, for short— in one of the modern lilongs in a house with metal window frames and linoleum floors still defined one's social position, even if home was an apartment with a communal bathroom and kitchen. And didn't people call this part of town, where the old foreign concessions had been, the "Upper Patch"—the zangzego? In contrast, Gendi was from the "Lower Patch," the hozego—the sticks. At one point, she had confessed to her younger sister that Xiaodi's address had been part of the attraction—in the eyes of people from Zhabei, Xiaodi lived in "Shanghai" proper—but where they lived wasn't really thought of as "Shanghai." This said a lot about the city's history.

Marrying a man from Shanghai proper was something to aspire to, especially for a girl as good-looking as Gendi. "Shanghai" was not merely a geographical concept—it meant much, much more. For example, Xiaodi was very different from the boys Gendi had grown up with. He was always neat and clean, and if she stood behind him, she could detect the scent of soap emanating from the nape of his neck. Back in their student days, even his dormitory bed had given off the bracingly fresh scent of detergent. He never used foul language, either. Where Gendi was from, girls and women cursed all the time. Xiaodi had fair skin, but the ravages of time had gradually robbed it of its luster, and his face had shriveled into something resembling a dried date. He had a gentle smile, and just as in childhood he had been his momma's good little boy, he had grown up to become Gendi's good little boy—at least that was how Gendi saw him. But how did he see her? Passive as he was, he had submitted willingly to the result of the struggle over him, namely that between Gendi and the women in his family. In other words, he was the spoils that went to the victor—Gendi. Like a princess in a fairy tale, he married the brave and wise champion. He did have standards, after all. His actions were guided by his weak character, albeit obscurely, which meant that he followed whoever was strongest. On the surface, his marriage appeared to be based on her looks and his address, but there was in fact a very practical arrangement underneath it all.

Lately, Gendi's life had developed a new rhythm. Because Xiaodi drove a cab, he worked a day and rested a day—thus Gendi also worked a day and rested a day. When her husband was at home, she spent the day cooking and serving him, ensuring that the breadwinner was well fed and well rested. Although she didn't have anything to say to him, she fussed over him like a mother hen, sheltering him under her wings. In short, Xiaodi had crawled out from under his mother's wings and burrowed under his wife's. It goes without saying that her feathers were much younger and fresher, and of course there was also the joy of sex! Naturally, after their son was born, he had to share that cozy nest with the baby. One day Gendi was walking down the street, and somebody convinced her to have her fortune told. Most of it was nonsense, except for one thing they said: "Your husband is also your son." For that, she gave them five yuan. On his days off, Xiaodi slept from three in the morning until noon. Gendi brought him his meals in bed, where he lay curled up beneath the quilts—it was a lot like feeding a baby bird. When he had eaten, he curled up and went back to sleep. Gendi had never been the recipient of this sort of pampering herself, not even during that special first month after their baby was born! Xiaodi would linger in bed until four in the afternoon, at which point he would languidly bestir himself and wander out to the lane. If Gendi was in the middle of a mahjong game, she would let him take her place and go back to cooking. The family of three would sit around the dining table eating and watching TV, until they eventually turned in for the night. At six the next morning, Xiaodi would set out for work. Gendi packed their son off to school, and her day of cultural entertainment began.

Mornings, she would go to the ballroom to dance. It was located in an addition to the teahouse in the park. Colored lights and streamers hung from the low ceiling, making it look like Christmas. With the curtains pulled over the window and blocking out the sunlight, it really did look like Christmas night. Since most of the dancers were middle-aged or elderly, the music was generally old-fashioned, with regular rhythms: classic waltzes, Teresa Teng songs, or the perky "light music" that lent itself to the quickstep or the rumba. The dancers were all regulars and knew each other, but they nonetheless observed certain proprieties. People didn't ask others to dance, as most arrived with partners. Anybody who came on their own, woman or man, was eyed with some suspicion. Even when the emcee called for people to change partners, these singletons were never invited, nor would anyone accept their invitations. Those who had partners simply exchanged partners. At the ballroom, those with partners were considered clean and above reproach; but the men and women who had arrived alone would sit dejectedly on the sidelines, sipping their complimentary refreshments and listening to one song after another. The revolving multihued lights cast bands of red and green over the dancers, obscuring their expressions and making it impossible to tell whether they were having a good time. Indeed, they appeared rather solemn as they danced their measured steps. It was only when the music stopped and the dancers left the floor that their happy and relaxed expressions were revealed.

Gendi had several partners—like her, they were members of the "forty to fifty" cohort. One of them was a security guard. He worked two days and rested on the third, and if his day off coincided with Gendi's, they would partner up. The other two were contingent workers and didn't have regular hours. When they had work, they didn't come to the ballroom, but when they were between jobs, they came every day. It usually worked out so that Gendi had someone to dance with, and in the event that none of her usual companions showed up, the old sophisticate—

"lokela" in the local parlance—who taught ballroom dance would offer to partner her. She had regular dance partners, so this wasn't improper. While Gendi was a good-looking woman, she wasn't much of a dancer—she was either going the wrong direction or stepping on her partner's toes. When the song ended, the dapper lokela escorted her back to her seat and would let a few songs go by before inviting her back to the floor. This was fine with her, as she wasn't truly dance-crazy. To her, it was just a pastime—and a way to prove she had a social life. She didn't get carried away, and when the time was up, she went home and cooked lunch.

Gendi made the midday meal mostly for her son's sake, since personally she could take it or leave it. She'd learned at the ballroom that a tomato and a cucumber were all she needed. Of course, this was also the time of day when she warmed up the young cobbler's meal. After lunch, it was time for mahjong. The table was just outside her back door. If it was raining, they'd bring their game inside to the furnace room. The other players were neighbors—two old ladies and a man they called Uncle Ye. The old lady who had introduced the cobbler to Gendi usually sat by and watched. When Gendi noticed the old lady's eyes starting to sparkle with interest, she would offer to give up her place. But the old lady always refused and would suddenly lose enthusiasm, saying that she didn't have any money for gambling, since every yuan and fen that came into their household was controlled by her daughter-in-law. Gendi wasn't much of a mahjong player, either, but when it came to games, even bad players could get lucky, so she didn't always lose everything. She had a flexible outlook—losing money was the same as buying a ticket. Just like ball-room tickets, her mahjong losses were no more than pocket money. Uncle Ye was a sharp player, and none of his three opponents was a match for him; but being kindhearted, he couldn't allow himself to take advantage of women or the elderly, so he didn't give it his all. The old ladies were tightwads, so the stakes were low and they played it safe. They didn't make big bets—they were looking for small but reliable gains. The atmosphere around the card table was rather sedate, so Gendi didn't get carried away by gambling, either.

Sometimes she would stroll around town with her next-door neighbor Jinrong. Jinrong was none other than the daughter-in-law whom the old lady had described in such terrifying terms—but in truth she wasn't that frightening. She was about two years younger than Gendi, and after being laid off, she had gotten an accounting license. Back then there weren't many people in financial services, unlike nowadays, when there's a surplus. Jinrong soon found a job in the accounts payable and receivable department of a medium-sized business. Unfortunately, the business was shut down, and she was out of work once more. At about that time, a new crop of younger and better-educated workers poured into the labor market, and Jinrong had no choice but to work for a small private company. At first, she'd looked down on Gendi for her humble background. Jinrong's parents lived only a block away from her husband's lane—and even closer to the city center, where every clod of dirt was worth its weight in gold. Developers had already turned most of the block into heaps of rubble, leaving nothing standing but the houses in the cul-de-sac, and that's where her parents lived. It was only a matter of time before they too would have to move out, and who knew how far away they'd end up? Jinrong no longer had much of an excuse to look down on Gendi, and once she got to know her, she discovered that Gendi had a lot more good points than the women who'd grown up in the longtang. For one thing, Gendi didn't hold grudges. When she still had her boxed lunch business, Jinrong had been one of the most vocal opponents and a leading strategist; but all of that was in the past—Gendi seemed to have forgotten all about it. In no time at all, the two women became fast friends. Even so, Jinrong limited her contact to walks around town and shopping trips to Tesco and Carrefour. She didn't go to the ballroom or join the mahjong game, either—not that either was against her principles; she just wasn't interested. A woman who was immune to the lure of gambling clearly had a great deal of self-control, but the flip side of that was inflexibility. Even her outward appearance hinted at this trait: she had well-balanced features and a good profile, and she looked youthful, but she never smiled, and that steeliness was off-putting. Her mother-in-law's impression that she was a hard woman was mostly on account of her face. The truth was, she couldn't help it—she had been born with a cold expression. It was entirely possible that deep down she was bubbling with life.

The old granny—Jinrong's mother-in-law—spent her days either sitting outside in the lane or watching Gendi and her friends play mahjong. At home in the evenings, she would talk about what she had seen and heard that day—like the woman from the provinces who stole a manhole cover and was apprehended right on the spot, or the VW Santana that knocked down a motorized bicycle. But strangest of all was the time a female passerby begged the cobbler to take out her earrings. She had fastened them too tightly, which had made her earlobes swell up, and that in turn embedded the earrings even further. To be sure, this was not the cobbler's usual line of work. So what happened? He helped her untwist them, and he didn't even damage the earrings. The woman complained bitterly, saying, "I don't want them anymore!" But in the end, she took them and carefully tucked them away before sauntering happily off.

There were many arguments over the mahjong table: the situation was constantly shifting, and the old lady found even this group's lackluster play quite exciting, for there was constant friction and endless squabbling—if it wasn't one thing, it was another. Jinrong exchanged only the most perfunctory words with her mother-in-law, and the old lady's son and grandson had even less patience with her; so the old woman just chattered on and on into empty air, with nobody listening—until one day a little tidbit caught Jinrong's attention. It concerned Gendi and Uncle Ye and suggested that something was going on between them. The old lady had wondered aloud what a sharp player like Uncle Ye was doing playing low-stakes mahjong with a bunch of ladies every day. Didn't that seem strange? Jinrong couldn't help but prick up her ears, and she heard her mother-in-law add, "I bet it has something to do with that floozie Gendi!" The old woman wore the same harsh expression that she typically wore when talking about her daughter-in-law—a look that combined disapproval and self-righteousness. This only went to show that Jinrong wasn't as impossible as the old lady liked to say; really, she just needed to have something to talk about. By the same token, it was a good bet that this bit of gossip about Gendi was baseless as well, but for some reason, Jinrong took her words to heart.

As we've already remarked, the fact that Jinrong's face betrayed no emotion didn't mean that beneath it all she wasn't roiled by intense feelings. Under the surface, she had a rich emotional life, just as rich as the inner lives of other women her age. This isn't to say these women were unhappy with their marriages—far from it!—but their inner lives and their marriages were separate matters. It's important to emphasize that their marriages were extremely stable; but it was that very stability that left them feeling bored and restless. By the time most women had reached Jinrong's age, their parents and in-laws were no longer underfoot, and their children had all grown up. (Jinrong's mother-in-law was still living with them, but she was going strong and wasn't a burden.) These women suddenly found themselves with time on their hands and energy to spare. Conversely, their husbands were at a low ebb—having fulfilled their obligations and with no new goals in sight, they lost their drive and became depressed. Physically, they were entering a new stage as well. They didn't have the kind of energy or stamina they'd had when they were younger, and they simply couldn't keep up with their wives. Jinrong gritted her teeth—this idle talk about Uncle Ye and Gendi made her face freeze up even more—but inside she was all churned up. She'd never given Uncle Ye much thought; and yet . . . why was it that even a nobody like Uncle Ye would find a woman of Gendi's ilk so appealing, while he ignored Jinrong? No matter how far she cast her gaze, there was no other man on the horizon—only Uncle Ye. She shuddered; she had reached a point in her life when opportunities were few and far between, and time was running short. At the company, everybody had called her "auntie"—she'd been surrounded by a bunch of twenty-somethings, and even the boss wasn't much past thirty. When she went shopping, the sizing and styles were all aimed toward young people—trendy young people. The salesgirls at the cosmetics counter would always say, "A woman your age . . . Aren't you finished with all that?" In fact, she felt more vital than ever; she was wiser, and she was full of passion.

The following day, Jinrong saw Gendi in the lane and started walking toward her; but then she flounced past in a sudden pique. Gendi had been about to say something to her, and finding herself suddenly facing nothing but empty space, she felt a bit discomfited; but she soon forgot all about it. Then one day when Jinrong was strolling down the lane, she walked up to the mahjong table outside Gendi's back door. The players were sitting elbow to elbow, their attention riveted on the game. Jinrong suspected it was all a ruse, a cover for hidden agendas. Her mother-in-law was sitting beside the table, and when she looked up, a look of mutual understanding seemed to pass between mother-in-law and daughter-in-law.

Thereafter, Jinrong continued to give Gendi the cold shoulder. Even a stupid person would have noticed, and Gendi was no fool; but at first she shrugged it off. *I wonder what I've done to offend Jinrong?* she thought to herself, and she decided to drop by Jinrong's and ask her in person. That's how Gendi was—uncomplicated and direct—but Jinrong was subtler. Her family lived on the ground floor, and the entry was on the back side of the building. Jinrong didn't answer when Gendi called to her, but since the door was open, there was nothing to stop people from coming or going. Thinking that Jinrong hadn't heard her, Gendi called out again, but there was still no response. After a few more tries, Gendi realized that Jinrong wasn't answering on purpose, and she went off in a huff. If Jinrong was going to ignore her, then she would ignore Jinrong right back. The next time they saw each other, they breezed past each other, their noses in the air; whenever they found themselves face to face, they quickly zigzagged, brushing shoulders, but no more. Gendi got a clear look at Jinrong's face, and what she saw was contempt, pure and simple. That was how Jinrong's mind worked—on the inside she was insanely jealous, but nothing showed on the outside but contempt. Gendi had no idea where this attitude was coming from, and her feelings of hurt and doubt were mixed with anger.

Gendi wasn't in the dark for long; longtang life was proof of the old adage "There's no such thing as an airtight room"—and if you lived in a longtang, the walls had ears. Jinrong's mother-in-law was a woman with stories to tell, and sharing them at home just wasn't enough. She had to tell the neighbors on the left and the neighbors on the right, and before long she was gossiping with the old ladies who played mahjong, until finally the news reached Gendi's ears. Gendi was furious, and as serious as this accusation was, she didn't know who to blame. The news had come to her by the most circuitous path possible, and tracing it back to its source would have been nearly impossible. She banished the mahjong table from her back door, and the old ladies tactfully went off in search of other pastimes. Only Uncle Ye came by again—twice—and twice Gendi slammed the door in his face, which only lent credence to the rumors. Gendi complained bitterly to Xiaodi about what had happened; but Xiaodi had acquired some wisdom in the course of his new line of work. Driving a cab had taught him a lot about the world, and he shared some of his experiences with her. He'd been living in this lane for decades, but he told her that since he'd been driving a cab, he had realized a few things about his home neighborhood. The longtang was a contentious place—people were jammed together, cheek by jowl, day and night. Given the close quarters, it was only natural that there would be some animosity; but because people were living right on top of each other, that hostility had to be kept under wraps—if people couldn't keep their negative feelings to themselves, how could they continue living together? That was why people who lived in the lanes kept what was in their hearts separate from what they showed on their faces—there was no connection between what people felt inside and what they showed to others. Forget about honesty—just go about your business and keep a pleasant expression on your face. That was enough. There was more than a little good sense in what Xiaodi said, but his words were tinged with resignation; it was the lazy thinking of a middle-aged man who'd been worn down by the years and had lost his edge. Instead of shaking Gendi out of her funk, Xiaodi's advice made her feel worse; but she absorbed his lessons and stopped associating with her neighbors in the lane. She also lost her appetite for going dancing, because social life was too demoralizing. She shut herself up at home, going out only to buy groceries or other essentials. The one other event of her day was warming up the young cobbler's lunch. She would bring it out to him, take a seat on the stool, and wait for him to finish so she could collect the bowl and chopsticks and take them home. She had an intriguing air about her as she waited; and she wore a defiant expression like that of a child, as if she were saying, *You people are bad. I'm not going to play with you anymore. I'm going to play with the little cobbler!*

3

Gendi and the young cobbler always spoke together in Subeihua, the dialect of their forebears in northern Jiangsu Province. The Zhabei slums from which they both hailed were full of country folk originally from that area. Their generation's version of the Subei dialect was a hodgepodge, lacking any specific sense of place; and yet it was still Subeihua, and when the cobbler heard her speak, it sounded like home to him. You could say that their friendship was based on their common roots. It was only natural for Gendi to tell the cobbler about her recent travails, which to his mind were no different from the commonplace troubles of his country kinswomen and their neighbors. But coming from Gendi, this lovely city girl with her brightly colored wardrobe, it almost seemed funny. She had bright eyes and white teeth, and a well-proportioned oval face. Her figure, which had been quite slender in her youth, had relaxed a bit, so that to the casual observer she seemed full-figured. Her hair, once a glossy black, was now shot through with silver and had faded, so when she dyed it, it turned a reddish color. She wore it in a tight perm, and when she swept it back from her face with a band and pinned it up, you could see her perfectly formed ears, from which dangled earrings of bright green jade set in gold. These made her rounded neck appear all the more luminous. She favored low-necked wool tops in pink or sapphire, unbuttoned to reveal the lace top of her camisole. She paired these with skirts, in a plaid or a splashy floral that matched the color of her top. On her feet she wore lambskin ankle boots, with spike heels as sharp as drill bits, or else big square heels. In short, Gendi's style was big and loud. It might strike the observer as a little bit country or a little bit Western, depending on who was doing the observing. No matter what she was doing—going dancing, strolling around town, shopping for food, playing mahjong out behind her house, sitting by the cobbler's stall, relaxing at home, or cooking in the shared kitchen—she was always put together: well-dressed, carefully coiffed, and made up. She regarded all of these as social activities—if she didn't, where else would she be able to wear her pretty clothes, nice hairstyles, and makeup?

But what was this overdressed beauty doing sitting in front of the cobbler's? There was something incongruous about it. On the other hand, people were used to seeing beautiful women sitting at the cobbler's stall. Heels took leave of shoe soles without warning, buckles broke, and handbag straps came off. At times like that, you needed a cobbler. For that reason, Gendi's presence wasn't especially remarkable. The only thing that made this striking woman notable was the gossip that had been circulating around the lane. Unlike the wily country girls the cobbler knew, she had a childlike quality. When she talked about Jinrong's contemptuous looks, she was angry: "She said I was sneaking around with Uncle Ye— but what about her? Uncle Ye doesn't even want her!" On the surface, this wasn't a very logical statement, but in fact, it had more than a grain of truth. The cobbler found this hilarious: "Look at you—aren't you gossiping about her, too? As the saying goes, if you don't want people to talk about you behind your back, then best not to gossip!" Gendi thought this very profound. She hadn't heard the saying before, and she recited it twice before she enthused: "A person would never know just by looking that you're a man of real quality!" The cobbler smiled, like an adult who'd been praised by a child. Gendi reached out and ruffled his hair, then picked up the empty pot and bowls and left.

The next day was Xiaodi's day off, and Gendi remarked, "That young cobbler may be from the countryside, but he's got some substance." She had memorized these words so she could say them out loud to her husband. In response, Xiaodi leaned back on his pillows and shared an anecdote about some people from the countryside, a couple of men he'd driven into town from Pudong. One of them had several sacks woven from cattails. Throughout the drive, Xiaodi could hear scratching and rustling coming from inside the sacks: there were crabs in them. They made a few stops, and each time the men got out, they would take one of the sacks. He listened in on their conversation—they were here to lay the groundwork for future enterprises. This demonstrated that country people knew how to think big. "Who knows," he concluded, "someday we may all end up working for people from Pudong!" Gendi countered, "And what would be the harm? At least they're willing to work, unlike Shanghainese, who want to take a day off for every day they put in at work." Xiaodi shot back, "What's wrong with working a day and resting a day? Some people just sit around *all* day and never do any work at all!" Gendi disputed this: "People who don't go to work are actually working all the time!" She proceeded to list all of the things she did in a day. Xiaodi took exception: "Oh, so it's the wife who takes care of the husband, is it?" Noticing his serious tone, Gendi humored him: "Of course it's the husband who looks after the wife, and that's as it should be." Her grandmother's mantra was "Marry a man, marry a man; clothes on your back and food in the pan." Xiaodi responded that in fact it didn't have to be that way, and that there were women who supported their men. Gendi told him to go find a woman to support him, and he told her to find another man who would look after her. "I want *you* to take care of me," she said. "Why would I want to go take care of another man?" "It does happen," Xiaodi said, and he told another story, this one about a man who was supporting a woman who used the money he gave her to take care of another man—his boss at the taxi company had seen plenty of crazy situations like this. They argued a bit longer about the question of who should support whom, until Gendi finally said she was going to cook lunch. She still had to warm up the cobbler's midday meal.

The following day, Gendi went to the cobbler's stall and told him about her argument with Xiaodi. Regarding the first issue—who supported whom—the cobbler believed there was nothing to discuss. In a partnership, one person tended the pot while the other tended the fire; neither could function without the other. As for the second situation, where the three people were linked together in a circle, like three fish biting each other's tails—they were humiliating each other, and if they kept it up, there would be dire consequences. The cobbler related the story of how God had punished mankind with the Great Flood, a tale he'd picked up from his perusals of *Reader* or some such magazine. That in turn reminded him of a legend the elders told in his hometown. In ancient times, there were people who didn't live by moral precepts: they had sexual relations in the Temple of Earth, and because of it there was a drought, which was followed by floods—not a single ear of grain made it to harvest time that year. Gendi was entranced; her mouth hung open and her eyes grew wide. The cobbler used to think that Shanghai girls had such big heads that they couldn't be bothered with others—but the truth was that they had tiny heads, and not much going on inside. They didn't have the slightest understanding of human nature or social mores.

Perhaps because she stayed longer than usual, or because she was especially chatty, the cobbler listened quietly. Or maybe it was the other way around, and he was chattering on while Gendi listened wide-eyed. When Jinrong's mother-in-law happened by and joined the conversation, Gendi abruptly got up and clomped off in her high heels. Although she had no solid evidence, Gendi saw the old lady as a prime suspect. For one thing, she had been a regular observer at the mahjong table; for another, she was Jinrong's mother-in-law. Gendi had little patience with narrow-minded people. Not once had Jinrong offered an apology or expression of goodwill; and not only had the gossip about Gendi and Uncle Ye not stopped, it was still spreading. She didn't know whether Uncle Ye had had any ulterior motives, but twice he'd gone looking for Gendi, found her at the cobbler's, and asked her to play mahjong—and twice she had refused. Her expression was as stone cold as could be, but Uncle Ye was all smiles. All he said was, "What's up? Have you found a new hobby?" She didn't answer; she simply glared at him. This exchange, filtered through Jinrong's mother-in-law's eyes and mouth, became yet another chapter in the scandalous exploits of Gendi.

Jinrong secretly compared herself to Gendi, and she always came out on top. Gendi was admittedly striking, both in her looks and in the way she dressed; but she was rather vulgar, and her style reeked of Subei bumpkindom. Gendi's speech was coarse as well, and often laced with profanity. In contrast, Jinrong had delicate brows, clear eyes, and a willowy figure, and she dressed with understated elegance. Without calling attention to herself, she was pleasing to look at. Her coworkers at the company may have called her "auntie," but she was still a white-collar worker—whether you were talking about social position or professional qualifications, she and Gendi were like apples and oranges. There was simply no comparison. So why did people find Gendi more attractive? She thought about their marriages: Gendi and Xiaodi had chosen each other without intermediaries, but Jinrong had approached her husband through an intermediary. When she and Gendi went shopping together, security guards and male salesmen had shown much more warmth toward Gendi. She had a natural ease and familiarity, which Jinrong disparaged—but Jinrong finally had to admit that this was why people found her so likable. In spite of herself, Jinrong took a leaf from Gendi. Set as she was in her formal ways, loosening up meant smiling and nodding when she met people on the street. Jinrong smiled so rarely that when she finally did crack a smile, it looked awkward. It just wasn't very natural. But a smile was still a smile, and better than no smile at all. People would go to the old lady and say, "Your daughter-in-law is happy today!" But the old lady never got to see those smiles, for as soon as Jinrong set foot inside her own house, her smile disappeared. That was her character—if she hadn't been gripped with such a powerful desire, she would never have made even this little detour from business as usual. Naturally, Uncle Ye was among the beneficiaries of this new bounty.

Now, nobody would have accused Uncle Ye of having loose morals, and he certainly didn't appear to have any improper designs on Gendi—he was simply bored. Every longtang in Shanghai had men like him—they bellied up to mahjong tables or stood around loitering where the lanes disgorged onto larger avenues. This isn't to say that men like this could only be found in the lanes—it was just that lane dwellers had to live their lives in plain view of their neighbors, so that everything private became public. Uncle Ye hadn't been born or raised in this particular lane, but his wife had. He'd married in, but since Shanghainese didn't harbor any prejudices on this account, Uncle Ye never felt discriminated against. On the contrary, people respected him. He'd worked in a factory that produced heavy machinery, starting as an eighteen-yuan-per-month apprentice and working his way up to foreman. He pomaded his hair and rode around on a Phoenix-brand bicycle, zipping down the lane like a flash of light. His wife came from a small family—just her and her mother—so he was master of the house. In the second half of the 1980s, his wife and some of her female coworkers started talking about going to Japan to work. At first it was just a joke, but to his surprise, a few of them actually went through with it, including his wife. She had always been a quiet and unassuming woman. She'd started in the role of his apprentice, ultimately graduating to his subordinate—in other words, she knew her place. But she had blossomed and was displaying newfound talents and abilities. If you lived in one of the lanes of Puxi, the moment you stepped out your door, you would find yourself in the thick of urban life in all its boisterous variety. You could go around wearing a blindfold and earplugs, and you still wouldn't be able to block out the sights and sounds of the city or shield yourself from the onslaught of knowledge. This was especially true for the women of Shanghai, who absorbed many of their ideas about life from the city around them. The urban core was overflowing with goods, and because the offerings exceeded what people needed for material survival, there was surplus, which could nourish the spirit. This suited the female temperament to a tee—it was the perfect union of reality and romanticism.

Uncle Ye's wife's trip to Japan marked a turning point, for things changed after that. At first it wasn't noticeable, but two years into her stint abroad, she made her first trip home, and everyone could see the writing on the wall. A taxi arrived from the airport, and soon there was a small heap of suitcases of all shapes and sizes blocking the lane; and one by one they all disappeared inside Uncle Ye's doorway. Unexpectedly, and after such a long separation, this much-anticipated reunion with his wife didn't rejuvenate him—instead he felt even more tired. She made several more trips back and forth, and when she finally came home for good, she opened up a little boutique near a cluster of hotels the next street over. She still wasn't very talkative, but when people passed by her shop and glimpsed her through the glass door, dressed in a black skirt and top, they often mistook her for a Japanese woman. People realized then that Uncle Ye's wife had changed.

Right at this time, the factory where Uncle Ye worked began its downward slide. First came the retooling, so they could manufacture different products; then came a merger, followed by a joint venture, joint investment, tax restructuring, private shareholding, then from private shareholding to an IPO, until finally the whole enterprise was bought up by foreign capital. People called it a "reorganization," but it amounted to profiteering from a shutdown. The officials who had been in charge of the factory were attached to new enterprises, while line workers took early retirement or else waited to retire. Mid-level cadres like Uncle Ye had another avenue open to them: a buyout of their seniority. The money realized from this was something tangible—he could take it home and put it in the bank, and he was very excited about it at first. But as those around him grew wealthier and inflation kept rising, his bank balance became increasingly pathetic. At the same time, Uncle Ye's attempts to find new work left him discouraged. He was an expert machinist, but there was no market for his skills; and the worst blow of all came when he went to the employment office and discovered that he was classified as elderly—and he wasn't even fifty years old. Uncle Ye couldn't stand the phrase "forties to fifties." It implied that he and his generation were the weak members of society, deserving of pity, unable to care for themselves and thus needing to be cared for. But nobody was going to take care of you—you were on your own. His wife had helped him apply for a job with a Japanese-backed company—something to do with being a manager of marketing, she'd said. It turned out that the so-called Japanese-backed company was nothing more than a small business set up by one of the Shanghainese who had gone to Japan with his wife. The business sold Chinese embroidery, lacquered chopsticks, sandalwood fans, and other handicrafts to Japanese people. Altogether, there were two offices and a handful of employees—the entire marketing department turned out to consist of Uncle Ye alone. The boss ran the business in a penurious fashion; perhaps she'd suffered too many hardships on the way up, because she was incredibly cheap with her employees. Unable to put up with this, Uncle Ye quit after a fortnight, even though it meant forfeiting his wages.

This misadventure inspired him to go into business for himself; and in this respect he was a lot like Gendi. At least it looked that way on the surface, as this cohort of newly unemployed workers had similar psychological experiences in common. But Uncle Ye was a man—he still had some ambition. One night, before he and his wife fell asleep, he broached the subject, suggesting that they close her boutique, pool their energies, and open up a large store together. Despite the fact that they were cuddling—she was literally tangled up with her husband at the moment—she was entirely clear in her own mind. "If you want to go into business," she told him, "I'll give you seed money and help you with strategy, but yours is yours and mine is mine." She'd been in the business world long enough to know that most business failures were caused by friction among friends and relatives. Until now, Uncle Ye hadn't realized just how far his wife had come—she was a superwoman, and it filled him with a combination of respect and fear. He had no choice but to back down. In the current labor market, there were only two possible jobs for a man like him: he could be a courier for an express delivery service, or he could be a security guard. The older he got, the less inclined he was to go out, so he whiled away the hours at home, sometimes dropping by his wife's shop to help unload merchandise; and most days he prepared three meals. He was living the life of a stay-at-home husband, while his wife earned money outside.

This kind of life had a tremendous benefit—it was humbling. Jinrong's mother-in-law opined that a crack mahjong player like Uncle Ye wouldn't be content to play the game with women unless he was harboring some ulterior motive. But the truth was more straightforward: Uncle Ye refused to gamble with his wife's money. He had a sense of right and wrong, which was why he would never stoop to the kinds of schemes Jinrong's mother-in-law suspected him of; and he spent time with Gendi because he got along with her. She was easygoing, not to mention quite funny. For instance, one time when she needed to draw a tile, she was afraid of drawing a bad one, so she asked Uncle Ye, who was on a winning streak that day, if he would blow on the tiles for good luck. He blew, but the puff of air missed the tile and landed on Gendi's hand. It was somewhat flirtatious, but there was nothing more to it. The moment it was time to cook dinner, Uncle Ye got up from the game table and obediently headed home, despite the fact that he was doing well. Whenever he needed to appear in public with his wife, he made sure that he was well-groomed—after all, he owed it to her—so he would restyle his hair with a blow dryer, put on a brand-new Western-style suit, and set out with her, his gaze never wandering. When Uncle Ye dressed up, he looked very sharp, and his newly humble expression made him seem especially kind and genteel.

Uncle Ye's good points were becoming ever more apparent to Jinrong, and she made a startling discovery: when she smiled at him, there was more to it than just a display of good manners—she felt genuine warmth. But, newly humble, Uncle Ye couldn't help feeling intimidated. And ever since the power dynamic between him and his wife had flipped, he couldn't look at a woman without feeling a bit afraid—a situation exacerbated by Jinrong's characteristically severe demeanor. A woman who went to work every day at a company wasn't to be trifled with. This was why he liked Gendi's company—she didn't go to work and she wasn't too serious. Of course, she was also very easy on the eyes, which was good for Uncle Ye's mental health. Jinrong had always ignored him, and he had long since grown accustomed to getting the cold shoulder from her. Suddenly, here she was, smiling at him, and his feelings of awkwardness and discomfort far outweighed any pleasant sensations he might be experiencing. Uncle Ye froze in his tracks, unable to respond. By the time he mustered a smile, Jinrong was gone, the long skirt of her green silk dress fluttering behind her as she walked. He felt deflated. The next time she smiled at him, it was dusk. A van had pulled up to the entrance of the lane. The door opened, and out stepped Jinrong. She stood and waited while someone in the van passed out a few parcels, gifts from the company, evidently—beverages, fruit, and sweets. Seeing Uncle Ye standing nearby, she smiled sweetly and said, "Give me a hand!" He bent over to pick up a flat of soda, and she put a box of assorted cookies on top of it; then she picked up a couple of plastic shopping bags and led the way.

Stepping lightly, she minced ahead of him in high, slim heeled sandals. Noting the heavy bags in her hands, he lamented to himself, *This world belongs to women now!* Following her into her home, he set the boxes down where she pointed, and he was about to go when she handed him a damp cloth to mop the sweat from his brow. She had pulled it out of the refrigerator, and it was sprinkled with Liu Shen–brand cologne. As Uncle Ye wiped his face, Jinrong asked, "Tell me, what new styles does your wife's shop have?" Caught off guard by this question, Uncle Ye blurted out, "You know, young stuff—bare-midriff tops, cropped pants, and skirts that barely cover a girl's behind." Jinrong's smile vanished, and her expression darkened. Uncle Ye realized he'd been too crude, and he clammed up. That's how he was—once he started talking, he couldn't shut his trap; shooting the breeze was a tradition in the factory. Jinrong knit her brows: "Right. Women my age can't keep up with the styles anymore." Startled, Uncle Ye hurriedly added, "Jinrong, you still look young and girlish." She laughed sarcastically: "You men only have eyes for girls—young girls!" Uncle Ye didn't dare utter another word, so he just stood there until Jinrong said, "Thank you, Uncle Ye." He knew he'd been dismissed, but as he reached the doorway, she called out to him—he still had the wet cloth wadded up in his hand. He mutely handed it back. Clutched in his fist, it had grown warm; but Jinrong's hands were as cold as ice. Uncle Ye walked down the lane toward home, overcome with a sense of defeat. Gendi had turned on him lately, but now Jinrong was acting nice. This was proof positive—women were an unsolvable mystery.

Depressed, Uncle Ye didn't go out for a few days; and Jinrong's mother-in-law stayed in as well. Jinrong had ordered Uncle Ye to move those boxes right under the old lady's nose, and she couldn't deny it was a blow;

the gossip about Gendi and Uncle Ye had backfired. Rumors spread fast in the longtang, but they also died down quickly, and before anyone knew it, the scandal had blown over. For the past several days, the lane had been quiet. The cobbler continued to ply his trade, and at noontime Gendi brought his lunch out in a metal pot. He liked to mix his rice, vegetables, meat, and soup together, and he would blissfully slurp it all down, so Gendi heated everything together and served it in one pot. She sat on the stool and talked while he ate; but today when he was through, she didn't leave right away and instead kept talking. She wanted to repeat for him verbatim what Xiaodi had told her and hear the cobbler's opinion.

"You may be from the countryside," she said earnestly, "but you are much more cultivated than a lot of Shanghai men!"

"You can find all kinds of people, no matter where you go," he demurred.

"I didn't mean to offend you!" She tried to explain herself.

He laughed. This woman was as naïve as a child, but she was utterly sincere. How mysterious women were! The two sat and talked, and before they knew it, the workday was over and it was time for Gendi to go home and cook dinner; so off she went. Before long, the cobbler had put everything away for the night, methodically placing his tools and supplies in their compartments in the metal tool chest. Then he went up the lane to Gendi's house, where he washed up and changed into clean clothes. If it was one of Xiaodi's days off, the cobbler would find Gendi already busy in the kitchen, boiling, sautéing, and frying. Xiaodi would be sitting at the kitchen table like a customer at a restaurant, waiting for his meal to be served. When he saw the cobbler walk in, he would politely ask him to join him, and the cobbler would always decline. But this time Xiaodi insisted, and he really meant it. Gendi also pressed him to stay and refused to give him back his suit of clothes. The cobbler had no choice but to take a seat.

Gendi set out another bowl, pair of chopsticks, and glass, and Xiaodi filled the cobbler's glass with red wine, addressing him as "Friend." Friendship meant that out in the world he would have one more helping hand, that he wouldn't have to stand on ceremony, and that they could eat and drink together. Smiling faintly, the cobbler raised his glass, toasted Xiaodi, and tilted his head back. He drained half his cup and took a few bites of food. Xiaodi also took a sip of wine and asked the cobbler how long he'd been in Shanghai, where his wife was, and what his life here was like. The cobbler answered each question in turn, and they traded a few more toasts and ate a bit more. The cobbler showed no effects from the alcohol, but Xiaodi's eyes were rimmed with red, and his skin had turned pale—he was looking like his younger self again.

"You've been away from home long enough, you're not a newcomer anymore—you're an old Shanghai man. No wonder you're so knowledgeable."

The cobbler knew that whatever he'd told Gendi, Gendi had told her husband, and he had to smile.

"I have a few interesting stories I'd like to tell you," Xiaodi continued. "I want to hear what you think."

The cobbler gestured to Xiaodi, urging him to please speak, and Xiaodi began. The first anecdote concerned something that had happened just the day before. He had picked up a passenger, a Shanghainese dressed in a Western suit and tie. The man was carrying a black briefcase with locks. When they reached their destination and the man took out his wallet, Xiaodi could see in the rearview mirror that the man had no cash, only credit cards. The man said, "Driver, please wait a minute. I'll go inside and get you the fare." With that, he got out. Xiaodi waited, and the man didn't come back; so he waited a little longer, but the man still didn't come back. Suspicious, Xiaodi got out of the car and went down the lane the man had disappeared into, only to discover that the lane was a narrow passage that was open at the other end. By then the man could have been anywhere!

That was the first incident. The second one had happened the week before, and it had also occurred when the time came for the passenger to pay. This particular customer's wallet was bulging with cash—but it was all foreign currency! The customer sheepishly explained that he'd just come from Hong Kong—could he pay in Hong Kong dollars? He would pay face value rather than going by the current exchange rate, even though the Hong Kong dollar was worth slightly more than the yuan. The passenger gave him one hundred Hong Kong dollars, and he gave the man eighty-one yuan in change. When Xiaodi took the money to the bank, they told him it wasn't Hong Kong money all—it was Peruvian money, and it wasn't worth a fen! That exotic bill now lay on the table. The third story had happened the previous month, and it was quite simple: Three men with provincial accents got into the cab. They told him right up front that they didn't have any money, but that he'd have to drive them to their destination whether he wanted to or not!

Xiaodi twisted his head around and looked at the cobbler: "Well, what do you think this means?" The cobbler's reply was brief: "The first two characters were con men; the last group were strong-arm robbers. But they had one thing in common—they were all after money."

"That's it! You hit the nail right on the head!" Xiaodi exclaimed. "Gendi said you were a wise man, but I didn't believe it. That's why I decided to ask you myself, and sure enough, she wasn't making this stuff up—there really was something to it!"

Xiaodi's face was completely flushed, for the wine had gone to his head; Gendi was also flushed, but from excitement. Leaning in close to the cobbler, Xiaodi asked, "Don't you think people today are a lot more prosperous than they were in the old days? In the beginning, Deng Xiaoping said a few people would have to get rich first; and now at least eighty percent of people have gotten rich—but as it turns out, people seem more short of cash than they ever were! How can that be?"

The blood had also rushed to the cobbler's face, but because his skin was darker to begin with, it was less obvious. He just seemed to glow, and he bent in closer to Xiaodi: "An excellent question, my friend. I can see that you have a deep understanding of our society. In my opinion, it's easy to fill a stomach, but the eyes are hard to satisfy!" Xiaodi slapped the cobbler on the shoulder and said, "I couldn't have said it any better myself!" That night, they got very drunk and didn't part until the wine was gone.

The next time the cobbler came over for drinks and a meal, Gendi spoke up as he was about to go home: "Xiaodi has to be at work all day tomorrow, so he won't be home for lunch or dinner. There's a lot of food left over, and what with the heat wave we're having, I'm afraid it's not going to keep. You could help us out if you ate here again tomorrow night!" The cobbler accepted, and the next evening, after he packed up his stall, he went to Gendi's. Seeing that she'd cooked some fresh dishes, he asked, "What's all this? You invited me over to help get rid of your leftovers." She replied, "Yes, but this is what I felt like eating!" The cobbler didn't touch the fresh food, and Gendi didn't pressure him; but when he wasn't looking, she slid a heap of it into his bowl. He could only shake his head. When they'd had their fill, two-thirds of the food was still uneaten, and Gendi took out a plastic bag and started dumping it all in. Snatching up a plate of stir-fried pork, soybeans, and wild rice stalks, the cobbler said, "Save this for my lunch tomorrow." Gendi refused, saying that tomorrow was another day, and he should have something different then. They fought over the serving bowl, tugging and pulling; and in the end the cobbler lost—not because Gendi was stronger, but because she was more determined.

After he got home that night, the cobbler chopped up half a cabbage and mixed in some chopped shrimp and a couple of beaten eggs to make dumpling filling. He then rolled out enough dough for skins and folded about three dozen jiaozi. These he set in a deep pot, which he immersed in water. The next day he would take them to Gendi's for lunch. He couldn't allow himself to freeload, or his friendship with Gendi would be a one-way street.

When noon rolled around, Gendi brought him lunch, but it wasn't jiaozi: it was rice, big fat spare ribs, and a soup of carp and tofu.

"Where are my jiaozi?" the cobbler asked.

"I ate them."

"They didn't have any meat. You got the short end of the stick."

"They were handmade—you can't beat that! I'm afraid *you* got the short end."

Once again the cobbler could only shake his head, and Gendi grinned with satisfaction: "You should know better than to think you can get the better of me!"

4

Although the meal exchange didn't continue, the hometown connection between the cobbler and Gendi deepened. When the cobbler closed up shop for the night and came to clean up and change at Gendi's, soon he wasn't just washing his face, he was shampooing his hair as well. Gendi would fill a basin with warm water and pour it over his head to rinse out the soap. One evening, some of the water trickled down his neck, and when he tried to get away, she chased after him. Eventually his shirt was soaked completely through. He stripped off the wet shirt and dried his now bare chest. He had a powerful physique; his was the body of a man who regularly exerts himself, and he didn't have an ounce of flab. Suddenly she realized that the cobbler was also very tall. Accustomed to seeing him sitting down, she had never noticed his height. Gendi dumped what was left of the water over the cobbler's back, and it glazed his dark skin with another shiny layer, the water droplets rolling off of him like big pearls. The pair carried on with this horseplay right there in the lane, in plain sight of everyone, but no one paid them any mind. They knew what Gendi was like—what would she want with a man like the young cobbler? Besides, he wasn't Uncle Ye. Uncle Ye himself had been awfully quiet of late and had been keeping to himself. He'd been spotted several times in his wife's boutique, sitting with his face hidden behind a newspaper. In fact, Uncle Ye was hiding—from Jinrong!

Ever since the day she'd had him carry all that stuff into her house, Uncle Ye had been afraid of her—not that he knew precisely what it was he feared. What could Jinrong do to him? But frightened he was. The woman who emerged from the van that day could have unleashed a stream of profanity at him, and he could have handled it; but confronted with warmth and a smile, he was at a complete loss. In fact, Jinrong's smile was stiff—it looked happy and angry at the same time. And then there were her eyes. They weren't like Gendi's eyes, which bored right into you—instead they looked everywhere but directly at you, and you couldn't be sure what they were hiding. And her hands—they were so icy, they made him shiver. Of course, it goes without saying that he hadn't noticed how attractive she was until now. She had a particular way of walking, which made the long skirts she favored float around her like petals on the breeze. She was petite and graceful, and there was no ignoring it. Gendi also had a nice figure, but like her personality, it was neither delicate nor subtle. Uncle Ye's wariness was complicated by temptation. He hid at home for two days, but he soon grew bored—if he went to his wife's boutique, he could at least watch people and cars passing by. But as luck would have it, Jinrong also came by the shop that day.

The company where she worked was in an office building nearby, and she often dropped by the shop on her lunch hour. Caught unawares, Uncle Ye was flustered; but before he could get up from his chair, his wife had stepped forward to greet her. At home in the lane, the two women were only nodding acquaintances, but here in the shop they were customer and proprietor, and in no time at all they'd struck up a warm conversation, exchanging pleasantries before turning their attention to the business of flipping through the racks of clothes. Uncle Ye's wife showed her all kinds of fabrics and styles, telling her where they were made, what international trends they reflected, and encouraging her to try some things on—she didn't have to buy anything, just have some fun with it. After carefully inspecting each piece of clothing, Jinrong picked out a high-necked top with a lacy yoke. She examined it again, then held it up to herself in the mirror. Uncle Ye's wife complimented her on the selection and urged her to try it on. Jinrong just smiled and looked at her reflection again, saying, "Some people say you have to be young to wear the things you sell here!" Uncle Ye's wife replied, "What nonsense! Fashion is made for individuals, not age groups—it's about sensibility." She swept a hand over a rack of clothes, like a pianist sweeping her hands over a keyboard. "Fashion has a life of its own; some trends are short-lived—those are what we call fads. Fads are about novelty and the unusual, but that kind of thing has no place in my shop." She was an experienced saleswoman, calm and poised. Jinrong slid the top back onto its hanger and returned it to its original spot, saying, "If only everyone saw it that way!" As Uncle Ye's wife tidied the racks, she remarked, "How others see things is their business. What's important is how *you* feel!" Jinrong looked at her intently, then said she had to head back to the office now, but that she'd return tomorrow. Uncle Ye's wife saw her to the door, and when she opened and closed it, the electric chime made a little "ding." Throughout the interaction, Uncle Ye had been cowering behind his newspaper.

As promised, Jinrong came back the next day, with a couple of young female coworkers in tow. While the girls rifled through the clothes racks, Uncle Ye's wife chatted with Jinrong. They acted like close friends as they shared personal stories and experiences. Uncle Ye's wife told Jinrong about the hardships she'd faced in Japan—how at first she couldn't understand a word anyone said, and how that had kept her from finding a job. But then one of the girls had to go back to Shanghai to tend to her ailing father, and Uncle Ye's wife filled in for her. The boss was a woman, and when she spoke to her, Uncle Ye's wife looked completely lost. The boss asked, "Do you understand what I'm saying?" Uncle Ye's wife didn't even understand the question. When she got to this point in the story, she couldn't help laughing. It was laughter well earned, at once self-deprecating and filled with pleasure at her own accomplishments. Uncle Ye, huddled behind his newspaper, listened in. He had heard his wife talk about her travails before, but never in such vivid terms. Jinrong also seemed livelier, and her laughter rang out loud and clear. After a bit, each of the girls found something she liked and went into the dressing room to try it on. Uncle Ye's wife went to the rack to get the top for Jinrong, but it wasn't there. She looked on another rack, but it wasn't there, either. Sounding a bit disappointed, Jinrong ventured, "Perhaps somebody bought it." Uncle Ye's wife said that wasn't possible—she kept a running tally of sales and inventory in her head. Turning to Uncle Ye, she asked him if he'd sold anything. "Why are you asking me?" he said from behind his newspaper, "You never let me wait on customers." Smiling slightly, she turned to Jinrong and explained, "It's not that I don't let him, it's just that he wouldn't know what to do—everything here is for women." The women searched the shop from top to bottom, even checking inside the cabinets, but the top was nowhere to be found. "Never mind," Jinrong said. "I've got to get back to work!"

"Come again tomorrow—it's bound to turn up. It was right under my nose. It can't simply have walked away!"

Uncle Ye's wife forgot to see Jinrong and the girls out when they left the shop. She stood in the middle of the floor, rattled: "Where could it have got to?"

The day after that, Jinrong didn't visit the boutique, afraid that she would come across as pushy or needy. Returning from work at dusk, she passed Uncle Ye at the entrance to the lane. She looked right through him and walked on by, unaware that he was quietly following, until he called out, "Jinrong." She jumped, and turned to see that it was Uncle Ye.

"What do you want?"

He had a mysterious look on his face and whispered, "Go inside and I'll tell you."

With some trepidation, Jinrong opened the door and went inside. There was no one home; the bamboo blinds were down, and the room was cool. Jinrong's house was like Jinrong herself, bracingly cold, but only on the surface. Uncle Ye thought back to the way she'd looked when she was talking to his wife—she had a vivacious side after all. Although she'd invited him in, she was giving him a look that struck fear in him. He drew himself up and cracked a smile, but it only made him look smarmy. Jinrong was filled with disgust—she'd forgotten that it was she who had made the first move.

"What do you want?" she asked again.

He took his hand out from behind his back and held something out to her—a plastic shopping bag.

"For you!"

She took the bag and pulled out a piece of clothing. It was the blouse they had turned the shop upside down for yesterday, mauve silk with delicate lace appliqued on the yoke. She shook it out and held it up to the light, gave it a good look, folded it up again, and threw it back at Uncle Ye. "Not very impressive," she sneered. "Stealing from your own wife so you can give a present to another woman!"

Turning bright red, Uncle Ye tried to defend himself: "I thought you liked it!"

"If you think I'd like something, then buy it for me!"

Uncle Ye started stammering and finally gave up trying to say anything more, while Jinrong flung the empty plastic bag back at him. It fell to the floor before it reached him, and when he bent to pick it up, he was so flustered that instead of grabbing the bag, he grabbed Jinrong's skirt. Raising her foot, she gently shook him off, and he let go. After a few failed swipes, he got hold of the bag and scurried out. The next day, Jinrong went to the boutique, and Uncle Ye's wife greeted her: "I found the blouse! It was right where it should have been. I don't know how we could have missed it." Jinrong said, "Sometimes you have to go in circles just to end up where you started, I guess!" With that, she took the blouse into the changing room. When she emerged, she examined herself in the mirror from several angles before deciding that the blouse looked good. Uncle Ye's wife said, "I told you it would suit you—didn't you believe me?" Jinrong said, "I know better now." She laid her money on the counter, and Uncle Ye's wife picked it up—they were doing business.

"Next time you'll listen to me, right?" said Uncle Ye's wife, adding, "Remember, the clothes in this boutique are ageless."

"I won't listen to anyone else ever again," Jinrong allowed.

From that day on, Jinrong and Uncle Ye's wife were fast friends, while Jinrong and Gendi went back to being nodding acquaintances.

Long before the gossip in the lane died down, Gendi had stopped caring what Jinrong thought. She had a new friend—the young cobbler. She spent all of her free time at his stall, keeping him company and knitting or doing crochet. If the cobbler had to leave his stall for any reason, say to go to the toilet or run an errand, Gendi called out to potential customers, took in items for repair, returned finished jobs, and took payments, dropping the cash into the cobbler's cashbox, an old Nestlé's coffee tin. She'd learned a bit of his trade and could do roughly half of the jobs that came in—or so she thought. The cobbler may have seen things differently. Once there was a job that Gendi gave up on, an old pair of leather shoes with broken heels, and the cobbler took over. He knew at a glance that they were counterfeit designer shoes. With the customer's consent, the cobbler proceeded to peel off the soles in their entirety, replacing them with rubber ones. Since nobody ever saw the bottom of other people's shoes, when he was through, they still looked to all the world like designer shoes.

The cobbler believed that people who wore designer goods were obsessed with appearances and didn't care about substance—as long as you gave them some face, they'd be satisfied. But on one occasion Gendi took a job that the cobbler refused to do. It was a pair of women's soft suede boots. The uppers were detached from the soles, and Gendi assumed that all they needed was to be glued back together, but the cobbler corrected her: "It may look like they've come unglued, but in fact they've been cut apart, with something very sharp." Gendi was taken aback and said that surely the customer hadn't realized. "Not necessarily," he replied, and Gendi was even more surprised: "Well, isn't she trying to cheat you?" The cobbler looked stern: "You mustn't talk that way. You know the saying 'Do no harm, only protect.' Anyway, there's nothing I can do to fix these." Gendi laughed and cuffed his head: "I refuse to believe there's anything you can't do!" The cobbler replied, "Being able to do everything is the same as being able to do nothing." Gendi looked baffled. "Even an all-purpose remedy is sure to be useless for something," he explained. "Take Wanjin Oil." Gendi laughed and swatted at him again, but he just laughed and blocked her, grasping her wrist. She tried to free herself but couldn't. "You're a strong one!" she said.

"A man who lets himself get slapped around by women loses stature."

"What are you talking about? You're as tall as a tower."

"I don't mean height, I mean reputation!"

His grip loosened as he spoke, and she twisted free. She made as if to slap him, and he stepped back, not realizing it was only a feint. She swiped at the air and brought her hand back, rubbing her wrist. "You're too rough!" she complained, but her expression said that she was impressed. She had realized he was a man, and a strong man at that.

Their mealtime get-togethers were confined to lunchtime, but now Gendi always took a little extra care and added special ingredients. She knew his taste—it was what she'd grown up with, tender and very salty: red-cooked fatty pork; oily stir-fried vegetables; chicken soup with cabbage and bean thread noodles; egg dumplings; shredded pork and greens over soft noodles, with a whole egg nestled inside. No matter how hot the weather was, the cobbler liked his soup piping hot, and he would slurp it down, with beads of sweat the size of soybeans rolling down his face and neck. A recipient of Gendi's tender ministrations, the cobbler was moved by her goodness, and he knew that her steadfastness and hospitality were the hallmark of her native countryside. When visitors from her hometown came to Shanghai, they brought home-raised hens, fish and shrimp from the local waterways, sheaves of sweet sorghum stalks, and wild mountain tea. They would give half of what they brought to Gendi, and she treated them like her own flesh and blood. The cobbler's mother-in-law was in town and dropped by the stall, occupying Gendi's customary spot, and Gendi stood aside. In the presence of a member of the older generation, Gendi and the cobbler were less relaxed with each other. Since the old lady was a woman of few words, the younger people followed suit, and the little group of three was largely silent. At some point, Gendi's and the cobbler's eyes chanced to meet, and the feelings that had been hidden passed between them. The cobbler looked away first, and after a moment Gendi, too, shifted her gaze. During her visit, it was the cobbler's mother-in-law who brought the noon meal, and the contents of the aluminum pot, made by the cobbler's wife, were inferior in both quality and quantity to Gendi's cooking; but Gendi knew that come evening there would be a delicious meal waiting for the cobbler when he got home—his wife wouldn't hold back. After work, he went to Gendi's to wash and change as usual, and she noticed he had a different smell—a sort of conjugal funk—and she kept her distance. His movements seemed rougher and clumsier as well. He turned the faucet on so hard the water came blasting out, and he shut it off with a jerk; and when he was putting on his shirt, he tore the armpit seam with his elbow and buttoned his shirt askew. Not having time to unfasten the buttons and do them over, he was out the door and had reached the entrance to the lane in no time flat, hurrying along as if he were being chased.

When his wife came up from the countryside, she never stayed more than a few days. During those brief interludes, the cobbler didn't bring his lunch for Gendi to heat up, but he still changed his clothes at her place mornings and evenings. Gendi's son—a stuck-up youth of twenty, currently in his third and final year of junior college—was always at home. Gendi and Xiaodi lavished love and attention on him, catering to his every need, but he answered them with silence. When the cobbler was in the house, he could be right in front of the couple's son, and the son would act even more as if nobody were there. The cobbler reflected that this boy was nothing like either of his parents, who were both so cheerful and straightforward; and he further concluded that only a pair as nice as they were could have raised such an ill-mannered child. When her son was home, Gendi waited on him hand and foot and didn't say a word to the cobbler. Only after she'd sent her son out on an errand did she turn and speak to the cobbler, but by then he too was on his way out. Watching their retreating figures, Gendi imagined that they were brothers, although brothers with a big age gap, in a family where the elder was helping his parents bring up the younger. The next day, she came by the stall and asked, "Are you going to bring food to reheat anymore or not? If you don't have leftovers, what are you going to eat for lunch?"

"I've been bringing cold noodles the past few days," he replied. "They don't need heating up."

Gendi went to open the lid of his pot, but he wouldn't let her. "Cold noodles three days in a row—are you going to have the same thing again tomorrow?"

"I'll worry about that tomorrow."

Gendi spun around and walked away, but she hadn't gone far when she turned back and flung a wad of bills at him: "Here's your gas money!"

He tried to refuse, picking up the money and attempting to press it into her hands, but she wouldn't let him. "You don't want me to heat up your lunches anymore!"

He was determined to give her back the money, and she was equally determined not to take it. Finally, he stood up, grabbed her by the wrist, and stuffed the cash into her hand, saying, "I will need my lunch heated tomorrow."

Mollified, Gendi accepted the money—but she didn't wait for the next day. When lunchtime arrived, she appeared with a pot half full of fish and shrimp. Snatching the cobbler's noodles, she slurped them down all in one go and sat down in front of him. Perched on the stool, she watched him eat, but neither spoke—they both felt hurt. He ate in silence, and when he was finished, she took the empty pot back home with her.

Life returned to normal, with the cobbler changing at Gendi's mornings and evenings, and Gendi bringing him his heated lunch at noon and sitting on the stool knitting or crocheting, keeping him company while he ate. But she wasn't as talkative as before, and there were long stretches where neither said anything. Uncle Ye and the others had found a new place for the mahjong table—since Gendi wouldn't play with them anymore, they couldn't spend hours playing outside her house. Instead they set it up beside the cobbler's stall, under the arch that ran across the entrance to the lane. The arch shielded them from the sun and rain, and this spot also caught the breezes that blew through the lane.

"Hey, cobbler!" Uncle Ye called out. "You're a strong one!"

There was a double entendre, which Gendi may or may not have caught, but the cobbler couldn't pretend he hadn't heard. He smiled weakly but didn't reply. Uncle Ye was undeterred: "A whole lane full of Shanghainese can't compete with you!" The new player at the mahjong table was a slacker who lived in the lane. A generation younger than Uncle Ye, he and his wife were living off of his parents. He spent his days pursuing leisure-time activities, looking for new ways to have fun and honing his slick patter. He picked up where Uncle Ye had left off: "Three stinking cobblers, Clobbering General Zhuge Liang!" This wasn't the least bit funny, but everyone at the table collapsed in laughter. Even the cobbler cracked a little smile, but Gendi wouldn't stand for it—she understood what they were talking about. Turning to go, she shot them a sidelong glance and said, "Who's really the stinky one? Sponging off a woman!" This was directed at Uncle Ye, and it hit home, for this was a sore point; but Uncle Ye wasn't the one who had said "stinking cobblers," nor had the epithet been directed at Gendi. Uncle Ye wasn't about to let this go, and when he spoke, his voice was gruff: "If you're going to accuse someone of something, you need to look them in the eye. Who were you calling 'stinking'?" Gendi laughed: "I was talking to the one who answered!" Taking the bait, Uncle Ye jumped up from the table and marched over to Gendi. With his face pressed close to hers, he said, "You, woman—you take on the colors of whoever you're with. If you go around with that stinking cobbler, you're gonna stink, too!" Gendi stood up with a flourish: "At least we've got each other—but you, you're such a loser, all you've got is your own sorry ass!" This time she was speaking directly to Uncle Ye, and this barb also found its mark. You couldn't live in a longtang and expect to have any secrets—you couldn't fool anyone. Uncle Ye turned bright red, took a step closer to Gendi, and threatened, "I'm gonna smack you!" Gendi moved closer to Uncle Ye: "Is that so?" Their foreheads were practically touching, and they could feel each other's breath on their faces. Gendi's eyelashes fluttered, the blood rushed to Uncle Ye's head, and he raised his hand to slap her in the face; but just as his fingernail was grazing her cheek, his hand went flying—the cobbler had blocked him. "What kind of coward strikes a woman?" the cobbler demanded. "Is she your wife? Find something else to do in your spare time!" Uncle Ye shoved him and realized how solid the cobbler was—his chest was as taut as a metal drum. Uncle Ye gave him another shove, but the cobbler didn't move a muscle or bat an eye, and Uncle Ye let out a stream of curses.

At this, the cobbler's face darkened, and he stepped out from behind his work table. Untying his apron as he walked, he said to Uncle Ye, "I had no intention of getting into a fight with you; but you've insulted my mother, and if I don't try to teach you a lesson, I'd be a bad, unfilial son. You've violated the Three Cardinal Hierarchies and the Five Constant Virtues—it's time to take your punishment!" Uncle Ye didn't have the faintest idea what the cobbler was talking about. All the filth he'd just spewed—"your mother" this and "your mother" that—had shot out of his mouth like pellets from a gun, but the cobbler cried, "That's an insult!" and punched Uncle Ye in the jaw. Uncle Ye staggered back a couple of steps, regained his footing, and rushed at the cobbler. All of the anger and frustration that had been building up inside him over the months and years suddenly merged into a mass of fury—directed toward the cobbler. Although the cobbler was young and vigorous, he was no match for someone who was going all out, and he fell to the ground under Uncle Ye's wild pummeling. Unwilling to stand by and watch, Gendi picked up the stool with both hands and started to bring it down on Uncle Ye; but he stepped aside just in time, and she ended up striking the cobbler in the face instead, giving him a black eye. Head down, Gendi charged at Uncle Ye again, and this time she rammed his chest with the stool. He stumbled back and landed on the ground in a sitting position, and Gendi moved in and pounded his face and head, repaying every blow that the cobbler had been unable to return.

The old ladies at the mahjong table had scurried off, and the young slacker who'd started it all was nowhere to been seen—he had washed his hands of the whole affair and had vanished without a trace. Calmly, the cobbler walked over to Gendi and pulled her off of Uncle Ye, saying,

"It's not good for two people to gang up on one." Uncle Ye was still on the ground, and he taunted the cobbler again: "Hey, cobbler—still think you want to do business here?" The cobbler replied, "Where I choose to do business is no business of yours—it's up to the government!" Uncle Ye sneered, "What makes you think the government even knows you exist? You and your rinky-dink repair shack!" The cobbler answered again, "The government doesn't just tell *me* what to do—it also has authority over you. If the government tells you to move out of your house, you better clear out, and fast!" After so many years in Shanghai, the cobbler was keenly aware of local sensitivities, and his words hit Uncle Ye where it hurt.

That afternoon, the mahjong game broke up, the cobbler closed early, and Gendi took him back to her place to wash up. She applied cold compresses to his bruised face, careful not to hurt him. At first the cobbler pursed his lips and exhaled slowly, but then he started to laugh, remarking that Uncle Ye really had guts, unlike your typical Shanghainese. They could curse you up one side and down the other, but when it came to real fighting, they were useless. Gendi moved the damp cloth from the cobbler's face to his back, and after the cool cloth warmed up, she tossed it into a basin and put her arms around him from behind. He didn't move a muscle; he could feel Gendi's soft breasts against his back. She was very warm, and the hottest spot of all was in the crook of his neck, where her face was. She opened her mouth and nibbled on his shoulder, then turned her face to the side and rested it on the bite marks. Her luxuriant and disheveled hair poured over the cobbler's shoulder, both prickly and soft against his skin. He tilted his head, pinning her hair against his shoulder. After a moment, Gendi spoke: "Cobbler, you really are something!" The cobbler broke free and turned around, thinking to himself that she was one very strong woman. They stood facing each other, and he studied her briefly, then said, "You always call me 'Cobbler'—I have a name, you know."

"What is it?" she asked.

"My family name is Xi—the xi that means 'mat.'"

"Is that a real last name?" Gendi interrupted.

"There's a tale in *Strange Stories from a Chinese Studio* with a character named Xi Fangping."

"Oh," she said.

"My family name is Xi, and my given name shares the character gen with yours. My name is Genhai."

When Gendi spoke again, she said just one word: "Genhai."

5

Gendi and Genhai's romance was red-hot. Anyone who saw the pot full of food that Gendi carried to Genhai at lunchtime would have been green with envy. Beneath the steaming golden surface of a pot of chicken broth, there might lie a pair of prawns, smoked fish, a chicken thigh, and an entire egg; or she might bring a braised pork knuckle, the rich, thick gravy mixed with rice. Genhai's contribution was to haul sacks of rice, bottles of drinking water, and cases of Sprite—the heavy lifting. He washed his face by Gendi's back door, quickly pulling off his shirt and washing his upper body, while Gendi soaped and scrubbed his back. Sometimes he helped her hang out the wash. The bamboo drying poles that extended from the walls of the house across the lane to the concrete eaves of Gendi's place were half again as tall as a person, so Genhai would put his arms around Gendi's legs and lift her up. As he lowered her, she would turn around, encircle his neck with her arms, and float to the ground. They were openly affectionate, but it hadn't gone beyond that. Intrigued, the neighbors were heard to remark, "Gendi and Genhai—their names are so similar, maybe they're related, like big sister and little brother!" Now that Gendi was calling Genhai by his name, everyone in the lane started doing the same. Gendi teased him: "Have you heard what people are saying? You should call me big sister." Genhai said, "Nope—I'm gonna call you little sister!" She put her hand over his mouth, but he managed to blurt out "little sis," and she laughed. Anyone who witnessed this spectacle was disgusted and fled in embarrassment, but the two of them were completely oblivious and engaged in more horseplay, until finally they settled down.

Their peaceful moments were truly peaceful, as they traded stories about the old days and discovered mutual friends and acquaintances. Genhai was from Yancheng, and Gendi's family was originally from Lianshui; and when Genhai insisted that the two places were very far apart indeed, Gendi protested that, on the contrary, they were both north of the Yangzi. Genhai found a piece of chalk and drew a map on the ground so that he could show her: "More than half of Jiangsu is north of the Yangzi River, starting at Chongming Island outside of Shanghai and going all the way up to Xuzhou, on the border with Shandong Province." Gendi countered, "Xuzhou doesn't count as 'North of the Yangzi.' In Shanghai, 'North of the Yangzi'—'Jiangbei'—means the people who speak that dialect."

"And which dialect would that be?" Genhai asked.

"The one you and I both speak."

"There's a huge difference between the way you speak and the way I do!" he laughed.

"It's still more or less the same."

Genhai shook his head: "Shanghai people think they're so smart, but they can't tell a dumpling from a noodle—it's all flour and water to them! They can't tell red from green or black from white."

"Jiangbei is Jiangbei," Gendi insisted. "It's just a manner of speaking."

Genhai shook his head again. "You're so mixed up, you don't know where your own hometown is. And you're so naïve—I bet if somebody sold you, you'd help them count the money!" Gendi inclined her head and met Genhai's gaze: "So I'm for sale, am I? Will you buy me?" Genhai answered, "I couldn't afford you." Gendi looked disappointed: "You're impossible." Genhai brought his hammer down hard on the sole of the shoe he was working on. "If Xiaodi wanted to sell you, I'd sell everything I owned to scrape together enough money!" At the mention of her husband, they both fell silent.

During this time, no matter how much Xiaodi pressed him to stay for dinner, Genhai turned him down. Gendi refused to intervene—all she'd say was, "It's up to him!" and she would see Genhai out, ignoring the look of disappointment on Xiaodi's face. Xiaodi genuinely wanted Genhai to stay—he thought of him as a close friend, a true kindred spirit. The more someone cares, the worse their suffering. Gendi and Genhai still hadn't been up to much; at most they would kiss and cuddle in the privacy of Gendi's house. If Xiaodi had been a brute like Uncle Ye, Genhai and Gendi might have shown more self-control; but Xiaodi was as weak as a newly sprouted pea vine, and the passage of years and the demands of earning a living had worn him down until he looked old and weathered. The situation was becoming unbearable for Genhai and Gendi. It felt like torture. Genhai was in his thirties and in robust health; but with his wife living in the countryside, he spent his nights alone. Gendi was somewhat older, but her blood was still hot and the spirit was willing. And then there was that other matter—how can we put it delicately . . . ? One time when Gendi was nibbling on Genhai's earlobe, she commented, "Did you know that eight or nine out of ten taxi drivers have the same problem? They can't do it! They're too tired, or they don't have any sensation. They sit scrunched up all day long, and they have prostate troubles." Yet what could she do? Xiaodi and Gendi's marriage certificate hung on their wall—all you had to do was look up, and there it was. But that certificate was twenty years old, and things had changed. Their heads had been in the clouds back then, and they had played their parts, struck their poses. Their old selves didn't even look like real people—their wedding photo was garish and crisply focused, and the young couple inside the frame seemed larger than life. Gendi was wide-eyed, while Xiaodi peered out timidly, like a blushing maiden. How could she ever treat a person like him badly? And then there was their son. He was constantly coming and going, never speaking to them. He had his father's face and body, but not his mien; his expression was cold and aloof, as if nothing could touch him. Gendi and Xiaodi were afraid of their son, and Genhai followed their lead. Whenever Gendi was getting close to the edge, her face took on a crazed expression, at which point Genhai would halt, and prying himself off of Gendi, he would go on his way. Soon after, they saw each other, and Gendi asked: "Genhai, do you hate the fact that I'm old?" Genhai didn't answer at first, but after a moment he leaned in and whispered in her ear, "Call me big brother!" In their hometown accent, the word for "big brother," "gege," sounded like "guoguo," which meant katydid. Both speaker and listener felt deeply pained; but the two of them weren't from Shanghai originally, and they knew that the awkwardness would pass—nothing lay ahead but happy times.

One day, Uncle Ye's wife had brought in three pairs of shoes for resoling, two men's and one women's. That afternoon, Uncle Ye and his friends set up the mahjong table at the entrance to the lane, and at a word from Genhai, Gendi took all three pairs of newly soled shoes and dumped them at Uncle Ye's feet. Uncle Ye was setting up mahjong tiles, and he spoke as he stacked:

"How much?"

"He doesn't want your money!"

"Now, don't get carried away with the giveaways—it's bad for the bottom line!"

"You can't put a price on artistry!"

Uncle Ye had long since dropped any pretense of politeness, but now that he'd gotten his ill will off his chest—not once but twice—he considered the matter closed. That's the kind of person he was: a man can hop in and out of a crucible of molten metal and be no worse for wear, but drop him in the midst of a bunch of women, and he'll be lost. Shanghai people have foul mouths, but their hearts aren't really in it; and ever since Genhai had taught him a lesson with his verbal barbs and hard fists, Uncle Ye had developed a respectful fear of the cobbler. When he was around Genhai, Uncle Ye was very careful about what he said and did. Genhai had a healthy perspective on things and knew when to forgive. At the same time, his opinion of Uncle Ye had gone up a notch or two. They didn't acknowledge any of this out loud, but you could sense an undercurrent of warmth.

It was another one of Xiaodi's days off, and Gendi was home as usual, waiting on the family wage earner. When the mahjong game was over, Uncle Ye didn't hurry home to cook dinner. Instead he sauntered over to hassle Genhai. "Hey, cobbler." Uncle Ye still insisted on calling him that, as if to maintain a particular stance. "Cobbler, Uncle Ye's got some free advice for you!"

"What would that be?" Genhai asked without looking up.

"A rabbit doesn't nibble the grass by its own burrow! You don't eat where you shit!" With that, he turned and walked away; but after a few steps, he turned again. Genhai was looking straight at him, and he knew that the cobbler had understood. Turning one last time, he went on his way.

Genhai was hammering nails into a shoe, and he was so flustered that he missed twice and bent the nails. On the third try, he hit his finger. Uncle Ye's words were a wake-up call, and Genhai realized that his conduct of late had been quite indecent. Gendi had an impetuous streak and would jump into things without regard for the consequences. He should have guided her with a firm hand—instead he'd followed her right into the fire. By now, everyone in the lane knew what was going on, and Genhai was filled with shame. When Gendi came by the stall the next day, he was noticeably more restrained. Not knowing what was behind his behavior, she turned up the flirtation a few notches, but he didn't respond. From his vantage point at the nearby mahjong table, Uncle Ye cast a few meaningful looks in Genhai's direction. Several times their eyes met, and each time they did, Genhai smashed his fingers with his hammer. The anger came bubbling up.

And so it went. Genhai didn't want to make an enemy of Xiaodi, but he ended up making one out of Uncle Ye. The more warnings Uncle Ye issued, the more he wanted to ignore them. He turned around to talk to Gendi, but she had already gone off in a huff. Seeing Uncle Ye's satisfied expression, Genhai looked into his eyes and felt the rage burning even hotter. For the rest of the day he was under a cloud. His tranquil existence had been shattered. He felt adrift—all of that newness and excitement had come at a heavy cost. His current state of gloom was the bitter fruit of those heady times. Genhai didn't close up shop until it was too dark out to see. He slowly put away his things and locked up the metal cabinet, secretly hoping that Gendi's son was already home. He got his wish—the youth, sporting hair freshly dyed the yellow of ripe wheat, was occupying his father's place at the table, wallowing in his mother's attention. Xiaodi was at work and wouldn't be home before midnight. As usual, the boy looked right through Genhai, and Gendi didn't look at him, either—he knew she was angry. He walked past the kitchen and went into the other room to change into his clean clothes. When he emerged, they didn't exchange their customary goodbyes.

Genhai stepped out into the lane. This particular lane wasn't very deep, so although it wasn't lit, the streetlights from the adjacent avenue afforded some illumination. The houses in the lane were Western-style, with wide staircases, arched doorways, and chimneys that ascended from pitched roofs. Once upon a time, these houses had been inhabited by members of the upper class, but later they'd been subdivided into countless flats, and countless new tenants had moved in. New structures had been appended to the original exterior walls and extended into the courtyards. Old balconies had been enclosed to form garrets, making the houses look bloated and ungainly. Below this clutter, the little lane was crowded and noisy. But when night fell, all of these blemishes retreated into the shadows, and the longtang not only appeared to have been swept clean, it looked quite dignified. In the old days, the larger street that passed by the lane had been a peaceful place, but more than half the houses there had been remodeled and converted into storefronts. These businesses sold one of two things—apparel or food and drink. This brought in a lot of foot traffic, and the number of cars also swelled. Genhai walked home along that road in silence, a knot in his chest. After a while, he turned down a narrow alleyway. It was lined with barbershops and "foot massage" salons. Although the blinds were pulled down, a little bit of light leaked out, along with some muffled sounds. Suddenly Genhai was seized with desire. He pictured pale limbs intertwined in novel and intriguing ways beneath dim lamps, and he felt both nauseated and full of pity. But the urge was powerful—his heart pounded, and he was shaking. Finally he went into a Chongqing style hot pot restaurant and ordered a super-spicy hot pot made with chili peppers and numbing Sichuan peppercorns. There was enough broth to serve four, but Genhai had it all to himself. Spread before him was a platter heaped with marbled beef, lamb, pig's brain, and blood tofu. He plucked these delicacies up with his chopsticks, one morsel at a time, and submerged each one in the boiling broth, swirling it around before popping it into his mouth. It was piping hot, fiery and tingling, rich and pungent—and all of this, combined with the thought of how much it was costing, brought stinging tears to his eyes. He was just like some old fat cat, except that he didn't know how he was going to pay for it! Stitch a ripped seam, five mao; punch two eyelets, one yuan; replace a heel, two yuan; completely resole a pair of shoes, five yuan. His own children had never eaten a hamburger or gone to KFC. He felt sick at heart, but the worse he felt, the better the food tasted. Cheeks bulging with the oily and spicy food, he felt tears rolling down his face, and his frenzy gradually gave way to a sense of calm. As he contentedly slurped his soup, he felt both satisfied and utterly ruined. Patting his now empty pockets, Genhai left the restaurant.

The restaurant was located inside the neighborhood wet market, which had already closed for the night; but there were other shops on the site as well, along with small vendors who had spread out their wares. The building was packed and bustling, and the roar of voices filled the air. He heard accents of all kinds—there were people from far and wide, dressed in dark colors and brusque in their movements, and one look told him they were peasants up from the countryside. Their faces were dark and weathered, but they were smiling. Grubby children chased each other through the crowd, while the adults cuffed them and cursed them roundly. The blaring of televisions and radios inside the stalls added to the din, which wavered in pitch and volume. Beneath brightly colored lights, the goods on display looked cheap and garish. Genhai felt himself sway; his foot was stuck between two stalls, but he managed to extricate himself and emerged at last from the clamor of this venal material world. The stretch of road that lay ahead of him was pitch-black. There were empty lots on either side—the people who had lived there had moved away, their demolished homes reduced to heaps of rubble; and in the meantime the developers had run out of money and put the project on hold. The land was nothing but a garbage dump.

At the distant edge of this wasteland, one row of houses was still standing—the end of the original longtang. Windows cast feeble lamplight onto the open ground, but in an instant the light was swallowed up. Genhai began to sweat, and when the night air came into contact with his skin, he felt somewhat refreshed. Although he was lucid, he couldn't control his body and hurried his steps—he wanted to slow down but couldn't, and he heard the wind whistling past his ears. He entered the dilapidated old house where he lived, pushing past other tenants who had come outside to cool off. Somebody shouted out to him, but they sounded very far away. Not knowing who had spoken or what they'd said, he headed toward the stairs to his garret without responding. He lurched to a halt. Waiting in the entryway in a bamboo chair was Gendi.

She had been there a long time and was sitting in a chair she'd borrowed from the neighbors, watching a miniseries on a television that someone had brought out of their apartment. When she saw him she stood up, but she looked hesitant and apprehensive. Gendi very rarely looked this way, and he felt sorry for her. The dried-food sellers from Henan who lived downstairs weren't home yet. Their door was closed and the passage was dark, and Genhai fumbled around in the darkness for quite some time, trying to locate the light cord. He could hear Gendi sniffling, and he felt the air stir. When at last he found the cord and turned on the light, their shadows leapt onto the wall beside the wooden stairs. They climbed the narrow flight, single file, while Genhai felt for his key. Unlocking the door, he pushed it open and they stepped inside.

Gendi took in the spotless and simple room. She had never imagined a man could be so tidy, with everything in its place. The straw mattress on the bedframe, the sheets spread over the mattress, the pillow and bed-spread—all were clean and smooth. There was a standing fan on the floor, and the floorboards had been scrubbed pale. Atop a dresser with three drawers sat an electric rice cooker, an electric wok, and an electric ket-tle. These appliances looked old—there were marks and dings here and there—but they had been polished till they shone. There was a basket with a small pile of soybeans, originally meant for Genhai's dinner, but he had already eaten. Such was the lonely and ascetic life of a man who had to live so far from his family. Tonight it had been invaded by the warm and vital body of a woman. Gendi held out a mug filled with pea and lotus soup. It was still warm. Genhai took it and set it in a basin of cool water. "This is my refrigerator," he said. "You don't have a TV, either," she responded.

When he opened the window, they were met with the scene inside the neighboring apartment—a mahjong table, so close they could practically see what tiles the players were holding. The two watched in silence, then Genhai closed the window, and they fell into each other's arms. Their bodies were damp with sweat, and they could hear each other's hearts beating. This time, the face that floated up into Genhai's mind's eye wasn't Xiaodi's but Uncle Ye's, with his menacing glare. Genhai pushed Gendi toward the side of the bed, and together they collapsed onto the mattress.

It was as if a dam had burst, sweeping away everything in its path. Summer was drawing to a close, and in the countryside it was time to harvest and replant. Everyone at home was too busy with farm work to come up to Shanghai to see Genhai—so for the time being, he was a free man. Xiaodi worked a day and rested a day, and Gendi went over to Genhai's every other day. The old houses, slated for demolition but still standing, were mostly rented out to people from the provinces, and since there was a lot of turnover, people didn't get to know each other. In this community of strangers, nobody noticed Gendi's comings and goings. She would show up an hour after Genhai got home. That way he could eat dinner and freshen up. It wouldn't be completely dark out yet—at first the room would be dimly illuminated, and the light would gradually fade until there was nothing but darkness. The two of them were covered with hot sweat, which soaked the woven mat; the blades of the old fan clattered, the volume rising and falling with each oscillation, but for all the noise it made, the decrepit old fan didn't really cool them, and they switched it off. They were breathing hard, but they could still hear voices drifting up from outside. Sometimes they got so warm that afterward they would open the window and lie sprawled across the bed in the inky darkness, watching the people across the way. After a bit, Genhai would hop over and close the window, and Gendi would get dressed and go home. The men from Henan were back, and they heard the babble of their voices through the thin floor. Not daring to turn on the hall lamp, the pair crept down the stairs, a patch of light from the garret illuminating their way. Gendi stepped outside. A cool breeze had sprung up, and the night felt crisp. Autumn had stolen in. The people who had spent their summer nights cooling off outdoors had almost all retreated indoors. Somewhere at the foot of a wall, crickets were chirping.

Gendi made her way along the broken pavement, flanked by the squat remains of abandoned houses. The moon was overhead, and it lit up an expanse of crumbled brick and tile. She suddenly felt disoriented, as if she'd been there before—indeed, she'd lived in this place all her life—but now everything lay in ruins. Empty door and window frames tilted at odd angles, there were jagged gaps in the walls, and potholes covered the ground. If she wasn't careful, she would stumble and become one of those women behind the window. When the breeze touched her hot, sweaty skin, she felt cooler, her entire body relaxed, and her cares melted away. She and Genhai were people with strong physical desires. This combined with the feelings they had for each other to give them great happiness. They were positively glowing, and they went around beaming. Because they enjoyed physical intimacy at night, their mood was placid during the day. Lunchtimes were no longer infused with passion; and Gendi went back to heating up whatever Genhai brought. They didn't act this way because they were trying to hide anything—rather, they had reached a state of deep fulfillment. After Genhai had refused him several times, Xiaodi abandoned his entreaties, and over time their friendship faded from his memory. And Uncle Ye? He assumed that his warnings had been effective and thus relaxed his vigilance. But beneath this tranquil surface, Gendi and Genhai were burning with passion, and when she thought about it during the daytime, Gendi cried out. What did she cry? *Gege, my dear gege, beloved gege, my hot gege!* The sound of the word "gege" in their country dialect made their hearts ache with homesick nostalgia.

Throughout this interlude of raging passions, Genhai never lost contact with his family at home in the countryside. The harvest was brought in, and the fields were replanted; the cedar in the courtyard was chopped down, replaced with a date tree; his parents suffered from various ailments that went away on their own; his eldest child had started school and was looking forward to the long National Day holiday in October. This last bit of news gave Genhai a start—the school had originally planned to bring the students to Shanghai during the break to see the Pearl of the Orient, but at the last minute the teachers had changed plans and were taking them to Nanjing instead, to see Sun Yat-sen's tomb. Genhai breathed a sigh of relief, and he and Gendi carried on as before. One day when they had finished, they headed downstairs. Gendi was leading the way, while Genhai followed behind, carrying a basin filled with water from washing and brushing his teeth. They moved with the languid steps of the sexually satisfied, and each time they plunked their feet down on the wooden slats, there was a hollow thump. Immersed as they were in their own contentment, they had gotten careless. Just then, one of the Henan fellows downstairs opened the door. The first thing he saw was Gendi's back, with Genhai right behind her. He gave Genhai a nod and a look of understanding that had more than a trace of a leer. Genhai realized he thought Gendi was *that* kind of woman—the kind of woman the men from Henan brought home with them from the back rooms of the barbershops and massage parlors that lined the half-lit street, the kind of woman who wrapped men in her chalk-white arms and legs.

The next evening, Genhai had returned to his lodgings and was cooking his dinner when one of the men from Henan knocked on the door and invited him downstairs for a drink. It had been a long time since any of them had invited him over—but here he was, back again. Genhai turned him down, but the man kept asking and even tried to pull Genhai along by the arm. Angered, Genhai freed himself with such force that the other man nearly tumbled down the stairs. When he regained his composure, Genhai forced a smile and explained that he was feeling tired and needed to get to bed early, but he'd invite them over another time. The Henan man went back downstairs, grumbling all the way. Genhai realized that he was shaking ever so slightly, and his heart was racing. He had eaten dinner, the dishes were done, and there was a book lying in front of him—but he didn't have the faintest idea what it was. He hadn't touched a book in ages, and the characters looked like strangers to him. Xiaodi was at home tonight, so Gendi couldn't come over, but the scent of her filled the room, soft and yielding, ripe through and through, and exuding heat. Hers was the scent of a woman who had borne a child but hadn't dried up—in fact, she was more fertile than ever. Later that night, Genhai called his wife in the countryside. He must have awakened her from a dream—she sounded befuddled and incoherent, like a little child. He asked her to bring their children to Shanghai, but she said the older one had school. He told her to ask permission for a couple days' leave from school, so that the family could have a long weekend. His wife said, "I'll talk to the teacher tomorrow, but I can't promise she'll say yes." Genhai replied, "Don't be long!" At this point his wife was fully awake, and she asked, "What's the rush? You're acting like the house is on fire." Genhai started to cry. "I miss you all so much," he choked. She'd never heard her man speak this way before, and she was quiet for a moment. "Okay," she said.

The next day, Genhai didn't go to the lane or set up his stall. Many of his regular customers came by to drop off shoes, but they left in disappointment. Others stopped by to retrieve finished jobs, and they too were disappointed. Gendi went over to the entrance of the lane several times, and when she didn't see Genhai, she grew suspicious. She thought about going over to check on him, but in the end she didn't have the nerve. She couldn't imagine what had happened. On the second day, he showed up with his two daughters in tow. It had never occurred to anyone that Genhai's children were both girls; what's more, they were fair-skinned girls, so they must have resembled their mother. They looked almost translucent in the sun. Because they had come to the big city of Shanghai to see their father, they had on new clothes. The older girl had already started school, and she sat on the stool, reading aloud from an English textbook. Her voice rang out bright and clear—she didn't suffer from stage fright at all. Her little sister scampered back and forth at the entrance to the lane—everything was new to her. Fearless, she marched right up to the mahjong table and looked at Uncle Ye's tiles. When he tried to shoo her away with the lit tip of his cigarette, she giggled and ran off; but soon she tiptoed back. Uncle Ye asked Genhai where he'd been the day before, and Genhai told him that there had been a meeting for him and the other street-side businesspeople. They'd been called on to form a team responsible for keeping public order, and Genhai was sporting a brand-new red armband emblazoned with the words, "Mutual Defense." Uncle Ye asked, "How long are those two little rascals going to be in Shanghai?" Genhai replied, "The older one has school, so at the end of the weekend, somebody from my village will come to take her home. The younger one and her mother will stay on a little longer, since right now there's no pressing work in the country." Gendi stood off to the side, listening in silence. She lingered a while longer; then she turned and walked away.

Authors

Chi Zijian was born in 1964 in Mohe in Heilongjiang Province on the Sino-Russian border. She is one of China's most well-known female authors. Chi's work often focuses on life in northeast China, especially Harbin, and features characters from indigenous peoples such as the reindeer-herding Evenki. Her novels include *A Peak in the Mountains*, *Puppet Manchukuo*, *Sunshine behind the Clouds*, *Last Quarter of the Moon*, and *Snow and Raven*, as well as several short story collections. Chi has won the Lu Xun Prize three times, as well as the 2008 Mao Dun Literature Prize and the 2004 Australian James Joyce Foundation Suspended Sentence Award. Her work has been translated into English, French, Dutch, Italian, and Spanish.

Fang Fang, born in 1955 in Nanjing, moved with her family to Wuhan, where she later attended Wuhan University. She subsequently spent four years as a dockworker to support her family, a period she recalls as instrumental to her portraits of a range of characters, from factory workers to intellectuals. Her work has become a prime example of "new realism" in Chinese literature. In her most recent novel, *Wuchang: A City under Siege* (2011), Fang chronicles the famous 1926 battle between warlords and Kuomingtong during the Northern Expedition. She won the Lu Xun Prize in 2010 and was named the 2011 Chinese Media Award in Literature Author of the Year.

Han Shaogong, born in 1953 in Changsha, Hunan, is one of the most well-known contemporary authors in China and a founding figure of the popular "roots-seeking" genre of Chinese fiction, which explored distinct rural themes and histories. After working for several years for the Writers' Association of Hainan, Han moved back to the countryside of his native Hunan Province, where he continues to write. His novel *A Dictionary of Maqiao*, first published in 1996 and translated into English by Julia Lovell in 2003, won the University of Oklahoma's second Newman Prize for Chinese Literature in 2011. His other works include *Ba Ba Ba* (爸爸爸, lit. "Da-da-da").

Jiang Yun, born in March 1954 in Shanxi, graduated from the Chinese Literature Department at Taiyuan Normal College and began writing fiction in 1979. Her major works include the novels *Secrets in Bloom, Prisoner of the Oak, My Interior, Glimmering in Your Branches, The Human World: The Tale of the White Snake Retold* (co-authored with Li Rui), and *The Age of Walking*, but she is also well known for her many collections of short fiction. Widely translated, Jiang Yun's works have been awarded the Lu Xun Literary Prize, the Zhao Shuli Literary Prize, the Beijing Literature Prize, and many others.

Li Tie was born in the 1960s. He has published numerous works of short fiction in major literary journals, and many of his short stories and novellas have been anthologized. Li Tie won the inaugural Youth Literary Award and the eleventh Hundred Flowers Award, and has won numerous awards for his novellas, including the inaugural Liaoning Prize, which he went on to win three more times.

Wang Anyi, arguably the most well-known contemporary female novelist in China, was born into a prominent family, the daughter of Ru Zhijuan, a well-known writer and Party member who was later denounced in the Cultural Revolution. She is among the most widely read and anthologized authors of the post-Mao era, and her acclaimed Shanghai-based novels have garnered international recognition. Her novel *Changhen Ge (The Song of Everlasting Sorrow,* 1996) was voted the most influential work of the 1990s in China and won the fifth Mao Dun Literature Prize in 2000. It was later successfully adapted for television, stage, and screen. The film, directed by Stanley Kwan, was produced by Jackie Chan. In addition to fiction, Wang has published essays, journalism, travel writings, literary criticism, and memoirs. In 2001 she was elected chairperson of the Shanghai Writers' Association.

Xu Zechen, born in 1978 in Jiangsu Province, obtained a master's degree in Chinese literature at Beijing University and is currently an editor at *People's Literature* magazine. Xu's realist fiction explores the lives of China's working classes and migrant workers. He has published four novels: *Midnight's Door, Night Train, Heaven on Earth,* and most recently *Jerusalem,* as well as a collection of short stories titled *How Geese Fly up to Heaven.* He has won several prizes in China. More recently he was the Writer-in-Residence at Creighton University in Nebraska in 2009, and took part in the University of Iowa's renowned International Writing Program in 2010.

Translators

Eleanor Goodman is a writer and a translator of Chinese literature. She is a Research Associate at the Fairbank Center at Harvard University and spent a year at Peking University on a Fulbright Fellowship. She has been an artist in residence at the American Academy in Rome and was awarded a Henry Luce Translation Fellowship from the Vermont Studio Center. Her book of translations *Something Crosses My Mind: Selected Poems of Wang Xiaoni* (Zephyr Press, 2014) was awarded a 2013 PEN/Heim Translation Grant and the 2015 Lucien Stryk Prize. It was also shortlisted for the International Griffin Prize. Her first book of poems, *Nine Dragon Island*, will be published this year.

Lucas Klein is a father, writer, translator, editor, and Assistant Professor at the University of Hong Kong, whose work has appeared in *Jacket, Rain Taxi, Asymptote, Cha, CLEAR, Comparative Literature Studies,* and *PMLA*, and from Fordham University Press, Black Widow, and New Directions. His translation of poetry by Xi Chuan won the 2013 Lucien Stryk Prize and was shortlisted for the Best Translated Book Award in poetry. His translations of seminal contemporary poet Mang Ke are available as *October Dedications* from Zephyr Press and Chinese University Press, and he is at work translating Tang dynasty poet Li Shangyin.

Charles A. Laughlin, currently the Weedon Professor of East Asian Studies at the University of Virginia, received his Ph.D. in Chinese literature from Columbia University and has published extensively on Chinese literature from the 1920s to the 1960s, including two books: *Chinese Reportage: The Aesthetics of Historical Experience* (Duke University Press, 2002) and *The Literature of Leisure and Chinese Modernity* (University of Hawai'i Press, 2008). Laughlin also edited *Contested Modernities in Chinese Literature* (Palgrave, 2005) and has published translations of poetry and prose by Yang Lian, Li Peifu, Ma Lan, and Song Lin, and the short stories "The Blessings of Good Fortune" by Guo Wenbin and "Song of Liangzhou" by Ge Fei.

Andrea Lingenfelter is a poet, translator, and scholar of Chinese literature. Her book-length translations include *The Kite Family* (Muse, 2015), a collection of surrealistic short fiction by Hong Kong writer Hon Lai Chu; *The Changing Room: Selected Poetry of Zhai Yongming* (Zephyr Press, 2011), for which she won a 2012 Northern California Book Award; and the novels *Farewell My Concubine* (Wm. Morrow and Co., 1993) and *Candy* (Back Bay Books, 2003). Her translations of poetry by modern and contemporary Sinophone writers have appeared widely in journals and anthologies, including *Granta, Chinese Literature Today, Pathlight, Zoland Poetry Annual, Mantis, Frontier Taiwan, Sailing to Formosa,* and *Chicago Review.* Lingenfelter received an NEA Translation Grant for *The Kite Family* and is a past recipient of a PEN Translation Fellowship. She is currently translating *Scent of Heaven,* a historical novel by Wang Anyi, for Penguin. She has also been awarded a Henry Luce Translation Fellowship from the Vermont Studio Center, which will support her collaboration with Hong Kong–based poet Cao Shuying on translations of Cao's poetry. She teaches at the University of San Francisco.